IMPRINT CLASSICS

SPOOLING THROUGH

An Irreverent Memoir

TIM BOWDEN

ETT IMPRINT
Exile Bay

Published by ETT Imprint, Exile Bay in 2024

First published in 2003 by Allen & Unwin

Copyright © Tim Bowden 2003, 2023

All rights reserved. No part of this book may be reproduced or transmitted in any form or by any means, electronic or mechanical, including photocopying, recording or by any information storage and retrieval system, without prior permission in writing from the publisher:

ETT Imprint
PO Box R1906
Royal Exchange NSW 1225
Australia

The Leunig cartoon is reproduced with permission of Michael Leunig. The newspaper clippings on pages 7, 94, 131 courtesy of the Hobart Mercury; page 170 courtesy of the *Launceston Examiner*; page 161 from TV Week; page 312 courtesy of the *Sydney Morning Herald*. Every effort has been made to contact copyright holders. The author and publisher would be pleased to hear from original copyright holders to rectify any omissions.

ISBN 978-1-923024-40-3 (pbk)
ISBN 978-1-923024-41-0 (ebk)

For Ros, Barnaby and Guy

Of All the Loves

Of all the loves that can be known
ONE has remained
NAMELESS;
IT'S the
LOVE of MICROPHONE
and it's the most
SHAMELESS!

Contents

Foreword by Maeve Binchy

1 Growing up *1*
2 Hot metal and copy paper *21*
3 Staying alive *47*
4 The clockwork tape recorder *77*
5 Orstraylian are you? *97*
6 The art of negative projection *122*
7 The fastest plucker on the island *144*
8 The man who was called God *176*
9 Far too dangerous! *210*
10 How are your teeth? *243*
11 Aussie is the place for me *277*
12 Naked came the stranger *314*
Postscript *335*
Index *338*

Foreword

Who are the right people to do a memoir? People who remember everything, see wonder and entertainment everywhere and who take their work but never themselves seriously. You could add in an ability to admit mistakes, that magic wisdom of hindsight in knowing when we were wrong over something, and the power to measure others by their personality rather than their so called achievements.

Tim Bowden does all this in spades.

He draws you into his eager, enthusiastic world peopled with a Cecil B. de Mille cast of thousands and somehow you share all the good and bad that happens to him - the heady days of being appointed with scant qualifications as a motoring correspondent, the inevitable fall from grace losing the post. If you were never in Tasmania he would make you ache to go there and regret that it wasn't the actual place where you were born. If you have worked on a newspaper like I have, you can recognise every single aspect of the *The Mercury* because all newspapers in the world are basically the same. Someone always thinks the editor is the cleaner or vice versa, someone always manages to shred articles on the way from the journalists to the sub-editors. And even if you do not work in a newspaper you have seen enough movies to feel at home when Tim starts to tell you about his early days.

We can wince with embarrassment for him when he is trying to show off in his local pub by ordering a liqueur since it was after dinner. 'What kind of Drambuie do you have?' he asked the barman, and for the rest of his life lived to be haunted by that one moment of youthful pretentiousness since the barman certainly wasn't going to let him forget it.

Not only would I like to have been raised in Tasmania, I would love to have known Tim Bowden's selection of relatives and friends and had the insight about them that he obviously did at an early stage. He sets us comfortably back in an Australia that is long gone, part of a world that has disappeared, where little boys on vacation with their aunts always came down to breakfast in plenty of time and then did not dig into the food until Grace had been said.

And then he takes us on his travels: the claustrophobia of near underwater living on board the Neptunia in a twelve-berth cabin under the water line. Not much privacy or chance for shipboard romance on the way to Europe on this particular voyage.

Then when he got to London he met the culture shock of Britain which not only the Australians but also the neighbouring Irish have encountered too. Things like the English almost fainting if you say 'Good morning' to them in a train, something most normal Australians and Irish people do automatically. He discovered too that being English-speaking but foreigners gives us an amazing advantage. They don't know what class we are. We could be extremely posh Ozzies or Micks for all they know or else the complete reverse. Once a fellow English person opened a mouth they would be placed immediately. With us however, it's a problem: they can't read us to place us and so they err on the side of assuming the best until proved otherwise.

There is the heart-stopping moment when he meets Ros Geddes and doesn't realise that she is destined to be the love of his life-and the even more electrifying one when he *does* realise this and we are so afraid she is going to tell him to get lost. If that had happened then one of the best and happiest marriages I know would never have taken place. It is too horrible to think what a huge consequent loss that would have been to all their friends, as well as to Barnaby and Guy.

I once drove with Tim and Ros from Sydney to Pacific Palms and I bemoaned the fact that I had to think up a column for my own paper back home. When we got out of their car I had a better column ready than I ever turned in before. Just by listening to his stories.

A friend already to hundreds and thousands of us lucky enough to have met him, to millions who have listened to him on radio and seen him on television, he will get an entirely new following with this book - readers who will believe they have lived through these escapades and met all these characters with him; people who will rightly think they know the real Tim Bowden and wish his story were twice as long.

Maeve Binchy

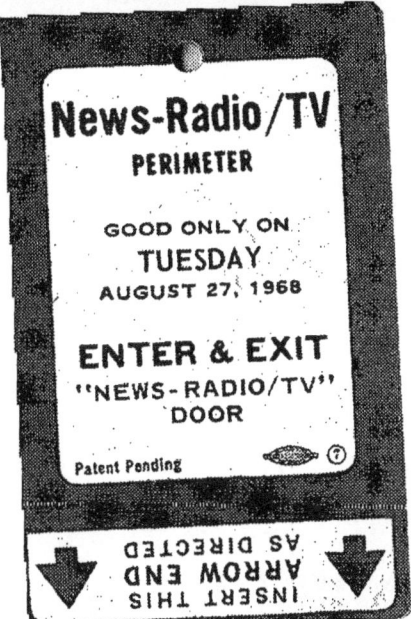

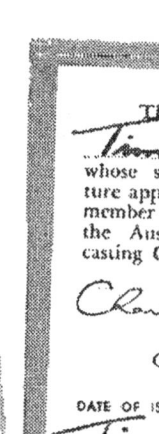
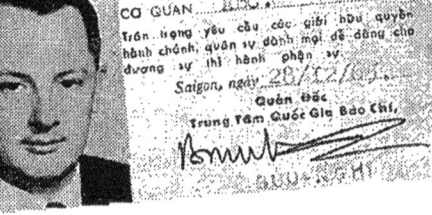
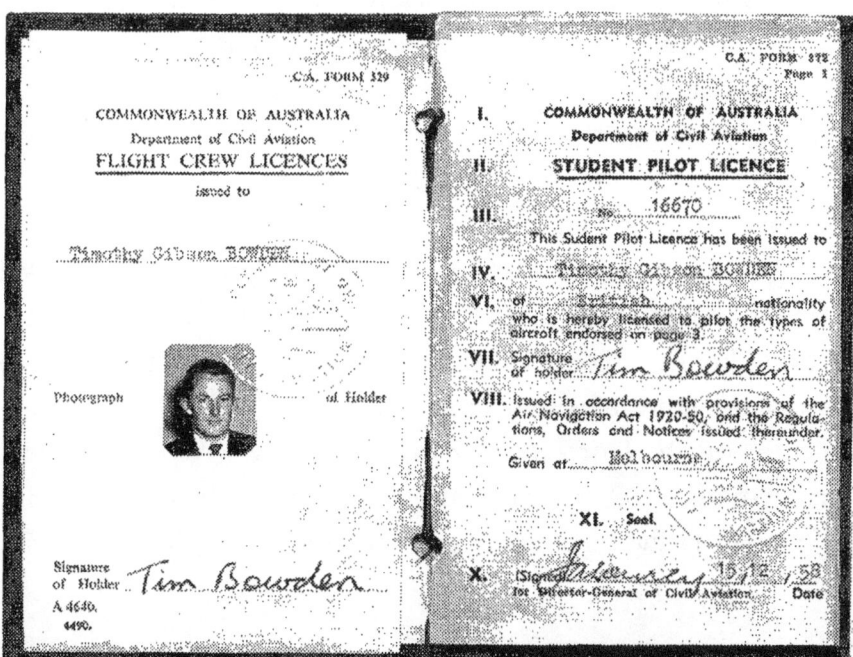

Growing up 1

My generation, born before World War II, timed things very nicely. We were too young for that war and for the Korean War. When I did compulsory national service-shedding my blood for my country safely in Brighton Camp, Tasmania - many instructors were Korean veterans, but even though successive Australian governments had eagerly sent our troops off to fight other people's wars since before Federation, no war came along for me. I was too old to be considered for Vietnam-although I did get there briefly as a war correspondent-and with a bit of luck my pre-war lot will sneak into the retirement villages and nursing homes before the hordes of greying boomers come tottering in to fight querulously over their access to the creaking aged care system.

I missed the Horses' Birthday-1 August-by one day, arriving on 2 August, 1937, at the Queen Alexandra Hospital in Hobart. A woman in the same ward as my mother rejoiced in the name of

Mrs Grubb. She asked Peg what she was going to call me. Peg said 'Timothy'.

Mrs Grubb said, 'I'm calling my daughter Marietta'.

There was a pause and then she said to Peg, 'Do you get it?'

My mother said she did. Marietta Grubb must be 65 now, and I'll bet she married early.

I consider myself amazingly fortunate to have grown up in Australia's island state. Hobart-born novelist Christopher Koch, who has written about the Tasmanian landscape more evocatively than anybody else, once wrote about the surge of excitement that returning Tasmanians feel as they fly over Bass Strait and catch their first glimpse of the island which 'causes a leap of the heart, like the sudden appearance of a loved face'. Rightly or wrongly, island people tend to think of themselves as being special, of embodying values necessarily different from 'the Mainland', as Tasmanians invariably call the big Australian island to the north.

The weather is an enduring topic of conversation in Tasmania because it has drama and immediacy-particularly in Hobart where the great guardian bulk of Mount Wellington can turn on a white Christmas and where, at any time of the year, winds and rain sweep down its flanks to the city with only a few minutes' warning. The winter light there has a low, translucent intensity I have seen nowhere else in the world. Although Tasmanian-born writers like Peter Conrad have written of the mountain as having a brooding, sinister--even malevolent-aspect, we never thought of Mount Wellington as anything other than a benign presence, a useful weathercock. 'What's the mountain doing?' my mother, Peg, would ask as if it had a life of its own. If it disappeared, you knew it would rain within five minutes.

Few capital cities can claim a more dramatic setting than Hobart, wedged as it is between the flanks of Mount Wellington and Mount Nelson, and the deep waters of the Derwent estuary. A capital city? Well it is, but 'big country town' would be a more realistic assessment. Even today my father's house on the lower slopes of Mount

Nelson has a sheep paddock beside it. When I grew up there Mr Livingston's dairy cows grazed nearby. As a small boy I helped deliver milk around Sandy Bay from Mr Livingston's horse-drawn cart, dipping the creamy unpasteurised milk from big wide-necked metal churns into billies left outside front doors. The horse knew the route intimately and would wait patiently at the end of a street before clip-clopping along keeping just ahead of our deliveries. I could hardly be called a city boy. In Hobart then there was no sharp barrier between city and the bush. Most of my contemporaries were as familiar with feeding the chooks as they were with catching trams in Elizabeth Street. We lived less than five kilometres from the General Post Office.

My parents thought life was pretty good in the 1930s, but the rise of fascism in Europe and the prospect of a world war weighed heavily upon them. That Australia should join 'the Mother Country' Britain in this struggle was taken for granted, despite the awful slaughter of young Australian men at Gallipoli and in France during World War I. My father's elder brother, Philip, had won a scholarship to Cambridge and was set on a career path in physics there that won him high acclaim and eventually a Fellowship of the Royal Society. In 1939 he returned briefly to Australia with a pessimistic outlook, telling my father, 'You are probably joining up to go away for ten years, and of course you must face the fact that you probably won't come back'. Yet there was never any question about not going. My father, then thirty-three, was a lieutenant, originally in the Signals and later in the Royal Australian Army Service Corps. He achieved field rank and was a major by the time the war ended, having served in Palestine, in Central Australia (after Prime Minister Curtin brought the Australian troops back from the Middle East in 1942) and in far north Queensland.

Australia in the early 1940s was an astonishingly Anglo-Celtic society. I don't remember seeing any black-skinned people in Hobart, no Africans, not even Indonesians, Thais or Filipinos. When some black Americans came ashore in Hobart from United States warships during World War II they were exotic creatures indeed, and when Indonesian and Thai Colombo Plan students first came to the University of Tasmania in the 1950s there was genuine (and friendly) curiosity by the locals about where they came from. There were Australian-born Chinese, of course, whose forebears had come during the gold rushes of the nineteenth century. They were as Australian as billy tea. Helene Chung, from Hobart, became the ABC's Beijing correspondent in 1983 but she couldn't speak Chinese.

As a small boy my father had listened as my grandfather read him the Uncle Remus stories written by Joel Chandler Harris. Set in America's Deep South, they involved a young white boy who used to be told stories by an old former slave about the antics of 'Brer' Rabbit and 'Brer' Fox and, I seem to recall, a tar baby! The tradition of those readings continued with me and they seem to have aroused my curiosity. Someone had told me that black A ericans were completely dark except for pink palms and the soles of their feet, so when I was about five years old I remember asking some black sailors from a US Navy ship on leave in Hobart if they would show me the palms of their hands. Fortunately they thought this was a huge joke, roared with laughter and cheerfully obliged. Their palms were pink. We didn't get around to the soles of their feet.

There were still horse-drawn cabs in Hobart during the war, perhaps gaining extra time because of fuel shortages. The few cars that were about sported gas producers mounted on their back bumper bars, a great cluster of tubes and a chamber that converted charcoal to a combustible gas. I was once taken for a ride in a hansom cab with a tall black canvas hood and side curtains. There was an air of some ceremony about this, and I recall being told it was something I should try to remember.

My first taste of schooling was a kindergarten at a girls' school called Fahan. The only other boy there was Michael Hodgman, later to become a politician in both federal and state parliaments and to be known universally as 'The Mouth from the South'. I was only at Fahan for about eighteen months before being enrolled at

Gladwyn, in Lord Street, Sandy Bay, a preparatory school run jointly by St Michael's Collegiate School for girls and The Hutchins School for boys.

Early in 1945 John Bowden was discharged from the army and I had a father again. John and Peg fell gladly into each other's arms and set about some post-war reconstruction in the family department. My brother, Nicholas, was born on 17 January 1948. For some reason my mother thought it some kind of badge of gynaecological honour to give birth without what were mysteriously called 'stitches'. When the phone call came through from the hospital announcing Nicholas's arrival (fathers were not wanted in delivery wards in those days), an eight-year-old Tim ran off down Mariing Avenue bellowing out to the world at large, 'It's a boy, eight pounds and no stitches!'

Post-war reconstruction continued steadily with another brother, Philip, born in 1950, and my sister Lisa the following year. Father had a stressful job in the car industry, but he revelled in family life. He built me a sledge that ran down wooden rails to a softish landing further down our sloping block. The rails were greased with dripping, left over from Peg's roast dinners. My friends and I hurtled down this thing with great glee. It is a wonder no one lost a finger or broke bones.

In the summer of 1948, when I was ten years old, my parents rather gamely took me on a major 100-kilometre bushwalk through the now internationally famous Cradle Mountain-Lake St Clair National Park. We had to carry everything with us on our backs of course-tents, food and cooking gear. Not water, because there was always plenty of that in the Tasmanian wilderness. It seems hard to comprehend these days, but plastic containers were yet to be invented. We had cylindrical aluminium containers with screw lids scammed from chemist shops-they were ideal for food storage, and waterproof. We carried rice, rolled oats, dried food and even tea in cloth bags. Rucksacks were fairly primitive, suspended on a metal A-shaped frame and leather strap that fitted just above your hips. The load sagged back making the damned things twice as heavy as they should have been. In those days only a handful of eccentrics went bushwalking. You certainly didn't expect to meet anyone else on the track in normal circumstances and you could reasonably expect to have the wilderness on your own.

I wrote an account of our trip which I still have because my aunt, Nora Bowden, was a shorthand typist and typed it up. It was my first attempt at oral history, I suppose, with myself as the source. There are references to 'the womenfolk' doing this and that, and some quaintly formal policeman-speak. We often 'proceeded' along the track rather than walked. Most walkers these days begin from Cradle Mountain in the north and walk south to Lake St Clair, but we did it from the south. We started on New Year's day, getting a lift to Derwent Bridge on the 'service car'-a large sedan or small bus which did the 'milk' run to Queenstown on the west coast, carrying papers, mail, general cargo and some passengers, stopping at Derwent Bridge near Lake St Clair on the way.

> We got to the service car and we heard that the driver had been drinking beer and sherry until 4 o'clock in the morning. We felt very encouraged as you may imagine. The driver drove very fast and it was very dangerous.

The main road to the west coast was an unsealed, pot-holed, corrugated goat track, but one bonus of starting from Lake St Clair was that you could organise a boat to save you the first day's walk. Our ten-day trek was not without incident. We got lost trying to find an allegedly idyllic high mountain plateau called The Labyrinth and had to scrub-bash down into a valley to spend an unscheduled night. (I did eventually get to The Labyrinth a decade later and it was truly magnificent, with little tarns and wind-sculptured King Billy pines surrounded by mountain peaks with names like The Acropolis and Mount Eros.)

We were only a day away from Cradle Mountain, our journey's end, when we were involved with a sad accident. As we rested beside the track enjoying our rations of restorative chocolate and the great

DRAMATIC DASH TO AID SNAKE-BITE VICTIM

POLICE and a doctor left Sheffield yesterday morning in a dramatic dash to aid a woman, believed to be a Sydney University student, who was bitten by a snake on the Cradle Mountain-Lake St. Clair track on Wednesday.

NEWS of the accident was conveyed 63 miles by a relay of messengers to Sheffield, the nearest town, but the woman's name was not known.

The party of which the woman is a member was on the third day of a 50-mile hike from Waldheim to Lake St. Clair, and three miles past Pelion, where the night was spent.

The woman was carried back to the hut and was reported to be unconscious on Wednesday afternoon.

The first messenger was exhausted when he reached Windermere, about 10 miles away, and the message was carried on to Waldheim and then to Sheffield by Mr S. Connell, who reached there about 1 a.m.

The road from Sheffield to Waldheim—about 42 miles—is fairly good, but after that there is only a hiking track.

The police party, with Dr L. Sender, left Sheffield yesterday morning and is not expected to return until today.

---

sweep of country looking back to a mountain called Barn Bluff, we heard the unmistakeable sound of someone running. A young man, without a pack, was thundering along and ran up to us with the terrible news that a young woman had been bitten by a snake near the Pelion Hut, a day's walk back, and he was on his way to raise the alarm and get a doctor from Sheffield, the nearest major town.

The circumstances of the accident were bizarre. The young woman was with a small group of Mainland university students. She dropped behind the group to have a piddle. Unfortunately, a tiger snake was on the other side of the log she chose for buttock support, and it reared up and bit her twice on her nether regions. The Tasmanian tiger snake is listed as one of the most poisonous snakes in the world. But it does not inject its venom directly into its prey. The poison runs down a grooved tooth. That is why Tasmanian bushwalkers always wear long trousers, never shorts. Should a snake strike, most of the venom doesn't make it through the material. In the case of the unfortunate student, the snake was able to deliver a full dose of poison into bare skin.

We were told later that due to the embarrassing position of the bite, the young woman made light of the incident, believing that the snake was unlikely to be poisonous. But all Tasmanian snakes are venomous and it was only when she collapsed that the true state of affairs was known. Of course a tourniquet was not possible and they carried her to the Pelion Hut while one of their party ran twenty kilometres for help. He met Graham Marshall, who had just climbed Cradle Mountain that day but who agreed to run on. Marshall had come eight kilometres when he caught up with us.

The first aid treatment in those days was to put on a tourniquet (if possible), cut the wound with a little scalpel, suck out the poison (difficult in the circumstances) and rub in some purple-coloured Candy's crystals. We carried the same kit in little wooden cylinders. Later research has shown the kits were all quite useless. The only hope for snakebite victims-other than to survive through good luck-was to be injected with antivenene, which was not an option. By the time we reached Waldheim, the lodge at the entrance to the park, we met the doctor and a police party on their way in. The doctor told us that the young woman would either be alive or dead. Sadly, she had died during the night in the Pelion Hut.

I put in the diary I dictated to Aunt Nora that a detective had come out to arrest the snake.

In 1949 Robert Menzies became Prime Minister of Australia and remained so for the next seventeen years. His avuncular figure, commanding presence and assured rhetoric seemed to embody a divine right to rule as he adroitly exploited the Labor Party split and fostered a xenophobic fear of Communism. The word inflation was never used because there wasn't any. Unemployment was similarly a non-issue. Most Australian men polished their Holden cars at the weekend, cheerfully kept up their mortgage payments on their three-bedroom houses on quarter-acre blocks, punted on the gee-gees, downed the amber fluid at the local pub (mercifully free of poker machines and loud music) and bred enthusiastically. Their (mostly) non-working wives looked after the kids and trotted out to the backyard Hills Hoists with loads of whiter-than-white Persil-laundered washing from the wondrous new machines that had replaced fired coppers, sticks and mangles. They delighted in their new refrigerators, vacuum cleaners and bright white enamelled gas and electric stoves. While not everyone was able to share these consumer joys, the voices of the poor somehow seemed muted. The war was well and truly over and it was time to relax and enjoy the peace.

In Tasmania, Robert Cosgrove's right-wing Labor Government had been in power since 1939, trees grew mainly to be cut down, rivers were to be dammed and tamed for hydro-electricity, and mining companies were allowed open slather on the island's west coast to set international benchmarks of environmental pollution. But this seemed to be how life was, and there was little, if any, environmental consciousness.

In the Bowden family, being the first born, I was rather indulged. I had riding lessons-they did not last long because one of my instructors said you could never be a proper horseman until you had fallen off and as it looked a long way down I lost interest-and there were piano lessons in the city at Miss Annie McGarry's rooms, up steep stairs in Elizabeth Street. The rooms were above a hairdressing salon, and the smells emanating from such establishments still take me back instantly to piano scales and the raw fear of tackling a new piece. I was cursed with a good ear, and soon learned to rattle along in the key of C or G, vamping songs and enjoying myself. But reading music was a challenge and I never made the breakthrough of transmitting those miraculous spidery annotations through my brain to my fingers. The music lessons petered out.

Reading was something I loved, however, and I started to write poems and plays when I was about ten years old. One surviving play was modelled on a radio serial for kids I used to listen to. It was called *Yes What* and during it a schoolmaster (played by Hal Lashwood) attempted to control a group of cheeky, wisecracking students. My tireless Aunt Nora actually typed out proper scripts from my scrawled dialogue and my school friends acted them out on the front lawn at one of my birthday parties. More classy entertainment was provided at another pre-pubescent birthday by Christopher Kimber, later a noted violinist, who played a solo from the open window of our living room.

Sometimes during the summer holidays we would stay with our neighbours, the Giblins, who had a shack on the east coast of Tasmania, south of Orford. The water there had-and has-a cobalt blue iridescence that reminded Father of the Mediterranean. Not only that, the beaches in the area were so dazzlingly white that it hurt to look at them in full sunlight. The waters teemed with fish that fought each other for the privilege of taking your hook. Spring Beach looked east over the Tasman Sea to Maria Island, which had been first named by the Dutch explorer Abel Tasman. Somehow Father convinced a bloke called Leo Ryan, who owned most of the land around Spring Beach, to sell him a couple of blocks at a fairly nominal price so we could have a holiday place in this most beautiful of situations.

Father couldn't afford a professional builder so he did most of the work himself with the help of a very handy bloke called Doug Burns. They constructed a vertical weatherboard shack with an open plan living room and kitchen alcove. Kitchens were invariably tucked away and hidden in those days, but Peg, as all her children called her, always said she wanted to be where the action was-a revolutionary concept then, but commonplace now.

When it was finished, my father, who during his wartime service in Palestine had been particularly impressed by the beauty of an old Roman resort town on the Mediterranean called Askelon (spellings vary, but that is how he remembered it), had the name ASKELON fashioned from wrought iron and nailed up on the front wall. It is still there and the Bowden family still owns the modest but comfortable weekender with million dollar views. In his eighties and early nineties, long after Peg died, Father would spend up to a month or more at Askelon on his own. He just loved being there. The fish don't bite quite as eagerly as they used to half a century ago, but you can usually get a feed of flathead every time you go out.

Before Askelon-and even afterwards-we would drive to Port Sorell on the north-east coast of Tasmania for our Christmas and summer holiday. Mary (Peg's sister) and Stuart Maslin had a cottage there called Sorlrite (It's All Right). I must report that three houses nearby were called (from the left): Weona, Soda-Wee and the less than inspirational Same Here. My older cousin Janne generally had a friend to stay, leaving her younger sister Toni-who was eighteen months older than me-as playmate. I insisted that I was going to catch her up in the age stakes, but strangely I never did.

After joyously boozy lunches the adults would enjoy their ritual afternoon nap. Toni and I would be banished to the beach to play. On one occasion I had the brilliant notion of tunnelling into a sand bank, and out again. It took some doing, but we did it, and were happily chasing each other in and out when about a metre of solid sand collapsed on top of me. Toni happened to be on the outside and let out her famous scream. (To this day she can turn on a scream that can shatter glass.) I can't remember much except the air being crushed out of my lungs and a leaden kind of blackness overtaking me. A man camping nearby came running and said 'Where's his head?' Toni pointed, fortunately to the right spot, and he grabbed a spade and got down to me before I stopped breathing permanently.

By the time we got back to Sorlrite it was drinks time again (well, it was a summer holiday). 'Guess what happened on the beach?' we said, but no one seemed very interested. I don't think our parents ever realised what a close run thing it had been.

Like my father (and his brothers) I was enrolled at The Hutchins School, then in Macquarie Street, Hobart. I don't know how my father afforded to send us all to private schools, although when

I asked him once he said he had a sympathetic bank manager. In retrospect he might have ensured I had a better education by sending me free to the Hobart High School. Hutchins in my time offered a bare-bones blackboard and chalk education in shabby classrooms with a mix of teachers ranging from the competent to the mentally disturbed. Facilities were minimal. The science laboratory was an absolute disgrace. About the only thing that worked was something called a Wimshurst machine with a wheel that spun around and generated a flash of electricity between two electrodes. What we did have plenty of was tradition. Buckets of it, ladled out every day. How lucky we were to be there, what a great school we were at, how it would shape our lives and so on. I think I would have preferred less tradition and a better education. But my father was right in one sense. Had I stayed in Hobart I would have networked very comfortably into the community. The Old Boy network is alive and well to this day. Fortunately Hutchins now dishes out a decent education as well.

Our day began with the Assembly, based on some English public school ritual. We sat on chairs in front of a stage while the headmaster and staff assembled outside, all wearing academic gowns. The headmaster, a classical scholar, Paul Radford, sported a mortarboard complete with tassel. They all swept down the aisle while we stood up, then sat on the stage facing us while we sang hymns (accompanied by the maths and science master Oscar Bigges pounding away on a battered piano), and endured prayers and whatever announcements had to be made. After that we stood up while the whole entourage swept out again. The gloss was slightly taken off the formality of the occasion by the fact that it all happened in the school gymnasium, the only auditorium big enough to hold everyone. My father had experienced the same ritual three decades earlier.

The senior school boys (from Year Seven up in today's system) had permanent classrooms in the Christ College block, and our teachers came to us. As our hormones were beginning to kick in there was a fair amount of crotch grabbing in the corridors and locker rooms (not a sensual experience I have to say, more like an assault) and talk about sex, of which we knew very little. Although towards the end of our final junior school year that summer my particular group had experienced wondrous and strange happenings.

One skinny lad had sprouted not only upwards, but outwards. We gathered, after school, in a secluded spot in front of a boatshed on the shores of the Derwent to take off all our clothes for a bit of sunbathing. It was really an excuse to marvel at the extraordinary protuberance that jutted out from the slender frame of our classmate. It was so big, and he was so skinny, it was a wonder he didn't pass out from lack of blood to the brain when it sprang to attention-where it remained for the rest of the public viewing. The rest of us couldn't rustle up a pubic hair between us, so we just gathered to marvel at the spectacle. We weren't allowed to touch it. We just looked, wondered and waited.

As soon as I was old enough to sleep away from my own bedroom without homesickness, I used to sleep over on Friday night and have Saturday lunch with my aunts Marge and Nora Bowden, four houses down the street at 27 Maning Avenue. This continued well into my early teens. They were exceedingly good to me and I was very fond of them. Their bookshelves were crammed with schoolgirl novels of previous generations and since I was a voracious reader I happily consumed Ethel Turner's *Seven Little Australians* and schoolgirl novels with titles like *What Katy Did* at home and at school.

Marge and Nora, both shorthand typists, worked at the Electrolytic Zinc Company at Risdon. Marge was born with a congenital deformity of the hip, its crippling effect unfortunately exacerbated by a botched orthopaedic operation attempted in her early teens. She could barely walk, but refused to use a stick, and led as normal a life as she could, although in constant pain. Nora was not well favoured, as they say, in the looks department. She had very bad eyesight and wore glasses with thick, bottle-like lenses. But she loved gardening and was cheerful and outgoing, although she had a rather flighty and nervous disposition. When I first remember going to No. 27 Maning

Avenue my aunts also had a delightful wire-haired fox terrier called Brock.

At No. 27 I slept in Dorothy Bowden's vacant bedroom. Dottie, my father's third sister, had moved out, eventually to go to Sale, in Victoria, to stay with her friends the Blackwoods. Donald Blackwood was then the Bishop of Gippsland, or 'the Gishop of Bippsland' as an announcer on the local radio station 3TR once inadvertently said. The great friendship of Dottie's life was with Ida Blackwood, the Bishop's wife. Tall, elegant, well read and compassionate in a deeply Christian way, Ida Blackwood was an ideal consort for Donald, a short, bustling little man whose feet seemed barely to touch the ground and who talked nonstop in a rasping, gurgling voice that was a legacy of being gassed in France during World War I.

I have no doubt that Dottie was deeply in love with Ida Blackwood, and remained so all her life. It was a love that I am sure never went beyond social hugs and kisses, but it was a powerful influence in my aunt's life. In her mid fifties Dottie managed to get a job as an advertising copywriter at Radio 3TR, Sale. As well as extolling the virtues of the local hardware or drapery store, she ran a book review program which, as tended to be the case with Dottie herself, became an indispensable part of the station's operations. Dottie had a great sense of humour, an insatiable love of Shakespeare (she used to write parodies for a Shakespearian society she belonged to), literature and creative writing. She was a great influence on me, urging me to describe notable events-such as the opening of the refurbished Theatre Royal in Hobart, once lauded by no less a figure than Sir Laurence Olivier. At that opening I sat high up in the gods, taking notes which I wrote up and sent to her so she could share the occasion. It was reportage long before I knew I would be a journalist.

In the summer holidays of 1951 Dottie shouted me a holiday during which I was to stay at Bishopscourt in Sale. I was fourteen and tremendously excited about the journey which included a flight by DC3 aircraft to Melbourne, and then a train to Gippsland. I was made welcome at Bishopscourt, slept the night and bounced down for breakfast. I was a bit late, and found them all standing behind their chairs waiting for me. 'Sorry I'm late', I said, sitting down and tucking into the bacon and eggs. Loaded fork in hand, I looked up. They were all still standing there-the Bishop, Mrs Blackwood, her older unmarried sisters Edie and May Pitt, and Dottie. Mrs Blackwood said in her gentle but firm voice, 'Now Tim, dear, we will say grace'.

Dottie and I rode bicycles every day to radio 3TR, Sale, where I experienced the daily life of a commercial radio station. Serials were big in those days, and were broadcast from huge acetate disks which played from the inside to the outer edge. I made my first broadcast there when Dottie included me in her books program. I reviewed one of C S Forester's *Hornblower* books and read my script to air live. I just loved being on the fringes of a working radio station. After the Bishop retired to Tasmania, Dottie continued her career in commercial radio working as a copywriter for 7HO in Hobart. She told me of one occasion when an announcer committed an atrocious spoonerism while reading an ad for Fullers Bookshop. She said 'Bullers Fookshop'. Things were very straitlaced in the 1950s and she sat at the microphone in terror, waiting for the roof to be pulled down. Nothing happened for about an hour until the studio door opened and the manager put his head in.

'Oh Miss Keating, I'm just going out for lunch and I thought I'd drop in to Bullers and get myself a...' The door closed gently.

Years later, after the Bishop died, Mrs Blackwood went to live with Dottie in her little cottage in Hobart but, sadly, developed dementia. She put on a wonderful front and to the casual observer was the same elegant, intelligent and courteous Ida Blackwood. Dottie cared for her with great love and devotion but was never without her trademark sense of humour. She told me once that Ida came out of her bedroom one morning and asked, 'Dorothy dear, who am I?'

By the time I was in the Intermediate class, Year 10, our collective interest was girls and how to get to them. Most of us signed up for dancing class, run by a formidable little woman called Mrs Donnelly. Like everything else at Hutchins, this class was held in the all-purpose gymnasium/assembly hall/theatre which had its splintered floorboards anointed with white slippery powder for those occasions. Girls from Hutchins' sister school, Collegiate, were there and also, to make up the numbers, some girls from the Fahan School in Sandy Bay. We learned the dances of our parents' generation to music banged out on the piano by a tall young man called Andrew Stein-polkas, barn dances, waltzes and the ubiquitous quickstep. The boys congregated nervously on one side of the hall, our hair slicked down with Brylcreem, wearing our best suits and ties. (We wore school ties daily anyway.) The girls, in their full-skirted taffeta dancing dresses, waited on the other side. We progressed around the hall, with our right arms jerking up and down with the music. This mechanical action was known as 'the Hutchins pump'.

Eventually we attended formal dances, some in the school hall. As the music struck up we made a beeline for the prettiest girls. The numbers were seldom equal, so there was invariably a sprinkling of girls left stranded on the sidelines, trying to look as though they were enjoying themselves as they sat stiffly through the dance. It was barbaric. When my own brothers and sister became teenagers a decade after me, I envied the easy companionship they had with the opposite sex. They were mates with them in a relaxed way that my lot found hard to achieve.

My classmates and I were much more innocent in sexual matters than any generation after us. Alan Goodfellow was dancing one night with a partner - they were practically welded together as they sashayed down the hall, right arms methodically doing the Hutchins pump. Alan's partner said to him, 'Have you got a cordial bottle in your pocket?' We tossed that one around in the locker room for weeks.

Not only did my generation dance to the same music as our parents did but there was then no teenage culture. There were certainly no teenage fashions as such, or even teenage magazines.

Essentially, girls dressed like their mothers, slipping straight from their school uniforms into the equivalent of twin-sets and pearls. In the early 1950s virginity was a ferociously guarded condition. If chastity belts had been available, they would have been worn.

But there were always other physical diversions. Australian Rules football matches against other Hobart private schools were keenly contested, particularly against the Catholic St Virgil's College teams where blood sometimes stained the mud. (I was not a footballer.) In the summer some of my contemporaries played cricket. I don't know to this day how you were selected. A man called Emerson Rodwell used to come to the school and coach at the cricket nets. I was never asked. A pity really. I love cricket now and in the early 1970s scored something of a journalistic coup by getting one of the first radio interviews with Sir Donald Bradman, who had agreed to speak about the controversial 'Bodyline' series of 1931-32.

I did manage to get into a rowing team, though, and rowed in a 'four' with moderate success. The rowing coach was our English teacher, a rumpled bear of a man, Russell Keon-Cohen. We called him 'Blurt' because of the frequent and unsubtle eructations that emanated from him unexpectedly. He was a good English teacher but didn't fit our headmaster's mould for a Hutchins pedagogue. His gown was always ratty, full of holes and chalk stained. You sensed he thought it a ridiculous garment anyway, which it was. We were always first in the school to know who had won the Melbourne Cup because Blurt would leave us to do some revision, and sensibly nick over to the pub across Macquarie Street to hear the big race on the bar radio. He was irreverently politically incorrect. I never heard him refer to a Roman Catholic in class other than as 'one of Hodgman's mob'. The 'Mouth from the South' and I were still pedalling in par-allel through the education system. He was the only Catholic in our Proddie lot but no one seemed to bother about that-certainly not Michael, although I never asked him what he thought about Blurt's crude stereotyping. Our mob didn't worry about those old sectarian hang-ups.

Like my father before me, I was a member of the compulsory school cadet corps. We were issued with woollen uniforms of World War II vintage. Our gaiters and belts had to be scrubbed with a substance called Blanco, and the brass collars on our belts shined with Brasso. We drilled with World War I vintage Lee Enfield .303 rifles with the bolts removed. Mine was dated 1912. I liked the cadets and became a sergeant, rather enjoying my lift in status above the humble privates. For several weeks a year we used to go to Brighton Camp, just north of Hobart, to live in army huts and play at being proper soldiers. This included sessions at the rifle range, where the bolts were returned to our venerable rifles. Unfortunately for my hearing, I was an instructor on the mound, with detail after detail of cadets blasting off .303 rounds for hours at a time. No one thought of ear protection then, not even a wad of cotton wool. I remember my head ringing for hours afterwards-a sure sign permanent damage was occurring. The .303 rifle was a very potent weapon. Although cadets was a senior school activity, puberty arrived late for some. I remember that one extremely small boy picked up his rifle and, holding the butt inches away from his shoulder, pulled the trigger before I could stop him. The recoil shot him straight back off the firing mound.

Due to my loathing and detestation of an awful teacher we called 'Goosy' Gerlach (because he sprouted hairs from ears, nose and everywhere else but his bald head) I had not done well in maths, geography or, sadly, Latin. Science was a dead loss too, but that wasn't Goosy's fault. After four years of secondary school we had to pass our Schools Board Examination to qualify for the final Matriculation year-a passport to university. I simply had to pass in French, and I remain deeply grateful to Lisl Mathew, a wonderful French teacher who joined the staff just in the nick of time to allow me to squeak past the post.

At the end of 1953, Paul Radford, the headmaster who had been there through most of my time at Hutchins, moved on and his replacement, Bill Mason-Cox, was like a breath of fresh air-for me, anyway. Radford had never cared much for me and the feeling was mutual. Now Cadet Sergeant Bowden had the time of his life in the final year at Hutchins. They discovered I could run, and I enjoyed training for cross-country with that wonderful feeling of being super-fit and just floating across the countryside as though high on drugs that I didn't then know existed. I managed to win the intrastate mile distance race against five other schools from northern and southern Tasmania, finishing in a respectable schoolboy time of 4 minutes 48 seconds. It was heady stuff, crossing the line with the whole school cheering me on. It also seemed a good moment to retire from all sport, so I did.

I even sang on the stage. To my surprise I was recruited for a production of the Gilbert and Sullivan operetta *The Pirates of Penzance*. I played Frederick, the lead tenor, who gets kidnapped by a band of pirates. The Pirate King was played and sung with some gusto by my friend Andrew Kemp. It is common these days for boys' schools to import real live girls for these productions, but not in 1954. Junior boys with rouged cheeks, frilly dresses, bonnets and great enthusiasm sang the treble choruses of the Major General's lovely daughters. My uncle, Don Lovett, who came to one of the performances, refused to believe they weren't girls. To this day I can sing just about all the choruses and solos of *The Pirates of Penzance* (including female roles in falsetto) and sometimes try to at parties, until stopped.

'Blurt' Keon-Cohen, the English master, who had fallen foul of a lethal combination of powerful mothers and headmaster Radford's distaste for him, was replaced by a wonderful teacher, John Kerr, whom we nicknamed 'Des', short for 'Desert Head'. Although he was only ten years older than us, he was follicly challenged. He came just at the right time for me. All my classmates went into the science and maths stream, and I was one of only two arts students. We worked alone in the school library and John Kerr was able to give us individual tuition in English expression and literature-the only subjects at Hutchins that I had ever really enjoyed or in which I'd achieved academic success.

The new headmaster wanted me to return for another year - doubtless with his eye on the inter-school athletics. There was even talk of reducing my school fees, but the suggestion was not seriously considered by me and certainly not by my cash-strapped father. In those days, if you managed just to pass the Matriculation examinations, you were awarded a Commonwealth Scholarship for free tuition at university. I was eighteen by then, and ready for life.

2
Hot metal and copy paper

The Mercury newspaper has its offices next to the General Post Office in Macquarie Street, Hobart. The white painted art deco frontage still looks today exactly as it did when I walked in the door as a newly appointed cadet reporter in 1955, sniffing that distinctive, faintly chemical, partly metallic odour emanating from the hot-metal printing process in the bowels of the building. The facade might look the same now, but the computers and new technology of the twenty-first century have swept away every trace of the newspaper production I was about to experience-a process, with links to Caxton, that was common to newspapers all over the world. *The Mercury* was independent in those days, owned by Davies Brothers Pty Ltd.

Stories-or copy-were typed onto small oblong pieces of copy paper (the same grade of paper that would hit the streets hours later), then were corrected by sub-editors who added headlines and sub-headers. The subs made the story fit the page layout decreed by the chief sub-editor who had to juggle the editorial material around the advertisements already blocked into the pages by the advertising department. The copy was then set into hot metal type on huge linotype machines (with a different keyboard layout from a typewriter), and manually slotted into columns in a broadsheet-sized metal tray. (Printers had the enviable and essential skill of being able to read type 'on the stone' as the freshly minted type was called as it lay in neat mirror image columns in a page-sized tray.) Ink was then smeared over the finished page, and several 'pulls' were taken onto single sheets of newsprint to be sent back to the chief sub-editor to inspect, but more importantly to the readers, who had the soul-destroying task of going through the proofs noting spelling mistakes, typographical errors, literals, and transposed lines. (I couldn't imagine a worse job, but those who did it were brilliant practitioners of their art. They are sadly missed today when stories can be sent directly from a reporter's computer straight into the paper with only cursory checks.)

The flat page of raised metal type would be taken to a press and a flexible matrix impressed. This could then be bent so a semicircular plate could be cast and bolted on to the cylinders of the printing press. A second plate would complete the circle. When the size of the paper had been determined, and all the finished plates were in place, the press would be run very slowly as the huge rolls of raw newsprint were coaxed through the labyrinth of cutters and rollers. The head printer would inspect the first finished and collated papers to see if the pages were in the right order and the ink evenly distributed. A few more adjustments would be made, and the speed would pick up. Minutes later the whole building would tremble as the big printing press began to spew out the finished papers into the conveyor belts that led to the loading docks where trucks waited in the early morning hours not only to deliver that day's *Mercury* around the city and southern Tasmania, but to make dashes to all parts of the island. If a catastrophic mistake was picked up at that point, the only way it could be fixed was to stop the press, set new type, and cast another semicircular plate to bolt back on to a roller.

All these mysteries were yet to be revealed when I arrived for work on my first day as a cub reporter. I was welcomed by the chief of staff, Dick Fulton, a big, bald-headed man with a gruff manner, a booming voice and a reputation as a tough disciplinarian. The reporters' room of *The Mercury* was on the second floor overlooking Macquarie Street. It was bordered by wooden bench desks, the edges of which were marked by the parallel burn marks of thousands of cigarettes smoked by tension-filled reporters over the years. It was a fairly stark space, with brown linoleum on the floor, a couple of wooden tables, a noticeboard at the end of the room with an airless sound-insulated phone booth in the far corner. A door near the phone booth led into the subs' room. The management of *The Mercury* was too mean to provide typewriters for its reporters. There were a couple of old chaffcutters for emergencies, but you were expected to buy your own portable.

Like all cadet journalists of the day I was started off in T & F - trade and finance. This page also included the weather and the shipping movements. Hobart was a major port in those days, particularly during the late summer when Tasmanian apples were exported not only to England and Europe, but all over the world. I was taken down to the docks during the afternoon to meet the harbour master and find out when ships were leaving, or expected. The shipping roundsman would also board passenger ships when they arrived to check if there were any famous people who might make a story. In the evening, after the Melbourne and Sydney stock exchanges closed, the stock details would come in by teleprinter. Bert, the one-armed messenger, would rip off the sheets as they came in to the teleprinter room at the other end of the building and tuck them under the stump of his missing arm while he ferried them down the corridor past the offices of the editor, deputy editor, news editor and the chief of staff and his deputy.

Spooling Through

I suppose it says something for the status of financial news in those days that the stock exchange was the responsibility of the cadets. The economy wasn't considered much of a story. There were no specialist financial journalists. Angus Small, a dapper, pipe-smoking New Zealander responsible for the T & F page, subbed them on this occasion, showing me what he was doing. It was my job to cut the rolls of the market prices into short sections and, with a large pot of Clag paste and a brush, stick them onto copy paper ready for numbering and subbing, which was done on one of the beaten-up wooden tables in the reporters' room. At 9 pm the pace was picking up, and the printers were howling for the stock exchange which they liked to set in type early, before the rush of late copy.

Small grabbed a great wedge of damp stock exchange and said, 'Be quick son, and bung this down the chute'.

'Where is the chute Mr Small?'

'In the subs' room. Where did you think it was, in the shithouse?'

I pushed open the door of the subs' room, where eight august gentlemen-there were no women subs in those days-were sitting around a kidney-shaped table. Seven of them had their backs to me. Facing me was the chief sub-editor, Lionel Miller, sitting in the cleft of the kidney, wearing a green tennis shade to protect his eyes from the overhead neon lights which were reflected on his bald head. (Perhaps he had seen a B-grade movie where all sub-editors wore eye shades.) I tapped one of the subs on the shoulder.

'Excuse me, Mr McWatters, where's the chute?'

'What do you think that is on the wall-a fucking mural?'

He gestured to a collection of pipes running up the wall. On one of them was a small metal flap. I lifted it up, and there was a swoosh of compressed air rushing past. It was a pneumatic system with single ended canisters, each with a spring clip to hold the copy securely, that went straight to the printers in the news room on the floor below. None of this had been explained to me by Small. I picked up my bundle of damp stock exchange, lifted up the metal flap, and stuffed it in. There was a loud farting sound and a bang. Some of the stock exchange was spat back at me. I grabbed it, pushed it back in and held the flap shut. There was a shudder, another loud bang, and the stock exchange--or what remained of it-was on its way.

I turned around to find all the sub-editors, their pens poised, looking at me in blank amazement. Lionel Miller broke the silence. 'What the fucking hell do you think you're doing?'

With all the aplomb of an eighteen-year-old on his first night at work I said, 'Just putting the stock exchange down the chute, Mr Miller'.

'Did you use a canister?'

'What canister?'

Lionel exploded. 'Jesus Christ! You'd better go down to the news room and see if they're getting it.'

I ran down the stairs, but approached the news room cautiously. That was wise, because I could hear the swearing as I got close. It was rather like those ticker tape parades accorded to returning successful cricketers. The uncontained stock exchange had burst forth from the pneumatic tube and exploded all over the room. I could see people running around trying to secure tram-ticket-sized bits of stock exchange. It seemed unwise to go in.

I returned to the subs' room. 'They seem to be getting it all right Mr Miller.'

Next morning the rises were mixed up with the falls, and there were big gaps in what should have been. It was not my finest hour on day one.

Lionel Miller, like Dick Fulton the chief of staff, had come to Hobart from the Burnie *Advocate,* a provincial paper on the north-west coast. As chief sub it was his job to assess the overseas news cables as they came in to the chattering teleprinters from news agencies like AAP-Reuters and Associated Press. He would then allocate space and decide what page and prominence a story would have. Miller was a competent newspaper sub, but he was not a worldly man. Not long after I arrived at the paper, he picked up a short overseas cable from the intray.

'Who's this Sibbeluss?' he asked the subs' table in general.

John Temple, a recently arrived Englishman from Reuters in London (and later to make his name with the ABC), asked Lionel how it was spelt.

'S i b e li u s', said the chief sub.

'Well', said John, 'I suppose I'd have to say he's the world's most famous living classical composer'.

'Well he's dead', said Lionel, and tossed the cable across the desk to Aubrey McWatters who tended to get the cultural stories because he had a Bachelor of Arts degree. 'Two lines of 18 point as a single column header on page 26, Mac.'

It was too much for Temple. 'Lionel, I think it should at least be a box on page three.'

'Nah, I've never heard of him.'

I was one of five first year cadets taken on by *The Mercury* in 1955. The others were Michael Philp, John Sorell, Kevin Randell and David Mitchell. I knew both Philp and Sorell. At nineteen Mike Philp was older than the rest of us, and had more life experience-most recently as a jackeroo in outback New South Wales. He was also an experienced sailor, and was soon helping to cover Hobart's keenly contested yacht races. John Sorell had been at Hutchins school with me, but we weren't close. He was a tall fellow with a rather aggressive manner that was fortunately more bluster than reality. Dave Mitchell, who grew up on Tasmania's east coast, was a tall rangy bloke and a brilliant Aussie Rules footballer who turned professional at the age of sixteen! Sorrell wasn't into sport, and derided Dave as a dumb football jock. They developed a friendly rivalry manifested not only in the reporters' room but in ferocious drinking competitions. Kevin Randell was from Hobart and was following in the footsteps of his elder brother, Ken, still one of Australia's best-known political correspondents and (in 2002) president of the National Press Club.

There is no better place to get a basic grounding in journalism than on a metropolitan daily newspaper. Dick Fulton took our training quite seriously. We were assigned to accompany experienced reporters on the daily 'rounds'-shipping, industrial, the courts, civic affairs and, on rare occasions, the political round. The chief political reporter, Eric Balfe, seemed immensely old to me. I suppose he must have been in his late fifties. The Labor premier Robert Cosgrove was still well entrenched in power, and in the mid 1950s the House of Assembly was a fairly tranquil beat. Eric Balfe had been in the job so long he knew all the politicians extremely well and they fed him with whatever information he needed to fill up his quota in the paper.

Shorthand was quite rightly considered an important tool of a reporter's craft, and we had lessons each week in the subs' room from the football writer Keith Welsh. His by-line was 'Drop Kick', but we inevitably called him 'Drip Cock'. This was partly because of Keith's avid interest in our sex lives. Philip Koch (brother of novelist Christopher Koch), a third year cadet who also attended the shorthand classes, had the reputation of being something of a stud, and Keith used to drive him mad with his innuendos and comments about his love life. One day Phil decided to put a stop to it. Keith had a school-aged daughter who used to come in to the office sometimes to see her father.

Phil pulled Keith to one side. 'Keith, you know how you think I can get any girl in this town that I want?' Keith said something like, 'Half your luck'. Phil went on. 'I'm fed up with all your comments in the shorthand classes about my sex life. If you don't cut it out, I'm going to knock off your daughter. Whatever you might think, I *know* I can do it. Not this week, not next, but sometime in the future I most certainly will.'

Drip Cock turned white. A few days later his daughter put her head into the reporters' room, saw Phil sitting at one of the desks, and scuttled around the edge of the room like a startled crab to where her father was sitting, spoke briefly to him, and fled. There were no more suggestive comments made to Phil. Keith was a nice man, and trying to teach us shorthand was often a thankless task.

After several weeks of trotting along with senior reporters on the civic, shipping and police court rounds, I was desperate to get my first story in the paper. Walking out the front door of *The Mercury* one afternoon I spotted a heavily laden cyclist, the flags and stickers on his backpack and saddle bags identifying him as a round-the-world rider. He was a Swedish lad and of course spoke English as well as I did. I whipped out my notebook and interviewed him about his Tasmanian experiences - *The Mercury* did then and still does love the local angle - and bullied a photographer to come out of the darkroom and take a photograph to go with my story. It actually made it into the paper, and I was very pleased with myself.

A week later I travelled to the quaintly named town of Bagdad (Jericho can be visited further up the Midlands Highway) about thirty kilometres north of Hobart. When I had interviewed the person I'd gone to see, I asked if I could use the toilet. It was the classic one-holer outdoor dunny. I had serious business to attend to and reached for the toilet paper-squares of newsprint punched on to a strategically placed nail. The piece that came to hand was my very first published story and picture of the Swedish cyclist. I thought seriously about what I should do, then used it. It was at least a variant on the old saw, today's news is wrapping tomorrow's fish and chips. It occurred to me at that precise moment that it was unwise to be too precious about the trade I had taken on.

The chief of staff, or his deputy, wrote reporters' assignments in longhand in a big diary that stood on its own sloping lectern in the reporters' room. Not long after my triumph with the Swedish cyclist I was tickled pink to see that I had been assigned to cover a story on my own - the annual general meeting of the Lenah Valley Progress Association. The only downside was the meeting was scheduled on a Saturday night. Lenah Valley was a suburb that pushed up into the lower slopes of Mount Wellington and was notorious for being either wet or cold. On this particular Saturday night it was both. I arrived promptly at eight and about five other people straggled in and sat in their damp overcoats on wooden benches. It soon became evident that the Lenah Valley Progress Association was in crisis. The election of officers came first. There were no nominations for president, and the incumbent said he wasn't standing again. After some persuasion he was prevailed on to saddle up once more. The secretary was equally reluctant, but bowed to pressure. However, the treasurer was adamant. He was out, and that was that.

I wasn't paying particularly close attention at that point, and was startled to find the president pointing his finger at me. 'Here's a young man who's obviously interested in the municipality or he wouldn't be here. I nominate him for Treasurer. What's your name son?'

'No, no-I'm from *The Mercury',* I squeaked. It was a good lesson though. If you are involved with any kind of association, never, ever go to the annual general meeting. It's far too dangerous.

The Mercury staff's favourite watering hole on a Saturday night was the back bar of Bert Dolan's Franklin Hotel, on the waterfront, only a few hundred metres from work. The front bar was rough and dangerous, but the back bar was small, cosy and the unofficial journalists' club. I thought I was a highly sophisticated young man. God help me, I even affected a green Trilby felt hat that I'd acquired somehow. One night I wandered in to the back bar of the Franklin around 9 pm. Mercifully none of my colleagues was there-but that didn't matter. Geoff the barman made sure everybody knew about my gaffe.

'Evening Tim.'

'Evening Geoff.'

'What'll you have, a beer?'

'No thanks Geoff, it's after dinner. I think I'll have a liqueur. What kind of Drambuie do you have?'

Geoff couldn't serve me because he was guffawing so much. He laughed till he cried, and then left me standing there while he rushed into the front bar to share the joke with his boss Bert. For years afterward he'd greet me with, 'What kind of Drambuie do ya want tonight, Tim?' and roar with laughter. He'd still be saying it if the pub hadn't been demolished.

The whole newspaper culture was fuelled by booze. The reporters were bad enough, but the subs were really dedicated pisspots. They used to hang their jackets on hooks in the passageway to the loo.

If you brushed against them, the flasks of spirits would clink together. Early one morning things got out of control when someone threw up in the lift. Not only was this considered an anti-social act but the editor, Roy Shone, slipped in the vomit on his way home. The chief of staff, Fulton, read the riot act, said there was to be no more booze on the premises and that if anyone was found with any alcohol they would be sacked as an example to others.

For a week the subs' room was a desperate, funereal place, the withdrawal symptoms rivalling the most torrid scenes in a Betty Ford Clinic. People snapped at each other and the usual blue fog of cigarette smoke was so thick that the subs on the general table could hardly see the sporting desk two metres away. It all got too much for Leon Searle, a sporting sub, who conned Bert, the one-armed messenger, to go down to the Hobart Hotel and get him a large can of Fosters. Bert, accidentally or on purpose, dropped the can on the concrete stairs on his way back but neglected to tell Leon. A tubby, vertically challenged feller with thick, bottle lens glasses, Leon slipped out of the subs' room, hiding his large chilled can of Fosters under his cardigan, and into the enclosed phone booth at the end of the reporters' room. At precisely that moment, Dick Fulton came into the area to talk to someone and stood with his back inches from the booth.

It was like a scene from a Mack Sennett comedy. Fulton heard the unmistakeable sound of a beer can being punctured. Inside the booth, a geyser of froth flew up and hit the ceiling. Leon bellowed 'Oh shit!' as Fulton wrenched the door open and said, 'What the bloody hell do you think you're doing?' Leon was still trying to tame the geyser and then grabbed fistfuls of copy paper and tried, ineffectually, to mop up. 'Just cleaning up a bit of water Mr Fulton.'

'Looks more like bloody beer to me', said Dick heading back to his office where he probably had a good laugh. Leon didn't get the sack, and the clinking flasks gradually returned to the subs' coat pockets in the dunny corridor.

Leon Searle liked a good party. His recipe for recovery was to leave a half-drunk long-neck bottle of warm Cascade beer under his bed which he would reach for and gurgle down immediately he woke the following morning, saluting the new day with a cry of, 'Ah, that's better'. Once, on a cold winter's night, he rolled himself up in a carpet during a particularly late session. When his hosts unrolled it the next day, there was Leon ready for action again.

My fellow cadet reporter John Sorell once scored the ultimate unwanted assignment to cover the annual general meeting of the Hobart Temperance Alliance on a Friday night. John (who in 2002 was still Director of News at Channel Nine in Melbourne, a job he has held for an extraordinary 27 years) was so cross that he went out on the town and got himself utterly blotto. He weaved in at 11 pm to write his story.

He had the program of the meeting to give him the basics, with the names of the office holders and the topics listed for discussion. His most immediate problem was to stay seated on his chair and get his fingers on the right keys of the office chaffcutter. Then he just made it all up. It was something like this: '"The curse of alcohol is the greatest social problem facing Tasmanian society today", said the President of the Hobart branch of the Temperance Alliance Mr Eustace Clatworthy at the annual general meeting last night. "Battered women and abused children are the victims of this vile and pernicious habit." ' At this point Sorell fell off his chair, but clambered back to continue fabricating half a column of fictitious bilge. It all went in the paper, and I don't think anyone ever complained or commented. I expect the Alliance members were grateful for any publicity.

I was fascinated by the magistrates' courts. The police roundsman, Rex Anthony, was a congenial bloke who taught me a lot. He would spend quite some time just yarning with the police in corridors, at the courts and at police headquarters, and in so doing picked up a lot of very good information. Sometimes I was quite shaken by the raw drama of the lower courts: sexual assaults, bashings, theft, fraud and traffic violations. Even the traffic courts could provide good theatre. There was one eccentric Hobart citizen who fancied himself as a bush lawyer and used to plead not guilty to parking fines, calling police witnesses with histrionic verbal flourishes, and mounting passionate civil libertarian defence arguments. He always lost, but was treated with remarkable courtesy considering the amount of court time he wasted. Although there were some moments of humour, my main memories are of sadness and tragedy. Anguished parents would come over to the press box after their sons or daughters had been found guilty of stealing, petty fraud, or illegal carnal knowledge, pleading for their children's names not to be put in the paper. We had to say we couldn't promise anything, it was up to the editor, but Rex was a nice guy and if the story wasn't important, or didn't have a news angle, it was quietly dropped.

Police time was still being wasted in those days on arresting alcoholic vagrants for being drunk and disorderly in a public place. One long-serving magistrate, then nearing the end of his time on the bench, was Hubert Mansel Brettingham-Moore. A poor, shabby wreck of a vagrant shuffled in to plead guilty to being drunk in a public place. Brettingham-Moore asked him if he had anything to say, and he hadn't. The magistrate looked down at his papers and record before sentencing him, and then looked up and beamed. 'Well, Bloggins, this is quite remarkable. I note this will be your one-hundredth conviction for similar offences. I was going to fine you ten pounds, but because of this notable occasion, I'll let you off with a fiver.' None of these drunks could ever pay the fine, of course, and they were locked up to do their time. At least they got a feed and a brief time to dry out.

When the Hobart police force introduced a system of junior constables they put the trainees out on the beat. They wore a distinctive peaked cap and weren't popular. One of the acned young trainees pulled in a vagrant on a charge of indecent language. He pleaded guilty, as usual, and copped his fine. What he had allegedly said was, 'You're not a junior constable-you're a junior cunt!' The sympathy of the court was not with the eager trainee.

There is an apocryphal story told about Brettingham-Moore which I like. He was supposedly presiding over a traffic court, and becoming increasingly irritated by the number of motorists caught speeding on Sandy Bay Road. Finally he rounded on the tenth defendant so charged, and said, 'I've had enough of this. I'm going to make an example of you'. He reached under the bench, produced a black cap, put it on and intoned, 'It is the sentence of this court that you be taken from here to a prison, and thence to a place of execution, and that there you shall be hanged by the neck until you are dead. And may the Lord have mercy on your soul .. .'

There was a stunned silence in the traffic court. Then someone jumped up at the back and said, 'You can't do that, you haven't got the authority'.

'Haven't I?' said Brettingham-Moore, taking off the black cap. 'Oh well-fined £10.'

The court administration was very blokey. There were no women magistrates, or court officials. The only women there officially were the court stenographers. In the case of a charge of indecent language there would be a pause, the Clerk of the Court would cough, and the stenographer-usually a woman in her forties who looked as though she'd heard it all before-would leave the court while the awful words were read out, then she would trot back in.

Stan Burbury (later Sir Stanley Burbury, Governor of Tasmania) was made Chief Justice in the early 1950s. He had been the Solicitor General and was an old friend of the Bowden family. He and his wife Pearl had a good sense of humour and, before high office stopped such frivolity, used to take part in the Hobart Repertory Society productions with my parents. (I saw him once doing a tremendous job as the judge in Gilbert and Sullivan's *Trial By Jury*.) When Stan decided to appoint a young woman as his Judge's Associate, he told my father and me that it took quite a bit of organising,

Spooling Through

but he got his way. One morning a senior police sergeant asked to see him in his chambers because he had a problem. He had to give evidence involving the use of indecent language in a Supreme Court hearing and asked if Stan's associate could leave the court while he gave it, to avoid embarrassment to her. Stan gave him short shrift, and told him to get on with it.

The next morning Sergeant Plod, perspiring freely, got to the difficult bit. 'I apprehended the defendant, Your Honour, laid my hand on his shoulder and said, "I arrest you in the name of the law". He said, "Fuck off you dead cunt"-and proceeded off in a westerly direction.'

Proceeding in a westerly direction went into the Bowden lexicon and is there to this day.

As a beginner I didn't do much direct reporting from the courts, an arena where shorthand was considered essential, but of soccer, which almost no one followed because Tasmania was an Australian Rules crazed island. That became my responsibility. I took over from a mild-mannered Englishman, Gordon Burnett, who had been a prisoner of war of the Japanese in Asia. The teams were migrants, many of whom had come to work on the Tasmanian Hydro-Electric Commission's dam projects. There were Italians, Germans, Serbs, Croats, Latvians and Hungarians. I don't remember an English team, but there may have been one. The games were often extremely vigorous. Sport in general was not my strong point and I struggled to get a working understanding of soccer and the rules. I never really understood what offside was. People would explain it to me patiently, but I never twigged. Describing the main game each Saturday was torture. It is a wonder I wasn't knifed behind the grandstand by a disgruntled supporter in the hope that my replacement might be better.

One Saturday afternoon I was sent to phone back the results of a country race meeting at Sorell, on the eastern side of the Derwent, about thirty kilometres from Hobart-probably because I had a car, a black side-valve Morris Minor. Mal Williams, from our rival paper the Launceston *Examiner*, was there too. Mal was not only an experienced journalist, but an experienced racing reporter. The only way to phone copy back to our respective afternoon papers was from a public phone box about a kilometre from the race track. I managed to get there first, and dialled the copy-taker at *The Mercury*. It was her first day as a copy-taker, and my first day relaying horse race results, and it wasn't a good double. Had I fluked an experienced copy-taker she would have sorted me out, and I'd have been out of there in minutes. As it was, it took about a quarter of an hour. I could see Mal pacing backwards and forwards outside the booth. Finally I burst out, apologising profusely.

'Jeeezus', said Mal. 'What do they do there at the bloody *Mercury*-carve it on to a bloody granite slab with a bloody cold chisel or something!'

My friend Mike Philp was in his element covering the yachting. At the tender age of twelve he had crewed for his father in the 1946 Sydney to Hobart yacht race in Colin Philp's big steel cutter *Southern Maid*. In the 1950s the Sydney to Hobart was a smaller, more relaxed affair with radio communications irregular and haphazard and corporate sponsorship way in the future. One year a yacht, appropriately named *Wanderer*, failed to finish. A week went by without any contact and there was some anxiety but it turned out the owner had got bored with the race and gone cruising.

In 1959, as the Sydney to Hobart race was nearing its end, the officials at the Royal Yacht Club of Tasmania in Hobart believed the race would finish at a convenient hour the next morning. So they had a few drinks at the clubhouse and went off home to bed. That same evening, Mike, cogitating in *The Mercury* reporters' room, wondered if they mightn't finish sooner. He checked with the Bureau of Meteorology on forecast winds, noted the last reported position of the leading boats and calculated that the winner could cross the line in the very early hours of the morning. On his own initiative he contacted the paper's chief photographer, Len Carter, and woke up the RYCT officials who blearily manned the box at the finishing line at Castray Esplanade. Sure enough, at 12.30 am the winning yacht appeared out of the dark, ghosting along in light airs. Had Mike not acted there would have been no officials there to record the time and the event-nor any photographs of *Solo* which won line honours that year.

One of the Sydney to Hobart yacht race traditions that has only intensified over the years is the end of race 'quiet little drink' in and around the fleet moored at Constitution Dock. The yachties start hitting the beer within a nanosecond of passing the finish line, and the drinking goes on through new year and beyond. On one occasion a photographer was needed to go down to the docks and photograph the winning crew. The only photographer on duty was David Baker, a small, rather shy man who usually covered the social round and general assignments, but not sport. David arrived at the dock carrying his big Speed Graphic camera with its trademark flashgun. Press photography was all done on big, single plate negatives. The yachties were shickered, of course, and a large, raucous crowd was applauding them from dockside. David jumped down onto the stern and asked the crew to bunch together in and around the entrance to the cabin, at the forward end of the cockpit. He had trouble fitting them all into his frame, and kept retreating towards the stern, asking them-as photographers always do-could they please get closer together. The crowd fell silent as David backed to within a few centimetres of the aft rail.

'Just a bit closer', pleaded David, then took a final, disastrous step back, and overbalanced. With great presence of mind, he carefully put down his camera on the deck as he fell backwards into the water. The crowd cheered, and a bedraggled David was pulled from the water to even louder cheers then sloshed back unhappily to his darkroom.

Some of *The Mercury* headlines were distinctive. There was a quite classy racehorse named Granny Smith, after the famous apple. The good burghers of Hobart woke one morning to see a bold headline over three columns of the sporting page:

Granny has it sewn up

The Roman Catholic Archbishop of Hobart, Guildford Young, was photographed walking down the steps of St Mary's Cathedral in formal regalia, flanked by his two civilian brothers. They did look a bit like plain clothes coppers, an impression heightened by the line below in large type:

Sex maniac at large - police warning

When the Shah of Iran was kicked off the Peacock Throne he lived in exile for a short while in the Bahamas-somewhat defiantly, according to *The Mercury*.

Shah sticks it out on resort.

Robber escapes with £1,235 payroll in snatch

conjured up a bizarre image for some.

The editor of *The Mercury* when I joined the paper was Roy Shone. Although to us he was a fairly remote figure, many years later I found a note in my papers from him, congratulating me on ferreting out and writing a story on my own initiative. That was unusual and many editors still don't bother with such encouragement. The reporters and news executives all wore suits to work but since he didn't have to leave the building and worked until the early hours of the morning, Shone was usually seen in a battered brown Harris tweed sports coat and rumpled grey trousers. One afternoon I was walking towards the lift on the ground floor with a new reporter, Barry D'Argaville, who had joined the paper from Sydney. Shone arrived at the same time and I stood back to let him go in first. D'Argaville barged in ahead of him and we all rode up to the editorial floor together. Barry pushed past him again when we left the lift, and out of the corner of his eye saw Shone walk through the door marked Editor.

'Why is he going in there?' asked Barry.

'Because he's the editor.'

'Shit! I thought he was the cleaner', Barry said.

Some of Shone's editorials were idiosyncratic. He became irritated by U Thant, the Secretary of the United Nations in New York, and referred to him in an editorial as that 'boob from Burma'. Wilfrid Asten, the president of the local United Nations Association, was outraged, and wrote demanding a retraction of this slur to the dignity of U Thant's office and to the man. Shone ran the letter but didn't see any need for an apology.

In 1956, one of the biggest stories in Tasmania, indeed one of the biggest national and international stories, began to run-and did so intermittently for the next decade. Sydney Sparkes Orr, Professor of Philosophy at the University of Tasmania, was sacked by the University Council allegedly for seducing one of his students-as well as for other allegations of professional incompetence and improper conduct. Orr was an activist who had published an Open Letter in *The Mercury* about general conditions at the university. The letter had been instrumental in instigating a Royal Commission in March 1955 into the running of the University of Tasmania. When Reg Kemp, a Hobart timber merchant, attended a University Council meeting a year later alleging that Orr had seduced a student, Kemp's daughter, Suzanne, the University Council quickly decided that Orr should be summarily dismissed.

At the last minute Orr offered to resign, with a six months' salary payout, but the council decided not to accept his resignation-an error of judgement that cost it dearly. That decision also set in train a succession of legal actions that split the Tasmanian community and academe, and provided a long-running saga of sex, intrigue, alleged attempted murder and bizarre evidence that included the psychoanalysis of dreams, links with the British royal family and enough salacious detail not only to fill the broadsheet columns of the nation's newspapers day after day, but to fuel a succession of books. One of the most recent books, by the Tasmanian writer Cassandra Pybus, was published in 1993, with the arresting title of *Gross Moral Turpitude*-a phrase taken from the lips of Justice Kenneth Green who presided over the first case that Orr instigated against the University of Tasmania, suing for wrongful dismissal. Litigation would continue for the next decade.

The evidence was sensational. Suzanne Kemp had kept a diary detailing the liaisons, and excerpts were read out in court. On several occasions there had been sessions with Orr at his family home, with his wife and children elsewhere in the house. Orr had bullied one of his lecturers, Yugoslavian-born Dr Kajica Milanov, a refugee from Europe, to interpret his dreams. The interpretations were included in evidence. Some of his colleagues spoke of Orr's conviction that he was the illegitimate son of King Edward VIII. (He did look uncannily like the abdicated monarch.) A limerick circulated in academic circles:

> A lunatic prof known as Orr
> Declared his mother a whore
> From the fantastic themes
> Of his Freudian dreams
> He deduced that his pere was Windsor.

Newspapers all over Australia could not get enough of the story and hot shot reporters from the Mainland came to Hobart to cover the court case using *The Mercury* as their base. I was too close to the story for comfort. Andrew Kemp was one of my best friends at school, and I knew the family well. Fortunately, as a second year cadet, I was too junior to be assigned even to help cover the story. Besides, my shorthand was abysmal.

Athol Bradley, a senior reporter on *The Mercury,* was a brilliant shorthand writer. Brad would go to the Hobart Supreme Court with his notepad and take down every word. During breaks in procedure and the lunch break, he would begin to handwrite his copy directly

Spooling Through

from his notes onto a small pile of copy paper he had in his briefcase. When the court rose he would return to the office with three-quarters of his work done. He just needed to write a lead, and finish off the last few hours of evidence, two-finger typing on his battered portable Underwood. By half past six he'd say, 'See ya later fellers', and walk out the door whistling, his felt hat tilted characteristically on the back of his head. Before he left, the gung-ho Mainland reporters (most of whom had tried to take it all down in longhand) would be frantically scrabbling through their scribblings trying to make sense of it. Inevitably they missed important exchanges.

Suzanne Kemp's diary was constantly quoted in evidence and, in the reporters' room, there would be a question, 'Brad, what was it that the professor was supposed to have said after they made love in his car near that beach? I can't quite make out my notes'.

Of course, the smartarse from the Mainland wouldn't have even a single word in his 'notes', but Brad would stop typing, and say, 'What's that mate?' He would patiently flip back through his notebook and give the exact quote, before continuing with his own work. Two minutes later, 'Brad, sorry to trouble you again, but .. .' I never once saw Brad lose his cool.

The Orr affair went on and on. Conspiracy theories were thick on the ground and in print. One key issue was academic freedom, which brought on board some supporters who couldn't stand Orr personally. Orr, an exceedingly difficult man, almost invariably turned on individuals who were trying to help him. He pulled on martyrdom like a well-loved overcoat in a Tasmanian winter and saw himself as a latter-day Dreyfus, or Oscar Wildean figure. He once compared himself with Christ.and should never have been allowed near the witness box. None of the court cases involving the university or individuals was ever instigated by anyone other than Orr. Somehow he always seemed to finish up in the dock, as though he was the defendant.

Sadly, the whole imbroglio took an enormous toll on the Kemp family. Andrew and Suzanne's parents, Reg and Pauline, died very young. My father died in his early nineties, and I enjoyed his friendship for just over sixty years. Andrew lost his father when he was twenty-four. He was well aware that it was the pressure of events that spiralled out of control that killed his parents. The trauma of those years shortened Orr's life too, and he died only three months after he eventually achieved a cash settlement from the University of Tasmania, ten years after he had been dismissed. He accepted $32,000 in May 1966-the same amount he had been offered by the university four years earlier. In a prolix statement, the University Council admitted that it stuffed up Orr's dismissal in the first place.

When the University of Tasmania celebrated its centenary in 1990, I met George Wilson who lectured me in history in the late 1950s. I remembered that George had been a prominent supporter of Orr, particularly in relation to the issue of academic freedom. In the course of conversation I said that Orr must have been a difficult man to deal with. 'Difficult? He was impossible', said George. 'One night I was up at Hytten Hall [one of the university residential colleges] with a colleague and Syd Orr trying to draft a statement to bolster his case. Syd was his usual infuriating self. At one stage I was out on the balcony grappling with my colleague who kept shouting, "I'm going to job him. I'm going to job him"'.

George told me of his reaction when he heard of Orr's death. 'I was down at the Travellers' Rest Hotel having a few beers after the rugby, and someone came in and said, "Syd Orr's dead". Do you know my first thought was, I wonder what the slippery little bastard's up to now?'

I was in Singapore for the ABC when Orr died and was sickened by an obituary which I considered to be an outrageous eulogy and which was published in *The Bulletin*. The magazine published the letter I wrote, in which I said that although it wasn't the most tactful time to 'raise my voice on the other side of the fence ... critics of Orr have always been labelled as vicious perverters of the truth'.

The simplest way to cope with the type of obituary I have mentioned (which just falls short of canonisation) is to prepare a glossary of terms. For 'philosophical idealist' read 'wishful thinker', for 'struggle for justice' read 'aggressive evasion of the point', 'uncompromising honesty' becomes 'that's my story and I'm sticking to it', and so on. I have always envied people who have been able to rationalise 'truth' as something they want to believe irrespective of what happened.

Orr, I suppose, will become a kind of folk hero, the little man who fought against the system for the principles of truth, justice, honour, etc. I don't suppose anybody ever spares a thought for the Kemp family, or wonders what became of them. Suffice to say that Reg Kemp died several years ago and the family has never recovered from the shock of 'The Orr Case'. But, of course, that is irrelevant to the canonisers.

Those who were in Tasmania at the time, and knew the people concerned, have always found it difficult to come to terms with 'mainland experts' chanting the gospel of the 'Divine Right of the Academic'. It is a pity that the University mishandled the manner of Orr's dismissal.

Wouldn't it have been so much better if Orr had accepted his dismissal and retired gracefully from the scene? (I can hear in my ears the wild screams of the Orr supporters.) At least the Philosophy Department of the University of Tasmania would have been able to attract a first-rate professor who would have been able to teach philosophy to students-denied the privilege of studying the subject through the efforts of the man who claimed to the last to have their interests at heart.

TIM BOWDEN
Singapore

The chair of philosophy at the University of Tasmania had been declared black after the Orr case and this was of some concern to me, as philosophy was one of my two major subjects at university. I had begun a part-time Bachelor of Arts degree, largely at the instigation of my father who would have dearly loved to have had a tertiary education himself. (Young people did what their parents wanted them to do in the 1950s.) We had no professor, although we did have the benefit of several visiting emeritus professors from the United Kingdom who knew Orr, and had no qualms about breaking the black ban imposed by his supporters on the faculty. One was Professor Levine, and another was Professor Alexander Macbeath from Queens University, Belfast, who had queried Orr's stated qualifications and achievements from that august institution.

Our lecturer was Dr Milanov, the Yugoslavian refugee from a Nazi prison camp whom Orr had inveigled into analysing his dreams.

The sun used to stream in through high windows at the back of the lecture hall where Dr Milanov was attempting to make metaphysicians of us. A mature student, an army captain, used to sit up the back. The soporific combination of the warm sun and Milanov used to send him almost instantly to sleep. I would watch fascinated as his pen formed a zigzag pattern across the page until the nib crashed off the edge of his exercise book onto the desk. He would then give a start, reposition the pen on a new line, and drop off again. At the end of the lecture his notes looked like the etchings of a barograph. I took pity on him, and gave him a carbon copy of my typed up lecture notes. He passed too!

My visits to university were regarded with deep suspicion by my chief of staff, Dick Fulton, who had odd ideas about tertiary education. After taking me to task about my many shortcomings, he warmed to his theme. 'Anyway, you should be more bloody grateful about what the paper is doing for you. Buying your textbooks and giving you all that bloody time off to go up to that university.'

Most of my university lectures were in the morning, and I was usually rostered on from 2 pm till 11 pm. I told Fulton I was very grateful for the books but, in reality, I wasn't taking any time off for lectures. He glared at me.

'Well you don't think you can do an honest day's work after you've been up there do you?'

He seemed to think my brain had somehow been 'milked' of a portion of useful function by academic activity.

Fulton came from the north-west coast and so, coincidentally, did many of *The Mercury's* cadets. The first to arrive were Alistair Edison and 'Bud' Eastley. If Bud had another name I never knew it. He was a tall, blond, surfer type. Al was of average height and stocky build. He was seventeen when he arrived, his dark hair slicked down with Brylcreem, zits on his face, and prominent, discoloured front teeth. Within weeks there had been a makeover. Al appeared with dazzling white false teeth, a short haircut and no Brylcreem. Even the zits had gone.

His explanation was pragmatic and succinct.

'I wasn't getting any fucks. A friend of mine told me to stop using hair grease, have my front teeth pulled out and get dentures.'

'But there was nothing wrong with your teeth!'

'Doesn't matter. It worked. Now I'm getting plenty of fucks.'

Soon two more north-west coast cadets appeared: Jim Dickinson, a rather shy, gangly youth, and 'Hooks' Wheat, a rather scruffy bloke with a knowing look about him. It was a wonder Hooks could spare the time from punting on the gee-gees to come to the office. I told him he was wasting his time once, and he rounded on me. 'Listen mate, I don't bet for fun, I bet to make money. I make more on the track than I do in this fucking place.'

I was incredulous, but he insisted it was true. 'OK. If I give you ten pounds [about a week's salary] would you be able to double it?' I asked.

'Sure', he replied.

I handed over my ten quid, and about five weeks later Hooks handed me twenty. 'I wouldn't do that again. I had to be too cautious, and do things I wouldn't have done with my own money. But I told you I could do it.'

Fulton did let a couple of southerners slip through the net, including Doug Blain, who was a year or so behind me at school. Doug's father, Ellis Blain, was a very well-known ABC announcer and tennis commentator.

I was still a second year cadet, all of nineteen years old, when Fulton came into the reporters' room one day and asked me, 'Your father's in the car business, isn't he?'

'Yes Mr Fulton.'

'Well you're now the motoring editor. Get on with it.'

I knew nothing about cars, but loved driving them. (Both Alistair Edison and Doug Blain must have been spitting chips about my stroke of luck, because they did know about cars and were motor racing enthusiasts.) I began a series of road tests of new models, using a stopwatch to do my own speed and acceleration trials. I used to take various friends to operate the stopwatch if they could spare the time. The road tests rolled along for some months until one of my timers begged me to have a drive. I resisted, for obvious reasons. But he persisted, saying he was a rally driver himself and no harm could come of it. He had been frustrated watching me belt a new car around winding Tasmanian roads, imagining how much better he could do it. He was used to driving a car with fairly indirect steering. The car I was testing was the opposite. Stan took off, and headed into his first bend with the straight-armed posture of a racing driver. Alas, he was not prepared for such direct steering and the back slid away. He over-corrected and took out a couple of white posts with the back mudguard. I had to say I had done it, of course, and the motor firm concerned complained to Dick Fulton that I had bent one of their cars. That was the end of my beloved road tests.

My motoring page appeared in the *Saturday Evening Mercury* edited by Vic Mitchell, who had his own office next to Roy Shone's. The SEM, as it was known, reflected Vic's own interests in many ways. He was very keen on page three beach girls-particularly in the summer months. There was enthusiastic coverage of all beach girl competitions-I think there was even a special SEM award. I found a clipping recently with a picture of an eleven-year-old junior beach girl in a one-piece bathing suit at the Sandy Bay Regatta. In fact, the junior competition went right down to one-year-olds, so prurience was abandoned somewhere down the line. We used to say that Vic would publish any girl in bathers who strayed in front of a lens.

Unkindly, we put this to the test one day. One of Hooks Wheat's mates-surprise surprise-was a jockey. Milton obligingly squeezed his spare frame into a bikini with a couple of oranges supplying the essential bulges. Hair was a bit of a challenge, but we made do with the end of a mop, tastefully arranged over Milton's brow and eyes. We posed him on the sloping front of a Volkswagen, and sent in the photo to Vic. Although it has to be said that Milton made a fairly ordinary-looking sort and I'd have thought that his big feet and prominent Adam's apple were dead giveaways, Vic took it seriously enough to put it in the paper.

Staying alive 3

It was possible to have a life away from *The Mercury* despite the shift work and uncertain weekends. I would have dearly loved - perhaps this was the unrealised ham in me - to have taken part in the Old Nick Company's annual university student review, but it was simply not possible.

For a brief time I joined the staff of *Togatus,* the student newspaper, but it was difficult as a part-timer to really feel like a proper university student. The curse of cynicism soon strikes the young reporter and the working life I led, covering police courts, accidents and fires, seemed to me light years away from the idealistic debates in the students' common room, even when I had the time to join them. Nor did I mind shift work as it made it possible to go to the beach in the mornings, when Tasmania's short summers allowed, while ordinary folk were slaving away at their nine-to-five jobs.

Then there was a brief flirtation with flying. When I was twelve, a family friend, Wilf Jowett, who worked in the Department of Civil

Aviation, shouted me my first flight in a Tiger Moth, piloted by one of Hobart's great characters, Lloyd Jones. (Wilf, even then, was courting my mother's sister Dot Lovett—I had two Aunty Dotties—but he didn't become my uncle until many years later. Wilf was a determined man and just kept plugging away doggedly until Dot finally said yes.) Lloyd Jones was an ex-RAAF Beaufort fighter pilot and veteran of the Pacific war, who found civilian life (and Tiger Moths) a bit of an anti-climax. But it was a terrific first flight for me from Cambridge Airport, east of Hobart. I had to wear one of those Biggles-style leather helmets, with a speaking tube plugged into the intercom system in the front cockpit. Lloyd Jones, who sported a trademark RAAF handlebar moustache, flew the aircraft from the rear cockpit. We seemed to take off in the width of a runway and headed off to Seven Mile Beach where Lloyd amused himself with a bit of low flying. The shallow sandbanks were above us, I recall, as we roared along the beach with the Moth's fixed wheels almost brushing the sand. He then climbed up and away for a few steep turns and a dive or two. It was just bloody wonderful. Moths were string-and-sealing-wax aircraft with a pedigree reaching back to World War I. They were chronically underpowered. I saw one flying backwards once at Cambridge against a stiff westerly wind.

The exhilaration of this flight stuck in my mind and I entered a flying scholarship that happened to be sponsored by *The Mercury* —that was a bit awkward and I knew I couldn't win it because I was a member of staff, but there was a chance of netting one of six half-scholarships on offer. The scholarship depended on a flying aptitude test. You were taken up in a Chipmunk monoplane trainer (it looked a bit like a scaled-down Spitfire and was a very sexy aircraft), shown the controls and what they did before you took off, and then when the pilot in the rear cockpit said to take over, you did. The idea was to fly straight and level for a while and then try a few turns. To my surprise I did quite well, having a natural feeling for the combination of rudder and joystick to bank the Chipmunk while making the turn. Lloyd Jones did the testing, his moustache as raffish as ever.

To my delight I did win a half-scholarship and was soon doing circuits and bumps in a Chipmunk—which happened to be a fully aerobatic aircraft. My first instructor, who wasn't much older than I was, soon got bored and we used to fly to a designated area to practise stalls and spins—or, I should say to practise recovering from them. To go into a spin, first you had to climb high enough, and then stall the aircraft by pulling back on the power, but holding the nose up until the Chipmunk literally fell out of the sky. It was never clear which way the aircraft would spin, but the trick was to work out whether it was to the left or the right and give full opposite rudder while pushing the joystick forward. In the excitement of it all I kicked the rudder the wrong way, merely increasing the rate of spin and my instructor had quite a job overriding my grim determination to kill both of us. We lost 1000 feet on every spin. He won control, put on power and pulled back to straight and level flight with drastic g-forces draining the blood from our heads and pinning us to our seats.

After this inept effort I was told to keep my bloody hands and feet off the controls, and we climbed back up to have some fun, looping the loop and doing slow rolls. Centrifugal force keeps you in your seat during a loop, but during a slow roll you hang upside down in your straps while chewing gum wrappers and junk on the floor fall down on the Perspex canopy under your head.

I did actually fly solo a couple of times—moments no trainee pilot ever forgets. Nick Tanner (who ran the Aero Club of Southern Tasmania after Lloyd Jones had to retire following a go-cart accident) was my instructor and we were doing circuits and bumps, and then lined up for a takeoff. Nick delivered the classic line, 'You take her around by yourself this time', and climbed out of the rear cockpit. I tried to pretend he was still there. It was an anxious time for both of us. I managed to take off all right—that's the easy part—flew around the airfield and lined up for the important bit. Normally a pilot who is running short on his landing approach just puts on a burst or two of power to get over the perimeter fence. Trainee pilots are supposed to get it right and if you do find yourself short, the drill is to abort the landing, go round and do it again. To my chagrin, I misjudged, and had to go around again. Nick probably wondered how many times this was going to happen, but I made it down on the second go. Then he made me do it again!

It wasn't possible to complete the course—I simply did not have the money to pay the other half of the scholarship on a cadet reporter's pay and I have to confess I found the maths involved a bit daunting too. Well, damn near impossible. Still, it was something to have flown solo in such an exciting aircraft. Stalls and spins are not recommended on the more sedate Cessnas used by trainee pilots these days.

Journalism might have paid miserably and had broken hours, but the holidays were generous to compensate—four weeks a year. In January 1956 Mike Philp and I decided to spend three weeks camping on Maria Island, off the east coast of Tasmania. The island is now a national park but was then still in its last stages of exploitation, with sheep farmers firing the timbered flanks of Mount Maria to generate more feed for their stock, and the remains of an abandoned cement works—with a huge chimney and silos—at the island's northern end. Maria Island was one of the first parts of Australia ever seen by European eyes, and was marked on Abel Tasman's charts in 1642. He named the island after Maria, the daughter of his patron the Governor General of the Dutch East Indies, Anthony Van Diemen. The land to the west (which he thought to be a promontory of the fabled Great South Land) was named after his patron when it was known to be an island.

As if Van Diemen's Land wasn't remote enough to ensure convicts could not escape, they were disbursed from the main penitentiary at Port Arthur on the Tasman Peninsula to Macquarie Harbour on Tasmania's wild west coast and to Maria Island in the east. In the 1950s you could still see the open-fronted remains of brick cells at an outstation near Chinamans Bay, towards the middle of the island. (By the end of the 1960s, the walls still standing in the 1950s were pushed over by vandals and became heaps of rubble.) Fortunately, some of the convict-built brick cottages at Darlington, the main settlement, were re-roofed with corrugated iron along the way and have survived.

Every enterprise that started on this spectacularly beautiful island went broke. A flamboyant Italian businessman, Diego Bernacchi, fell in love with Maria Island and settled there in the late nineteenth century. He planted acres of grapes and planned to make the island a great wine producing centre. 'King Diego' even managed to get Darlington re-named as San Diego but his pastoral dream was brought down by the economic depression of the 1890s.

Mike Philp and I planned to camp on the western side of the island—we were not quite sure where. So we chartered an aircraft from the Aero Club of Southern Tasmania, filled some sacks with tins of food and sawdust, which we hoped to drop near our camp site, and set off to reconnoitre. We found a dropping zone on top of some cliffs and chucked out our sacks of provisions, which burst like bombs as they hit the ground. We hoped we could find them again.

Maria Island is divided into two parts by a narrow sandy spit separating Chinamans Bay from Riedle Bay on the eastern side. We planned to take a dinghy, pull it across the isthmus and, with the rest of our camping gear, row it along to a lovely little cove we had seen from the air. A professional fisherman from Orford, Fred Gourlay, towed our small boat behind his fishing dory across to the island, and waved us farewell. Mike and I struggled across the isthmus with our boat, tent and provisions only to find a dangerous surf running on the ocean side. It was too risky, said Mike, to launch the dinghy with all our gear. What we should do, he said, was walk the dinghy along the beach through the wash of the surf, and launch it from the safety of a rocky point that would give us shelter from the swells. (There was only room for one of us and the gear in the boat anyway. The other would have to walk around the shoreline to our camping place—with luck locating our aerial drop on the way.)

Mike was far more experienced with boats than I, but I argued that it *was* possible to launch the dinghy and I was buggered if I was going to trudge around the beach in the wrong direction from where we wanted to go when we could stick to plan A. We argued for a while until Mike said that I could do what I liked but he was taking his own gear out of the boat. He watched impassively as I rowed through the broken foam in our little cockleshell, copped a big breaking swell that half swamped the boat, which broached and was tipped over by the next wave. I have to say that Mike came into the water at that point and helped recover what we could of our gear and bring the boat ashore again. As well as tipping the boat over I had also managed to strain one of the wooden oars. One of my better performances, really. Fortunately Mike was (and is) a very equable feller and I don't think he even indulged himself with an 'I told you so'. We then did what he had suggested in the first place and pulled the boat around in the wash of the surf to the shelter of the southern rocky point of Riedle Bay. There we dried out our gear as much as we could in a few hours and Mike made an ingenious repair of the oar using some fencing wire and splints of driftwood.

Shouldering my wet pack, I began to walk around the ocean beach and then follow the coastline as closely as the cliffs and scrub would allow. I caught occasional glimpses of Mike and the dinghy, sometimes disappearing completely in the trough of a big swell, making his way across Riedle Bay in a stiffening onshore easterly sea breeze. I found our tinned supplies dented but otherwise OK, noted their location and finally reached the cove where Mike and I intended to camp for three weeks. But the beach that had looked so attractive from the air was stony and not sheltered from a heavy surge sweeping in and out. I walked down to the beach to see if I could see Mike, when I noticed an attractive young woman rock-fishing. This was a surprise as we expected to have this side of Maria Island to ourselves. She hadn't seen me, and the roar of the wind and waves drowned my approach.

'Er, hello, good morning.' She nearly threw her rod into the kelp with shock. We had hardly time to exchange more than a few words when a very fit young man in shorts bounded over the rocks towards us, and said (rather belligerently I thought) in heavily accented English, 'What are you doing here?'

'I'm on holiday, and a friend of mine and I have come to camp here for three weeks.'

He seemed unimpressed with this news and said he thought there was a much better camping spot further up the coast! I was slow on the uptake. They were on their honeymoon and had come to what they hoped was one of the most private and secluded places in the world.

This was my first meeting with Olegas Truchanas, adventurer, canoeist, explorer and conservationist who was about to make his name in the fledgling Tasmanian environmental movement. He had fought with the Lithuanian resistance movement in World War II and emigrated to Australia in 1948. Ten years later he became the first to canoe down the entire length of the Gordon River from its headwaters in Lake Pedder to Macquarie Harbour on the west coast and was a passionate advocate for letting Tasmania's remaining wild rivers run free. (Tragically he was killed in 1972, trapped underwater in his canoe while negotiating rapids on his beloved Gordon River.)

Olegas, being Olegas, had pitched their small tent halfway up a cliff, in a small cleft. It looked so precarious that it seemed to me one incautious move in the night by either Olegas or his bride, Melva, could have been fatal. By this time Mike Philp had arrived off the entrance to the cove in the dinghy and we could only gesticulate at each other, but he clearly could not land, and headed off to the shelter of Whalers Cove about a kilometre further around the coast, which was his only alternative.

To the evident relief of Olegas and Melva, I headed off to meet Mike at Whalers Cove which was a beautifully sheltered inlet, with a creek of pristine water running down from the high country. It was the perfect camping spot, and Mike and I could barely tear ourselves away to walk to other parts of the island. We did have to make a few expeditions, however, to cart our bent tins from the airdrop site. The labels had parted company from most of them, so we weren't sure whether we were opening a tin of stew or canned peaches. It didn't seem to matter much. Most of the time we ate fresh fish including as many crayfish as we wanted. Mike even managed to catch crayfish by lying on a rock, reaching down and grabbing them by their front feelers! Leaning over an overhanging bit of granite to catch a crayfish requires immense patience since the slightest movement of Mike's hand in the water made an eddy that spooked them back into their crevices. I had brought a mask, snorkel, flippers and a spear gun and used to skewer delicious trumpeter among the kelp—our only way of getting them, as they do not take a baited hook. We found weathered fragments of whale bone near our camp, a legacy from the slaughter of whales in the nineteenth century.

We had to keep a lookout for snakes and Mike shot quite a number around our camp with his .22 Browning rifle. Once he was squatting naked on a rock in the creek washing his socks when a sixth sense made him look around and there was a big black snake coiling up a foot behind him. Mike jumped into the water, flat out, like a frog.

Most of the time we didn't bother about clothes except when an occasional 'Yoo hoo' was heard from afar. I didn't have a wetsuit, and the water was very cold, even in Tasmania's short high summer. I could only stay in for about ten minutes before becoming a shivering wreck. For some reason we had a flagon of autumn brown sherry in our grog supplies that was so foul we didn't drink it. Desperate for underwater warmth I started the dangerous habit of gulping down a tumbler of this sherry and heading back again into the water. The underwater scenery had a surreal look about it, but the sherry didn't help me to spear fish, unfortunately. A medico told me later I was doing something that was very dangerous as alcohol dilates blood vessels and can lead to hypothermia.

Olegas and Melva did drop round for an occasional evening meal, and crayfish boats used to overnight in Whalers Cove. We became friendly with a Swedish skipper, Peter Svensen, and his offsider. 'Gom unt 'ave tee, viz us', Peter would shout after he moored for the night. Mike and I would row out and Peter would have scaled and filleted fresh trumpeter from that day's catch which was sizzling in the frying pan by the time we got on board. We had good conversations in his snug little fo'csle. He had a different way of cooking crayfish tails. He dipped them in boiling water just long enough to set the surface like a soft-boiled egg. Then he popped the flesh out of the shell, cut it into chunks, and fried the just translucent jelly in butter. They were great days.

We arranged to be picked up by yacht, and some of our friends came along for the ride and spent a few days at Whalers Cove. They ruined a splendid photograph of me posing proudly with a huge brown-banded morwong I had speared. Closer inspection of the background shows two of my 'friends' exposing themselves, and a third giving a single finger salute.

Looking back, and despite the generous holidays for journalists, I wonder now how I fitted in so many bushwalking adventures in the few years I was at *The Mercury*. But Tasmania was such an exciting place physically that it seemed criminal not to experience as much of it as possible—a legacy, I suppose, of my ten-year-old's walk through the Cradle Mountain–Lake St Clair National Park with my parents.

In the early 1950s the south-west region of Tasmania was as remote and unknown as Sir Arthur Conan Doyle's *Lost World*. From Macquarie Harbour on the west coast (where convicts had laboured in the constant drenching rain to harvest the incomparable boat-building timber Huon pine) round to South-West Cape, this wild, beautiful and mountainous wilderness was almost totally uninhabited. Deny King and his family scratched out a living from an alluvial tin mine in Port Davey (and got supplies and equipment in by boat from Hobart) and the Clayton family lived on the northern shore of Port Davey where Clyde was a cray fisherman. The two families lived in total isolation. This wilderness began just to the west of Mount Wellington, unbelievably close to Tasmania's capital city.

A jewel in the crown of Tasmania's natural assets was Lake Pedder, about eighty kilometres due west from Hobart and headwaters of the spectacular Gordon River which had scored its way through deep rocky gorges over the millennia to the upper reaches of Macquarie Harbour. Lake Pedder, a shallow lake of peat-stained water, was fringed on its eastern side during the summer months by a dazzlingly white beach of glacial sand so big and firm that light aircraft could safely land on it—depending on how full the lake was in a particular year.

Lloyd Jones and the chief engineer of the Aero Club of Southern Tasmania, Alan Hume, were among the pioneers to use this unique landing strip in 1947 flying a Tiger Moth. Carrying their return fuel in a jerry can, they coaxed the tiny biplane up to 5000 feet to clear Mount Wellington, and headed west. It was a cloudless day, but Tasmania's weather can change in hours, and invariably comes in from the west. Lloyd told me that he bounced the wheels of the Tiger Moth on the sand in a practice touchdown and it seemed firm enough. They committed to a landing and switched off the engine. It was an extraordinary moment which both men remembered vividly. There was total silence and absolutely no wind. They climbed out of the aircraft and stood for the first time on the beach. Something made them drag the Moth around so that it faced the west, where the peaks of the Franklin Range rose up like so many jagged teeth. It was breathtakingly beautiful, but they did not linger and began to refuel their fragile aircraft. Were they to crash on take-off or be forced down it was unlikely anyone would ever find them.

Without warning a sudden 60 km/h gust of wind howled across the dark, rippling waters of Lake Pedder, almost flipping the Moth on its back. Had they not faced it to the west they would have lost their aircraft. Unnerved, they took off without further delay and flew back to Cambridge airport. Later, heavier aircraft would not be so vulnerable to such rogue westerlies, and by the time I started to learn to fly in 1956 the aero club was running regular flights in and out of Lake Pedder using Austers and a more substantial four-seater Percival Proctor.

Four of us decided to fly in to Lake Pedder, camp there for a few days, and then walk out. We camped behind the sand dunes, and fluked some warm sunny weather. Lake Pedder was shallow, and its water, the colour of strong tea, used to warm up quite quickly in direct sun. To swim you had to walk out at least two hundred metres to be waist deep. It would have to be one of the great swimming experiences of all time, surrounded by spectacular mountains, with that improbable glistening white beach on the eastern edge of the lake. Swimming there reminded me of a wonderful practical joke perpetrated on Peter Tanner, the older brother of Nick (who had risked sending me on my first solo), who had flown in to Lake Pedder for a swim with the then secretary of the Aero Club of Southern Tasmania, Patricia Dalton, a couple of years earlier.

Unfortunately for Peter and Pat, he had telegraphed his intentions of doing so a few days earlier. A plot was quickly hatched by other club members. Very early in the morning of Peter's jaunt, another aircraft flew to Lake Pedder and straight out again but left behind a pilot, John Stanwix, who concealed himself behind the sand dunes. Peter Tanner and Pat Dalton landed on the beach in an Auster Aiglet at about 10 am. It was a vintage Tasmanian summer day. Leaving their clothes on the beach they headed out into the lake in their swimmers, walking and wading until it was deep enough to swim. To his intense surprise, Peter heard the unmistakeable sound of an aircraft propeller being turned over. They thought they were the only people there. An artist, Harry Buckey (who had been an RAAF pilot), was somewhere about painting in the Franklin Ranges, and the brief thought crossed Peter's mind that the old boy had gone mad and was trying to steal his aircraft.

Peter started to run towards the beach, but as he laboured through the shallow water it was like those nightmares where everything goes into slow motion. He had hardly covered thirty metres before the mysterious figure had started the engine, climbed into the Auster and taxied towards the end of the beach, gunned the engine, and become airborne. The Auster seemed to be wobbling about strangely, but eventually gained height and headed east. It disappeared from sight, apparently in a spin, behind the rocky spire of Mount Anne. By this stage Peter smelled a rat, but what could he do? Their kindly colleagues left them on the beach for the entire day before they flew in to pick them up. (The experience did no harm to their burgeoning relationship, because they were married not long after and still are.)

We camped for a couple of days at Lake Pedder before walking out via Mount Picton to the Arve Valley behind Geeveston, picking up a lift on a forestry road there, and on to Huonville and Hobart. It was only a two- or three-day walk at the most, so we weren't particularly fussed about it. One of our party, Graham Jack, did not have the time to walk out and flew back to Hobart. That left three—myself, my friend Mike ('Spike') Bryden, a veterinary student, and Leon Searle, the sports sub on *The Mercury* whom Dick Fulton had surprised in the reporters' room phone booth with his clandestine can of Fosters. I'm not sure whether Leon had ever been bushwalking in his life, but the genial, stocky little guy was always game for anything.

We set off towards the south-east in fine, warm weather and in high spirits, covering our first day's target of sixteen kilometres with ease. It was wonderful Tasmanian high country walking, with quite a good track through knee-high scrub, normally covered with snow in winter. Occasionally a tiger snake, sunning itself on the narrow track, would rise up and slither away at high speed, generally causing the person leading to find an excuse to tighten their bootlaces or pack straps so that someone else could take the lead. We only had a small two-man tent for the three of us, but as we only had two nights on the track, we were prepared to make do.

By midday on the second day we reached the saddle leading to Mount Picton, where we were to head down into the Arve Valley. A surveying party camped there had been waiting ten days for clear conditions to climb the mountain and take some sights. I knew the surveyor, Chris Butler, who had taken me, fresh out of school, as a novice chainman (assistant)—in reality another pair of shoulders to carry supplies—to Mount Murchison on the west coast a year before.

'How long have we got to go to reach the forestry road?'

'About four hours if you keep at it.'

They were running short of food, so we gave them all of ours. After all, we'd be back in Hobart that night.

From the ridge we could see where we had to go, and could pick out the Arve River glistening in the sunlight as it snaked through the thick forest on the valley floor. I was leading the way, and managed to lose the not-too-well marked track. We stopped to decide whether we should retrace our steps and find it, and agreed that would be a bore, and we would head off down into the valley and make our own way.

The open high country soon became thick and heavily timbered as we descended into the valley. By keeping to the ridges as we went down, we could just get through. By four in the afternoon we knew we weren't going to be in Hobart that night. A westerly change swept over, soaking us with misty, cold droplets of rain. We were unaware we were heading into virgin Tasmanian rainforest, home to the island state's unique horizontal scrub which is like a huge barbed wire entanglement, throwing off horizontal and vertical limbs, all knitting together in the moisture-filled valleys where it proliferated. We were a sad and thoughtful threesome as darkness overtook us. We had to move dead logs to make enough space to pitch our little two-man tent in which there was no room for our packs, nor even our walking clothes: they had to stay out in the rain. Throwing in our sleeping bags and our still dry sleeping clothes, we drew lots for the central position. Leon scored. There was no way those on the outside would keep dry, pressed against the thin fabric of the tent.

First light revealed a dripping, dank world. Emerging naked, shivering and hungry, we quickly pulled on our wet walking clothes. We weren't thirsty. Water was the least of our problems. Why had we given all our food away?

Heading down and following the creeks would eventually bring us to the river. We knew the logic of that, but the reality was different. Often, the ridges we were following curved around taking us back the way we had come. Our packs were filling with water and getting heavier. The straps wrenched at our shoulders as we climbed through the fiendish tangle of horizontal scrub, its limbs as thick as small tree trunks. Occasionally we could hear rushing water below us, but could not see the creek sometimes twenty or so metres below us. The limbs of the scrub were greasy and treacherous. Once my foot slipped, but fortunately my sodden pack went on one side of the branch, and I went the other, so I was counter-balanced and saved from a bad fall to the unseen ground—often six metres or more below. When we were able to reach the floor of a particular valley, we struck thickets of *baura*, a three-metre-high tangle of meshed green tendrils that would have been completely impassable even if we had had a bush knife or machete with us. The only way to get through was to hurl your body at it, then your companions would walk over you and do the same for you. One of us found a few bits of barley sugar and some chocolate in a pocket—and some utterly useless dehydrated soup cubes. We could feel our strength ebbing away. All we could do was keep struggling, pushing and climbing through the horrendous wall of entwined greenery that threatened to entomb us. At least when we were moving we were warmer. Stopping to rest caused us to shiver and shudder in uncontrollable spasms as our bodies tried to preserve our core temperature. The spectre of hypothermia stalked us as we kept battling, desperately, to reach the Arve River while our strength held out.

As darkness pressed in, we knew we had to camp again and to create space for our tent we had to move rocks and logs. The rain never let up. Although our bags and sleeping clothes were damp, they were essential to our survival. As before, we left all our gear in the rain, stripped naked and one at a time wriggled into the tent and into our sleeping bags, lying there shivering and exhausted until communal warmth enabled us to sleep. At least it was my turn in the middle.

We woke to another wet, cold morning, and struggled into our sopping walking clothes. That day was a blur of effort and exhaustion, trying to keep heading east, but in reality going where we could force our way through the appalling density of the rainforest floor. Occasional patches of sword grass cut our arms, hands and the webbing between our fingers, but our extremities were so cold and numb that we felt little pain.

We did have a compass, but that was almost useless because we could only go where the terrain would allow us. I do remember having a stand-up argument with Spike Bryden that the compass was obviously wrong. He said that with the greatest respect for my bushwalking skills and sense of direction he would rather trust the compass. Commonsense prevailed. We didn't talk much, actually. All of us were conscious that if we slipped and broke a leg, no one would ever find us and we had a growing feeling that we mightn't get out of it anyway, although none of us said so. (Thirty years later, a fourteen-year-old boy absented himself from a school excursion to climb Mount Picton, headed down into the same valley and vanished. His body was never found.)

To add to Leon's woes, he was a heavy smoker and his last packet of cigarettes and matches dissolved in the relentless rain. Spike and I weren't smokers and were unsympathetic to his lamentations, but had we known the tortures he was going through—going cold turkey from one of the most addictive substances on earth—we would have been kinder to him. When he wasn't cursing not being able to have a ciggy he switched to tucker and fantasised about huge steaks, mashed potatoes and peas. We could all relate to that.

By 4 pm we knew we had to spend a third lost night in our tiny tent. Spike scored the prized middle berth. By this stage our sleeping clothes were so damp there was hardly any point in changing into them. As we huddled together for warmth, the cuts on our hands and arms and the abrasions on our legs from slithering over rocks began to ache unbearably.

Our morale was at its lowest the next morning. It was still raining, of course, and a deep hunger gnawed at our bellies. One at a time we shed our sleeping clothes and stumbled naked into the cold rain. Spike was first out, and as he pulled on his soaked trousers and shirt—shivering uncontrollably as he did so—he gazed up at the dripping rainforest canopy that blocked out the looming sky. He said simply 'Geez, what a bastard!' It was.

Spike told me later that on that ghastly third morning he doubted whether we could get out of it. I had come to the same conclusion, but we never said so to each other. There was an unspoken feeling that if we said it out loud, it would be true. We hadn't eaten for three days and nights, and every movement was becoming an effort. We had become automatons, three gasping, aching, soaked, desperate people just concentrating on survival.

By what should have been lunchtime we weren't even sure we were still heading for the river; all we knew was the dispiriting combination of horizontal scrub, thickets of *baura* and the cursed, constant, cold, pissing rain. We couldn't rest because as soon as we stopped the uncontrollable shuddering started. We'd moved beyond shivering. In front lay the same unchanging wet labyrinth of thick scrub, gullies and rushing creeks.

By 4 pm on that fourth day we noticed an axe mark on a tree, the first sign of a human presence since we had so joyfully and confidently headed into the valley. It took a few moments to register. Shortly afterwards we stumbled on a track, which we were able to follow to the longed-for Arve River. There was no flying fox or other way to cross the deep, dark and swiftly flowing river so we went back to see where the track went. To our great joy it curved back towards the river, and we saw a rough timber hut. From that moment we knew we'd make it. It was about 5 pm when we stumbled through the door. It was still raining.

Our sanctuary was a timber-getters' hut. Some wonderful person had left a box of matches on a shelf and dry firewood in a corner. We soon had a fire going and a billy of water, into which we were going to put the now sodden soup cubes, the only food we had not given to our surveyor friends at Mount Picton. To say we were looking forward to it was an understatement.

Before the billy had time to boil there was a knock on the door. A pair of sturdy boots could be seen in the gap between door and step. We thought it might be timber workers wondering what we were doing in their hut, but when I opened the door it was to see the utterly unexpected figure of my father John standing there with his friend Mac Urquhart who had pioneered many of Tasmania's bushwalking trails. We were utterly overjoyed to see them and, when the excitement of this unlikely meeting had subsided, Father said he had been worried about us being overdue. He discussed the situation with Mac and they decided to drive down to Geeveston and up the forestry access road in the hope of finding us. They had an esky full of food prepared by my mother. An egg-and-bacon pie, sandwiches, cold meat, bread rolls, fruit and cake. We fell on this like the starving men we were. My father and Mac were so embarrassed by the primitive spectacle of our group ripping into this tucker they walked outside until we had something in our bellies. I have never enjoyed food more.

(As we had notified the police before we set out on our Lake Pedder to Geeveston walk and were already overdue, I asked my father to drive us to the Geeveston police station to confirm our return before we drove back to Hobart. About two weeks later Spike Bryden's mother had a call from the police asking if we were back, because we were about to be reported missing!)

That night we slept in our own warm beds in Hobart—it was a curious and sudden transition from total hopelessness and despair to complete security. On the way back in the car the three of us resolved to have a survival dinner at the Dutch Inn, a restaurant in Battery Point, Hobart. To the surprise of the amiable proprietor, Mrs Van Dongen, we ate our way through a four-course meal—twice! Leon Searle, who wasn't used to bushwalking and probably never did it again, left his sodden pack with all his gear in it in the Bowden garage. It festered there for two months before I could convince him to come and take it away. My mother was fearful it might explode, or at the very least spontaneously combust. I suspect he just chucked the whole caboodle into the garbage.

The experience did not put me off bushwalking, but made me more careful about keeping to tracks. And its lasting legacy was my attitude to comfort. I have never, never again worried about having a 'wet arse and no fish' as they say in Tasmania. What is a few hours of cold discomfort when you know there is a warm fire and a change of clothes at the end of it? Although I have had brushes with death on the roads—as most of us have—and in war zones and in aircraft in later years, I have never since then been faced with a struggle for survival over such a long period. It was an experience I am pleased to have had, but am not in any hurry to repeat. And I was lucky to have had two steadfast and good mates with me who didn't panic. I lost touch with Leon when I moved away from Tasmania and, sadly, did not meet up with him again before he died, but Mike Bryden (who became a distinguished academic and recently retired as the Professor of Veterinary Anatomy at Sydney University) and I are still good friends.

In the summer of 1957 I had to sacrifice my university vacation (and get time off from *The Mercury*) to do National Service training. This was a severe and unwelcome interference with partying and drinking. The arrival of rock 'n' roll had liberated us from Glenn Miller and our parents' dance music, and we twisted and gyrated with the heady freedom that Bill Haley and the Comets and the early rock 'n' rollers gave us. To this day I still give fervent thanks for 'Rock Around The Clock' and 'Twist And Shout'.

National Service was compulsory for all eighteen-year-olds. Most did army service. A period of six months' basic training was followed by two years in the CMF—Citizen Military Force. University students did three months' basic training in the summer vacation and three years in the CMF. There were two university platoons in my intake, 5 Platoon and 9 Platoon. The officer in charge of Brighton Camp had strange ideas that the university platoons would be the jewels in the crown of his national service intake. We soon disabused him of this notion, proving that our happy band of scholars had more than the average number of conscripts who could not keep in step and had difficulty in carrying out a simple order. I scored 9 Platoon to my great relief, as 5 Platoon seemed closer to our CO Major Smith's idiotic notions of elitism. They actually wanted to win the drill competition.

Although some of our group found army life a bit of a shock—sleeping in dormitory style barracks and taking group showers—I wasn't fussed by any of that and with some other blithe spirits in 9 Platoon set about the important work of seeing how much drill we could avoid and how often we could go AWOL at least to the local pub at Pontville, which was seriously out of bounds. One of the early things we realised about the army was that we didn't have to make any decisions. The army provided us with bedding, accommodation and food, instructed us how to make our beds and tidy our lockers (and inspected them to make sure we'd done it properly), told us what time to get up in the morning, what to wear, and made sure we went to breakfast. (Whether we ate it was up to us.) It then marched us around in circles, or put us in the back of a truck and drove us to a rifle range where we tried to hit a target with a bucking .303 Lee Enfield rifle, exactly the same vintage as the Anzacs carried when they landed at Gallipoli in 1915. We also fired Bren guns, Owen guns and hurled an occasional live hand grenade. No one even considered ear protection, of course, and my high frequencies, already damaged by Sergeant Bowden's duties in the school cadets, were further assaulted.

With the need to take any decisions about daily life removed from us, we set about amusing ourselves as best we could. Camp was 'dry', of course, so a hut mate, Nick Evers, and I thought of a great scheme to make money. We did get a few days' leave from time to time, and as beer was too impractical to carry, we decided we'd smuggle small flasks of scotch, gin and vodka back to camp in our kit bags. We actually got away with this, but there was a bad flaw in our business plan. Our fellow nashos were beer drinkers to the core. We had to drink it all ourselves. The army was soon right on to this possibility and instituted a crude but practical way of stopping the smuggling of spirits. Those on guard duty simply dropped the kit bags of returning nashos from a great height onto the road outside the guardhouse. The distressing sounds of breaking glass could clearly be heard. If it wasn't liquor that was smashed, but a jar of mum's Anzac biscuits—too bad.

Occasionally we were issued with blank cartridges—the .303 brass casings were crimped in where the bullet would normally be. These were for firing at each other when we played war games. Some care had to be taken with firing too close to an 'enemy' because a wad was discharged which could cause serious damage if it hit someone in the eye. More robust blanks could be made by smuggling back live ammunition from the firing range, and removing the bullet. This was done by inserting the tip of the bullet into the top of the rifle barrel—a .303 bullet is slightly larger than the barrel and is compressed and spun by firing it—and wiggling it until the steel bullet came free. One night in Hut 30 I was making some of these illegal blanks when some bright spark picked up my rifle and hammered it down on the floor. How was I going to look on parade the next morning with a cheeky little reversed bullet jammed in the top of the barrel? I simply could not get it out and, in desperation, decided to blow it out.

I did not share this decision with anyone, and around me my hut companions were sitting on their beds reading, or shining the brass on their belts and powdering their gaiters with Blanco for the all-important morning parade inspection. Pointing my rifle to the ceiling, I pulled the trigger. To my intense surprise, nothing happened. I ejected the cartridge, and tried again—still nothing. By that time I was getting a bit blasé, and slipped a third cartridge in and got ready to pull the trigger. Now, anyone who knows anything about guns and rifles will know that I was courting death. To try to discharge a firearm with a blocked barrel will almost certainly explode the whole thing. In my case, I was compounding the danger because, although the cartridges weren't firing—they had become damp—the percussion cap was going off, and just pushing sticks of cordite into the barrel which was becoming even more of a potential bomb.

On the third try I fluked a dry cartridge. There was a tremendous explosion, and the trapped bullet—fortunately—left the top of the barrel, spinning madly, and proceeded to ricochet around the upper walls of the hut. A great gush of fire and smoke followed it from my rifle as the accumulated cordite exploded. The effect of this on a peaceful hut can be imagined. Most hit the floor and scrambled under their beds. No one was hurt. But I was now in grave danger from another source. Quickly we chucked my rifle under the hut, opened the doors and windows to get rid of the smoke and distinctive smell of cordite, and all resumed our peaceful activities. Our NCOs were quickly on the spot, sniffing suspiciously. Someone had discharged a rifle. Had we heard anything? Yes, we'd heard something, but it wasn't here. God knows how we got away with it. As soon as they safely could my hut mates declared that I was not only a silly prick, but the most stupid bastard God ever shovelled guts into and a prime candidate for having my testicles anointed with black boot polish. But there was no way I could get my gravely abused rifle clean, and I was charged with having a dirty barrel the next morning! It certainly served me right, and it was better than being dead.

Several of our NCOs were proper soldiers, veterans of the Korean War. (Our fearless CO was a part-time CMF man.) We also had several newly graduated officers from the Duntroon Military College, swaggering around with their two pips. One, a huge, truculent and over-muscled thug, had an inferiority complex about university students and proceeded to give us merry hell in ways that only basic training situations could provide. Nick Evers, a braver man than I, decided that we'd get our own back for all the hours of extra drill and unpleasant abuse that this prick had visited upon us. Every day a duty officer was rostered to be present—and to eat the same food— in our mess. At the end of our meal we had to scrape our plates out into swill bins and then rinse them. We waited until our *bête noire* was rostered on, then lovingly prepared a plate of slops brimming with gravy, mashed spuds, beans, carrots, stewed fruit and spit for good measure. Nick, a big feller, but not as big as the Duntroon thug we were aiming for, was—very unfortunately—jostled as he passed by, tipping all this muck straight into his lap. Pure accident, everyone agreed. But Nick said that this bloke watched him like a hawk for the rest of the intake. This particular recent Duntroon graduate needed a war, although my friend Spike Bryden said he would probably have been shot by his own men first. One of his favourite punishments was to get the university student national servicemen to drop down on their hands and knees to polish the nail heads in the floors of the huts to his satisfaction. So unspeakable was his behaviour towards us that a second assault on his person was planned and successfully executed. Again, the scene was the mess hall, on one of his duty days. Enough purgative to move the bowels of the earth was added to his lunch by a national serviceman cook, sympathetic to our cause. It was certainly enough to move his. We had the quiet satisfaction of seeing him run urgently from the mess even before he finished his first course.

The professional soldiers in Brighton Camp must have marvelled at the training films we had to endure—World War II Pommie stuff in black and white showing us scenes of English fields and hedgerows, and how we should conceal ourselves in the shadows thrown by copses and hawthorn hedges. Jungle warfare, more likely to involve our armed forces, had actually arrived in New Guinea in 1942. We found the hygiene lectures amusing, with the horrors of venereal disease graphically illustrated—they managed colour for that part of our training. We were shown an American film of GIs filing out of a bordello looking pleased with themselves. Then some gruesome close-ups of the diseased male members of those who had not taken precautions. Our medical corps instructor was Corporal Bell—we called him 'Happy Clappy'. He was a small, bald man with a heavy Scottish accent, no top teeth and a consequent lisp. He impressed on us the importance and necessity of using army issue condoms when we went on leave. 'If you come back here and thell me you've caught it off a lavathory theat, all I'll thay ith that'th a bloody funny plathe to take a woman.' He also explained that the issue was two condoms for a long weekend and one for a short.

That we should be so lucky. There were probably more virgins in our platoon than a nunnery. Nick Evers and I decided that we'd take Happy Clappy up on his official offer the next time we went on leave. I don't know about Nick, but my chances of getting lucky were exceedingly remote. We presented ourselves at the RAP (Regimental Aid Post) in our best going-on-leave uniforms. Corporal Bell was bandaging someone's foot. We couldn't see who it belonged to, which, as it happened, was unfortunate.

'What do you want?'

'We're going on leave and we've come for our issue.'

Happy Clappy seemed to be playing dumb. 'What issue?'

'The frangers you said we had to take with us on leave. Condoms, frenchies, rubbers. Things you put on your dick.'

There was a bull-like bellow and the camp adjutant, Major Smith's deputy, hopped into view. 'Call yourselves men', he shouted, beside himself with righteous moral rage. 'Get out of here. You'll be hearing more about this.'

Nick and I shook our heads and returned to our platoon, ready to march out of camp. As we passed the CO's office our platoon was told to halt. 'The two privates who just attended the RAP are to report immediately to Major Smith's office.'

We marched in, crashed to attention in front of Smith's desk and saluted. He seemed strangely friendly. 'Take your hats off and sit down. Now I'd like you to think of this interview not as a formal one between privates and their commanding officer, but more like a father talking with his sons. Because I'm very concerned about the moral welfare of the young men in my charge.'

Nick and I exchanged a glance, and I decided not to chance my arm by calling him 'Dad'.

Smith (a devout Roman Catholic) leaned forward across his desk. 'Now it has come to my ears that several of my national servicemen—you—have been to the RAP asking for contraceptives before you go on leave. Is that the case?'

Nick said, 'We were obeying orders, Sir. Corporal Bell advised us to do so when we went on leave, at the last hygiene lecture'.

'I don't know how that happened, and I'll deal with Bell later. But I find it very disturbing that young men like yourselves are taking such action. Does this mean that you two boys are going on leave with the deliberate intent of having sexual intercourse?'

I decided that this was really none of his bloody business, and the father-to-son stuff was getting out of hand. 'Well Sir, you never know your luck. In any case I have no intention of blowing them up as balloons, or making water bombs on a tap.'

'Father' Smith went ballistic and ordered us out of his office. We didn't get any army condoms nor, it has to be reported sadly, did we get lucky on leave.

All in all, National Service wasn't too arduous. We did get very fit, and made some good friends. Nine Platoon was regarded (with some justification) as the larrikin university group, a status we rather gloried in. But towards the end we decided it would be absolutely insufferable if that do-gooding, army-loving bunch of 'conchies',

5 Platoon, actually did win the drill competition. About a week before it was due to take place we smartened ourselves up and did some serious practice. We didn't win—I think we came second—but we trounced 5 Platoon to our intense satisfaction.

Before we were discharged from Brighton Camp, 9 Platoon was put into the RAASC (Royal Australian Army Service Corps)—by coincidence the same corps my father had served in during World War II. For me that meant driving trucks around, the same GM 6 × 6 monsters that Father would have driven. They did not have synchromeshed gears, and you had to develop the arcane art of double-declutching to change gear up or down. I rather enjoyed this, but the crunching of cogs by some of my fellow recruits was cruel to hear. The steering wheel on the 'blitz wagons', as they were called, was made of wood and quite small in diameter. We learned quickly to keep our thumbs on the outside, as a large bump would spin the wheel out of your hands with such force it could easily break them.

I only went to a couple of part-time night 'parades'. We new nashos quickly realised that life in the CMF was a relaxed affair compared with the spit and polish of basic training. I was promoted to Lance Corporal by my CMF publicity-hungry CO as soon as he realised I was a journalist. But I didn't even have time to get my solitary glorious stripe sewn on my sleeve before our unit was disbanded. My brothers, Nick and Philip, nearly had to fight in a real war—Vietnam. Fortunately their birth dates were not drawn out of the obscene lottery barrel that their baby boomer generation was subjected to in the 1960s.

One compelling reason to celebrate the end of my national service training was that I was deeply smitten. I met petite and dark-haired Penny Ford at a party, and she seemed to like me too. Penny was three years younger than me and in her last year at Fahan School, but that seemed unimportant. We managed to see a lot of each other as the year went on. Fortunately her mother Marjorie did not seem too dismayed by this older journalist taking out her eldest daughter, and often produced the sherry decanter when I called. I did get some mild ribbing from my fellow cadets for dating a schoolgirl, but that ceased as soon as they met Penny.

Penny's best friend was Rosalind Geddes, who had come to the Fahan School three years earlier. Her father had been a tea planter in Ceylon (Sri Lanka) but was kicked out after the war when the country became independent. Ros was actually born in Sri Lanka, and had gone to school for a time in southern India. (She could swear in fluent Tamil—a good party trick.) Red-headed Ros and I became good mates, but I only had eyes for Penny. To the dismay of the two maiden ladies who ran the Fahan School, Ros decided to leave after her Schools Board Certificate and get a job. She was a bright student and they even offered to waive her school fees for her to matriculate, but Ros was adamant. Her parents were not well off, nor coping all that well with non-colonial life and her two younger sisters were still at school.

Ros saved enough money from her job with the AMP to buy a 1929 Willys car. It was a singular vehicle. The interior was in bad shape, so Ros pulled out all the tatty inner lining of the roof and sides and painted it a bright pink. She then pasted a collage of magazine colour pictures over the inside of the roof. Like an army blitz wagon it did not have synchromeshed gears, and double-declutching was essential. Ros did not have a licence, so I taught her to drive. On the day of the licence test, Penny sat in the back of the Willys, charming the young policeman assigned to the test. I sat in the front, surreptitiously double-declutching for Ros with my right foot on the clutch pedal. We all had a lot of fun, and when we got back to the police station the constable reluctantly left the back seat and Penny's charms and awarded Ros her licence. As we got back into the car, he called out to Ros, 'Now go away and learn to drive'. Ros loved her Willys car, but no one told her about putting oil in the differential so the transmission seized terminally a few weeks later. Alas, she couldn't afford to have it fixed.

Staying alive

Drink driving was illegal in Tasmania in the 1950s but breath tests had yet to be thought of, and the technology invented. The practical result was that people didn't worry about it all that much. The young men of the day boozed happily and drove as if there was no tomorrow. For some of them there wasn't. My mother owned a little Fiat 500, which was really a two-seater, although there was a token back seat. The canvas top could be rolled right back to create a sports car effect. The tiny 500 cc engine sounded like a lawnmower. It had an ingenious transmission which, if you judged the revs right, meant you could change gear without using the clutch. It also had, for some curious reason, a hand throttle. It wasn't anything like a cruise control—computers were yet to happen. It was simply a metal ring which you pulled towards you to increase the revs, and then locked on by turning it to the right. I am not proud of the following story now, but feel compelled to tell it as a cautionary tale.

One Saturday afternoon I was driving down to Clifton Beach, south-east from Hobart, in the Fiat 500 with a friend, Neville Henry. We were happily drinking from large bottles of Cascade beer. As I drove past Cambridge Airport on what we called 'the Cambridge straight'—Tasmanian roads snaked around a lot—I had a bright idea. I checked it out with Neville who thought it was a hoot. I pulled on the hand throttle so the Fiat was doing a steady 80 km/h. Neville reached across from the passenger side and steered from the bottom of the steering wheel, so his arm could not be seen from the front. I then stood up in the driver's seat and turned around so that my back was to the oncoming traffic, lifted up my bottle of beer and drank from it to the bemusement (and I suspect horror) of the drivers of cars coming the other way.

A late night diversion only ever attempted when exceedingly 'elephants trunk' was to 'climb the horse' in the Queenborough Cemetery in Sandy Bay. One of the graves there was topped with a full-sized bronze statue of a horse. There were all kinds of apocryphal stories about it. One was that the person buried there had been a rich old man who had married his housekeeper in his last years. The gossip was that she had married him for his money, but to disprove this slur, she sank it all into having a life-size bronze horse specially commissioned and cast. Whatever the circumstances of its existence, it stood proudly on a high plinth, surrounded by a cast iron fence topped with arrow-like spikes. (When the cemetery was resumed as part of the Sandy Bay campus of The Hutchins School, the horse was removed to the more appropriate venue of the Elwick Race Course where it can still be seen.)

Climbing it was so dangerous it was important to be drunk. You had to clamber over the iron spikes on the low fence, and reach up to the top of the plinth at full stretch to find a loose bolt near the horse's rear left foot. Vertically challenged people had to jump up a bit to grasp it, which meant risking a fall back onto the spikes of the fence. Having grasped this bolt, you could then lean out (over the spikes) and pull yourself up to the top of the plinth. Mounting the horse was almost as dangerous. The only way I could do it was to throw my body across the horse's back, reach up for one of the bronze ears and pull myself into the sitting position. But it was wonderfully exhilarating when you made it. This had to be done fairly quickly because people living nearby were fed up with drunks and used to call the cops.

One night my fellow cadet Mike Philp lost his grip on the bolt at a crucial moment and fell back towards the spikes. Somehow he twisted his body around in mid-air, and kicked up and over, landing on his hands on the ground two metres below, badly breaking his left wrist. To make matters worse, the cops arrived, trapping us like roos in a spotlight, saying they had six local complaints about the noise we were making. A couple of young constables whipped out their notebooks and began taking down our names and addresses. To our everlasting relief, an old sergeant summed up the situation and decided we weren't a bunch of yobbos and vandals who had come to desecrate the cemetery, and told his troops to put their notebooks away. He gave us a verbal bollocking and told us to clear off.

Our first port of call was to the casualty department of Royal Hobart Hospital to get Mike Philp's busted wrist seen to.

Mike was proud of his physical fitness, and anxious to have his body back in full service. He advanced the theory that a broken bone was like a weld—when it knitted, it was actually stronger than it was before. The day his plaster came off he demonstrated this to my mother in the Bowden kitchen by falling forward on his hands. There was a horrid snap as his wrist broke again, and it was back to the RHH.

I used to spend quite a lot of time with Mike, as our shifts often coincided. He had a flat on Sandy Bay Road, overlooking the Derwent River. Being a handy kind of bloke, he constructed his own hi-fi system. He decided to advance his appreciation of classical music by giving himself repeated doses of composers whose music had to be worked at a bit. But after two weeks of Bruckner symphonies, he'd had enough. 'How are you going with Bruckner?' I asked him one day. 'I'll show you', he said. Taking the vinyl records out of their sleeves he threw them like Frisbees across Sandy Bay Road and into the Derwent River.

One morning, over the strong coffee Mike liked to brew, we were arguing about social responsibility. I said that he didn't have any. 'What do you mean? I work for a newspaper that brings news and services to the public', he said. 'That's just a job. I mean contributing to the community without getting paid for it.' He countered quite pertinently that I wasn't very socially responsible either. 'OK', I said. 'We'll donate blood. That is something that is a benefit to the community that we don't get paid for and is an utterly altruistic act. Come on, we'll do it now.'

As we drove to the Red Cross, Mike told me that I would have just ordinary blood, but his would be special. It would be so potent and strong that old age pensioners would be given teaspoons of it and gain years of added life. I said that was total bullshit and that his blood would be as mundane as mine.

After being tested and bled, we were given the obligatory cup of tea. The nurse came in and thanked me for coming, and said I was 04 positive.

'But Mr Philp, you're the man we want!' It turned out that Mike had a RH negative blood group that was as rare as hens' teeth. Weeks later I saw Mike walking up the street wild-eyed and pale after an emergency call. 'I've been called in to give blood twice in six weeks!'

I said it served him right for being so egotistical.

The clockwork tape recorder 4

Sometimes chance or unexpected events can engineer major shifts in a life and a career. So it was for me when in 1958 a former Repertory Society mate of my parents, James Pratt, came to Hobart from Sydney to act briefly as Head of Talks at the Australian Broadcasting Commission. I was at work when my parents entertained him at dinner so didn't meet him, nor did I hear the conversation. 'What's the boy doing these days?' Jim seems to have asked. Peg and John told him I was a reporter at *The Mercury*. 'Get him to come and see me at the ABC and I'll see if I can give him some work.'

(During the war Jim used to take my mother out from time to time in his car. She was perfectly safe sexually-Jim was 'a confirmed bachelor' as the saying went-but she was probably more physically at risk than my soldier father. Jim was an atrocious driver. Peg said he used to drive straight through intersections shouting cheerfully, 'Please God let nothing come'. Twenty years later when something did, Jim was badly smashed up and never drove again.)

The ABC offices and studios were less than a hundred metres from *The Mercury* in Elizabeth Street, opposite the General Post Office, so soon after Jim made his offer, and wondering vaguely why I was doing this when I already had a job, I presented myself to Mr James Pratt, and his Talks Assistant, a dark-haired young man of serious demeanour, Anthony Rendell.

It turned out Jim was in town because the previous Director of Talks had just retired and the man from Head Office had come to do some moving and shaking. A new director still had to be found, but in the meantime Jim was rampant. Anthony Rendell (who had just come to Hobart from Adelaide) told me many years later that he went on a steep learning curve as Jim rushed around grabbing air time and starting new programs including *People Talking* and *Ideas and Opinions*. He would get groups of people in to have a discussion on current arts or social issues, and then demand they do it all again if it wasn't lively enough. One of his new Talks initiatives was a 5-minute slot at 5.55 pm each week night called *Tasmania Today* which featured a topical report—an interview or colour piece—reflecting the events of the day, or indeed the week. There was no television in those days, and radio was big. Jim and Anthony needed to find a freelance interviewer to expand the Hobart Talks empire and thought perhaps it might be me.

I knew none of this when I was given a tape recorder and told to go to the Hobart Town Hall where wool auctions were underway, record the yips and yelps of the bidding as a bed of sound, and then find a wool buyer and interview him about his life and his job. Anthony would show me how to edit it all together when I got back.

I was given a clockwork tape recorder to carry out this assignment. That may sound like a line from the *Goon Show*, but it was true and actually quite a smart idea that preserves battery life. Most of the battery power in portable recorders was used to drive the spools and move the tape across the recording heads at 7½ inches per second. Very little power was used for the actual recording on the magnetic tape. The clockwork recorder was called a CEB. It was housed in a red-vinyl-covered box with a shoulder strap so the reporter/broadcaster could walk about with both hands free. On the side was a hinged brass handle which could be folded out to wind up the spring when it started to run down. A fully wound spring was supposed to give you four minutes of recording, but experience was soon to show me that you only got three and a half minutes with luck. Like an organ grinder, you then had to give it some surreptitious turns while your subject was waxing lyrically away. There was also a 'level' meter with a graduated scale and needle. On the right side was a curved red line which indicated over modulation. The trick was to keep the needle just hovering on the beginning of the red line. In really noisy surroundings you had to wind back the recording level or the tape would be oversaturated with sound and therefore distorted.

Attached to the CEB was a big, black STC directional microphone with a silver grille, specially designed to strike fear into the heart of a nervous subject. It certainly had that effect on me as I tried to remember all the things I had to watch and at the same time remember to interview my wool buyer.

Anthony showed me how *always* to do a sound test on the spot before doing an interview—because something might happen to the tape or the settings on the way to the location. It was excellent advice which I have always followed. He also said to play a bit back at the end of the recording before leaving. It is far easier to do it again at that point than reach the studio close to deadline with what turns out to be a blank tape. The CEB had no internal speaker, but you could play back using the microphone as a speaker. The sight of a reporter with his microphone pressed to his ear added to the *Goon Show* overtones of the exercise.

Somehow I got away with this first interview, although paralysed with nervousness. As instructed, I first recorded five minutes of 'actuality'—the distinctive shouts and cries of a live auction. The wool buyer I approached for an interview was terrific. Like most of his colleagues he could have talked under wet cement, but he was lively, amusing and informative—a dream interviewee for my first go. (I didn't manage anything as successful for at least six months!) I even remembered to wind the spring up while I was doing the interview, which was just as well. Tape slowing down during recording causes a reverse effect during playback at the correct speed—the interviewee's voice gradually rises in apparent mounting hysteria until (again like sound effects from the *Goon Show*) it turns into complete gobbledygook.

Back at the ABC Anthony Rendell demonstrated how to link up three Byer tape recorders, with two machines patched into one. My edited interview with the wool buyer was on one, and the bed of sound on the other. He then skilfully married the two together—and all this outside a studio, in a little cupboard of a room near the Talks Department. My item went to air that night.

I was instantly hooked on radio. How many words would I have to write, I wondered, to capture the magic of actuality—the sounds and feeling of being there. And I loved the extra dimensions added by the wool buyer's voice. Apart from his amusing tales, there was so much extra to pick up from the way he spoke—his personality, his credibility, irony and humour. I doubted that the printed word could get anywhere near it and I still believe in the unique power of radio to create pictures in the mind.

Big Jim Pratt was pleased with my first effort, and so was Anthony. Pratt did think that my voice was a bit light and might need to be worked on. I can't remember what they paid me, but it was probably about three guineas. They asked me to keep in touch and do more assignments. That was just fine by me. There was no conflict with the 'hard news' job I had with *The Mercury*, although the boundaries started to blur a bit when I did current affairs interviews for a national ABC program *News Review*, which at that time followed the 7 pm news from 7.15–7.30 pm. (Jim Pratt's stentorian tones introduced the program behind a suitably rousing fanfare.)

I had come into contact with broadcasting at a fortuitous time. The freedoms offered by quarter-inch magnetic tape were very new.

Until its introduction in the 1950s, sound could only be stored on disc, either 78 rpm records or acetate discs which were expensive to produce and could only be played a limited number of times before they wore out. There were wire recorders, but they were difficult to operate (the hair-thin wire would often break and had to be knotted together if the resulting tangle could be sorted out) and editing was virtually impossible. During World War II ABC war correspondents—like Chester Wilmot—and their brave technicians even managed to cut discs on the battlefield using cumbersome equipment that needed a van to cart it about.

The liberation given to broadcasters by portable recording equipment and access to editing was heady stuff. It was a technology that would endure for half a century and I was in there on the ground floor. Oddly, radio technology changed less radically than newspapers over time. My print journalist colleagues were gazing into the green screens of early computers by the end of the 1970s as hot metal and copy paper vanished without trace, but I continued to edit tape the same way I had always done—with a splicing block, a razor blade and special sticky tape—until I left the ABC in the early 1990s. (Robyn Williams still edits his *Science Show* into the twenty-first century in this manner. His office floor becomes littered with varying lengths of tape snipped from his interviews on a rusting Tandberg tape recorder that probably has valves, as he holds the digital revolution idiosyncratically at bay.)

Splicing blocks were an undreamed of luxury in 1958 as I marked broadcasting tape with a white chinagraph pencil and snipped unwanted sections out with scissors, always cutting on an angle to make sure there was not a 'blip' as the edit ran past the replay head. I used two fingers to marry the joins together roughly in line, put white editing tape over the back of the tape and trimmed off the excess along the edges with scissors. Unwanted 'ums' and 'errs' and other verbal stumbles soon littered the floor of the Talks offices. In later years my friend Professor Hank Nelson (who worked with me on several major oral history based radio series in the 1980s) used to call this audio detritus 'the confetti of stumbling lips'.

The ABC technicians (or Postmaster General employees as they were in those days) didn't like producers and reporters cutting tape. Apart from the expense of mutilating quarter-inch recording tape (all the tapes were erased and re-used after the programs they contained went to air) they saw this activity as a threat to their expertise and future employment. It was not permitted to put a tape to air which had splices in it, in case the tape broke during transmission. So we used to make up fag ends of tape on spare spools on which we dubbed (copied) the interview material to be edited. These reels of 'cutting' tape were so intensively used they often finished up with a splice every few centimetres. The edited speech was then dubbed back onto a pristine, numbered ABC tape for transmission. Some sound quality was lost by doing this, but it was compensated for—we thought—by the more succinct broadcasting that resulted from our cut-editing. We used to slice up our tapes in the privacy of our own offices, carefully cleaning up the detritus of stumbling lips from the carpet in case we were sprung by the powers that be.

Curiously, I can't recall ever discussing my moonlighting with *The Mercury* and if they knew (and I can't believe that they didn't know) they must have been unconcerned. As it turned out, my time with *The Mercury*, like King George VI's life many years previously, was slowly slipping away. I still enjoyed working there but was not as excited by the job as I was with radio.

With my encouragement Penny had joined the paper as a cadet reporter, but working in the same office (she was doing her best to break out of the mould of the social pages which is what female reporters were supposed to do exclusively) hadn't been such a good idea after all. Although I was slow to pick up on it, my colleague Doug Blain was white-anting me by wooing Penny. We coincided once by accident at the Ford family home. I was walking up the drive after visiting Penny, and Doug had mistimed his arrival and was walking down. He was taller than me and was standing on higher ground. I had to stand on tiptoe to try to punch him on the nose. He did not respond, confident in the knowledge that he had the high ground in the emotional stakes as well. I drowned my sorrows in drink and maintained my friendship with Penny's friend Ros Geddes. We were friends but not romantically involved. Ros moved to Sydney to train as a nurse, but we kept in contact. This was fortuitous as we were married ten years later.

It was Dick Fulton's paranoia about my university work which caused me to part company with *The Mercury* shortly after I had put my cadetship behind me and become a fully-fledged D Grade reporter. Perhaps foolishly I had given him a list of the days I had exams and asked if I could either be rostered off or put on day work on the day before each exam. The old bugger put me on the 'dog watch' on purpose, which meant that I wasn't able to leave work till after 1 am on the day of an exam.

The ABC's new Director of Talks, Lucien May, had been appointed from Adelaide, as had Anthony Rendell, and they knew and liked each other. He was the thinnest man I think I ever saw, and wasn't much more than five feet tall. He looked like a dwarfed Andy Warhol, although I wasn't aware of Warhol then. He had a thick thatch of long blond hair that used to flop over the edge of his big horn-rimmed glasses. He was ambitious and needed more of my time than I could give him while I was still at *The Mercury*. (It was a feather in Lucien's cap that, while on secondment with the BBC, he had discovered the joys of the program *My Word* with Frank Muir and Denis Norden—teamed then with E Arnot Robertson and Nancy Spain—and successfully argued the case for the ABC to buy this long-running and popular series.) I told Lucien of my troubles with Fulton and exams, and he suggested I resign and come to the ABC as a full-time freelancer. He couldn't offer me a job, but said there would be enough assignments to keep me going.

This seemed just fine to me, so much to Fulton's surprise I resigned from *The Mercury*. I bore him no ill will. Underneath his blustering manner he did care about the advancement of the cadets under his care. We parted on good terms, even though leaving *The Mercury* was regarded as a rat act. You were supposed to stay for life and staff ungrateful enough to leave became non persons never to be mentioned, certainly not in print. This attitude changed only if someone became really famous. The writer and adventurer Alan Villiers once worked on *The Mercury* before he hitched a ride on a four-masted grain clipper out of Hobart and never came back. He and Denis Warner, a distinguished Tasmanian-born war correspondent, were the only departed staffers to score honourable mentions during my time with the paper—always with the same bracketed qualification: ('. . . a former member of the literary staff of the Hobart *Mercury*').

My main bread and butter programs as an ABC freelancer were the prestigious Sydney-produced *News Review* and the local 5-minute daily *Tasmania Today*. Cracking *News Review* was crucial to my being able to eat. It was edited in Sydney by a great character, Fred Simpson, who had a wonderful feel for good radio. Although Tasmania was not in the forefront of national news, Fred loved a slightly off-the-wall story or colourful interview. You only had two minutes—sometimes with luck two and a half minutes—for an item. Every week day at 10 am I would meet Anthony Rendell in Lucien May's office, we would survey what was happening in the news and Lucien would ring Fred in Sydney and try to sell him a story. Knowing Fred's idiosyncrasies Lucien was quite brilliant at this. Then it was up to me to justify the power of Lucien's sales pitch. Fortunately there was always the tape editing process to sharpen things up and repair any of my own botched questions and I became adept with my scissors and sticky tape at removing the confetti of stumbling lips, including my own. The item was fed to Sydney on a booked land-line around 4 pm, and then I had an anxious wait until 7.15 pm to find out if I had made it. I didn't get paid unless my story was used.

Probably because we were trying harder than other BAPH states (ABC jargon for Brisbane, Adelaide, Perth and Hobart—the capital cities outside the Melbourne–Canberra–Sydney axis) I scored better than a 50 per cent success rate. But not every day, of course.

The ABC manager at the time was Wilbur Reed who seemed puzzled by having me about the place. Perhaps no one ever explained to him who I was or what I was doing there. He knew that I wasn't on staff. We would nod to each other in the brown linoleum-floored ABC corridors. One afternoon when I was running a bit late with the *Tasmania Today* for that evening, I was pushing a trolley with a tape recorder (with my precious edited program on it) into the lift when the right-hand spool dropped off the machine and with unerring accuracy disappeared into the crack between the lift and the floor. Fortunately broadcasting tape was fairly robust stuff, and I jammed the door open with my foot and started hauling up my program like a fishing line while the spool unravelled down in the depths of the building. I knew that I could re-wind it on another spool later on, and salvage my program. As I did this, my neck festooned with loops of recovered tape, I became aware of Wilbur's presence. (He had skin problems and his hands—which he was fluttering nervously—were always covered in white bandages.)

'What on earth are you doing?' he wanted to know.

'Oh just getting *Tasmania Today* ready for tonight, Mr Reed.' At that point I fished up the last of it, the lift door closed and I sank from his view.

Lucien May was a very knowledgeable radio man and a hard taskmaster, for which I suppose I should have been grateful. He and Anthony were determined to make me a competent broadcaster. Although Lucien seemed more approachable than my old chief of staff at *The Mercury*, he was an unpredictable and neurotic man. Anthony told me later that he could sense by the way his boss said 'good morning' whether it was going to be a difficult day. Lucien was marvellously gifted in almost every way apart from human relations. Anthony, being on staff, was more vulnerable to Lucien's emotional whims, but it didn't take much to dent my fragile confidence. One aspect of broadcasting that I found most difficult was to arrive somewhere and actually describe what was going on, straight onto tape. I was more comfortable interviewing and writing backgrounders. Curiously enough this nervousness about directly describing events has stayed with me through a lifetime of broadcasting—but it caused me considerable grief when I was making my first half-hour radio documentary.

One way to augment my fees for short interviews was to attempt a documentary for national broadcast. Lucien asked me to submit some topics, and we agreed I should do a definitive program on scallops—the succulent bivalve as an enthusiastic commentator once called them. Tasmania was famous not only for its apples, but for its scallops—before a spiked dredge and over-fishing wrecked this formerly profitable industry. I threw myself into a frenzy of scallop research. The distinctive shape of the scallop shell was depicted by the ancient Greeks and Romans and in more modern times as the logo of the Shell oil company. Dr Bill Bryden, the obliging Director of the Tasmanian Museum and Art Gallery, swotted up on the classical scallop story and I interviewed him on the clockwork CEB tape recorder. A key part of this exercise was going out on a scallop trawler in the D'Entrecasteaux Channel, south of Hobart, to record interviews with fishermen—all kinds of strange objects appeared in their scallop dredges—about how they caught scallops and why. I recorded the sound of scallop dredges being dumped down on the deck, and the flapping, clapping sounds of live scallops trying to return to the deep.

Unlike oysters and mussels, scallops are rather lively creatures and swim quite fast by opening and closing their shells. They are filter feeders and use the tides as well as their swimming ability to extract phytoplankton from the water. They even have a number of opalescent eyes on the edge of their mantle to avoid predators, mostly starfish. To catch these smartly swimming critters, fishing boats have to act co-operatively and motor backwards and forwards, keeping quite close to each other so that the frisky scallops, which jump out of the way of one dredge, are picked up by one coming the other

The clockwork tape recorder

way. At the same time the fishermen have to be careful that they don't snag each other's dredges, which are open fronted cages suspended from steel cables that bump along the seabed.

I also interviewed chefs about how to cook scallops, and consumers about why they liked them. This was to be the definitive documentary on scallops after all, so after weeks of work I took the edited and finished program to play it to my new boss. Lucien swung his chair around towards the window of his office facing Elizabeth Street, put his feet up on the desk (his forelock of blond hair partly obscuring the left lens of his glasses) and listened impassively while thirty minutes of things that you might never have wanted to know about scallops were revealed.

At the end he lifted his feet from the desk, and swung his chair around to face me for the first time.

'I have one question to ask you,' he said silkily.

'Yes Lucien?'

'How do you catch scallops?'

The bastard was absolutely right of course. At no stage had I described (with the sounds of it happening) how the scallop dredge was winched onto the deck, and the contents sifted of dross and old car tyres, to capture the furiously flapping succulent bivalves. Radio is essentially 'pictures in the mind' and I had failed to deliver essential scenes. He said he couldn't pay me until I fixed it up. I was desperate. Car repayments were coming up and I was even behind with my board at home. What to do?

My only option was to fake it, and I went down to Hobart's Constitution Dock where the scallop fleet was in but getting ready to go out again. 'Hey mate, do you mind starting your diesel and rattling your dredge a bit for a broadcast?' The skipper was a nice guy, and said he would do it. Hoping that no car horns would intrude at critical moments and with adrenalin fuelled desperation, I stood on the dockside and described what I should have described while at sea.

Lucien subjected himself to the whole documentary again, but this time smiled beatifically and said, 'Now I know how scallops are caught', and to my great relief accepted the program.

Although Hobart (and Tasmania) is now famous for its chic restaurants and clean green innovative cuisine, it was something of a culinary desert in the late 1950s when Lucien came up with the bright idea of doing a Christmas special. I was told to wind up my tape recorder and go down to Wrest Point, Hobart's biggest hotel (where the Casino now is) and interview the chef about Christmas recipes.

If I expected the head chef of Wrest Point to be called Maurice Cordon Bleu or some such I was soon disabused of that notion: the chef was Les Smith, and he didn't even run to one of those tall white hats. At least he took time out from his busy day to be interviewed so I got the spools spinning up to speed on the CEB and began:

'Mr Smith, I wonder if you could share with our listeners some of your special ways of preparing a Christmas turkey?'

'Sure', said Les wiping his hands on his apron. 'I roast 'em, steam 'em, or barbecue 'em.'

'And what about vegetables?'

'Much the same really.'

I didn't seem to be on a rich vein with the main course, so I switched to dessert. 'Mr Smith, I'm sure you must have a special recipe for Christmas pudding you can recommend.'

Les brightened up and winked at me. 'Sure I have. Ya get a can of Tom Piper in one hand, and a tin-opener in the other ... ha ha ha ha.' And I'll bet that was what Wrest Point diners finished up with.

Some years later Doug Fleming, the BBC's representative in Australia, summed up that era of Australian cuisine by telling me how he called in at a country pub once for lunch. He thought a mixed grill would be the safest, and asked the waitress if it was possible to have a glass of wine.

'What do youse want—sweet sherry or port?' Doug said that a glass of claret or Riesling might be better. 'Well I'll ask the barman', she said reluctantly, giving the strong impression that this was well outside the call of duty.

They did manage to rustle up a bottle of quite reasonable red, which Doug drank with his chops, sausages, lamb's fry, chips and tinned peas.

On his way to the loo he heard the waitress say to the barman, 'Joe—ya know the Pommie bastard who ordered the wine?'

'Yeah.'

'He drank the whole fuckin' bottle!'

It made one proud to be Australian really.

Towards the end of 1959 the interminable process of getting a part-time Bachelor of Arts degree was in sight. It had taken five long years, and I felt that life was passing me by. I was twenty-three and most of my school friends had either set off for Europe or left Tasmania to attend other universities. Phil Koch and John Sorell had left *The Mercury* and were already in London. Phil was working as a sub-editor with AAP-Reuters and urging me to follow.

I needed little encouragement. I wanted to travel the world and, in particular, to go to England. It wasn't only that my generation had been brought up to think of Britain as 'home'; I also had cousins near my own age there, living at Cambridge where my Uncle Philip was a don at Caius College, and also Director of Surface Physics at the Cavendish Laboratories. Those Bowdens lived in some style in a university-owned house, Finella, on The Backs near the river Cam, not far from Kings College Chapel. My Aunt Dottie had spent some time there in 1948 when she travelled to Europe with the Bishop and Mrs Blackwood and 'to the Holy Land' (including a train trip through Iran and a flight in a De Havilland Comet jet aircraft, just before they started falling out of the sky). She had idealised the Bowdens' life at Finella to me as only Dottie could do. Even before her visit I had fantasised about going there one day. As a boy I even used to dream about it.

I decided to set off for Europe in mid 1960 after my graduation ceremony in May and, more practically, after I had saved some money to pay my fare. I was managing to live as an ABC freelancer but that was about all. Lucien was also being more than usually demanding about my broadcast techniques and program making and I decided I needed another job. The Launceston *Examiner* had a Hobart office, and I went to see the manager, Wyn Salisbury, to ask for work. I was up front about what I wanted and said I could only work for six months if they could give me afternoon and evening shifts as I needed to keep working for the ABC as well. They had a vacancy for a D Grade. Wyn Salisbury was a nice guy, and agreed to all these conditions. God knows why.

Lucien was surprised (and a bit chagrined I think) to lose me as a full-time freelance, but agreed to employ me in the mornings. He also stopped riding me so hard in case he lost me altogether. I was a busy little Vegemite, but managed to keep all these balls in the air and, indeed, bank my entire *Examiner* salary. The *Examiner* reporters were a good bunch and welcomed me on board. John Dingwall, for instance, was later to make his name as one of Australia's most creative script writers and directors of television drama and feature films—including *Sunday Too Far Away*, *Phobia* and *The Custodian*. Another reporter, a New Zealander, Barry Holland, headed to London a year after I did and we shared a house in East Finchley with Mike Philp and the re-toothed and re-furbished Al Edison. Former *Mercury* cadet Dave Mitchell also joined our merry band at one stage.

The amiable Wyn Salisbury was a contrast to both Dick Fulton and Lucien May. In Hobart, the *Examiner* had a small office. Wyn presided over a happy ship and we tried not to let him down. Unhappily, however, I did just that. I can't recall the exact details, but in juggling my two jobs I forgot to cover an assignment. I arrived at work to find a personal note from Wyn pinned to the noticeboard.

I opened it and my blood ran cold. It was brutal and to the point. I had failed the paper and him. My dereliction of duty was inexcusable and he was formally reprimanding me accordingly. If such a thing happened again he would have to reconsider my future with the paper. As I stood there, ashen faced, letter still in hand, Wyn walked through the door. 'Oh hello Tim, did you have a good weekend?' he asked in his usual genial way. He hung his narrow-brimmed Akubra hat on the rack and disappeared into his office. I showed his awful rocket to Barry Holland. 'Oh, that's just Wyn. He can't bear to discipline anyone to their face, so he writes these shocking letters and just behaves as though nothing has happened.'

On 20 April 1960 Hobart was inundated by a once-in-two-hundred-years event, a huge flood. A cloudburst high over the Derwent Valley and Mount Wellington funnelled floodwaters through narrow valleys trapping people in their houses. Some had to break through to their rooftops and be rescued by boat. By the time the inundation reached Hobart, the Hobart Rivulet—long concealed and constricted by shops and bridges built over it—could not cope with the rampaging floodwaters which tore a devastating swathe through the business district causing millions of dollars worth of damage. It was a big story, and the ABC wanted coverage not only for *News Review* but for local programming. The damage to the CBD could be seen clearly, but what about the rural communities to the west whose plight was still not known? I decided to hire a car and head up the Derwent Valley towards New Norfolk to investigate. Arthur Wyndham, our acting Program Director who was normally stationed in the Sydney head office, asked if he could come for the ride. I was glad of his company and, as it turned out, his broadcasting expertise.

As we drove up the Derwent Valley it became obvious that the flood had been an extraordinary event. Grass and debris were strung up in the telephone and power cables seven metres above the ground. Some of these had been brought down by the force of the waters. Then we noticed that some of the houses had sheets of corrugated iron missing from their roofs. The penny dropped—this happened when people had to break them up from the inside to sit on their roof ridges to await rescue by boat. I soon found some survivors to interview and their stories were graphic and compelling. When I felt I had enough material I suggested to Arthur that we drive back to Hobart.

'I don't want to tell you how to do your job, but have you considered taking your tape recorder into one of these houses that has been completely flooded and describe it?' That, of course, was my weak point—my hang-up about describing events as they happened, particularly in front of a professional. I said, 'What would you do in a case like this?' Arthur, who had come into the ABC as an announcer and was used to describing everything from Royal visits to Anzac Day marches, could barely keep his hands off the microphone. I was very happy to learn and said so. Arthur delivered a classic demonstration of how to use sound to bring a word picture to life.

He positioned himself outside the open front door of a drowned house. Before he switched on the recorder he explained what he was doing. 'I'll start out here to get the outdoor acoustic, and keep talking as I walk in. Then we'll hear the change as we go inside, that boxy echoing sound, and then we'll just play it by ear.'

'I wonder', intoned Arthur in his rather plummy ABC announcer tones, 'what it's like to go inside a house that has been completely covered by water? The front door is open, so let's go in. My first impression is the smell. The carpet is inches deep in stinking mud'. At this point he inclined the microphone down to record the sound of our feet sloshing along the muddy carpet. 'The pictures have all been swept off the walls, and the force of the water has broken out the front windows. I'm walking down the hallway towards the first door on the left.' More sounds of feet squelching through the mud. The acoustic changed again as we walk into what is left of the front parlour, with Arthur picking up on detail like some ornaments still surviving on the mantelpiece. 'The cushions are totally sodden as you would expect [picking one up and sloshing it back on the soggy sofa]. Now let's go through to the kitchen and see what has happened there...'

And so it went, a lovely lesson in how to explore that feeling of being there which radio does so well, using actuality sound augmented with observations of telling detail like a child's rag doll caught in the flattened palings of the back fence. Arthur ended it, like the true pro he was, by walking out the front door into the open air acoustic where he had started and speculating whether the owners would ever live in it without fear of such a thing happening again. It was a lesson in the basics of radio description that I have never forgotten. I ran Arthur's piece with my edited interviews and even Lucien was unstinting in his praise of our efforts.

(It had rained 250 mm in 24 hours. Ten people were injured. Remarkably no one was killed. Ten houses were completely destroyed, 200 more badly damaged and 1000 homes significantly damaged by floodwaters. The total damage was estimated at 150 million dollars.)

I passed my last university exams at the end of 1959 (I had majored in Ancient Civilisations and Philosophy) and even managed a couple of distinctions in Philosophy. Getting that bloody degree had been a major hassle and hurdle in my life and I really did it because my father wanted me to. Graduation didn't take place until May 1960, and I felt I couldn't deny my parents and fond aunts the chance to see me in my hired gown and mortarboard, as it was the only time in my life I would wear it.

The cheapest way to get to Europe then was by ship. I booked a passage on *Neptunia*, a Lloyd Triestino liner, in a sixteen-berth cabin (on, not below, the water line) for the princely sum of £109. I was to join the ship in Sydney and then call at Melbourne, Adelaide, Perth, Jakarta, Singapore, Cochin (India), Aden, Suez, Messina, Naples and Genoa. We would have a day's sightseeing in each of these exotic places. The whole voyage would take five weeks. My plan was then to buy a Vespa motor scooter in Genoa (duty free)

TIM GETS AROUND

The voice which has introduced many Tasmanian ABC programs to mainland and Radio Australia listeners belongs to young Hobart journalist Tim Bowden.

Since joining the ABC Talks Department in Hobart a little over a year ago as a free-lance interviewer, Tim has followed up many Tasmanian stories for National News and Scope, and Tasmanian documentary programs.

Tim uses a portable tape recorder to get his stories — and takes it to some very unusual places.

He has, in fact, cultivated a "go anywhere, do anything" approach which has produced some remarkable off-the-beaten-track programs.

Last summer he went underwater diving on Tasmania's wild west coast with a team of skin-divers who were looking for sunken wrecks of historical interest.

As well as putting together an on-the-spot documentary of the expedition, Tim used a fishing boat's radio to broadcast an actuality description.

Tim was on the spot just a few weeks ago when the recent heavy floods swept through Hobart — incidentally nearly sweeping him away too.

Tim will be leaving Hobart shortly for the Continent, where he hopes to continue his experience in radio interviewing.

He has just graduated as a Bachelor of Arts from the University of Tasmania after some years of part-time study.

After his overseas trip Tim hopes to return to Tasmania to continue his radio work.

Tim Bowden interviews Mr H. Menzie, skipper of the cray boat, "Mavis."

and ride it over the Brenner Pass in late summer, through Austria and France, to England.

I thought it a good idea to travel with someone—in hindsight not a good decision, because travelling alone invites more varied experiences and more freedom to take advantage of changes of plan. This is not to denigrate the amiable nature of Nic Stilwell, a recently graduated engineer who was also ready to see the world and who agreed with the basics of my plan.

As it happened, the graduation ceremony was hardly worth waiting for, although I did manage to save some more money in the meantime. It took place in the Hobart City Hall, a large barn of a venue with a raised stage at one end. I knew that somewhere in the crowd were my proud parents and aunts, but I never saw them. After we lined up to doff our mortarboards to the Chancellor of the University of Tasmania, Sir Henry Baker, I had expected to meet up with my family. But the university had decided to save money on the morning tea, and we were told to march in line up the street to another venue for our tea and cakes. Stupidly I did this, rather than—as some other smarter souls did—ignoring these arrangements and spending time with my family in the City Hall. So my parents never really savoured this moment of robed glory after five years of encouragement (perhaps nagging might be a better word), and I made small talk with people I didn't know and then went home. Despite the anti-climax I felt an exhilarating surge of freedom. (Even now, four decades later, I still have stress dreams about having to pass my final exams.)

After fond farewells I took off for the Mainland, with my pack on my back and not a care in the world, for some boozy farewells with my schoolfriends who were becoming veterinarians and doctors at Brisbane and Sydney universities. At St Lucia, in Brisbane, my mate Spike Bryden said it would be fine to doss down with my sleeping bag in his college room. 'We'll fix you up with a gown so you can eat in the dining room.' It all worked out. I did see some of the lecturers eyeing me off with some suspicion, but nobody challenged me during the four days I spent living in Emmanuel College, carousing and driving to the Gold Coast (then splendidly undeveloped) with my student friends.

In Sydney a similarly bibulous lot of university student mates decided to come down to the docks to see me off. They swarmed on board and continued the party. Sirens sounded and there were stern warnings that all non-passengers should leave the ship. One of my friends, Ted Lilley, had passed out and we took photographs of him in one of the lounge chairs, cradling an empty beer bottle and plastered with signs that said NOT WANTED ON VOYAGE. Ted was carried off in time, but as *Neptunia* pulled away from the Overseas

Terminal, with streamers billowing and last goodbyes being shouted, I heard familiar voices beside me as I stood at the rail. Two of my farewell party were still on board!

'No worries', they said cheerfully. 'We've done this before. We'll have a few more drinks and give ourselves up before we go through the Heads. They'll take us back in the pilot boat.'

Eventually, as the lights of Sydney retreated behind us, they made their way to the bridge and confessed. The Italians were not amused but, as predicted, they were ejected on to the pilot boat after we cleared the Heads and disappeared into the dark shouting cheerful goodbyes.

5 Orstraylian are you?

Ocean liners were the jumbo jets of our day for cheap travel abroad. Although my twelve-berth cabin was close to or below the water line it was at least airconditioned and I didn't plan to spend a lot of time there anyway-some wag immediately put up a sign, THE BLACK HOLE. We had the run of the ship-apart from first class-with our own swimming pool, lounges, bars and generous deck space for games of quoits or deck tennis-even a gymnasium to take off those extra kilos that the dining room would surely put on. Even in tourist class we were very nicely done by, thank you. Waiter service, a four-course meal with multiple choices and free red wine-as much as you could drink-at lunch and dinner. It was like being in Europe before we left. All the ship's announcements were made in Italian and English and the food and wine were splendidly Italian.

The passengers were a mix of Italian migrants to Australia going back to Italy for a holiday and Australians, young and old, heading off to Europe. The only slight downer was that there seemed to be about twice as many young single men as young single women. A number of the girls were from New Zealand, many of them bound for Perugia in northern Italy where they planned to study Italian. Unfortunately for us, our extremely smooth Italian purser, effortlessly bilingual and handsome as a movie star, was called Romeo and the New Zealand girls were far more interested in him than in any of us.

With a great deal of eating and drinking ahead of us, Nic and I were more than averagely interested in who would be sharing our table. Passenger ships then—perhaps still—insisted on seating passengers at certain tables and refused to allow any changes. We scored an extremely boring young Australian dentist named Barry and a monstrously bigoted and loud-mouthed Danish seaman in his forties who hated all Italians with a ferocious passion and spent the entire voyage telling us why. There were only two pluses at mealtimes, the food and the wine. Conversation was heavy going and to survive twice-daily contact with these two nerds Nic and I used to have wine-drinking competitions at lunchtime out of sheer boredom, and sleep it off in the black hole. Our first lunch together was on a Friday. Barry ate one spoonful of soup, put his hands to his throat in great alarm, jumped up and rushed from the dining room. I thought he must have been overtaken with a sudden bout of seasickness, although the ship wasn't moving much. It turned out that Barry was an extremely devout Catholic and as he swallowed his first mouthful he realised to his horror—with Purgatory staring him in the face—that it was pea and ham soup. He had eaten meat on a Friday!

Neptunia was a narrow-gutted ship. If stabilisers had been invented by then, the Lloyd Triestino line didn't think they were necessary. A day out of Adelaide, headed for Perth across the Great Australian Bight, we encountered huge swells rolling up from the Southern Ocean all the way from Antarctica. We were broadside on, and *Neptunia* rolled atrociously with great crashing sounds coming from the galley and the dining room in a state of barely controlled chaos as chairs slid from side to side. Waiters staggered around leaning against the angle of the roll to feed the few passengers who actually made it to the dining room. Most stayed in their bunks. It was actually quite dangerous to move about the ship, particularly on staircases.

Nic, being an engineer, quizzed one of the officers on the critical angle from which the ship could not recover. I think it was 60° so he suspended a beer bottle on the wall of our cabin and marked an arc on each side to 60°, ending with skull and crossbones. We would lie on our bunks watching this damn bottle inch towards the point at which the ship would roll over and we'd all die. I think we had a couple of 50° rolls during this time.

Perth was our last port of call in Australia, and when we finally pointed our bows north-west into the Indian Ocean, we felt our voyage had really begun.

Jakarta was our next port and a stunning experience for my first day in a foreign country. In brilliant sunshine and full tropical humidity we steamed slowly through fishing traps, suspended from rickety bamboo platforms, into the port of Tanjong Priok, where armed soldiers watched us unsmilingly from the wharf. Getting off the ship was an ordeal with complicated paperwork and temporary visas. We were practically strip searched to make sure we weren't carrying any foreign currency ashore and we were allowed 100 rupiahs for an English pound. The black market—had we been able to exploit it—was five times that. A group of us hired a car and driver with the idea of avoiding the usual tourist experience. Our guide, who spoke some English and wore a President Sukarno-style *pitji* (black cap), was peeved that we did not want to visit every museum and monument in Jakarta.

Initially we were shocked at the extent of the city's poverty but fascinated by the way people lived life on the streets, bathing, washing, excreting and, I suppose, drinking from the fetid waters of the *klongs*—the canals—most of which were filled in during the modernisation of Jakarta which has occurred over the last half century. We made our guide drop us off at the entrance to a market, and plunged into an area where tourists did not usually go. We were greeted with enormous cheerfulness and friendliness by the stall holders who tried to sell us everything from blue coloured eggs, strange tropical fruit we could not identify (purple mangosteens and bright red, spiky rambutans) to live chickens. The sights, colours and smells were not only exotic but exciting. Cheerful urchins in ragged clothes followed our every move. One picked my pocket, but our watchful guide cuffed the boy on the head and returned my Parker pen to me. I have never forgotten the romance of that incredible day when I became instantly fascinated by Southeast Asia—although it would be another five years before I lived and worked there.

We drove up into the hills to Bogor where President Sukarno had a palace and where we saw spotted deer grazing behind a huge white iron fence. Hungry for interaction with the culture and ordinary Indonesians other than tourist traps, I decided it would be a bonus if we could visit an Indonesian family in their house.

Our lugubrious guide—who had at least given up trying to take us to museums and monuments—dutifully went to a house we indicated and presumably said to the owners that he had these mad English people with him who had asked to visit. We were on the outskirts of Jakarta by then, in a semi-rural area almost certainly covered by skyscrapers today. The house I had selected at random was actually a small fish farm, on a half-acre block. It was surrounded by ponds with fish in various stages of growth. We were shown around with great courtesy by the husband and wife who obligingly netted some fish to show us. Then we were taken into their timber house which was quite large, with bare wooden floors, basic furniture and a big portrait of President Sukarno on the wall of their living room.

What happened then haunts me to this day—an inevitable clash of cultures where trying to do the right thing according to one's own cultural standards became a disaster.

The couple spoke in Indonesian through our guide and asked if we would like a drink. We were hot and thirsty and thought this was a splendid idea. But we had that absurd English tradition of saying, 'Oh no thank you'. In the English way, the host then insists, and you then say, 'Yes, thanks very much'. But it never got to that. We had refused their hospitality and were shown out almost immediately with some coolness. The situation was irrecoverable, and I have long agonised over it. Since then I have never refused the offer of a drink in any circumstances!

We only had six hours on shore, but those few hours gave an unforgettable experience of another culture. Travel by ship gives a wonderful sense of actually going somewhere, a sense of journey and distance simply not present when you are strapped into a seat in an airconditioned metal tube being transported across the world in a matter of hours rather than weeks.

Singapore was next on our itinerary and even in 1960 it seemed incredibly sophisticated after Jakarta. The black-holers went shopping in the good-humoured chaos of Change Alley where I decided £27 sterling was a bit steep for the portable typewriter I needed to buy. Someone told me to wait till we got to Aden, but before that we were to visit the ancient fishing and trading city of Cochin on the south-west coast of India. Again, a group of us tried to avoid being taken on a tourist tour and do it alone but it was an enormous hassle. Beggars—some without limbs and several with grotesquely swollen legs caused by elephantiasis—and small boys constantly badgered us for money. We did tour a small Portuguese church built in the fifteenth century and some forts in the English quarter but our hearts weren't in it and our bodies were wilting. I had brought with me some Australian pennies which had kangaroos on them (as well as a British royal face), and just as we were about to go back to the ship I decided to reward the shoals of small boys who had been pleading with us for money all day. I threw my pennies up into the air and the urchins scrabbled urgently for them in the dust. Their anticipation quickly turned to fury. What was this? They wanted real money—and hurled the useless Australian pennies back at me.

As *Neptunia* steamed towards Aden through the Indian Ocean, some of the twelve denizens of the black hole got lucky—despite the regrettable male–female imbalance against us. Finding privacy was an even bigger challenge than latching on to a girl. Don, a New Zealander in the bunk below me, threw caution and communal graces to the winds one night and brought his girlfriend back to the black hole. There is nothing more intensely frustrating than trying to sleep when a couple are getting into it enthusiastically only centimetres away.

I became friendly with a Maori girl—one of the few New Zealanders on board not going to Perugia to learn Italian. Neither she nor I was keen on a public tryst in the black hole. I had a brilliant idea. The Indian Ocean nights were just wonderful, balmy and warm, with stars blazing down from clear skies. I grabbed my sleeping bag and the two of us made our way up towards the bow, past the anchor winches and bollards where passengers are not supposed to go.

I unrolled the sleeping bag and we began to canoodle. Unfortunately there was more light about than I realised, and those on the ship's bridge were taking an intense interest in how things were going. I imagine the conversation went something like this (in Italian of course), 'Shall we switch on the spotlight now?'

'No, no, wait for a minute ... NOW!'

It was intensely embarrassing. The harsh, revealing glare of the spotlight was followed seconds later by a visit from the smirking ship's bosun who told us passengers weren't allowed in this area and we had to go. It was also the end of a potentially beautiful friendship.

The political situation in Aden was tense, with the British occupation of its garrison challenged by nationalist Arab guerrillas. We were advised, through our urbane purser Romeo, that it was not advisable to enter Crater City where all the main tourist attractions were. The alternative was to shop at the seedy collection of stalls along the harbour front. The intrepids from the black hole talked with some British soldiers on duty at the port, and when they said things weren't too bad in Crater City, although they couldn't guarantee our safety, we decided to risk it. This was also my last chance for a duty free typewriter—not that I wanted to die for it.

Mohammed Ali, an obliging taxi driver, drove us through the narrow pass to Crater City and we had a great time, taking in such delights as the Queen of Sheba's reservoirs (cut into solid rock) and a camel market. I bought an Olivetti portable for £22 sterling, which was a bit better than the Singapore price. We were all safely back on board by 5 pm with the ship due to sail at 6 pm. I wandered to the rail where the Aden bumboats below were offering duty free goodies ranging from French brandy, cameras and binoculars to improbable aphrodisiacs like Spanish Fly. To inspect an item you pointed to what you wanted and the bumboatman threw up a line. You hauled up the camera, or whatever, and then either sent it back, or bargained and paid for it.

I am deeply ashamed of what I did next. There is no excuse at all. I was uncomfortable with the bargaining process—as many Australians are—and considered I'd been ripped off in various ways from Jakarta to Aden with just about everything I had bought, so I pointed at a large pair of binoculars. The bumboatman removed them from their leather case, and I hauled them up on a rope, then scurried away from the rail and down to the black hole with my ill-gotten gains.

Several things happened. The ship, unfortunately for me, did not sail on time. For the next two hours (and I knew this because various black-holers came to tell me) the trader I had robbed screamed and shouted for justice and cursed me roundly in Arabic and English. My cabin companions took a high moral tone on this, as well they might, and sent me to Coventry. Even my travelling companion Nic thought it was a bit off, but at least he was still speaking to me. After an hour and a half of this I could stand it no longer. I put on a disguise of a floppy sun hat and dark glasses and poked my head over the rail.

'There he is', howled the bumboatman, who spotted me in a millisecond and cranked up his lamentations. I fled below for the second time until *Neptunia* finally sailed.

'What a rotten thing to do... how could you... I'll bet you are proud of yourself now, robbing that poor wog...' There was nothing I could say.

Mutterings and mumblings continued about my unspeakable behaviour in the confines of the black hole as we headed up the Red Sea towards the Suez Canal. The plan was that while *Neptunia* was negotiating the canal, passengers could elect to take a bus trip to Cairo, visit the pyramids and rejoin the ship when it reached Port Said and the Mediterranean. As we steamed towards Suez, a number of traditional Arab feluccas with their distinctive gaff-rigged single sails headed towards us. Cameras clicked as it was a lovely sight. But they did not pass by after all, turning towards us, and coming alongside. They threw up grappling hooks and ladders and within seconds traders poured onto the deck, pulling up bags of merchandise behind them. There were alabaster heads of Queen Nefertiti, pearl-embossed wooden platters, leather camels (allegedly stuffed with soiled medical dressings as a gesture of contempt towards the tourist infidels), riding crops with concealed stilettos, paintings, jewellery, leather pouffes and bric-a-brac of every imaginable nature.

Thoroughly chastened after Aden, I bargained for and bought an embossed wooden platter for my aunt in England, and returned to the cabin. It was like returning to a thieves' kitchen. The high moral tone had vanished. Almost to a man my cabin companions were knocking off stuff from the traders with élan. Taffy the Welshman, who had been perhaps the most critical of me after the binoculars incident, was shameless. 'Look, I've got two camels, a wooden plate and a riding crop.' The Australians and New Zealanders from the black hole soon bettered his score, with alabaster busts, lapis lazuli brooches and a plethora of stuffed leather camels. Intrigued, I went on deck to find the Egyptian traders beside themselves with rage, literally running around in circles while their stuff went off as quickly as the proverbial bride's nightie. I heard no more of Aden.

Nic and I elected to join the Cairo and pyramids bus tour and journeyed for hours across the desert, occasionally sighting the sweet water canal that took the waters of the Nile to Suez. The Cairo Museum was dark and dingy compared with other museums I had visited, but the contents of the shabby glass cases were stunning. As I stood marvelling at the fabulous, intricately worked lapis lazuli embossed gold mask that covered the head of the young pharaoh Tutankhamen, I heard a north country English voice behind me. 'I wish aa'd been with Howard Carter when he found all thaat stoof.' I was stupid enough to ask him why. 'Aa'd have melted all thaat gold down and made a fooking fortune.'

With only hours at our disposal we simply had to roll along with the tourist nonsense. It was quite impossible to avoid riding towards the pyramids on a camel. The camel driver asked my name. By an extraordinary coincidence, the camel I was riding was called Tim. Nic and I did the Great Pyramid of King Cheops inside and out. Dutifully filing up through the stone passageway to view the huge granite sarcophagus in its centre, I was reminded of the story of the World War I Australian Digger who must have walked the same way. He was shown the eternal flame, flickering in its stone lamp, and asked how long it had been alight. 'Oh for five hundred years, Sir', said its guardian proudly. 'It has never been allowed to go out in all that time.' The Aussie took a deep breath and blew it out. 'Well it's fucken' out now.'

Nic and I and a few others were determined to climb to the top of the Great Pyramid. In those days there were no rules about such things and little public awareness of conservation. We asked the bus driver not to leave without us, implored everyone we knew not to let him do so, and headed up. The stone blocks at the bottom of the pyramid are at least two metres high, but we found that they had crumbled on the corners, and there was a kind of trail where others had gone before. It took us twenty minutes to get up, and the view was well worth it—but our bus driver was already tooting his horn impatiently down below. The bus looked like a Dinky toy, we were so high. We scrambled down in ten minutes, and were so stiff for the next three days that we could barely get up and down the staircases of *Neptunia* to eat.

Now that we were in the Mediterranean we were impatient for our voyage to end, although we had a day each in Messina and Naples before berthing at Genoa. There Nic and I installed ourselves in the Genoa Youth Hostel, incorporated into an old castle, whose plumbing seemed also to date back to the Middle Ages. We both decided to buy new Vespa motor scooters, which was just as well as the day after we bought them, disaster struck. My bag was stolen from under my bed with both our passports, all my traveller's cheques, camera—not the typewriter fortunately—the ill-gotten binoculars and £20 sterling. Nic still had his camera and some traveller's cheques. But we couldn't cash them without a passport.

The Vespa people were very helpful and duplicated our paperwork. The Italian police gave us a letter (which listed all the things which had been stolen) which we could produce in lieu of a passport until we got new ones. The British Consulate in Genoa was less helpful (Australian passports did identify us as British subjects in those days) and refused to issue documents which would enable us to get to England. Instead they told us to go to the Australian Embassy in Rome. We would have enjoyed the trip more if we hadn't been so anxious about our passports.

Our Australian embassy people in Rome weren't very pleased to see us, and said the British Consul in Genoa should have fixed us up there. I had the strong feeling that the woman diplomat who interviewed us thought we had sold our passports on the black market. (Not even a signed letter from Prime Minister Robert Gordon Menzies—that could be obtained by departing travellers like me who knew a Federal Member of Parliament—which stated that 'any facilities or courtesies which may be accorded the bearer whilst absent from the Commonwealth will be greatly appreciated' broke any ice at the Embassy.) During the three days it took to verify who we were and construct the new passports, we 'did' Rome, seeing the Forum, Catacombs, Colosseum and the Vatican, but without enthusiasm. Finally our passports were ready. We opened them up gleefully. I was astonished to find Nic's 'orrible face gazing at me from my passport, and my face in his! 'Goodness me, that has never happened before', said the consular official in an irritated voice. As we watched, he tore the photos out, restuck them in and embossed them again with the official stamp. It looked as bodgie as all get-out and I had visions of being stranded on some lonely border accused of having a forged passport.

It was now September and we were not only worried whether we could get to England with the little money we had left, but whether we could make it over the Italian Alps through the Brenner Pass to Austria before it snowed. To economise we slept out when we could—on one occasion asking an Italian farmer if we could doss down in his private forest—conquered the Brenner in brilliant sunshine with superb views of alpine peaks all around us, and had a rare beer to celebrate. Our Vespas never missed a beat as we made a beeline for Calais and England.

The stresses and strains of our emergency dash were showing. Nic and I had developed a system of tooting on our horns in a particular way to indicate whether we wanted to stop or slow down so we could communicate. We used to start off as early as we could each day and then stop around nine or ten for a light breakfast of coffee and bread rolls, which was all we could afford. One morning in Switzerland Nic said it would be nice to find a Swiss café with a flowered pergola and a view of the mountains for our morning coffee. I was less fussed about the view and keener on the coffee. We rode on and on and on. Nic was in the lead, still searching for his ideal. Desperate for a caffeine hit I signalled that I wanted to draw up alongside his scooter to talk. He stopped. I said I only meant him to slow down, but before I could mention coffee he said, 'Well, why didn't you give the right signal then?' and took off. By the time I caught up with him we were in a Swiss town with a cobbled main street. This time I tooted to stop, and we pulled up alongside each other.

'Look Nic, I don't give a fiddler's fuck about the rose trellis and views of the mountains, I just want a cup of coffee. The first café we see will just be fine by me.'

Nic was still holding out for his scenic idyll. We both got stubborn. I can't remember why we started hitting each other, but it must have looked quite comical from afar, both astride our spluttering scooters and belabouring each other's torsos with wild punches in the middle of the street. I said, 'Well you can go and find your own fucking café, I'm leaving. And furthermore, if we don't meet up again—well bad luck'. Nic said, 'OK, that's fine by me', and took off. By this stage we were completely self-contained, with our own gear and our own scooters, so there was no practical reason to stay travelling together.

I guessed I would never see him again, but I did. By complete coincidence we met on the same Channel ferry a week later and patched things up.

The white cliffs of Dover looked strangely familiar as we neared the English coast—just as they looked in the postcards. Nic and I parted more amicably this time and he headed off to London while I began to navigate my way to Cambridge to fulfil my long-held dream of visiting the Bowden family. I found the countryside incredibly ordered and tidy compared with Australia. Even the roads were edged with a concrete border that meant you couldn't pull off until you came to a special bay called a 'lay-by'. I had a twinge of homesickness for Australia's splendidly untidy gum trees and the freedom to pull off the road wherever you wanted. Still, it was a relief to be driving on the left again and talking to people without waving arms and stammering in schoolboy French.

I had a childhood dream of simply turning up at Finella—and did just that, even though it would have been more polite to tell them precisely when I was coming. In Britain, one does not just 'drop in'. Finella, on the Backs at Cambridge, was a university house shared between two families, the Bowdens and the Bicknells. I fluked the correct driveway, fortunately, and rode my scooter into the Bowden courtyard. A young man with curly hair and glasses asked if he could help me. I said, 'I'm Tim'. It was my cousin Humphrey who went into full welcome mode and ushered me inside to meet my aunt Margot. Piers, the eldest son who at twenty-four was the closest to my age, came home for lunch. He was a research metallurgist doing important work in electron microscopy and we established a fine rapport. Jonathan, eighteen and the youngest son, was still in his last year at school so I didn't meet him immediately, and Sophie (then fifteen) was a delightful, shy young girl who was very welcoming. Uncle Philip didn't get back until late that night, as he had been to London where he was on the board of General Electric.

Science was God at Finella. All the boys did science degrees. Even Jonathan, the rebel who wanted to be an artist and eventually became one, had to do a biology degree first. Philip's original speciality and PhD topic was friction—the physics involved in what happened when metal surfaces were rubbed together. Physics students to this day probably study his classic work, *The Friction and Lubrication of Solids*. When I went to stay at Finella he was at the height of his career, not only heading the Department of Surface Physics at the Cavendish Laboratories, but a Fellow of the Royal Society. Philip was a great friend of the scientist and novelist C P Snow, later Lord Snow. In Snow's books on academe—one was *Corridors of Power*—Philip was the model for Francis Getliffe, the caring, ethical scientist.

Although he was three years older than my father, sadly he had only eight more years to live before being cut down by lung cancer. Both Philip and Margot made it clear to me that I was to consider Finella my home while I was in England, and I did. Curiously enough, although science and physics dominated the lives and careers of most of that family, the conversation around the dinner table was more likely to be about literature, music, drama or art. The Bowden half of Finella had a generous dining room with a table of baronial proportions and a bay window that looked out over sweeping lawns running down to a magnificent cedar of Lebanon. (Philip's Tasmanian origins were symbolised by a small, struggling snow gum that gradually established itself beside the big bay window.)

All meals were served at the large dining table and were cheerful, lively affairs. Margot produced wonderful roasts and casseroles wheeled in on a trolley from a tiny cupboard of a kitchen. Philip carved at the far end of the table and, after the meal, the dirty plates were placed on the trolley and pushed back into the kitchen where the family rallied around later to clear up. Philip served superb wines. He was on the Caius College wine committee—the only committee of the many on which he served that he really looked forward to attending. The college committee did its own tasting and imported directly from France.

Margot presided over the large rambling house with great style as she dealt with a constant flow of family and guests. She was a gracious hostess, a great connoisseur of art—the paintings at Finella seemed to change by the month—but had a rather shy, diffident manner. The family loved to tell the story of how she once attempted to sack the part-time help, a Mrs Mottley, whose rudeness and sloppiness had gone beyond the pale. 'You must do it, Margot', they said. 'Do it now.' Margot headed for the kitchen, stayed away for some fifteen minutes, and returned to the living room pale and shaking, demanding a gin and vermouth. 'Did you get rid of her?' the family asked eagerly. Margot said she had, but it was simply awful.

The next day Mrs Mottley turned up as usual, and just kept coming. Apparently Margot had been so discursive in sacking her . . . 'Thank you for helping us out for so long . . . your work has been much appreciated but . . . the time has come for a change . . .' that Mrs Mottley thought she was being praised for her work and getting a pay rise!

The Bowdens' generosity to me was extraordinary. Philip was aware I was short of money and organised me a temporary job in the Cavendish Laboratory which involved some typing and checking the references for a publication—for English expression, spelling and layout, not, of course, for scientific content. I was able to explore Cambridge and experience some of its student life with my cousins—mostly in pubs—and prowl around Kings College Chapel, museums and galleries. I went to a performance of the Cambridge Footlights, where Peter Cook, Dudley Moore, Jonathan Miller and Alan Bennett were polishing up their *Beyond the Fringe* routines which were about to revolutionise British comedy. Philip gave me £50 (a huge sum in 1960) so that I could accompany my cousins on a university skiing holiday to Zurs in Austria before joining the Bowdens for Christmas and their traditional fireworks party, with imaginative Bowden-designed pyrotechnics and much hilarity.

It was all great fun, but by January 1961 I had to face up to reality. One possibility was getting a job with the British Colonial Office. I had seen an advertisement in *The Times* (which still had its front page devoted to classified advertisements) for the position of Radio News Editor Uganda. The qualifications called for experience in both radio and newspapers—not all that common in those days. Working in Africa? Why not! Momentous and life-changing decisions are often taken by young people in a cavalier way. I was prepared to give Africa a go, and sent in an application. My friend Philip Koch gave me some unfortunate advice. 'The Poms don't think you can do any job unless you are at least twenty-five. Best bump up your age.' This I did, but was badly caught out when the Colonial Office required a birth certificate.

Nevertheless, I set out from Cambridge to London for my interview thinking I might have a real chance. The second class carriages were crowded, and I splurged another five shillings to experience the splendours of first class. It was a morning commuter train, and I opened the door of a 'dog box' carriage with eight seats. A businessman was the only occupant, working at some papers on his knees.

As I opened the door of the carriage he looked up. So I said, 'Good morning'. He took off his reading glasses and looked at me curiously. 'Do I know you?'

'No', I replied.

'I see. You're just being cheerful or something are you?'

'Yes.'

Satisfied he need not bother about me any more he muttered, 'Good morning' and returned to his work. We did not speak for the rest of the journey. It was my fault. I had broken the code.

Perhaps it was a harbinger—in terms of not understanding the British way of doing things—of what was to come later that day when I navigated my way to the gloomy pillared halls of the Colonial Office and at least arrived on time for my interview.

I faced two men. One was the organisational man from the Colonial Office. He was fat, wore a bow tie and horn-rimmed glasses and had an unnerving similarity to the feared BBC inquisitor Robin Day. The second man was a journalist, a rather pleasant chap, who asked me questions about what ratio of local to overseas news I would put in news bulletins for the native Ugandans, and so forth. That was on the rare moments in the interview when I wasn't being fanged by his colleague.

The first to speak was Robin Day. 'Mr Bowden, you claim in your application to be twenty-five years of age. Yet by your birth certificate and simple arithmetic you are unquestionably only twenty-three. Would you care to explain the discrepancy?'

I mumbled something about British prejudice about people under twenty-five, and ground to a halt. It wasn't a good start. I was relieved to be asked some questions by the journalist, with whom I got on well—or thought I did.

Robin Day was soon at it again. 'Mr Bowden, I note from your application that you have a Bachelor of Arts Degree from . . . the University of Tasmania I think it was . . . and you majored in Ancient Civilisations and Philosophy. Which of those subjects would you like to address?'

Unwisely I chose philosophy.

'Which area of philosophy should we talk about?' he asked with a slight smile that chilled me to the marrow. Even more unwisely I suggested metaphysics, and we finally narrowed it down to Immanuel Kant. 'Would you describe yourself as a logical positivist Mr Bowden?'

At this point Mr Bowden was so stressed he could barely remember what a logical positivist was. It had been a long time since Philosophy II. 'Look, can we move on to Ancient Civilisations, which was my real forte', I said.

'With pleasure.' Robin Day was homing in for the kill, and I was like a rabbit trapped in a sharpshooter's spotlight. 'What do the following names mean to you Mr Bowden?' He rattled off six.

'Look, I'll be perfectly honest, I've never heard of those gentlemen.'

Robin Day leaned back in his chair with a smirk of quiet triumph. 'Gentlemen, Mr Bowden? They're places!'

I didn't get the job.

By now completely broke and fairly desperate I borrowed £50 from Uncle Philip and headed for London—but not to Earls Court where the Australian ghetto was already attracting the satirical attention of Barry Humphries, then in London understudying the role of Fagin in the musical *Oliver*. (The actor playing Fagin was no fool—he didn't miss a performance the whole time Barry was breathing down his neck.) I managed to inherit a rather roomy basement bed-sitter that Phil Koch was just vacating in Hampstead. Plans to join archaeological digs in Palestine or Egypt or shouldering the white man's burden in Africa had gone on the back burner. I turned back to the trade I knew, and pressed the buzzer on the front door of the ABC's London office in a rather gracious Georgian building in Portland Place, not far from the head office of the BBC.

I had an appointment with the ABC Manager in London, one William Bearup, who had been exiled there after losing a power struggle with Charles Moses, the legendary and long-serving ABC

General Manager renowned for his abilities to wield an axe, metaphorically and practically. (He kept a competition axe in his office and would shave the hairs from his arms and occasionally from the arms of his visitors to demonstrate how sharp it was.)

It was my first experience with a speaking security system and I jumped back when a voice said, 'Who's that?'

'Er, me! I mean Tim Bowden.'

'Push the door open and come in.'

Bill Bearup's office was in the basement, with glass doors opening out into an elegant courtyard. He was a small man, sitting behind a very big desk. There was no small talk.

'Good morning Mr Bowden. What exactly did you want from us?'

'Well, some work Mr Bearup.'

'No, no, we don't have any of that.'

On my way out a nice man with white hair, John Warren, introduced himself to me. 'I'm the admin man. I gather you didn't have much success with Bearup.' I admitted as much. 'I'd suggest you take yourself over to the General Overseas Service of the BBC in the Aldwych. The Pacific Service there broadcasts to Australia, and the bloke in charge, John Terraine, is an Englishman who actually likes Australians. I'll give him a ring and tell him you might drop by.'

I was already finding out that although I had come 'home' to England from Australia, the sense of family was rather one way. On hearing an Australian accent people would say with faint amusement and a good measure of condescension, 'Oh, you're Orstraylian are you?' It was the kind of reaction that spawned the comic character Bazza McKenzie, the archetypal Oz in England who certainly knew when the Poms were coming the raw prawn. Nicholas Garland drew the comic strip, and Barry Humphries provided the dialogue. It used to be run in the satirical magazine *Private Eye*. 'As dry as a Pommie's towel' or locating sheilas that 'go off like an alarm clock' were expressions symptomatic of an Australian penchant for rewarding perceived Pommie pomposity with earthy home-grown vulgarisms.

Australians did have one thing going for them—no one knew exactly where we fitted in the complex British class structure. We weren't Oxbridge, red-brick university, or grammar school, nor were we Cockney, Scots, Welsh or North Country. We were treated with a certain amount of innate suspicion, but with luck we could slip in between the cultural cracks. I was about to be the beneficiary of this uncertainty.

While the BBC's HQ at Broadcasting House was a solidly Anglo-Saxon bastion of breeding and upper-class plummy accents, Bush House at the Aldwych, where the General Overseas Service operated, was a wonderful polyglot mixture of just about all the races of the world. There were the African Service, the Chinese, French, Hungarian, Russian, South American and many more services, broadcasting in the languages of those countries as well as in the official voice of Britain—the General Overseas Service (GOS) of the BBC (later renamed the World Service). There were sub-strands like the North American Service and, indeed, the Pacific Service. Bush House was funded by the Foreign Office and run by the BBC. Its job was to reflect British interests to the world, and while propaganda obviously played a part, it was painted on fairly lightly. The mainstay of the service was, of course, the BBC news, widely respected for its accuracy and relative impartiality.

The Pacific Service—which included Australia and New Zealand—was run by John Terraine, who was just about to make his name as a World War One historian with a seminal biography of Field Marshal Douglas Haig. (In later years he wrote and presented several major historical television series, the best known of which was *The Great War* which used a skilful blending of movie footage and still photographs.) When I first met him he was spending most of his time writing his manuscript on Haig and came to the Pacific Service mainly to keep a light hand on its helm, and to drink and sleep.

Spooling Through

On the second floor of Bush House I presented myself to a snooty receptionist who told me to wait while she phoned to see 'if you are expected'. There was no security in those days. I was told to take the lift to the seventh floor and was ushered into Terraine's office by his extremely buxom and glamorous secretary, Vera. John Terraine was then in his late thirties but had lived fairly hard if the startlingly deep pouches under his eyes were any guide. He asked me a few perfunctory questions about where I had come from and what I was doing, then took me into the main Pacific Service area, an open plan office jumbled with desks and tape recorders, and introduced me to an amiable New Zealand producer, Basil Sands.

'Try him out on something', said Terraine and disappeared back into his office. Basil didn't seem to mind having me foisted on him and said there was an interview he wanted done. Fortunately the BBC had moved beyond clockwork tape recorders and issued freelancers with an EMI reel-to-reel portable recorder housed in a green box with a carrying strap. BBC radio producers like Basil used to commission items from freelancers, and then edit the tape brought back for broadcast. The craft of tape editing was jealously guarded by the BBC technicians who rightly saw their jobs under threat by producers—and certainly freelancers—who could do their own. Producers in Bush House had won the right to cut edit tapes in their offices before taking the cut tapes into a studio to be mixed under technical supervision into the finished program. Beside their desks producers like Basil had tape decks called Ferrographs, which had a splicing block mounted at the front and were excellent for cutting and splicing quarter-inch tape.

I was desperate to get my hands on one of these machines so I could whip my first interview for Basil into shape before he heard my mistakes—botched questions or failure to follow up an obvious lead. But Basil wouldn't let me. He quite rightly wanted to hear the raw tape to see if I knew what I was doing. It became obvious to him, after my first effort, that I had interviewed with editing in mind. In other words it is far better to repeat questions, or seek a better answer to a misunderstood question, on the spot. You can't re-record your questions later because the acoustic circumstances of the interview are usually impossible to duplicate. I must have passed the test because I was asked to put up some ideas for interviews and was given work.

The standard BBC rate for a 5-minute (or less) item was five guineas. My Hampstead bed-sitter was four guineas a week. One interview meant I was housed, a second took care of food and a third interview in a week meant I was drinking as well. Any more was a bonus. I found a restaurant in Hampstead that served a three-course meal for three shillings and nine pence. I cooked breakfast in my own room, on a small gas stove. The standard London bed-sit fit out included a washbasin with hot and cold taps. It was considered bad form to piss in it. The bathroom and toilet were down the passage.

Life seemed pretty good. I managed slowly to enlarge my stable of producers who wanted my interviews for their magazine programs. I even managed a couple of programs for the Home Service, at the holy of holies, Broadcasting House. No one seemed to worry too much about my Australian accent. Tapes of the time reveal that I was starting to sound a bit plummy myself. Essential osmosis I suppose, but English people picked me as an Oz in seconds. In the cold weather I took the London Underground to work but as the weather warmed up I rode my scooter past Lords Cricket Ground, down Park Lane, past Buckingham Palace and through the Mall on my way to the Strand. It felt like a daily tour around the Monopoly board.

My biggest problem was to find a desk and a phone. English people very seldom agreed to an interview on the first phone call. 'My secretary will ring you back.' But there was nowhere to ring. Prowling around the sixth floor of Bush House one day I found a room with a newspaper and magazine rack in it and, joy of joys, a desk and a telephone. I kept an eye on it for a few days and no one seemed to be using it. Keeping myself fairly portable—I could snatch up my briefcase and be out of there completely in seconds—I gave my extension to the BBC switchboard and was able to confirm my interviews. The same snooty receptionist who had guarded John Terraine from me now asked my visitors 'if they had an appointment with Mr Bowden'.

In those more relaxed days ID wasn't required. Carrying a BBC issue tape recorder was enough. I went to a press conference at the Savoy Hotel one day, and was royally entertained with gins and tonics and elegant sandwiches. Not that I made a welter of it, but during lean times I would shoulder the EMI recorder and ask at the Savoy reception where the press conference was. There was almost inevitably one going on and I could eat and drink stylishly for free.

After about three months in my acquired office I looked around one morning and saw a bald-headed chap looking quizzically at me through the door. 'Just using the phone for a moment', I said cheerily, grabbed my bag and was off like Bazza McKenzie's bucket of prawns in the sun. By then I was doing so much work for the Pacific Service that I was given part access to a spare desk, phone, and Ferrograph tape recorder to edit on.

The BBC Club was dangerously close, just across the Strand. That's where I first met producer Gordon Snell, who was helpful in introducing me to some of his colleagues in the North American Service. (Our paths would cross again in Australia in the 1970s after he married Maeve Binchy, the London correspondent of the *Irish Times*, who had not then made her name as a best-selling novelist.) I had a few pints one evening with John Newell, an ex-Cambridge graduate who ran a weekly science program *Science and Industry*. We got on well after a marathon session of pint after pint of flat English bitter, and he agreed to try me out on a job or two. I'd only done a couple when I was summoned to the office of George Steedman, who was in charge of the Pacific and North American services. He'd heard some of my interviews, of course, and wanted to meet the Australian freelancer who'd joined his merry band. Steedman—inevitably called 'Buckmaster' by his loyal troops—was an intimidating bloke to meet. He had the disconcerting habit of rolling his eyes up under his lids so you could only see the whites. In the course of our chat he asked me what were my preferred interviewing fields. On the spur of the moment I said 'Science' because I'd just done a couple of jobs for John Newell.

Buckmaster's eyes swivelled completely up into his head. 'Who told you to say that?' he snapped back at me. I honestly didn't know that he was an absolute science nut, who would have liked nothing better than to be doing what I was doing. In fact, after he retired from his eminent BBC job he came back and worked for *Science and Industry* as a freelancer! At least he didn't put a black ban on me.

By doing my own editing, I not only ensured quality control over my own work, but ensured that the producers I was working to would have more time to go to the BBC Club or have long lunches. I got lots of work, and they didn't have to worry about processing my raw tapes. While as fond of a drink as any journalist, I did have to make sure I earned the wherewithal to buy it. Terraine, supremo of the Pacific Service, used to drink at the Surrey pub, not far from the BBC Club, across the Strand. The Surrey was where expatriate Australians hung out, and could get their beloved Fosters on tap. The downstairs bar and dining room was perpetually crowded with homesick Australians, mostly from Earls Court, downing cold ones and offering unflattering commentary on their host country and its warm beer. The graffiti in the toilet took Pom-bashing to a high art. I was devastated when Freddie, the English owner of the Surrey, had all the graffiti painted over. It was a great blow to the social historian.

There was a small upstairs bar which sold the usual range of draught English ales and bitters where John Terraine would hold court when the quaint British licensing hours allowed. The pubs would open at 11 am and close at 3 pm, opening their doors again at 6 pm. Terraine's usual routine was to get into his office about 10 am (having worked on his Haig manuscript until late into the night and early morning). From 10 till 11 am he would take care of his in-tray, shouting as he dictated to the long-suffering Vera with whom he used to have a series of steaming altercations which I think they both enjoyed. By opening time he would be panting for a drink.

I would be beavering away at a Ferrograph, cutting and editing tape. The door to the Pacific Service office would open, and Terraine's glowering face would appear around it. 'Bowden', he would declaim in an injured, accusatory and reproachful tone, 'they've been open for *ten minutes*'. Well, he did authorise my cheques. I would leave whatever I was doing and go to the top bar of the Surrey where John would preside until 3 pm. At five minutes past he would ask Helen the barmaid for another half pint of bitter. She would refuse as the law dictated and a ferocious argument would ensue. John wouldn't get his drink, and would stomp back to Bush House and into his office where he would fall into an armchair and sleep heavily until 6 pm when it was time to go back to the Surrey. Sometimes I used to manage to slip away and get back to work, but often not.

One afternoon after a particularly punishing session at the Surrey, I decided to give Terraine a fright. I climbed out of the Pacific Service office onto a small window ledge seven floors up with a sheer drop to an interior courtyard, edged along to Terraine's office window next door, and knocked on it. He was sound asleep in his armchair, and woke up to see my peaky face glaring at him through the window from the outside. I pulled the window open, climbed through and walked past him without speaking back into the main office. He claimed later it took years off his life. When I sobered up I had a bit of a think about it too. I have no head for heights and am prone to vertigo.

Terraine's affection for Australians came partly from his work as a World War I historian, and from having been sent to Australia for a familiarisation tour by the BBC. He found an extraordinary number of ABC managers (including Wilbur Reed of the bandaged hands in Tasmania) who seemed determined to take him on personally conducted tours of broadcast studios. This was not in the mainstream of John's interests, and he generally managed to find some blithe ABC spirits who rescued him from studio tours and took him to the pub.

One of John's favourite stories about his down-under odyssey was the time he became exceedingly friendly with an Australian girl. They went back to her flat. Things progressed and, just as John in fine priapic splendour was about to consummate their love-making, the young woman seized him by the shoulders, looked him straight in the eye and drawled: 'You won't do any good up there!'

The art of negative projection 6

In 1961 Harold Macmillan was Prime Minister of a Conservative government, his walrus whiskers and aristocratic drawl making him an irresistible target for the *Beyond the Fringe* satirists who were then taking their anarchic comedy from its Cambridge beginnings to London. The biggest international story was the ill-judged and failed United States invasion of Cuba resulting in the Bay of Pigs fiasco which blighted President John F Kennedy's 'Camelot' administration. The Cold War was at its most frigid. In May, a British public servant, George Blake, was sentenced to forty-two years in gaol after spying for the Russians. The following month the charismatic young Russian ballet dancer Rudolf Nureyev defected to the West while in Paris. But the Russians had scored a great coup in April by launching the first man into space to orbit the earth, Yuri Gagarin.

I was more preoccupied with getting work and making a living through the BBC than worrying about the Cold War. In one vintage British radio comedy show there was a radio reporter called Cecil (pronounced, with a lisp, Cethil) Snaithe. This unfortunate chap was always finding himself broadcasting from exceedingly hazardous situations. These sketches invariably ended with a blood curdling scream from the intrepid reporter as Cecil succumbed to yet another frightful accident. I had a soft spot for Cecil. John Newell, the producer of *Science and Industry*, loved adventurous radio and in a desperate attempt to get enough work, I used to volunteer for some hazardous assignments.

I had Cecil Snaithe definitely in mind when I leapt off a tower in a simulated parachute jump with a British army training unit, tape recorder running. Another time I was lucky enough to get a very funny interview with a solemn dog psychiatrist, surrounded by the yips and yelps of pampered poodles and neurotic Pekinese. So when John heard about a man who trained guard and killer dogs, I was sent off on the train to Sussex to get the story. The guard dog trainer, Mr Derbyshire, seemed as savage as his Alsatians and Rottweilers.

I introduced myself as being from the BBC. 'I'm fed up with you poncy, wet-behind-the-ears reporters coming down here thinking you're going to interview me and then just stuffing off back to the office. Have you any idea what it's like to be attacked by a vicious dog?'

I said I hadn't, and hoped I never would. That seemed to inflame him further.

'Well bugger you then. You can piss off right now. The only way you'll get an interview from me is if you let me demonstrate what it's like to be bitten by one of my dogs. This is the deal: I'll dress you up in protective padded clothing, and hide you in the woods and set a dog on you. It's all right, I'll be close by to pull him off, but try not to fall over. They aren't supposed to go for your face, but sometimes they get excited and forget. Then I'll give you an interview about how we train them. That or you can leave now.'

I couldn't bear the thought of going back to London empty-handed. Besides, I needed the money. He strapped padded guards over my arms and legs and I struggled into a big military greatcoat that covered the padding and the rest of my body. That was how I found myself standing under a big oak tree, whispering nervously into my tape recorder.

The dog hunting for me was a big Alsatian, and he didn't take more than a minute to suss me out. I'd stopped talking by then, too. Those guard dogs don't bother to bark, they just move in silently. I was in deep fear. As the dog leapt at me I instinctively put my right arm up to guard my throat. In a split second he had bitten my arm three times. The power of his jaws was awesome. I could feel the bones in my arm buckling under the pressure. There was certainly some nasty bruising over the next few days despite the padding and the coat. The dog, having been muzzled, glared at me with mad yellow Hound of the Baskerville eyes, clearly disappointed at not being able to finish me off, but the trainer was as good as his word and gave me an excellent interview. Edited together with my yells of terror, the item was a hit with John Newell. (The dog did growl obligingly for the tape while it was trying to chew my arm off.) Derbyshire told me during the interview that it was possible to call the guard dogs off, but the killer dogs (which were trained by being teased and goaded to a frenzy by their trainers until they hated all human beings) were uncontrollable once they were unleashed.

Other assignments were less physically risky but hazardous in their own way. One of the perks of Bush House work was to think up people you wanted to meet, and put up a proposal for an interview. I had long admired the work of Frank Muir and Denis Norden who had not only written the radio comedy *Take It From Here* that was very popular in Australia, but were the mainstay of the witty and erudite *My Word* (and *My Music*). In 1960 Muir and Norden were working in television at the BBC's White City studio complex.

On reaching their office my nervousness was compounded by the fact that they were both two metres tall. They welcomed me in a kindly way and asked how I wanted to handle things. I said I would interview them both together and produced my list of carefully worked out questions.

'Could you tell me how you manage to work so well together on your comedy scripts?'

Norden shot a glance to Muir to respond. 'Well, in the first place', Frank said in that wonderfully mellifluous voice with its slight lisp, 'it was very difficult to get a pen that was big enough for two hands to hold . . .'

My heart sank—I was about to be sent up rotten. But they were nice men and, to my intense relief, they took pity on me so that I came away with quite a reasonable item.

The writer E Arnot Robertson was a friend of the Bowdens in Cambridge, and she arranged tickets for me to attend a recording of *My Word*. Arnot and the journalist Nancy Spain verbally sparred with Muir and Norden on the program which was recorded in a small theatre before an audience. They all came on stage in fairly good form from a well lubricated dinner. Although the broadcast program was only half an hour, they recorded for at least twice as long and edited together the best bits. That is why if any listener bothered actually to count up the scores as broadcast, they wouldn't make any sense at all. But no one minded.

The highlight of each show was the embroidering of a quotation by both Muir and Norden in a hilarious and improbable story which invariably ended in an atrocious pun. For example, the line, 'You can't have your cake and eat it', would be taken up by, say, Muir who would weave a discursive story about an Eskimo who used to get very cold when he was hunting and built a fire in his kayak with disastrous results. The conclusion? 'You can't have your kayak and heat it.' Devotees of the program will have read the many books that followed these erudite and funny programs over the years.

Later I asked Arnot how much lead time Frank and Denis had to work out their wonderfully witty and intricate stories. She said that in the early days of the show, they were given the quotations cold, on the spot. But they became such a feature that the BBC relented and used to give them their quotes at the beginning of the dinner before the recording.

Another broadcaster I much admired was Alistair Cooke, whose weekly talk *Letter from America* was already a well established feature not only on the BBC, but in Australia. When I heard he was in London I arranged an appointment at his Park Lane hotel. (At the time of writing he is still broadcasting *Letter from America*—now into his nineties—forty-two years after I met him.)

My first question, serious and rather portentous, was something like, 'Mr Cooke, at this moment in Australian history we seem to be torn between the old ties with Britain and the new realities of American world influence—how do you think Australia should resolve this dilemma?'

Cooke wasn't as benign as Muir and Norden. He snapped back: 'I don't know, what do you think?' I stopped the recorder in dismay and confusion, as I hadn't come prepared for a debate. Cooke told me to start the recorder again, and I ground out the same question. Again, he asked what I thought. I mumbled something about, with luck, getting the best of both worlds.

'Yes, well that's the kind of confused and muddled thinking that will almost certainly lead to utter disaster. And furthermore...'

It was not a happy occasion and that was one item that died on the cutting room floor.

One of the Pacific Service producers for whom I worked was a New Zealander, John Laird. He, too, used to like interviewing much admired figures, but he was bolder than I was. John decided he wanted to interview Bertrand Russell, who was then ninety and passionately involved with the nuclear disarmament movement. In fact, he refused to talk about anything else. Lord Russell, with his shock of white hair, thin, lined face, piercing eyes and long stringy neck looked a bit like a startled ostrich. He spoke in a high rasping whisper—for reasons John was about to discover.

After Russell had gone around the tracks on tape with his views on the threat to the civilised world posed by nuclear weapons, Lady Russell came in with a tray of morning tea. As they sat making small talk, John was offered a plate of shortbread biscuits and passed them on to Lord Russell who waved them away and croaked: 'No thank you. I shall never eat again.'

John Laird didn't know what to say to that, but Lady Russell later explained that the venerable philosopher had throat cancer and could only take liquid food. (He was 98 when he died in 1970.)

Thinking back, I realise I've always been more interested in the stories of 'ordinary' people (who tend to have extraordinary stories) than I have been in interviewing celebrities. But in the London days a job was a job, and I had to eat. On occasions the two could be married comfortably. I was asked to interview a former Hungarian entrepreneur who had started a chain of restaurants in London called The Guinea and the Piggy. The idea was simple. You paid a guinea, and then could stuff yourself with as much food as you could keep down, ranging from a bewildering array of entrees and salads, through myriad main courses, served on a buffet, as well as a cholesterol-challenging array of sweets and puddings. It seemed churlish not to sample a guinea's worth. I asked the restaurateur how he could possibly make a profit if, for example, everyone made a beeline for the caviar and hogged it. He explained to me that human nature (or greed) was such that people tried to have a little bit of almost everything on offer, which was impossible, but helped the bottom line.

On another occasion I found Sir Compton Mackenzie to be a fascinating old man. I spoke to him at the Saville Club, the theatrical club where he took me to lunch. Mackenzie was deaf and shouted out the names of well-known actors in the dining room in case I missed them. 'See? There's Sir John Gielgud over there. And there's Alec Guinness at the next table.' The old boy wanted to come to Australia to present a television documentary series for the ABC, but nothing came of it and he died not long after I saw him.

Amnesty International had not long been formed when I interviewed its founder, a deceptively mild-mannered lawyer, Peter Benenson. He made a big impression on me by his absolute determination to do something about political prisoners rotting in gaols all over the world, without having been charged or with no prospect of a fair trial. He spoke beautifully, with such logic and well-expressed reason that it seemed inevitable that Amnesty would become a major force against personal injustice in the world.

John Betjeman, the Poet Laureate, was as whimsical as his poetry. He was over the moon about the talents of Barry Humphries who, he said, was one of the world's great poets—apart from his success as an actor and satirist. I had already beaten a path to Barry's door to record some of Mrs Norm Everage's impressions of London and the Poms. The future Dame was working on an Australian household alphabet in rhyme:

> 'A' is for Apron, in plastic or cloth. It protects all your dresses from hot fat and broth.
> 'B' is for Bathroom where dirt I deplore—you ought to be able to eat off the floor!
> 'C' stands for 'cuppa', refreshing and hot. It won't taste the same if you don't warm the pot...

Mrs Everage was getting a bit jaded by London and the weather (this was during the time Barry was in *Oliver* understudying Fagin who never got sick) and he ended one of our interviews by saying that London was a good stepping off point. 'And, Mr Bowden, I think I'll be stepping off *very* soon.'

It was all very well getting a couple of interviews with Barry (both he and I needed the money) but what on earth was I going to do with them. I was supposed to be reflecting positive views of Britain for its international broadcaster and while satirising Australians in London was funny, it was hardly in the British national interest. One of the Pacific Service producers I worked to at that time was Michael Williams, a Welshman whose perspective on the English was not all that different from mine. We hatched the concept of 'negative projection'. By broadcasting Humphries sending up Australians in London we were showing how broadminded the BBC was. Even the pro-Australian Terraine's eyebrows shot up when we expounded this theory. I only got away with it twice. Bill Peach, who had joined the Pacific Service as an exchange producer from the ABC, thought it was a hoot. (Bill and Shirley stayed away from the Australian ghetto in Earls Court too, and had a flat in Camden Town, where I used to join them occasionally on Sundays for a game of tennis.)

Michael Williams became a great friend and, always conscious of the duty of the BBC's General Overseas Service to boost British exports, he was entranced to learn of a little firm in the Midlands that still manufactured leg-irons for export to African and Middle Eastern countries. He couldn't resist accompanying me to highlight that telling example of niche marketing. We decided to tie in a few other stories, one of which involved a hairy-chested Outward Bound school in Wales, by a happy coincidence quite close to where Michael's mother lived in Bangor, and a visit to Lord Montagu of Beaulieu's vintage car museum in the south of England. The good lord had recently featured in Britain's tabloid newspapers following a bit of alleged hanky-panky with a Boy Scout. He invited us into the kitchen of his manor house for a cuppa before I recorded an interview with him among the car collection which included a rare Stanley Steamer. Lord Montagu's wife, an attractive, long-haired county 'gel', was there when we arrived. Before he could introduce us, she announced rather aggressively that she was leaving. As she strode towards the door Lord Montagu asked, mildly enough I thought, where she was going.

'Out!' she snapped, banging the door behind her. We left as soon as we decently could.

My growing testiness with brass warming pans and thatched cottage tea rooms confirmed that I was unlikely to become an expatriate.

The very neatness of the English countryside made me yearn for that wonderful Australian untidiness—in a landscape sense—with its sprawling eucalypts and freedom to pull off the road without finding a lay-by or having a concrete verge to stop you. I missed the space and the big skies. The clouds over London seemed to hug the chimneys of the grubby brick terrace houses which, in those days, still spewed out coal-fired smoke.

One of the services that I provided for newly arrived Australian friends was to introduce them to English beer. I would take them to a pub where they served keg bitter—which had the advantage, for Australian tastes, of being reasonably cold and had bubbles in it. The Poms, of course, preferred their pints of flat bitter served at room temperature. (I did develop a taste for English beer but it took a while.) The most alien beer to Antipodean tastes was draught Bass. It came out of the tap warm, flat, and without the trace of a head. John Terraine said you could always tell draught Bass drinkers because they wore cloth caps and had burst veins in their noses and cheeks. He told me of overhearing two draught Bass drinkers commenting on their freshly poured beers.

'A beautiful drop', said one, holding his pint of warm brew up to the light. 'Aye', said his friend, 'but I think I'll warm mine in my hands for a bit longer'.

My strategy for incoming Australians was to tip off the barman to be ready to tap an emergency half-pint of cold keg bitter. I would then order my friend half a pint of draught Bass, which looked like warm piss. Some would allege it tasted like it. My friend would sink his top lip into the frothless brew and take a tentative sip. Reactions varied, but were never good. Some screamed and ran to the toilet to spit it out. Others swallowed and shuddered with fear and loathing. 'Geez, if that's English beer I'm never having another.'

'Just a minute', I'd say, and order half a pint of keg bitter, which was not only cold, but effervesced. 'Christ, that's better', my friend would say. If I'd given him the keg brew in the first place he would have complained almost as vociferously. I did this as a selfless public

The art of negative projection

B.B.C. POST

From our special representative
LONDON. — "Report from London," one of the B.B.C's regular magazine programmes to Australia, is at present being produced by Tim Bowden, a former Hobart journalist.

Tim, a former member of the literary staff of "The Mercury," broadcast for the A.B.C in Hobart before going overseas last July to try his luck in London.

He rode a motor scooter across Europe from Italy to London, and began freelance interviewing for the B.B.C. Overseas Service, broadcasting to Australia, Africa, North America, and Asia.

Always keen to get his tape recorder into "off beat" and unusual situations, Tim has gained interesting experience. For one B.B.C. science programme he flew a home-made hovercraft while on an actually broadcast.

He has also commented on demonstrations of rocket-assisted aircraft ejection seats.

On one occasion he was knocked flat on his back while recording the blast of an underwater explosion designed to shape steel into rocket nose cones, near London.

During the compilation of Australian programmes, Tim has interviewed such personalities as the script writers Frank Muir, Denis Norden, Arnol Robertson, Australian author Russell Braddon, and Nancy Spain.

After some months freelancing he was offered a contract with the B.B.C. to produce "Report from London," which is part of the Corporation's Pacific Service.

Before returning to Australia in about 18 months time, Tim hopes to broadcast in East Africa, in Tanganyika, or Uganda.

● Tim, who is the son of Mr. and Mrs. J. G. Bowden, of 37 Maning Ave., Sandy Bay, is pictured at the B.B.C. studios in London. He is preparing his "Report from London."

service to my fellow countrymen arriving in London.

But I enjoyed the work I was doing and was delighted, after several months working out of Bush House, to be offered a contract to produce a Pacific Service program called *Report From London* for six weeks. This meant that I would be hiring freelancers, instead of being one. As I would be joining the staff temporarily, I would have to be vetted by the security service (either MI5 or 6, I supposed). Further good news was that I would be allowed to freelance for my other regular gigs on top of my £25-a-week contract. Life seemed pretty good. Spring was in the air and, as I rode down the Mall on my Vespa, in front of Buckingham Palace in bright sunshine with daffodils bursting out all over in the nearby parks, I pulled up beside a mutton-chopped old gent driving a Bentley. We caught each other's eye, and although I should have known better after my experience in the first class carriage in Cambridge, I remarked cheerfully what a great day it was. 'Yes, but we'll have to pay for it later on', he said gloomily, and we both drove on.

Being a lover of classical music, I used to keep an eye out for good concerts. When I first arrived in England, the legendary Sir Thomas

Beecham was still conducting. I made a mental note to go and see him, but the old boy died before I was able to do so. I did see the venerable Sir Adrian Boult in action at the Festival Hall and of course 'Flash Harry'—the urbane Sir Malcolm Sargent, who was famous for his stewardship of the annual Henry Wood Promenade Concerts in the Albert Hall.

There were other agreeable diversions. Malcolm Playford, an Adelaide lawyer married to my cousin Peg, arrived in London unexpectedly on business. He was on generous expenses and staying at the Savoy. He asked me to lunch there and I arranged to pick him up from Liverpool Station on my trusty Vespa. Malcolm is very tall and was smartly suited. I tied his lawyer's briefcase on to my luggage carrier with string and we pulled up in front of the Savoy's imposing entrance. The doormen in their ornate uniforms and top hats didn't miss a beat, they simply untied Malcolm's briefcase and directed me to where I could park my battered scooter. Then Malcolm and I had a most expensive lunch on Malcolm's faraway client.

As the summer progressed I laid plans for a better assault on the Continent than my first experience had offered. The Bowdens in Cambridge invited me to join them for a summer climbing holiday in Switzerland. I planned to ride my scooter through France to Spain (and the Balearic Islands) before joining the family in Switzerland. My cousin, Piers, and I planned to meet in Corsica, and camp and climb the mountains in the high country there. Flushed with BBC loot (and mindful of Arnot Robertson's freelance dictum: 'The worst thing that can happen is nothing') I made my farewells from Bush House and hoped I would still be able to pick up work again when I got back after a couple of months in the sun that seemed so scarce in Britain.

In Paris I tracked down Alistair Edison whom I'd known at *The Mercury* and who was staying with an elderly Tasmanian, Miss Mary Adams. She ran a school teaching English to the French and Al had fallen on his feet as usual, getting rent-free accommodation for talking Strine to French English students. At the same time he was learning French himself, and the lucky bugger was one of those people born with an ability to absorb another language through his skin. One of his pupils, Gerard, was a nightclub singer who took us to off-the-tourist-track nightclubs on the Left Bank, where enchanting *chanteuses* entertained locals with songs of great wit and political satire. I couldn't understand the subtleties but it was fantastic entertainment and a wonderful welcome to the 'real' Paris. Al swore that he saw Jacques Tati (M Hulot in *Mon Oncle*) standing in a doorway in Montmartre one day, dressed in Monsieur Hulot's trademark raincoat.

I ate and drank my way south towards Spain and Barcelona, and across by ferry to Majorca where I soaked up sun like a salamander. The wine, food and accommodation were not only cheap but excellent and I combined underwater snorkelling in the crystal clear Mediterranean with touring around the island. The post-war tourist boom was just beginning in the Balearic Islands and on the Costa del Sol where the beaches were dotted with pink and blistering English (and some German and Scandinavian) persons. The only reason to leave was to get to Switzerland to join the Cambridge Bowdens at Zinal for their summer walking and climbing holiday.

The distances were ridiculously short compared with Australia, and it only took me a couple of days to ride from Spain up the coast via Perpignan (sneaking around the edge of the Pyrenees) and into France. Zinal was in the French-speaking part of Switzerland, and I chugged up towards the high country through picture postcard Swiss farms backed by snow-covered peaks. The Bowdens were staying in the rather sinister-sounding Hotel de Diablons. It was an Edwardian-style hotel built originally for nineteenth-century English alpine summer climbers. Nothing seemed to have changed in the interim. The bookshelves had a selection of English novels written in the 1890s. Each evening, after rambling and picnicking in the high country among the wildflowers, we would gather in the lounge after dinner to hear a most professional trio from Zurich (I found out later they played for their holiday) perform chamber music. It was the first time I can remember hearing Beethoven's *Archduke* trio, and I think of the Hotel de Diablons every time I hear it.

Philip Bowden, generous as ever, subsidised my stay at Zinal, and included me in a rock climb with a Swiss guide. My cousins Piers, Humphrey and Jonathan were all experienced rock climbers. I had never been rock climbing, although I liked walking up mountains for the view. Rene, our guide, was horribly fit and we practically ran up the first thousand metres until we reached a sheer rock cliff. High above I could see a vicious looking peak, reminiscent of the Matterhorn, towering into the sky with a number of lesser pinnacles in front. We roped up. I was just behind Rene, then Piers, Jonathan and Humphrey. It soon became obvious to me that Rene was trying to kill us all.

It was all very well telling me to take the weight on my feet whenever possible, but I was forced to scrabble with my fingertips in rock clefts to stop falling. To my horror I realised that Rene was going to take us up and over the top of all the pinnacles before we tackled the main peak. Looking down, I saw another party walking up a much easier way and mentioned this. That was when Rene called me a *crapaud* (toad). The dreadful realisation dawned that Rene (on behalf of the rest of us) was actually looking for the most difficult route. That is, apparently, what all crazed rock climbers do. I honestly didn't think I would get off that mountain alive. To show how easy it was, Rene sang songs and did little dances on murderously exposed spots. At one stage I found myself clinging to a razor-backed ridge with the ends of my fingers cold in the shadows on one side of the mountain, and the backs of my hands warmed by the sun on the other, sending showers of little stones down 1000 metres on *both* sides. Rene shouted back at me that I was an *escargot*. I knew what that meant all right.

Somehow they hauled me up to the top of the highest peak. I was exhausted and in need of some Dutch courage from a Spanish wineskin I had carried with me. A photograph was taken, which I later sent as a postcard to Rosalind Geddes then nursing in Sydney, and with whom I kept in touch from time to time. I found the descent even more scary than the climb and swore a solemn oath that although I liked climbing mountains, I was never going to go on a serious rock climb again. Rene tried to ingratiate himself at the end by saying we were the best party he had all summer. We were probably the only party he'd had all summer.

Piers and I decided we would meet up in Corsica and do some less hazardous mountain climbing there. I rode my scooter down to Nice, on the French Riviera, to catch a ferry to Corsica. I had to ride over mountains so steep I actually had to slip the clutch of the Vespa deliberately to get over them. Other motorcyclists were walking beside their machines to make it. That wonderful Vespa never missed a beat the whole time I owned it.

Approaching Nice I smelled a familiar scent and realised I was riding through a line of huge gum trees. Underneath one of them was standing a beautiful, long-haired girl wearing a wide-brimmed hat, white dress, a sketchbook under one arm and a small rucksack at her feet, hitchhiking. I screeched to a halt and met Monique, an art student from Paris, also heading for Nice. It seemed churlish not to give her a lift.

We seemed to get on just fine, and Monique's English was marginally better than my French. I asked her if she would like to have dinner with me and she accepted. It was a great meal, but rather more expensive than I had in mind as she ordered *langouste* (lobster) at a price which would have kept me in fuel for a week. We drank lots of wine and I asked her where she was thinking of staying the night. I told her I was going to sleep on the beach at Nice. What fun, she said, and thought she might join me. I thought this sounded pretty good too and we actually did drive to the beach and lay down our groundsheets and sleeping bags. It was a fine night, with stars blazing down, and we embraced and kissed tenderly. The debacle at the bow of *Neptunia* flashed in front of my mind, but this seemed open ended. To my surprise I found she was crying silently, her cheeks wet with tears. I asked her what was the matter?

Her mother was gravely ill, she managed to communicate to me, which was why she was heading back to Paris. She was planning to catch a train from Nice the next day, but that would be very slow. Across the water we could hear and see aircraft landing and taking off from Nice airport. It would be much quicker if she could fly back to Paris. There might even be a flight tonight, late as it was. The only problem was she could not afford the fare. If I could lend it to her, she would promise to pay me back. Not only that, she would be happy to see me in Paris at some future time where she would make me very welcome indeed. She knew that I had hoped to make love to her on the beach, but she felt so miserable about her mother that her heart wasn't really in it. But in Paris things would be different.

So with a little balloon over my head saying 'sucker' we rode towards Nice airport on the faithful Vespa. At the ticket counter the French airline clerk said that, sadly, there were no seats left on the last flight to Paris. Monique really turned on the pathos and the charm, and to my dismay, got a seat. I lent her ten English pounds—a lot of money then. She kissed me joyously and rushed to the gate for her flight. I drove sadly back to the beach at Nice and pondered how things might have been as her aircraft roared into the air and turned slowly over the bay to head to Paris. Why hadn't I been a hard-hearted bastard and not lent Monique money? I was sure I'd been conned and that I would never see my £10 again.

(I was absolutely wrong—but the story does not end well. Three months later I had heard nothing and had written off the ten quid. Then a letter from Paris arrived at my Hampstead address, with £10 enclosed. In the letter Monique said that she had often thought about me, my generosity and what a nice feller I was. She was looking forward to meeting me in Paris whenever I came that way, and she would make me *very* welcome. Would I please write and tell her that the £10 had arrived safely. The address was indecipherable! I even took it into Bush House and got someone from the French Service to try to figure it out. I took a stab at it, and wrote a letter. It was returned to sender. About four weeks later another letter from Monique arrived saying she was worried and sad that she had not heard from me. Had I received the £10? And when was I coming to Paris? Her same scrawled address might well have been in Babylonian cuneiform. Her letters stopped. We never met again.)

The ferry dropped me off at Bastia, on a promontory at the northern extremity of Corsica, and I rode down the east coast to the capital Ajaccio where I had arranged to meet Piers. The country was wild and beautiful, and almost completely tourist free. I snorkelled at deserted beaches and rocky coastlines, and looked at the distant high mountains Piers and I planned to climb. Apart from Corsica not being 'discovered' by tourists, there were other reasons to be wary. The French colony of Algeria, just across the Mediterranean in Africa, was in a virtual state of war with a virulent independence movement clashing with an equally brutal French administration determined to hang on no matter what. Corsica, too, wanted independence from France, and there had been bandits in the mountains there since living memory.

I scootered merrily into Ajaccio where I was to meet Piers at the railway station. My schoolteacher Lisl Mathew's French lessons failed me at a crucial moment. I stopped at a café where several rotund Corsican peasants were enjoying a pastis or three. I tried to ask one of them where the railway station could be found.

'Excusez moi, ou est la guerre?'

This produced an alarmed reaction.

'La guerre monsieur? Non, non!'

I came at it from another tack. 'Oui, la guerre! Chemin de fer, chouf, chouf, chouf.'

'Ah ha! La gare!!'

I had not mastered the difference in the pronunciation of 'war' and 'station'. The bloke I had asked burst into roars of laughter and rushed inside to tell his mates. He never got around to telling me where the station was, but I found it somehow, and Piers as well.

The high country of Corsica is superb—in many ways reminiscent of Tasmania—with clear mountain streams, easy walking and small stunted pine trees. We had flawless weather so didn't bother to pitch our small tent but slept out under the stars while we climbed three mountains, including Corsica's highest, Monte Cinto (2865 metres). It wasn't technically challenging and we carried our lunch up and ate it on the summit surveying almost the entire island.

One night we lay in our sleeping bags gazing up through the clear air at the blazing firmament. Satellites were then rather new and we started talking about them. 'As if to illustrate our conversation,' I wrote in a letter home, 'one sailed serenely and clearly overhead. Then we started to talk about shooting stars and were rewarded by a graphic display. Remembering H G Wells' story *The Man Who Could Work Miracles* we thought we'd better not mention comets and suppressed a desire to command the earth to stop turning'.

Our descent from the mountains was risky. Some idiot had started a forest fire. The fire-fighters who were first on the scene knew that it wasn't us, but as we drove further down towards the plain, the village people preparing to fight the fires themselves were convinced we had started it. There were angry shouts, and a few rocks thrown at us, so the only thing to do was to open the throttle and hope we'd make it, which we did.

Back in Ajaccio we rented a room from an ancient and voluble old crone who nearly drove us mad. The toilet was a long way from our room, so we pissed in a wine bottle and hid it under the bed. The accommodation included lunch, so we fronted up for some spaghetti and bread rolls. Just as we were about to eat, our ancient concierge signalled we were to wait. The poor old thing clambered upstairs to our room and returned with our wine bottle three-quarters full of stale piss which she plonked triumphantly on the table. I fell about laughing, but Piers—being British—was utterly disgusted. Eventually he saw the humour in the situation. I said it might have been marginally better than the vin-very-bloody-ordinaire that had been in it originally.

The art of negative projection

After I had been holidaying on the Continent for more than two months my funds were running low, and I wondered if my freelance empire was still intact at Bush House. I pointed my handlebars towards Calais and London looking neither right nor left except to avoid accidents. Fortunately I had not been forgotten at the BBC, and there were even assignments waiting for me.

There was a problem of where to live, however, since I had surrendered my bed-sitter in Hampstead before I went on holiday. Various former Tasmanian colleagues were homing in on London, including Al Edison and Barry Holland with whom I had worked briefly in the Hobart office of the Launceston *Examiner*, so I found a tiny two-storey terrace house for rent at 93 East End Road, East Finchley, in the north London area. Both Barry and Al needed to find work, but I thought we could cope with the £10-a-week rent. We had to endure a forty-five minute Underground journey to the city, but then so did lots of Londoners.

Gradually the 1955 line-up of the Hobart *Mercury* cadets started to clock in to 93 East End Road. Mike Philp arrived, broke, from the United States having had incredible adventures in a big three-masted schooner in Guatemala (about which he should write a book but probably won't). Some months later big Dave Mitchell arrived from Paris where he had remarkably landed a job as a political journalist with Agence France Presse, alongside the famous Australian journalist Murray Sayle—Dave had to handle copy in French and turn it into Franglais (even though his command of French was circa Scotch College, Launceston, Tasmania 1954). If Drip Cock had called by we would have had a quorum for a shorthand class.

The little terrace house in East Finchley was bursting at the seams. As the lease was in my name, I tried to keep things within bounds, paying the rent, being our charlady, and making sure the antique furniture was not permanently disfigured by grog rings. Mike Philp did a bit to help, but Al was on shift work and Dave was the house slob. The film *The Odd Couple* had not yet been made, and when I saw it in New York some years later, I almost had to be carried out of the theatre helpless with mirth. I was Jack Lemmon and Mitch was Walter Matthau.

One evening Mitch came home and smelled cooking. He came through to the kitchen where I was making a Spanish omelette. 'Gudday mate. What's for dinner?'

I exploded. 'Jesus Christ, what do you think this is, a fucking hotel? Here I am slaving my fingers to the bone in the kitchen, doing all the fucking work, while you never do anything to help. How do you think this place runs with passengers like you just taking and giving fucking nothing?'

Mitch took a step backwards. 'It's all right mate, there's no need to get upset. If you want me to help, I'll help. What do you want me to do?' I thought about this, and realised there was nothing he could do. The dinner was just about cooked, and as far as the washing up was concerned, he wouldn't even know where the detergent was kept.

'Oh I dunno—you could take the kitchen garbage out the back and put it in the rubbish tin.' I went on cooking, and realised a few minutes later that Mitch was still wandering around looking lost with the package of scraps still in his hand. 'What's the matter now?'

He looked embarrassed. 'Mate, where's the back door?'

He'd been living in the place for six weeks and he had never been out the back! Not that there was much to see. A pocket handkerchief lawn that we actually cut with the kitchen scissors because there was no lawnmower.

At Bush House, Cecil Snaithe was back on the job. An interview behind the scenes at a travelling circus nearly ended in a Snaithe-like bloodcurdling scream when I strayed too close to the cage of a Bengal tiger which took a savage swipe at me through the bars, then I was knocked flat on my back by the blast of an underwater explosion in a tank, used to fashion nose cones for rockets. I caught bronchitis while on assignment on a lightship supply vessel in the North Sea and decided the world's worst job would be a crewman on one of

The art of negative projection

these tethered, manned lightships which just heaved and rolled all day and night on station.

A more gentle job was to interview a nice old man who specialised in detecting art forgery not only through the analysis of paint pigments, but using X-rays. He produced a fake and a genuine fourteenth-century painting, to demonstrate the deception. He offered me a cup of coffee, and for some reason I dropped in my two lumps of sugar from a great height, and splashed coffee on the fourteenth-century original. My interviewee jumped two metres in the air and clapped the soles of his feet together as he frantically wiped the drops off the painting while I wiped drops of sweat from my brow. Permanent damage was averted, and I asked him how much the painting was worth.

'About five hundred guineas.' He was quite sporting about it and gave me a good interview despite my crassness. Perhaps his adrenalin was still pumping. Mine certainly was.

When asked to do a feature on the British Customs service for a program *Calling Australia*, I took a train to Tilbury and boarded the liner *Oriana*, recorded my interviews, and was invited by the Chief Customs Officer to have lunch in the first class dining room before the ship sailed. As I tucked in to the four courses I vaguely heard announcements for all non-passengers to leave the ship. A steward asked if I would like a brandy with my coffee and I could see nothing wrong with that idea. Then I heard a gentle clearing of a throat and turned around to see the First Officer in full uniform standing behind me. 'I don't wish to hurry your lunch Mr Bowden, but we are holding the ship for you . . .' They couldn't sail without their Customs clearance. I hurried on deck and down the gangway. As I did so a voice said: 'Righto Joe, let 'er go', and the great ship cast off her last link with the land and set off for Australia.

At the Martin Baker Aircraft Company I was to see a demonstration of a new ejection seat developed for the RAF which could even be employed close to the ground. It shot the pilot 100 metres into the air so that a parachute could be safely deployed. Fortunately

Cecil Snaithe was not required to do this—a dummy strapped in a capsule did the job for my tape recorder. Afterwards I was taken to the executive dining room, surrounded by RAF Wing Commanders and Squadron Leaders. It was the morning that the Russians had put the first man into space. Yuri Gagarin had orbited the earth before being safely returned. I heard the news at 8 am, and thinking I was on safe ground, I said to the Public Relations Officer next to me (who happened to be a Wing Commander) that it was amazing news about the Russian spaceman. 'What spaceman?' he asked. I explained that the Russians had put a man in space that morning.

'Is he back?' (I had a feeling they thought he might drop in.)
'Yes.'

The Wing Commander turned to his colleague on his other side. 'Bill, how are your daffodils coming along . . . it's the horticultural show next week . . .' To my astonishment they talked about growing flowers for the rest of the lunch, and the Russian space breakthrough was not mentioned again.

After more than two years in Britain I was feeling a tad homesick. Perhaps the long Underground journeys from East Finchley to Trafalgar Square were partly responsible for this. Tube travel was, and is, a solitary experience despite the thousands packed into the subterranean carriages. Eye contact was avoided, and casual conversation a no-no—for quite sensible reasons. The Japanese do the same in their even more crowded underground trains. With personal space so cramped, such group anonymity is a useful survival mechanism. The noise of the trains rushing through the tunnels made conversation almost impossible anyway. But sometimes the trains would stop, without any explanation, for minutes at a time. Then the silence of a crowded carriage hung heavily in the air. Suppressed claustrophobic thoughts would surface with the knowledge that we were all a long way below ground. Yet I was living in the land that spawned the Goons and eventually Monty Python. During one of these long silent stops a voice from the back of my carriage screamed one word: 'SMALLPOX!' (There was a scare at that time.) As ever, London commuters remained impassive.

Towards the end of 1962 decision time was upon me. It was made clear that if I applied for a BBC producer's job that was coming up in the Pacific Service at Bush House I would probably get it. This was an enormous compliment, and probably a job for life. It was something I had never envisaged happening. Yet I felt strongly that I wanted to return to Australia, to complete the cycle as it were, before committing myself to being an expatriate in London.

Two things happened to cause me to cut the painter with Britain. Mike Philp had taken off to Belgium to help a wealthy American, David Louthan, buy a 65-foot steel-hulled schooner, *Moonglow*, in which he proposed (with Mike's help) to sail around the world. Mike wrote to me saying that a berth was available to me as a crew member for five weeks during a shakedown cruise in the Mediterranean. If everything worked out I could probably stay with *Moonglow* and sail to the West Indies.

Then a letter arrived from my father saying that through the good offices of his boss, Len Nettlefold, a supernumerary berth was available to me on a cargo ship which would sail from England to Australia in November. I could sign on for a symbolic shilling and get home for nothing.

It all seemed too good to pass up.

The fastest plucker on the island 7

I paid my symbolic shilling to the Shaw Saville Line for my passage on MV *Canopic,* due to sail from Tilbury at the beginning of November, thus leaving the five weeks to frolic in the Mediterranean. David Louthan's *Moonglow* looked very fine to me as she lay at anchor in San Remo, fresh with Falmouth paint. I was greeted by her sailing master, Christopher de Grabowski, a lean, bearded man who looked every inch a sailor-which, as I was about to discover, he certainly was. I was dismayed to learn that Louthan had been called away to Singapore on business and that Chris and I were the sole crew. We would have to sail *Moonglow* to the Balearic Islands by ourselves; David and the rest of the ship's company would join us in Palma de Mallorca. As things turned out, it was just as well I'd arrived when I did. Although I was 'green as an Irish pasture' (as Chris later described me in a sailing article he wrote) I was at least another pair of hands. Even Chris, who had sailed single-handed across the Atlantic, would have been unable to manage *Moonglow* on his own. We eyed each other off warily as he invited me down below to stow my gear in one of the two forward cabins.

I had never been on board such a luxurious yatch. There were two heads (lavatories) and a big comfortable saloon and David's stateroom with a double bunk and lots of storage. Aft, and on deck, were the wheelhouse and small navigation cabin where Chris and I effectively lived while we were underway, taking alternate three-hour watches. The masts and stays were festooned with complicated halyards and pulleys with which I was expected to become familiar—'so you can locate the right ropes in the dark', said Chris ominously. Having only done day sailing I had not considered such a possibility. Sensible sailors went home at night in my experience. The boat was stacked with a wondrous variety of tinned food ranging from basics like potatoes and carrots to delicacies like squid preserved in its own ink, olives, tinned ham, anchovies and a well stocked liquor locker bursting with Scotch, gin, vodka, cognac, Campari, Tio Pepe sherry, vermouth, beer and French wines of every imaginable variety. Chris, probably noting the gleam in my eye, turned off *Moonglow*'s fridge saying it was a waste of bottled gas!

My new skipper wasted no time in licking me into shape: he roused me from my bunk at 6 am and had me scrubbing the decks with Teepol, pumping out the bilges and even polishing the brasswork before giving me a rundown on the basics of how the schooner worked. This wasn't quite the holiday I had envisaged from London but it was certainly character forming. My taskmaster was a colourful character. Gloomy and moody, as Poles often are, he was actually Count Christopher de Grabowski—although there were times during the next few weeks when I mentally dropped the 'o' in his title. His background was like something out of an Ian Fleming novel. He had been displaced from his land in Poland first by the Germans and then by the Russians. He didn't talk about himself very much, but from Mike Philp and others who knew him, I gathered he was in the Polish diplomatic corps before the war, and a navigator with the Polish Free Airforce during the war, first in Britain and later in North Africa. Mike said that he spoke Polish, English, Italian, French, German and Arabic quite well, and could get by in Spanish, Russian and even Flemish. While Mike was helping to outfit *Moonglow* he'd watched Chris learn enough Flemish in five weeks to carry on useful conversations in Belgium.

Despite having fought for Britain during the war he was unable to get British citizenship and was still a stateless person when I joined *Moonglow*. He had some kind of refugee document that enabled him to travel, but not to settle. Doubtless this made him even more irritable and moody—apart from the legacy of his apparently stormy relationships with women. But fortunately he had friends in San Remo and it was decided we would cruise from the Italian Riviera to the French side, finishing up in St Tropez. I wondered if I might get a glimpse of the French film star Brigitte Bardot. From there, Chris and I would set off for Palma de Mallorca.

Chris's friend, Duke Gian Marco Borea D'Olmo, who lived in San Remo, only had one arm having lost the other in a plane crash while flying in Mussolini's air force during the war. He had already met David Louthan through Chris and had agreed to sail with *Moonglow* to the West Indies. Gian Marco came on board with his wife Fiorenza, born a baroness, their twelve-year-old son, Gian Battista, a marquess, and his eight-year-old sister Ottavia, a countess. Another friend, the glamorous Lahra de Galard, was a French countess. Chris, of course, was a count, and I was, well, a commoner. It was decided that I should be upgraded. As I had started to grow my first moustache—every man does it once in his life—I was seen to have a rather military look and was dubbed 'Major' Timothy Bowden, with an Honourable slapped on the front for good measure. As Chris later wrote, 'If ever a blue-blooded crew manned a ship, I had it on that short voyage'.

The voyage was a notable cultural experience for me. All the adults were fluent in English, French and Italian, and when they thought of it, spoke English so I could be included. But the children only spoke French and Italian, so the conversation would often abandon English to include them. La Comtesse Lahra de Galard used to favour French, but choice of language really depended on what they were talking about. For example, Italian topics would be discussed in Italian—but they would switch to French in mid-conversation for no discernible reason. I felt a linguistic moron, and wished I had paid more attention to Lisl Mathew. Somehow in Australia it hadn't seemed relevant.

Chris had described St Tropez as a kind of quaint marine Greenwich Village, full of fake Brigitte Bardots and beach bums—and a great deal of charm. We lingered there for a few days but he was keen to put to sea where he was closest to personal happiness. By then he had decided that at least I knew one end of the ship from the other.

Our route to Majorca lay across the Gulf of Lions, known to all but me for its unpredictable weather. Even Chris, however, was surprised by what it threw at us. We didn't get away from St Tropez until late afternoon, and it took an hour and a half for the two of us to raise the big schooner's sails and snug her down. We were too preoccupied to pay much attention to some low flying military aircraft until one dropped a practice bomb just in front of our bows. In blissful ignorance we had been heading into a protected military zone.

The barometer was plunging and a stiff south-easterly continued to strengthen. Just after midnight Chris called me on deck to take a reef in the mainsail and staysail—tying the sails around the booms to reduce the sail area. We had to run down-wind while we were doing it. Steering at night on a slight reach and a tumbling sea was an exacting business and the compass needle in the dimly lit binnacle seemed unwilling to stick on my ordered course of 230° south-west. I became disoriented and hypnotised by the needle and corrected the wrong way, causing Chris to bound up from below, toothbrush in mouth, beard flecked with foam, saying: 'Damn it all, if I can't even go down to clean my teeth for five minutes without you going all over the shop, how the hell am I going to get any sleep over the next three days!'

Sleep came fitfully in the deckhouse and when Chris woke me at first light I felt utterly and nauseously seasick. *Moonglow* was pitching violently and rolling in a great, grey sea with the wave tops whipped away in a smother of foam by the now roaring wind that was working up to a full gale. Down below there was utter chaos as badly stowed gear, books, cushions and packets of food were thrown around as if in a giant washing machine and an improperly fastened skylight added salt water to the mix. We sat in the deckhouse and tried not to be thrown about. A few hours later, with the wind gusting 40 knots, Chris shouted that we couldn't hold our course anymore and must hove to. This meant lowering all sail except a storm staysail which would keep our bows just off the wind. I'd hoped that actually *doing* something would make me less seasick, but the reverse was true.

We retreated to the deckhouse where at least the lashed wheel was doing the steering. Chris, who said he'd never been seasick in his life, seemed to be getting happier the worse the weather became. Munching cheerfully on some bread and cheese (I had to avert my gaze) he announced that the barometer was still falling and we were now officially in a full gale. So much for a peaceful autumn cruise in the Mediterranean. As it happened we were lucky to have plenty of sea room. Freak storm conditions and torrential rains, we found out later, had hit Barcelona with such force that some 800 people were drowned in flash floods.

The Mediterranean is a shallow inland sea, and strong winds whip up steep and very nasty swells. It was reassuring to have *Moonglow*'s solid steel hull underneath us as the big seas boiled past and the wind screamed through the rigging. And that is what went on for the next 24 hours. I was not only wretchedly seasick the whole time but constipated as well. Perhaps it was raw fear of how I might have to manage things if my bowels did move. Chris said brightly that at least things were emerging at one end.

Just as I thought it was impossible to be more miserable, my skipper ordered me forward to secure a hatch that wasn't properly fastened down near the bow. As I made my way forward I was seized with a sudden bout of nausea. I hooked my arm around a stay on the starboard side and vomited violently—and the wind whipped it all accurately inside the hood of my oilskin. That was my lowest ebb. The best option seemed to let go the stay and end it all!

That night the wind died away briefly and there was an electrical storm with thunder like gunfire and enormous crackling flashes of lightning that lit up the sea and sky almost continually. Then the wind howled in again, from the opposite direction! Although we were still hove to, now it was at least pushing us in the right direction. At first light a little land bird fluttered weakly on to our lee rail for a few minutes and then was swept away. We were at least 160 kilometres from the nearest land, so it was difficult to imagine it surviving.

On the morning of the third day I was inexplicably feeling better and managed a mug of coffee and some bread and cheese. The wind, although still gusting at 50 knots, was behind us, and the swells roaring past us were still steep and intimidating. One option was to run before the wind but Chris was unsure how *Moonglow* would behave in a following sea. There was a possibility she might broach, with disastrous consequences. But, being Chris, he decided to give it a go. He eased the big schooner's head away from the wind, and for a few gut-wrenching seconds we wallowed in a trough before our stern was picked up by the next rolling monster of a wave. We were off, creaming down the swell in a smother of foam, on a fantastic ride—actually *surfing* in a 65-foot steel schooner. Fortunately our little storm staysail gave just enough stability to keep us straight in the trough while the next swell picked us up and threw us forward again. Before long Chris was confident enough to give the wheel to me, and we both whooped and hollered with the sheer exhilaration of it all, surfing towards our landfall, the Balearic Islands. We even had bursts of sunshine through the clouds. To add to our joy, Chris managed to find Beethoven's *Eroica* symphony on the radio which seemed to surge in concert with our wild ride. At last, the storm was over. (Chris took a photo of the Hon. Major Timothy Bowden at the helm, a trace of anxiety on his face—we must have been at the bottom of a trough—with a wall of water tumbling down behind *Moonglow*'s stern, and used it in an article he wrote later for a yachting magazine.)

Chris expected to make our landfall at the small island of Minorca by 8 pm, but he had not been able to get a sun sight with his sextant for three days and was relying on dead reckoning—more difficult than usual because we had been forced to heave to for some 48 hours. He was understandably smug when the loom of a lighthouse rose above the darkened horizon just where he had predicted.

The next morning we hung about at the mercy of light airs and a calm sea. What a contrast! Chris became impatient and hit the starter button of *Moonglow*'s big diesel. There was a nasty 'thud'—and silence. The Polish count soon worked out what had happened. The following seas we had so joyfully surfed down the day before had deposited dollops of sea water into the stern exhaust outlet, and had then run down into the engine. It should have been sealed off with a plug. Now we had a diesel full of salt water. There was no alternative but to sail into the great natural harbour of Port Mahon. Chris, humming quietly to himself now that he had another challenge to surmount, got out his charts.

Although Minorca boasted one of the world's great natural harbours—five kilometres long and over one kilometre at its widest point—it was protected from invasion and bad weather by a long narrow channel between rocky cliffs that led in to the sheltered basin of the main harbour. This channel, only a few hundred metres wide, was at least a kilometre long but our problem was that we had to sail through with no engine and very little breeze.

We set every stitch of canvas we had, an exercise which took several hours to accomplish. *Moonglow* must have made a fine sight as we neared the narrow entrance to the harbour. As we did so, the breeze dropped noticeably. By that stage we were past the point of no return, and pressed on. (I had the anchor ready to drop in an emergency.) As we sailed silently and majestically up the narrow channel, tourists flocked out onto their hotel and apartment balconies on either side, photographing what may have been the biggest vessel to come in to Port Mahon under sail since the days of Nelson. (The British first captured the island from the Spanish in 1721.)

Inside the main harbour we could see a small island on which stood a Georgian military hospital, its whitewashed walls gleaming in the sunshine. It would not have looked out of place anywhere in the British Empire, including Tasmania.

We still had to get close enough to the port area to row our dinghy in. Chris started to get fancy, and had me running backwards and forwards to the jib sheets as he tacked towards his goal. By now there was practically no wind at all and he nearly stalled on his last turn. We both held our breaths as *Moonglow* faltered, but just made it onto the last tack. Chris signalled for me to drop anchor and we celebrated our achievement with one of David Louthan's fine malt whiskies.

Port Mahon was a pleasant place to spend a few days. The British had built a gin distillery in their time there and Minorca was also famous for the invention of mayonnaise—said to have been sampled on a farmhouse salad by the Duc de Richelieu, who named the olive oil and egg yolk blend 'Mahon-aise'. Chris rang David Louthan (by then back in London) who arranged for a diesel mechanic to fly in from Madrid to give the engine a full overhaul. Fortunately he found that the salt water was not in there long enough to do significant damage.

A week later we sailed for Majorca, the main island in the Balearic group, where we were to meet David and Gian Marco. The Mediterranean turned on its usual trademark weather and the voyage was without incident—until its final moments. The only berth available to us in the marina at Palma was right at the end of the wharf, on an angle. Chris, conscious that the eyes of the cognoscenti of the

Palma Yacht Club were upon us, had to reverse in to this awkward berth. He told me to be ready to jump ashore and take a half-hitch around a bollard when he gave the word. I had been practising my half-hitches and was confident that nothing could go wrong.

'Now', shouted Chris, giving *Moonglow* a touch of forward throttle. I jumped ashore, ran to the bollard and, in the stress of the moment, forgot how to do a half-hitch. I tried one way, then another. I didn't have time for a third go because the skipper with a bellow of rage left the wheel, jumped ashore, snatched the rope from my useless hands and tied the half-hitch before leaping back on board again. It was at that precise moment I realised I didn't have a big future as a yachtie.

Later, having a drink at a nearby bar, I met a young Englishman, Tony Van Hee, who was looking for a yacht to sail on as crew. He was a dedicated sailor and had been shipwrecked in a yacht on the northern coast of Spain only a couple of weeks before. I introduced him to Chris who later suggested to David Louthan that he give him a trial on the way to Gibraltar. This all worked out and Tony eventually sailed with *Moonglow*, not only to Gibraltar, but on to the West Indies. By that stage I had decided not to go to Barbados, but to stick to my plan of a free voyage home from London on MV *Canopic*. I sent a telegram to Al Edison offering him my berth and he immediately resigned from his job and got ready to head for Gibraltar.

Moonglow was a different ship with her owner on board. The fridge sprang into life and we feasted on exotic Spanish delicacies washed down with the best grog. There was lots of laughter and jollity as we set sail for Gibraltar. Even the Polish count seemed more relaxed. After all, he was now the sailing master, not the captain. The weather stayed benign as we sailed and motored towards Gibraltar. About a day out from the famous rock, David Louthan was at the helm under bare poles and power as we passed another yacht heading the other way. We shouted pleasantries at each other and David, on impulse, swung the wheel over to do a tight celebratory circle.

Unfortunately he forgot about the ship's log, a speed and distance recording device trailing from the stern at the end of a long, tightly braided rope, which promptly wrapped itself around our propeller, stalling the engine.

David looked chagrined, but he couldn't blame anyone but himself. What to do? I said that I had an underwater mask with me and would be prepared to have a go at cutting the log line off the prop if a good lookout could be kept for sharks. I put on a long-sleeved shirt to protect me (I hoped) from the barnacles on the steel hull, and Chris rigged a rope around my waist so I would stay with the ship, which was drifting in quite a strong current. It was a bugger of a job, actually, and I kept being banged against the hull by the current as I sawed away with a sheath knife at the cord tightly wound around the propeller shaft. It took a long time, as I had to keep coming up for air. Finally I cut it all away and was hoisted back on board to loud and relieved cheers from my shipmates. My shirt was stained with red anti-fouling paint and it was only then that I learned that my loyal friends thought this stain was my own blood from barnacle wounds. They didn't want to tell me until I'd finished the job!

I planned to fly back to London from Gibraltar in time to brief Al Edison on what he hoped would be the adventure of his life so far. I still felt ambivalent about giving up a voyage to the West Indies, but reasoned that if I was passionate about being a yachtie, I would have persisted. Perhaps my four weeks alone with the Polish count had some influence on this decision, but in fact I had been lucky to have such an experienced skipper on board when we ran into the full gale. By now I'd also been away from home for more than two years and felt it was time to return.

Al took to nautical life with great gusto—so much so that after *Moonglow* reached the West Indies and Chris had to leave for other sailing commitments, David appointed Al skipper while he returned to work. After Al had enjoyed some weeks of idyllic life in and around the waters near Barbados, David realised that he could not afford to keep *Moonglow* and instructed Al to entertain prospective buyers until he sold it. The newly-promoted skipper lived the life of Riley, immersed in rum, women and song until, to his great distress, *Moonglow* was actually sold. I can claim to have changed Al's life to some significant extent because he became a yachting enthusiast, juggling journalism with sailing. Eventually he acquired a succession of cruising yachts and in 2002 he and his partner Joan were in the Mediterranean near St Tropez—appropriately enough—sailing their latest yacht, a 34-foot sloop *Celebration*.

Sadly Christopher de Grabowski was lost at sea in January 1964 while skippering the 58-foot schooner *Enchantress* from Charleston to the Virgin Islands. His body was never found. Mike Philp told me he had a wonderful photograph of Chris, face turned towards the sun, at the helm of *Moonglow* as he sailed from a cold northern winter towards the Mediterranean. When he heard that Chris had been lost at sea Mike wrote on the bottom of that image: *Wherever the storm takes him, he goes as a guest.*

Back in London it was time for lunch with Philip Bowden at the Athenaeum Club as a farewell gesture after my two years in England. Although he had enthusiastically embraced British establishment values Philip retained his essential Australian iconoclasm and after lunch in the funereal atmosphere of the dining room (where my presence must have significantly lowered the average age of the members there below seventy-five) he decided on a whim to take me on a tour of the club. He charged into the toilets to show me strange, historic grooming instruments chained to the wall and, finally, into the library, where no one had spoken audibly for the last 200 years. Uncle Philip flung open the double doors and announced loudly: 'And this is "The Silence Room".' It was straight from a Giles cartoon. Florid, be-whiskered, angry faces appeared from behind books and newspapers and glared at us. Philip seemed unperturbed.

Despite his Fellowship of the Royal Society and his brilliant work as a physicist at the Cavendish Laboratories in Cambridge, Professor Philip Bowden was never awarded the knighthood which his contemporaries believed he should have had. Perhaps his Australian origins were not helpful. As I left him after our Athenaeum Club lunch neither of us dreamed that he had only four years to live. We met again briefly at Cambridge in the spring of 1968 when I was married—the reception was at Finella—but by then he was gravely ill with the lung cancer that killed him six months later. He was cut off in his prime, at sixty-six, although Bowdens are usually a long living lot. Philip's eldest brother, Eric, was eighty-six when he died in 1980, and my father John was ninety-one when he exited in 1998. My childhood fantasy of going 'home' to England had been well and truly realised by the generous welcome given me by the Bowden family at Finella.

Unlike the liner *Neptunia* two years earlier, which called at ten ports, MV *Canopic* did not stop anywhere between Tilbury and Perth. As a supernumerary passenger, I qualified for the officers' mess and fortunately did not make it to the captain's table. The captain, a crashing bore and arrant snob, was travelling with his rather horsey looking wife—which meant, said the bosun, that we would have foul weather the entire trip. Had there been a parson on board as well, he said, there would almost certainly have been a typhoon thrown in for good measure. Another supernumerary passenger, the ship's doctor, a young Englishman who had only recently graduated, was deemed suitable material for the captain's table. I, on the other hand, being a journalist, and socially suspect, was banished to the only other table in the mess with the ship's two young merchant navy officer cadets. This was perfectly fine by me as they were pleasant young men and vastly preferable to the bunch of alcoholic crazies and misfits at high table.

The politics of the dining room were like this: the captain had had a row with the chief engineer on their previous voyage and they hadn't made it up. Therefore they were not on speaking terms. Like all chief engineers of that generation, our man was deaf, and made a point of turning his hearing aids off when he came to dinner. The captain, who was usually the only one talking, pontificated on anything from the Common Market to test cricket and droned away keeping his voice low so the chief engineer couldn't hear him anyway. The chief engineer was a total alcoholic who hadn't been into the engine room of any of his ships for five years. The deputy chief engineer (who had to do all the work) just sat at the table and ate his dinner without saying anything. The radio officer didn't appear for the first week because he had got drunk and fallen into Tilbury Harbour's waters which had given him gastroenteritis. The first mate was a dour Scot who seemed competent enough but who didn't like the captain or the chief engineer. The second mate was a quietly spoken Londoner who hated being at sea, and pined for his wife and children. When he was off duty he sat in his cabin making woollen rugs for the family home. John, the doctor, didn't talk much during meals because the poisonous vibes around the table exacerbated his mild stutter to the point where he didn't dare risk saying anything. The cadets and I had quite a jolly time nearby. The food—there was full steward service—was excellent and wine and beer were free.

To stave off boredom I helped the cadets look after the pet dogs travelling by sea because of Australia's strict quarantine regulations. We had three Labradors, three poodles and two corgis. Every day they had to be fed and watered, groomed, exercised—their turds cleaned up—and kept healthy. The notes that their anxious owners had provided for their care made amusing reading: 'Trudy is a sensitive little poodle and thrives on a little social life. Please give her a drink of milk and a yeast tablet in the morning.'

Some of the more congenial officers, the ship's doctor and I got together a scratch musical group in the evenings with three guitars, my ukulele and a penny whistle. The radio officer, when he emerged, turned out to be a virtuoso on the whistle and knew the lyrics of countless dirty ditties. Had it not been for my daily doggy duties, time would have passed even more slowly than it did. I read a lot, had afternoon naps and began to wonder what I would do when I got back to Tasmania.

The first mate spent almost the entire voyage calculating how he would berth the ship at Fremantle in time to begin unloading cargo at 9 am on a Monday morning. And so it came to pass that although he had done this with great skill he had no way of knowing that our arrival day was also the wharfies' annual picnic, so the ship lay alongside at great expense for an extra 24 hours. It was a relief to leave my companions of five weeks in Melbourne and head for Hobart in time for Christmas.

I felt a mounting sense of excitement as I glimpsed the north coast of Tasmania from the aircraft crossing Bass Strait. It was not only the thought of seeing my family and friends after two years, but the prospect of immersing myself in the beauty and isolation of Tasmania, pointed up by living for two years in London with its gloomy lowering skies and vast population. It was necessary to complete the cycle, to return to my roots. I was in absolutely no doubt about this despite having to knock back the job with the BBC.

I was quite shocked to see the deterioration in the health of my mother, Peg. When I left she had been a healthy, active woman who used to play an occasional game of social tennis. But while I was away, a small gynaecological procedure had gone horribly wrong and she had haemorrhaged on the operating table. In this emergency she had been given a mismatched blood transfusion which nearly killed her. One of the side effects of this accident was the sudden onset of virulent rheumatoid arthritis, an awful disease which can attack every moving joint in the body, fingers, toes, ankles, knees and hips. Nothing seemed to ease her distress. She tried gold injections, even homoeopathic remedies. Only large doses of cortisone seemed to give her any relief. But that was a double-edged sword, leading to circulation problems, gut disorders, oedema and a plethora of other disabilities. Walking was agony, as was almost every movement. But she remained cheerful and outgoing, never talking about herself and, as the years went on, coping with major operations to hip and bowel without complaint, despite being in constant pain. She tried anything to beat that cursed arthritis. Someone once told her that she should get as much sulphur as would cover a sixpence, mix it with a jigger of gin, and drink it before breakfast every morning. She did this for weeks, before confessing to her doctor. It tasted foul and didn't do her guts much good either. Nor did it have the slightest effect on her arthritis. Nevertheless, she continued to run the house as she always had, somehow producing the same fantastic food despite her disabilities.

I loved being back in Australia. Tasmania was even more beautiful than I had remembered, with its clear, translucent light and splendid mountains. We had Christmas at the family weekender Askelon, and I had a sentimental visit back to Maria Island which reared out of a Mediterranean-blue Tasman Sea, its coastline dotted with pristine beaches where few footprints ever marked the glistening white sand. In Europe there would have been resorts and cable cars.

The question of what I was to do to earn some money had to be faced. After the holiday season ended I wandered in to the ABC in Hobart where my old friend and mentor Anthony Rendell had become Supervisor of Talks, after Lucien May's sudden death. Television had come to Hobart in my absence and was about to reach Launceston and the north-west coast later that year when the transmitters were finished. Anthony told me there was a Talks job going and encouraged me to apply for it, saying there would be opportunities to travel to Hobart probably as often as once a week if certain television programs he was planning were approved by management.

With about as much thought (but with very different consequences) as I had given to my application for a journalist's job in Uganda, I banged in an application for the Launceston job and was successful. For the first time since I left *The Mercury* I had a permanent job again. Had anyone told me that I would be working for the ABC for the next thirty years I'd have said they had to be joking.

I bought an FJ Holden on hire purchase, and set off for Launceston. A friend told me of a three-bedroom flat that was available for rent in Welman Street, East Launceston. The place was too big for me, so I hunted around for flatmates. My old friend Mike 'Spike' Bryden, newly graduated as a vet from the University of Brisbane, had joined the Department of Agriculture in Launceston and needed somewhere to live. So did another veterinary friend of his, Graham Gregory, who was also starting work with the Ag Department. The ABC studios were close at hand in Brisbane Street and a newly arrived journalist with ABC News, Terry Brown, a big, amiable New Zealander, was another who was looking for digs. Two vets and two journalists prepared to co-exist in our big sprawling apartment which occupied the whole upper floor of quite a large house and which we christened Welman Towers. Our landlord, 'Scotty' Jantzen, and his wife and small daughter lived underneath. 'Scotty' wasn't averse to a drink, and on occasions when his wife sent him up to tell us to quieten down a bit, we would offer him a beer and he wouldn't leave.

Sharing a flat with vets had its moments. I came home one evening to find a very strange, unpleasant smell permeating the whole place. I followed my nose to the bath, where two pairs of overalls were soaking. Both Graham (we always called him 'Dr Greggers') and Spike had spent the day pulling bits of foetus out of a cow. The calf had been dead in its mother for three months. One night I came into the kitchen to start cooking a meal to find Dr Greggers spaying a cat on the kitchen table.

'Are you going to be long?' I was hungry but Dr Greggers seemed preoccupied.

'I should have been finished ages ago. I can't find its bloody ovaries.' He was pulling bits of intestine out of an incision, inspecting them, and stuffing them back. This went on for a while, and then I came back for a closer look.

'Greggers, I'm no expert in these matters of course, but what are those furry bobbles between its legs?'

'Shit! It's a bloody tom.' The recently graduated Dr Greggers shoved everything back inside, sewed up the incision, castrated the cat, and I was able to start cutting up the onions. One way or another that cat wasn't going to breed.

The ABC studios in Launceston were in a ramshackle brick building that had been extended over the years to encompass extra offices. In my new job I was responsible for a local 15-minute magazine program, imaginatively titled *Northern Tasmanian Magazine*, for which I had to record material not only in Launceston, but along the north-west coast in the main centres of Devonport and Burnie. *News Review* was still going in Sydney, and there were some new Tasmanian-based radio talks programs like *Good, Bad and Indifferent*, a weekly half-hour arts show which Rendell had started. I hadn't ever done much live broadcasting and needed to know how to get myself on the air when contributing an item for *Tasmania Today* (which was still going strong). The Launceston manager, Fred Fry, was used to reading the news and not much else. He puffed up the stairs to the studio, threw some switches on the panel to show me what to do, but after about twenty minutes the head technician, Bill Tanner (who had a jaundiced view of new, young staff members like me), put his head through the door, saw me sitting in the driving seat and thought he had me. 'Can you explain why the station has been off the air for the last fifteen minutes?' he asked. Fred had to take the rap.

Then there was television. Each specialist department in Hobart—Rural, Talks, Music and Light Entertainment—was allotted ten minutes each in the 9.30–10 pm slot to showcase their wares. The Music Department might put on a short musical studio recital, the Rural Department might interview an expert on animal husbandry with some associated film footage, Light Entertainment might field a stand-up comic or some live light music, and Anthony Rendell would commandeer a lecturer from the university (or a visiting expert) to give a commentary on some world hot spot. It was all very messy and fragmented. The same thing was happening in all the other BAPH states—Brisbane, Adelaide, Perth and Hobart—but the precious air time was jealously guarded by all the departments. One of the advantages of working in a small organisation is that people sometimes actually talk to each other and Anthony, with the help of

He'll play you a tune
ON HIS TEETH!

● **TIM BOWDEN, the man with the musical teeth, apparently likes them to be heard and not seen. He's the only TV interviewer in Australia with musical teeth.**

Tim is the ABC's talks officer in Launceston, seen during ABNT3's opening night programme Northern People.

In the programme Tim interviews well-known Tasmanian historian Mr. Karl von Stieglitz, and Mr. Mont Turner jun. who will soon start a wildlife sanctuary in Launceston's Punch Bowl Reserve.

From history to animals is a pretty wide field to cover in two interviews within half an hour—and Tim Bowden is well qualified for such diversified activities.

He has been filling the newly created position of talks officer in Launceston for four months after returning from England.

Tim spent two years with the BBC after working in Tasmania as a journalist and freelance talks man with the ABC.

He worked on such programmes as Calling Australia and Report From London, which are widely distributed by the ABC and Australian commercial stations.

Tim has earned himself a reputation as a man with an eye for the unusual.

For example, in England he did an interview with a man training police dogs, who insisted that Tim should have first-hand knowledge of his subject or no interview. So Tim stood, microphone in hand, describing the approach of a savage dog, and listeners were able to hear his yell of pain as he was bitten.

Other unusual spots in which Tim has found himself include the ejector seat of a jet aircraft ground-trainer, the pilot's seat of a hovercraft, and on board a lightship in the North Sea.

He interviewed a singing penguin at Edinburgh Zoo, and since returning to Tasmania interviewed a talking dog at Ulverstone.

And those musical teeth. Yes, Tim can actually play tunes on them, and has proved it!

On the ABC's national radio programme Scope he has played his teeth twice—the first time as a mere demonstration and the second time in a three-man jazz band.

The trio, consisting of trumpet, ukulele and Tim's teeth, played When The Saints Go Marching In.

But Tim Bowden has a more serious side, too.

For example, he has interviewed famous conductor Sir Malcolm Sargent, and has produced a 20-minute radio documentary on the Farnborough air show.

Since returning to Tasmania Tim has done a TV film report on the decline of the coal-mining industry in the Fingal Valley, as well as chairing a TV discussion on problems on the Hobart waterfront.

With TV coming to the North, Tim will probably be seen frequently on Channel 3, doing all sorts of things from serious work to the "gimmick" jobs he seems to attract like a magnet. #

AUGUST 3, 1963—TV WEEK—Page

a sympathetic program director, Chris Symons, got everyone together to discuss pooling their television time so each could get a full half hour a week from 9.30 pm. This would stop the daily scramble to fill ten minutes and mean that something of substance could be organised for a half hour. I think Hobart was the first ABC branch to do this and for us in the Talks Department it meant a weekly current affairs magazine program—something which was not then being done in any other state. (*This Day Tonight*, the first half-hour national television current affairs program, did not start until 1967.)

Anthony called our new baby *Week*. With hindsight we both agreed that it was not a felicitous choice. Announcers would say: 'And for another *Week* program, tune in at the same time next week...' and worse. *Week* went to air at 9.30 pm each Wednesday night. Its first compere was a former Navy submariner, the heavily bearded Norman Dahl. (Beards were a rarity then, particularly on television.)

Going to air was a nail-biting experience in those days before videotape. The News Department had a monopoly on most of the sound-on-film cameras and first call on the all-important film editing section. (They did, after all, have to put a thirty-minute news bulletin to air each night without the luxury of being able to take in material live from other states.) The only way we could use film to illustrate local stories was to hire a freelance cameraman to shoot 16mm silent film, scrounge some time with a film editor, and run it with live commentary and/or music from disc. Without videotape, which is mostly used as a time-shift device for current affairs programs, all our interviews or discussions had to be live! We tried to keep a handle on international and Australian politics using academics and political scientists from the University of Tasmania but our bread and butter had to be local affairs. In view of Tasmania's rabid north–south rivalry it was essential that we tapped stories from all over the island.

In Launceston I needed a freelance cameraman: enter Bob Montgomery—always called Monty. He was the Cecil Snaithe of cinecameramen. There was nothing Monty would not do for a film. He was a big, roly poly, good-humoured bloke who reminded me somewhat of Yogi Bear. When I wanted to do a story on the fledgling abalone industry, based at Bicheno on the north-east coast of

Tasmania, which was already exporting to Southeast Asian markets, I asked Bob if he could swim and he said yes. The fact that he had never dived or used an aqualung seemed irrelevant. We needed underwater shots of divers cutting the oval abalone shells from the rocks and putting them into mesh bags.

Monty located an underwater housing for his Bolex 16mm camera and the abalone divers managed to squeeze his portly frame into a spare wetsuit. They gave him a five-minute course in how not to kill himself by using an aqualung (if you don't breathe out continuously as you rise to the surface you can burst your lungs), estimated how much lead he needed on his weight belt, and then Monty jumped overboard. He sank straight to the bottom and had to leave behind his camera in its heavy housing just to get up again. The divers lightened his weight belt and Monty returned to the depths to recover his camera. But whenever he lifted his head, his face mask leaked and filled up with water. I was an amateur spear fisherman and was in the water with a mask and snorkel to see what was going on. Monty was as game as Ned Kelly. Determined to finish one shot, he kept filming as the tide rose *inside* his face mask over his nose and eyes before he was forced spluttering to the surface. The abalone divers were laughing so much they could barely get to Monty to help him. Although he had never filmed underwater before, Monty's exposures were spot on and the action was graphic and beautifully captured. Although underwater photography is part of the furniture these days, it wasn't in the early 1960s and the film created great interest.

I became friendly with the Agricultural Department's entomologist in Launceston, Don Cunningham, a delightful man and a good communicator. In those early days of television there was a fascination in getting cameras into unusual situations, so when Don said there was a good story in bees Monty managed to hire a micro-lens. I left Monty to it on this occasion and he filmed happily away with bees buzzing all around him as Don revealed the workings of a hive. Monty got wonderful close-up images of worker bees constructing the hexagonal beeswax columns and filling them with honey. Rather than try to write a commentary on a topic I knew absolutely nothing about, I invited Don to come to the studio and give a live commentary on the footage as it was screened.

This idea of having an expert in the studio to comment on film stories as they were broadcast was something I was keen to develop and an opportunity to do more came with a decision to film the annual mutton bird harvest. Monty and I flew to Trefoil Island off the north-west coast in a light plane to film action. The workers on this unattractive job were from Cape Barren Island, in the Furneaux Group, Bass Strait. The short-tailed shearwaters fly thousands of kilometres from the Aleutian Islands in the northern hemisphere to hatch their young in burrows tunnelled into the sandy soil of Bass Strait islands. The young mutton birds look a bit like mini-versions of Sesame Street's Big Bird, covered with fluff, and stuffed full of fish oil by their attentive parents. They are harvested by workers putting their arms down the burrows and pulling them out. (An occupational hazard is grabbing an equally surprised tiger snake which has taken over a burrow.) The whole mutton birding process is ghastly. The luckless chick has its neck wrung, head wrenched off and the contents of its stomach (mutton bird oil is a valuable by-product) squeezed into a 44-gallon drum. The carcase is then gutted and plucked. During the short season the whole of Launceston seemed to reek of mutton bird oil. Roasted mutton bird was highly prized as a local delicacy, although I could never understand why.

Even in those days there was a vigorous debate about how many mutton bird chicks could be taken without threatening the survival of the species, with the Bass Strait Aboriginal people arguing that it was a traditional hunter-gathering activity for them which should be exempted from any quota imposed.

Just as Monty and I had finished filming this brutal harvesting process, a man rushed down the tussocky hill towards us. 'Are you the blokes from the ABC?' We said we were. 'Ya simply gotta come back and film old Charlie in that hut up there on top of the hill. Charlie's the fastest plucker on the island.'

Monty and I looked at each other and agreed this was an opportunity not to be missed. Charlie was an impressive plucker, indeed, redoubling his efforts as Monty filmed him, almost disappearing in an eruption of fluff and feathers.

Back in Hobart I asked Dr Eric Guiler, then a lecturer in the Department of Zoology at the University of Tasmania, to give a live commentary on the mutton bird story. Eric, an engaging Irishman with a great sense of humour, agreed to do the job. As we viewed the edited film and worked out what should be said, I told Eric about the fastest plucker on the island, and dared him to mention it on air.

I did not think to mention this, however, to Bruce Allen, our producer, who had the challenging task of pulling all the threads of *Week* together. Norman Dahl had 'moved on' as they say, and our new compere was a serious young man, David Wilson, who came to the ABC Talks Department from his former job as Secretary of the Youth Hostels Association of Tasmania. We only had two cameras in the studio, one for David's to-camera links, the other juggled by Bruce to cover studio interviews or film still photographs and captions as required—backed up by the compere's camera while it wasn't being used. Each of the studio camera operators was linked to our producer by microphones and headsets, as was the floor manager, who roamed around cueing us to the right cameras and relaying any other instructions from Bruce by gesture, or verbally if there were no microphones open.

David announced my mutton bird story, and I introduced Eric Guiler briefly in the studio. The film rolled and I asked Eric questions as it progressed. Up came the plucking sequence, but there wasn't a peep out of Eric. Unwisely I said, 'Dr Guiler, I believe that some of the men are very fast pluckers'.

'Oh yes indeed they are', shot back Eric. 'But the women are much faster pluckers than the men!'

We lost it. The camera guys locked their cameras into position and turned away, trying to stifle helpless laughter. Bruce cut sound from the studio as we all fell about, including Eric. The film continued silently to air without commentary. In desperation Bruce spoke through the loud speaker system directly to the studio floor. 'You idiots have ten seconds to pull yourselves together.'

Reality reasserted itself. 'And Dr Guiler, would you say that the mutton bird harvest is endangering the species?' Eric pontificated away and we got through.

What with travelling to Hobart at least once a week for *Week* and keeping my radio commitments up, I was as busy as the proverbial one-armed paperhanger with the crabs. I also found a girlfriend, Fiona, who was a just-graduated schoolteacher working on Flinders Island. She and her fellow schoolie Sandra used to escape from the island at weekends whenever they could and there were joyous times at Welman Towers.

It was in Launceston that I had an experience which, had I realised it, pointed to an area which in future would become an important part of my work. One day I was working in the Talks office when a very old man asked to see me. Jack Williams, from Lefroy, was in his early nineties. He had a passion to share his memories of growing up in this small Tasmanian bush town, and of his early career as a bushman and timber getter. He was a veteran of the Boer War. Jack prepared some talks which I recorded and broadcast. I wish now that I had recorded more with him. To my shame, it was he who insisted that his memories be preserved. Unfortunately there was no formal sound archives system in the whole of the ABC in those days, and certainly not in Tasmania. In 1985 when I managed to start ABC Radio's Social History Unit in Sydney I was trying to locate early Australian memories and remembered old Jack. David Wilson, my colleague in Hobart, was keenly interested in early Tasmanian history and made copies of Jack's tapes. I rang the then retired David, who said, 'I did have them—but you have forgotten that my house was burned out in the 1967 bushfires. They were lost along with everything else I had.'

Rural broadcasting was a big part of the Launceston ABC's regional output, and the Rural Department Representative was Craig Sambell, a young West Australian who had only recently emerged from broadcast training—in the days when the ABC had such facilities. Much of his work was done in the early morning, broadcasting the details of stock sales, river heights, rainfall, and detailed area weather forecasts. Rural trainees were a lively lot and Craig used to tell me hair-raising stories about practical jokes played on rookie broadcasters when they were doing their first live-on-air stints. This invariably happened while the Rural trainees were reading out lists of river heights or lamb sale auction results. Craig said an unkind colleague crept under the broadcasting desk one day and set alight to his script. He had to try to stay calm while trying (a) to put out the flames and (b) finish what he was reading before it was consumed by fire. He swears that another trainee was assaulted in a unique and vulgar way from under the desk. As he broadcast earnestly away, his fly was unzipped and a string tied around his penis. The practical joker then started to pull on the string, while the hapless Rural rookie was drawn further and further under the desk and away from the microphone.

Unfortunately for Bill Tanner, the head technician in Launceston, Craig's mind used to dwell on these alarming practical jokes while he was droning away through his river levels and rainfall readings on the early morning shift. Bill would be dozing in the control room when Craig would suddenly cut himself off the air and scream with demented laughter (possibly with relief that he was safe from such assaults on his person in Launceston). Listeners were unaware, but Bill got it at full volume. It was difficult for Craig to explain to him why he did this.

The news editor of the Launceston news room was Hedley Farquhar, a tall, lean man with heavy horn-rimmed glasses. Hedley was very good at his job, but exacting and uncompromising in his standards and sometimes a difficult man to work for. His *bête noire* was the Hobart News Editor, Warren Denning, a pioneer of the ABC's independent news service in Sydney, who had been exiled to Hobart for reasons I never found out. I didn't work to Hedley, so we got on just fine. He was very droll and good company. (He left the ABC in later years and successfully stood for state parliament, becoming the Minister for Health in a Labor government.) Hedley was a fanatical trout fisherman. The *crème de la crème* of trout fishing occasions—and people from all over the world would come to Tasmania for it—was the annual Shannon Rise, at the outlet from the Penstock Lagoon. At a pre-determined time each year, the white caddis moths would hatch, and flutter into the air to mate. Trout used to migrate to the Penstock for this event, and go into a feeding frenzy while anglers lashed the waters with their lures on either side of the shallow stream. The phenomenon was created artificially by the Tasmanian Hydro-Electric Commission's Great Lake dam complex. So there was a great wailing and gnashing of angling teeth when the Commission announced it was going to cut off the flow from the Penstock for—I presume—practical reasons rather than the total bastardry alleged by the trout fishing fraternity.

Hedley knew that if he asked Warren Denning for the day off to go fishing he wouldn't get it, but he just couldn't stay away from the last ever Shannon Rise. So, uncharacteristically, he rang in and reported sick and headed for the Penstock. Monty was assigned to cover this historic event for ABC TV news. But he only had a limited time on site if he was to get his film back for processing and the evening bulletin. The white moths were whirling around photogenically and the trout were eating them enthusiastically as they dropped into the swirling waters of the Penstock's outfall. But the anglers weren't having much luck at that particular time. Suddenly Monty saw someone hook a trout and zeroed in with his lens as Hedley played and landed a nice fish. Hedley had chosen a bad day to take a sickie. Not only did his nemesis Warren Denning see Hedley absent without leave catching a trout at the Shannon Rise on his television screen that night, but it was also the day President Kennedy was assassinated in Dallas. Not a good time for a news editor to be away from his post. Monty had to keep out of Hedley's way for a while. Hedley swore he'd done it on purpose. I was at the Penstock, covering the last Shannon Rise for radio, not for *Week*, and broke the news to Hedley about President Kennedy. (You always remember where you were on that day.)

We kept experimenting with *Week*. There were no similar programs anywhere in Australia to measure ourselves against. The closest would have been Bob Sanders's *People*, but that program concentrated on personality interviews and couldn't be described as current affairs. State politics in Tasmania was very sedate at that time and it was sometimes difficult to mount a program that would command viewers' attention. These days we are swamped with current affairs programs on television, but in 1964 the cynical catch-phrase about the genre, 'You can't miss with animals, kids and two-headed people', hadn't yet been coined. Sometimes we tried to put on stories that were simply fun and attention-getting to attract an audience. I heard that a team of Oxford and Cambridge university students had competed against each other in a piano smashing competition. The pianos had to be pulverised into pieces small enough to pass through a 9-inch square aperture. The British pop star and political anarchist, Screaming Lord Sutch, was involved as the umpire. It also had *Goon Show* overtones about it. What sounds the pianos would produce as they were demolished could only be guessed at.

As luck had it, Sutch was due to tour Australia and was to be in Hobart in November. I convinced Anthony Rendell that it would be a coup for the ABC (and *Week*) to stage a world championship piano smashing competition in Hobart under the benevolent stewardship of Screaming Lord Sutch, during which local university students would compete against a team of world-champion axemen, of which Tasmania had an extraordinary number. We would go for the world record in piano smashing, no less, which had been captured from the British by the Americans in seven minutes flat.

● SEVERAL HUNDRED people who went to Franklin Square, Hobart, yesterday, found that the scheduled piano-smashing contest had been cancelled, but "Screaming Lord" Sutch who was to have been judge consoled them with an impromptu performance.

We would stage this important cultural event in Hobart's Franklin Square, in the centre of the city, and televise it for later broadcast.

Anthony convinced our new ABC Manager, Arthur Winter, that this was a good idea, and I negotiated with the Hobart City Council for permission to use the square (and put down timber decking so as not to damage the flagstones), the university students' union and the Tasmanian Axemen's Association to provide the piano demolition contestants, which they were delighted to do. Screaming Lord Sutch sent word that he thought it was a wonderful idea and he'd be there with knobs on. To give the event some useful purpose we agreed to donate proceeds to the Musicians Benevolent Fund. We bought a couple of second-hand pianos for a song (as it were), booked the Outside Broadcast van, and got ready for the big day on 31 July 1964.

Unfortunately David Wilson overdid the publicity the day before. We wanted to get a good crowd, so not only did David plug the event on air, but *The Mercury* and *The Examiner* took it up as well. A political storm broke round our ears the night before the big day. The joyous anarchism of the event was not appreciated by some citizens who complained not only to the papers but to the Minister for Education that it was entirely inappropriate for the ABC to be smashing pianos, those symbols of middle class gentility and culture. If this went ahead, they said, it would encourage gangs of piano smashing youths to break into Tasmanian homes and demolish the family upright. The Minister rang the ABC manager, Arthur Winter, to see if he could put a stop to it. For good measure he also hit the phones to the City Council to revoke our permission to use the Franklin Square, the Police Commissioner to ban the event on the grounds of public safety, the University Council to forbid the students taking part, and the Tasmanian Axemen's Association to put the kybosh on their participation. We were outgunned.

The spectre of political interference in the programming of the ABC was raised—and headlined in the newspapers—but we had to agree with Arthur Winter that once the shit had hit the fan, piano smashing could not be defended as a serious issue. Poor Arthur— he was a wonderful man and the best ABC manager I ever worked to. The Deputy General Manager of the ABC, Talbot Duckmanton, rang him from Sydney to ask what the hell he thought he was doing. Arthur had difficulty finding the right words. Anthony and I backed him to the hilt and our great international contest had to bite the dust. The out-of-tune Allisson & Allisson (1887) and even more venerable Collard & Collard (1870) were saved and went to good homes.

Nevertheless, more than two hundred people turned up at Franklin Square the next day to protest at the International Piano Smashing Competition being cancelled. Screaming Lord Sutch (the unsuccessful candidate for the seat of Stratford-on-Avon and the leader of the National Teenage Party) turned up in top hat and cloak and gave an impromptu, unaccompanied concert to mollify the crowd.

(*Week* continued until 27 June 1966 when it became *Lineup* for three nights a week. It was such a rating success that ABC chiefs travelled from Sydney to Hobart to look at what was going on. The concept was eventually taken up in other states, and Tasmania's *Lineup* became the model for the first national television current affairs program *This Day Tonight* which was transmitted live to Sydney, Canberra and Melbourne in 1967, Monday to Friday, compered by Bill Peach.)

Thanks to Arthur, neither Anthony's nor my career suffered as a result of the piano smashing debacle. Anthony was appointed as the Talks correspondent in New York several weeks later, and I was slotted in behind him as Acting Supervisor of Talks in Hobart while that job was advertised. I settled in to the new job with gusto, juggling the television and radio components of my Tasmanian Talks empire, comprising talks officers David Wilson and John Roberts, as well as commissioning freelance contributors for programs like our arts magazine *Good, Bad and Indifferent*. After some three months I had a call on my internal office phone.

'Is that Tim Bowden?'

'Yes.'

'My name is Arthur Limb, I am the ABC's chief accountant. I just rang to tell you that you have spent the entire Talks budget for this financial year in three months.'

As God is my witness, I said, 'What budget?'

I didn't know I had one. I thought that broadcasters broadcast and authorised payments to bring that happy state of affairs about. Arthur Limb said it might be a good idea if I dropped by to see him.

He was an understanding fellow, but incredulous that I knew nothing of the ABC's budgetary structure. But why would I? I asked. I had come onto the staff from being a freelance and Anthony had handled all the paperwork while I was in Launceston. Arthur, nevertheless, was unsympathetic about the bottom line—the Talks pot was empty and I couldn't have any more money.

One of the strings of my Tasmanian empire was religious broadcasting. We used to pay clerics to write and record 10-minute inspirational talks like *Daily Devotional*. The arts program, *Good, Bad and Indifferent*, was organised and compered by the talented Barbara Manning. Contributors to *Week* would have to come on without being paid. I called a meeting of our regular contributors, told them the bad news and said that in the interests of public service broadcasting they would have to work for the next nine months for nothing, or we would have to take the programs off air. To my relief and some astonishment they all agreed to do this. I decided that wherever my future lay in the ABC it was almost certainly not as an administrator.

Total budgeting (where ABC departments are charged for everything from paperclips to studio time) then was years ahead. One way I was able to keep *Week* afloat was to make use of the ABC's Outside Broadcast van. This great pantechnicon came complete with a staff of thirty, four cameras, operators to man them (there were no women camera operators in those days), drivers, riggers and someone to make the tea. Then there were at least twelve extra people needed to man the mountain and hilltop relays for the direct links path to the television tower on Mount Wellington and ultimately to the Hobart studios. The great advantage to me was that getting this travelling circus on the road didn't cost my budget a brass razoo. The OB van was sent up to cover the annual show at Oatlands—a small hamlet almost halfway between Hobart and Launceston. We intended to film the wood chopping events, and interview some of the contestants, one of which was the then world champion Doug

Youd. (The Minister for Education did not intervene on this occasion.)

Unfortunately our links path to the chopping venue was blocked by the branch of a big pine tree. I said to the director that I'd fix it and who better to get than a professional axeman. I saw this bloke in his best whites walking past the OB van and explained our dilemma. 'No problems at all mate, I'll fix that for you. But I can't use my championship axe.' I cast about and found a real backyard beauty with a loose head and an edge about as sharp as the side of my finger. This nice guy eyed it off with some disdain, but obligingly shinned up the pine tree (getting resin on his immaculate whites) and hacked off the offending branch. I thanked him, and he walked off.

One of the locals who had been watching all this came up to me. 'Do you know who that was?' I said I had no idea. 'That's Doug Youd.' I had asked the world's champion axeman to hack off the pine branch with a blunt axe.

As it happened, I was never confirmed in the Supervisor of Talks job. I saw a job advertised in the staff bulletin for Talks Officer, Singapore. Without any real hope of getting it, I bunged in an application. Not long afterwards the ABC's new Federal Director of Television Programs, Ken Watts, came to Hobart to interview me. We got on well (my BBC experience seemed to impress him) but I still had no high expectations. To my utter delight and astonishment, I received a letter saying that I had won the Singapore job. Later I found out this had been against the wishes of my boss, Alan Carmichael, the Director of Talks in Sydney. The Singapore Talks job had been advertised at a lower salary than the other two overseas Talks jobs in London and New York. Carmichael wanted it re-advertised because he said it would not attract a high enough standard of applicant. Watts trumped him by saying he had found just the man for the job in Hobart—me! I wouldn't have quibbled about the salary anyway. I was about to become a foreign correspondent in Southeast Asia!

Arthur Winter released me quickly from my Hobart job, and David Wilson took over. I flew to Sydney for a head office briefing (Alan Carmichael, an immensely civilised man, didn't seem to mind having been rolled in the process of my appointment) and I was booked to fly to Singapore in late April 1965. Bill and Shirley Peach were back in Sydney after Bill's stint with the BBC and he was working with Channel Ten. The Peaches threw a farewell party for me, and I looked up Ros Geddes, then nursing at Prince Alfred Hospital, and invited her to the party. We hadn't met since I left Tasmania for London in 1960. We delighted in each other's company as we always had, still without any romantic attachment.

The man who was called God

8

There could not have been a better time to be sent to Southeast Asia as a foreign correspondent. In 1965 the Menzies-inspired fantasy that Australia was somehow linked to Britain by some kind of spiritual-and economic-umbilical cord was being replaced by a belated but timely awareness that we had better take account of where we actually lived. The Vietnam War was hotting up with President Johnson pumping in half a million US troops to keep the 'Commies' at bay, and President Sukarno's declaration of a war of confrontation *(Konfrontasi)* in 1963 against the newly federated Malaysia-which he regarded as a neo-colonialist plot-had Malaysian, Australian and British troops in battle against Indonesians in the former British Borneo, now Sarawak and Sabah. Despite the sideshow of *Konfrontasi* the British were preparing to leave their former colonies of Singapore and Malaya to decide their own regional destinies.

As far as news gathering in Asia was concerned, the ABC was ahead of its time. When I took off from Mascot in a Qantas Boeing 707 in some style (even humble public servants like myself travelled first class overseas until Gough Whitlam ended all that in 1972), the ABC had permanent correspondents in Tokyo, Jakarta, New Delhi, Saigon, Kuala Lumpur and Singapore—where the Southeast Asian office was located. We also had stringers in major centres like Manila, Bangkok and Hong Kong. China was shut to western correspondents in the time of Chairman Mao.

Such was the hunger for news from the region that what Prime Minister Lee Kuan Yew said in Singapore that day could make it onto an Australian domestic news bulletin, as well as onto Radio Australia. (Conversely, Singaporeans couldn't have cared less about what was happening in Australia as I was to discover quite quickly.)

The ABC's News Department (which controlled the ABC's overseas news gathering) regarded Talks Department officers as arty-farty types, certainly not trusted to report hard news, but because I was a 'proper' D Grade journalist—thanks to *The Mercury*—I was allowed to file for News as well as Talks.

It was early evening when my Qantas flight touched down at Paya Lebar Airport on Singapore island, and as the door swung open, I breathed in the heady, humid, spiced—slightly crutchy—scent of rotting vegetation and a whiff of cloves from *kretek* cigarettes. I was twenty-eight years of age, single, and couldn't believe my luck at scoring this assignment and I felt, correctly as it turned out, that I was on the brink of adventures that could hardly be imagined.

My fellow Tasmanian, cinecameraman Neil Davis, had had precisely those feelings when he landed at the same airport a year before to work for Visnews, the international news film arm of Reuters news agency. He, as I, marvelled at the sight of people virtually living on the street in the benign balm of the tropics, patronising the pavement street stalls, eyes flashing, burnished skin shining under the pressure lamps of the outdoor markets and the animated chatter in Cantonese, Malay and English. Neil had based himself in Saigon as the Indochina war quickly became the world's biggest ongoing story and I was looking forward to meeting up with him again.

It was alleged by some of my colleagues there was a kind of Tasmanian mafia at work in the ABC's Asian operations. Davis (who worked administratively to the ABC's Singapore office) was already in action in the region, Philip Koch (another refugee from *The Mercury*) was in Jakarta and Tony Cane (from the ABC in Hobart) was about to be posted to New Delhi. Now I had arrived to swell the Tasmanian ranks and further fuel the allegations.

There had been a changing of the guard in the ABC's Singapore office, and not before time. The previous representative, Ted Shaw, was a Walter Mitty character who claimed in his cups—where he was most of the time—to have broken wild brumbies in far north Queensland, played test cricket for Australia and to have interviewed Adolf Hitler in the Berchtesgaden before the war—all about the same time. 'Eva Braun was with him the second time I saw him. You could see a woman's touch—the curtains had changed.' Ted, like all good liars, was never short on descriptive detail to flesh out his fantasies. He seldom went anywhere but his favourite local bar and explained his absences from the office by saying he was at Phoenix Park, where British military intelligence was located. He had been appointed by the previous general manager, Sir Charles Moses, whom he managed to entertain so well every time he came through Singapore that any discrepancies in Ted's ramshackle operation were overlooked. He had enormous *chutzpah*.

Neil Davis loved outrageous characters and was fascinated by Ted's wild and ingenious stories—but he spent most of his time away from Singapore and only had to have fleeting contact with him. Hitler's interlocutor and wild brumby buster wasn't able to charm his new boss, Talbot Duckmanton, who didn't share Moses's penchant for heavy boozing and unsportingly had ABC accountants take a close look at Ted's books. He had been recalled to Sydney by the time I arrived.

The new Singapore Representative was Peter Hollinshead, who had just turned forty—a forceful journalist from the stable of the ABC's News Department. His wife Val, a big, gregarious blonde who in her day had marched with the surf lifesaving flag along Coogee beach, quickly became known to the correspondents in the region as 'Mother Asia'. Peter was the antithesis of Ted Shaw; he was a straight-talking, competent hard-news man, fiercely loyal to his staff, and expecting nothing less in return.

The ABC office was in a rather dilapidated three-storey building at 302 Orchard Road, just across from the smart, newly-built Indonesian Embassy, unoccupied due to President Sukarno's *Konfrontasi* with Malaysia. There were still empty building blocks covered in *lalang* grass on Orchard Road in the mid 1960s, now the high rise heart of Singapore's premier shopping and business district. The building housed some eight local staff, including a driver for Peter Hollinshead's official black Holden. Omar, a skinny Malay of indeterminate age, sported the worst fitting pair of false clackers with bright orange gums it has ever been my experience to see. We always meant to club together to buy him some better dentures, but never got around to it. There was a small 'studio' of sorts with soundproofing and some run-down tape recorders and switching gear presided over by our technician, Lee Kim Chwee. Peter (a dreadful man for bestowing enduring nicknames) immediately dubbed Kim Chwee 'Carrier' because of his insistent call of 'Hello Carrier' when he was trying to get through to Singapore Telecom to access a broadcast land-line to Sydney.

Singapore was a wonderfully exciting place then, and was yet to experience the spectacular development that transformed it into the ordered and controlled metropolis we know today. You had to step carefully to avoid falling into deep and malodorous concrete monsoon drains. The pavements were cluttered with *makan* (food) stalls selling everything from noodles to turtle soup served in the luckless creature's own shell. As soon as the sun set, the Orchard Road night market would set up, pressure lamps blazing under temporary canvas awnings, displaying tropical fruits and vegetables, cooking utensils, ceramics, hardware, clothes and vinyl records of Chinese popular songs. Chinatown was an exotic place to visit, with its crowded shop-houses and stained walls, their cracks sprouting tufts of grass and optimistic tree seedlings. Coffin makers worked alongside tinsmiths and pavement cobblers, while the click-clack of wooden sandals on the paving stones seemed in syncopation with the buskers sawing away on their single-string Chinese violins. Small boys ran among the crowds with tin trays carrying glasses of fragrant Chinese tea and wizened old grandmothers in traditional dress shepherded their button-eyed grandchildren through the chaos. Before the bulldozers had completely cleared it all away in the 1970s a survey was done asking tourists what they wanted to see in Singapore. Chinatown was near the top of the list. The clearance went on, and the ubiquitous high rise flats took the place of the old shop-houses. The Singapore authorities simply said, 'Why should our people live in squalor?' They had a point. Colourful it may have been, though hardly sanitary. But it was the smelly, vibrant, slightly raffish Singapore I knew and loved in the mid 1960s.

On my first night on Singapore Island I was taken to the famed Bugis Street by some members of the Singapore Foreign Correspondents' Association which I was about to join. We sat outside at oil-cloth-covered tables in the warm tropical air, sniffing the heady mix of cooking smells (garlic and five-spices with a whiff of monsoon drain), drinking cold Tiger beer and ordering *sate* and Hokkien noodles from the plethora of restaurants and food stalls happy to supply us. We watched the parade of rather obvious transvestites—tall and with large Adam's apples and big feet—sashay past in their form-fitting dresses under the glare of the hissing pressure lamps before disappearing into the shadows to prepare for their next outing. I was in distinguished company. Dennis Bloodworth, the Far East correspondent for the London *Observer*, was there partly because he was entertaining his colleague Gavin Young who was about to go to Vietnam. Dennis tended to stand out in an Asian crowd because he was two metres tall. Gavin was also a tall man, a seasoned correspondent and traveller, and they were amused by my reaction to this new, exciting Asian ambience. So when a taxi driver in a stained T-shirt and baggy khaki shorts ranged up and offered to take us to see a dirty movie they could see I was intrigued. I confessed I'd never seen one, and on a whim they said, 'Let's all go'.

We were driven to a sawmill in the semi-industrial suburb of Geylang. The projector was up on a platform among the saws and their electric motors. This was the dress circle. Down, literally, in the pit, in the sawdust, was a motley collection of drunks including some British and Australian sailors.

Dennis (who had a Chinese wife and spoke fluent Cantonese) fell into animated conversation with the projectionist who eventually managed to put on the first film. It was a frightful, grainy, black and white film of obese European men with their socks on having sex with rather blousy women. There were tedious blurred close-ups of genitalia while they humped away. It was a depressing spectacle and not the least bit erotic. The audience in the pit started to get restive. 'Put on some technicolour cunt', shouted an Australian voice from below. The projectionist hastily obliged, but by that stage we were all bored and left.

There were only three hotels of any note in Singapore when I arrived, the Adelphi in downtown Singapore and the Cockpit and Goodwood Park in the upper Orchard Road area. I was put up in some style in the Goodwood Park until longer-term arrangements could be worked out. Peter Hollinshead said to enjoy it while it lasted and 'tuck into a few good steaks' which was his idea of living it up.

I presented myself for work at 302 Orchard Road. Peter welcomed me, showed me my office, and asked me if I played tennis. I said badly, but I could hold a racquet. 'That's good', he said. 'There's nothing much going on at the moment. I don't suppose that'll last, but there's no use twiddling our thumbs waiting in this dump. We'll go down to the *padang* at 11 am and then have a few beers and a curry afterwards.' There was a tennis net but no boundaries to the 'court'. Our loose shots skimmed unrestrained into the distance, but were immediately chased and brought back by small, smiling Malay boys happy to earn a few Straits dollars for the service. The other players were Hollinshead, Singapore correspondent Tony Ferguson, and a local character we called 'The Colonel' or 'Mac'. Ron McInnes was an Australian major who had stayed in the army after the war, and had been involved in the Malayan Emergency. He looked a bit like Ronald Colman, with slicked-back hair and a trimmed moustache, and was eking out a precarious freelance existence in Singapore including shooting news film for the ABC using a battered Bolex 16mm camera held together with sticky tape. After our tennis we piled into the official Holden, driven by Omar of the amazing dentures, and were taken to the Tanglin Club where we had a swim in the pool and the promised curry lunch. If this was ABC life Singapore style, I was all for it.

One of my first assignments was to cover a lunch held by the Singapore–Australian Alumni Association, to be addressed by Prime Minister Lee Kuan Yew. It was an occasion of some cultural embarrassment—not because I was surrounded by Chinese speaking with broad Australian accents, lashing into the cold ones and asking for news of the footie from Melbourne, but because of my unawareness of Chinese banquet etiquette. The first dish to arrive at my table was a 'hot and cold' dish. Proud of my newly acquired chopsticksmanship, I hoed into it and had lunch. I could see the rest of the table eyeing me with some curiosity. Replete, I settled back to wait for the speeches. But it was the first of fifteen dishes! I just had to watch all that glorious food pass by.

When Lee Kuan Yew spoke, he indulged in his favourite sport of Australia baiting. The Prime Minister said he was happy to send his most radical and pro-Communist students to Australia, because it wasn't long before we turned them into comfortable members of the bourgeoisie that were no threat to national security at all. This got up the nose of the Australian High Commissioner, Bill Pritchett, who pointed out to Lee in his speech in reply that it was jolly nice of Australia to give up places at our universities to his students when we needed them ourselves! In my time in Singapore I formed the opinion and still firmly believe that Lee Kuan Yew's ambivalent attitude to Australia and Australians has nothing at all to do with being Chinese. It was the Oxbridge graduate's thinly veiled contempt for Australian 'colonials' that influenced his opinion of us.

Soon after my arrival in Singapore I heard that the last Lancaster bomber still flying in the Pacific was being flown back from Australia to England to an aviation museum. It was due to pass through Singapore and on to the Butterworth air base near Penang on its slow and stately progress to the UK. Ever the frustrated aviator, I managed to wangle a ride on that leg to do a story for the ABC, and went out to Singapore Airport to watch it land. The big four-engined plane, straight out of a World War II film, sank majestically towards the tarmac on its landing approach. It touched down a trifle heavily I thought, and immediately rose up before its tyres again hit the tarmac. In fact, it landed three times in this manner before eventually taxiing to its berth.

It had been difficult to find a crew with current operating certificates on a big four-piston-engined vintage aircraft like a Lancaster bomber. The pilot was a retired Qantas captain who naturally enough had not flown Lancs for twenty-two years. The co-pilot had more recent experience flying big multi-piston-engined planes. Somehow an engineer with valid papers was found and a crew cobbled together.

Perhaps unwisely I asked if I could fly in the rear gunner's turret, a Perspex bubble that stuck out from the tail. I had read so many hair-raising stories of rear gunners, whose casualty rate was legendary. If the poor buggers weren't killed by fighters approaching from the rear, they often—due to communications being cut from the cockpit—failed to hear the order to bail out of a stricken plane, and went down with it. I can tell you from personal experience that they must have felt terribly exposed watching all that flak rising up towards them at night over German cities. The rear gunner suffered greater vulnerability. He was beyond the heating system in the main cockpit area and so had a suit that was a forerunner of the electric blanket. Also he was on an oxygen line in the unpressurised Lancaster. If the oxygen failed he might just be in dreamy hallucination or unconscious for most of the trip, and with luck regain consciousness as they came in to land. But there were cases of crews finding they had a rear gunner frozen to death in the rear turret—flak and bullets cut communications, destroyed his heating, and left him to freeze.

The Perspex bubble of the rear gunner's turret extended under your feet, so I had almost complete 360° vision, except for the area immediately behind my head. We flew low (1500 ft) over the rice fields, rubber plantations and Malaysian jungle, the big bomber jumping and heaving in the unstable, hot, tropical air. I am not prone to airsickness, fortunately, because I couldn't have told anybody and there were no sick bags.

I was able, however, to listen in on the conversations in the cockpit, and became aware that it was like listening to an instructor talking to a trainee pilot. Without doing disservice to our skipper, I had already been told by other crew members that they would have been happier if the co-pilot had been in the main pilot's seat. As we headed out over the milky-blue waters of the Straits of Penang four Sabre jets from the RAAF base at Butterworth ranged up alongside us, flaps down, as they struggled to slow down without stalling, to stay with us in formation. Rear Gunner Bowden had a good view and was able to wave to the pilots from my Perspex bubble. Then I heard, with mounting concern, the skipper being talked down by his deputy. 'Watch that airspeed ... more flap ... level her out now ... stick forward ... [more urgently] stick forward! ... NOT TOO FAR ... stick back now, STICK BACK ... [crunch].' We were down, and this time did not kangaroo down the runway like the last effort in Singapore. I'm happy to report that they made it safely to England.

After a couple of weeks in Singapore Peter Hollinshead thought it was time I did some real work and started familiarising myself with the area. He despatched me to former British Borneo to cover the Allied military operation there, starting in Kuching, the capital of Sarawak and moving onto Sabah where most of the sporadic fighting was going on with Indonesian troops on the border. In Singapore I was no longer living at the Goodwood Park Hotel. I had taken Peter at his word as far as the dining room was concerned but it was not tucking into the steaks that did me in but the grilled trout, specially flown-in Sydney rock oysters and sautéed frogs' legs. Graham Taylor, the Assistant Representative in charge of administration, was surprised that I was costing so much and called for the receipts. So another arrangement was made for me at the Cockpit Hotel where I was limited to the set price menu—which was no great hardship. Hollinshead shook his head over the frogs' legs, but it was not only that episode that caused him to bestow my first Singapore nickname. The ABC contingent was invited to a private home to enjoy a Malay curry, eaten in the traditional style, with the right hand. I was entranced with the flavours and the method. Hollinshead saw me from across the room with dripping hand and curry plastered across my face from ear to ear. 'Muldoon the Glutton, the man who ate his mate' he hollered across the room. I became 'Muldoon' from that moment.

I flew to Kuching by De Havilland Comet, comets being the first commercial jet airliners to go into service in 1952, before they were withdrawn after several aircraft inexplicably fell out of the air killing all on board. The problems of metal fatigue in jet aircraft were not immediately apparent. The original Comet aircraft had square windows, and the fatigue started in one corner and opened up the whole aircraft like peeling a banana. The problem was eventually solved, and Comets were flown widely by many airlines in the early 1960s. I flew on a Malaysian Singapore Airlines Comet Mark IV to Borneo, with oval windows. The landing was exciting because the main runway at Kuching was a tad on the short side and didn't leave much margin for error. The pilots used to bang the Comets down onto the runway as quickly as they could and immediately hit reverse thrust. We shuddered to a halt only metres from the end of the strip. On descent I caught a glimpse of Borneo's extraordinary topography, great mountain ranges covered with triple canopy rainforest, except for the huge rivers which looped across the lowlands like great serpents before discharging their brown waters into the otherwise blue South China Sea.

Kuching was a sleepy ex-colonial town which had surged into the news with a plan to 're-settle' the Chinese in the area into what were virtual concentration camps, because of their alleged Communist sympathies. Singapore, then still federated with Malaysia, took a dim view of this. The rivers provided the only access to the interior—as they always had, even when we were flying by helicopter. The jungle is so dense and forbidding that the choppers flew along the rivers, which at least gave the crews a chance of getting out alive if they had to put down. Freelance cameraman Lee On Wing and I climbed aboard a big twin-engined Wessex Mark V helicopter, which was based on the British aircraft carrier *Albion*, on station just off the coast. As we put on our life-jackets, one of the crew told us that if we went into the river on no account were we to inflate them while we were still in the aircraft, or we'd never get out. We were bound for Long Jawi, the most isolated military outpost in Sarawak, near the Indonesian border. Despite its landlocked location, its support base at Nanga Gaat, on the confluence of two rivers, was officially a 'ship' in the naval tradition. As we clattered up the lower reaches of the mighty Rejang River we could see the longhouses of the indigenous people of the region. The Ibans and Dayaks were tough, resourceful people who lived near the rivers where they subsisted on fish and limited rice grown on rough paddy on land reclaimed by burning the jungle.

We were to overnight at Nanga Gaat before flying across the mountains to Long Jawi which was garrisoned by a Malay regiment. Later that afternoon I found myself water-skiing behind a Royal

My first baby photo, shortly after being plugged into an electric light socket.

At Coles Bay near Mount Amos on Tasmania's east coast, aged ten, with friend.

My sister Lisa (5), proudly togged out in her first school uniform complete with gloves.

My mother Peg hated being photographed but used Hobart street photographers to send occasional snaps to my father in Palestine in 1941.

Lieut John Bowden, about to go to war. My mother Peg's expression sums up her feelings.

School army cadet Tim Bowden (16) with his younger brothers at Brighton Camp, Tasmania. From left: Nicholas (8) is relaxed while Philip (6) seems a trifle over-awed.

My big moment of sporting glory—winning the State Combined Public Schools mile race in 1954 in the mildly respectable time of 4 minutes and 48 seconds.

My broadcasting mentor and much loved aunt, Dorothy Bowden, at the 3TR Sale microphone in the early 1950s.

The Hutchins School production of The Pirates of Penzance in 1954. From left: Roland Whitchurch as Mabel (borrowed from Friends School for the gig, his voice broke only days after the last performance), me as Frederick and my friend Andrew Kemp as a memorably rambunctious Pirate King.

The denizens of Hut 30, 9 Platoon, Brighton Camp, Tasmania, in the National Service intake of January 1957. Front row from left: Michael Edwards, Robert Bye, Peter Heerey, Tim Bowden, 'Perry' Mason and unidentified. Back row from left: Tony Crawford, Ross Jones, Nick Evers, Gordon Baxter and David Allen.

A carefree frolic in the shallow waters of Lake Pedder before three of us nearly lost ourselves for good and all.

I was not aware until much later that my so-called friends had 'flashed' behind me during the photographing of a magnificent carp I speared at Whalers Cove, Maria Island. I was so proud of it too . . .

After five, long years of part-time study, I received my Bachelor of Arts degree from the Chancellor of the University of Tasmania, Sir Henry Baker, in 1960.

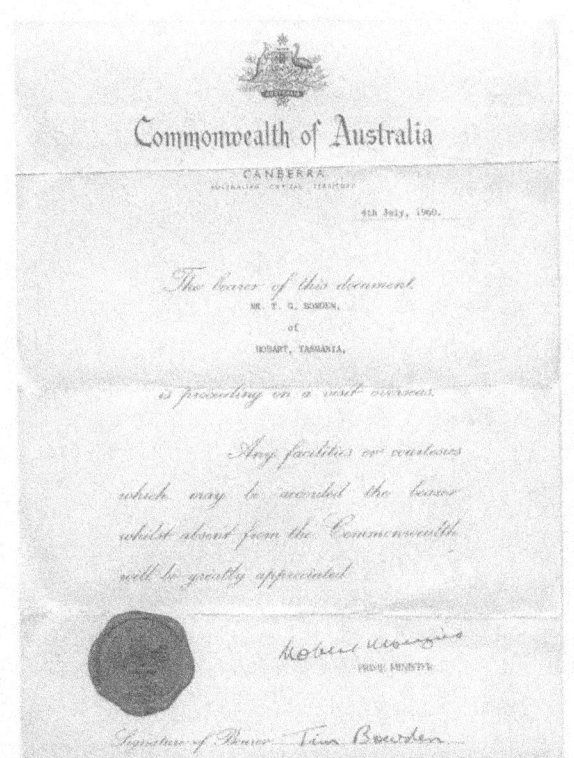

If you knew a Federal parliamentarian, overseas travellers in the late 1950s and early 1960s could actually get a letter from the Prime Minister— no less—as a personal testimonial. Ming obliged, but somehow the moment never arrived to use it.

My student friend, Ted Lilley, was overcome by events on MV Neptunia before I sailed from Sydney in 1960.

My trusty Vespa (pictured outside my Hampstead cellar bedsitter) took me to France, Switzerland, Spain, Sardinia, Corsica and Italy without missing a beat.

The Polish Count, Christopher de Grabowski, and his 'green as an Irish pasture' crew member on board Moonglow *in San Remo. At that stage he had me up at six every morning to shine the brasswork.*

The only way I could face the descent from my first (and last) major rock climb was to absorb some Dutch (Spanish?) courage from a wineskin. I sent this hero shot as a postcard to Ros.

Rosalind Geddes graduated as a fully-fledged nursing sister from Sydney's Royal Prince Alfred Hospital in 1962

My Singapore boss, Peter Hollinshead, in reflective and relaxing mode, camping on the tiny island of Babi Kechil, off Mersing, on the east coast of Malaysia, circa 1966.

The indomitable 'Mother Asia', Val Hollinshead, having a cuppa at our camp on Babi Kechil.

Talks Officer, Singapore, recording a radio commentary from the steaming East in the ABC 'studio' in Orchard Road, 1965.

Author, Ros and Neil Davis at a Singapore restaurant in 1966.

One of my least-favourite and anachronistic assignments—recording taped Christmas messages from Australian troops in Borneo in 1965 for later broadcast in Australia.

American Marines force South Vietnamese peasants to link hands and walk across their fields—as human mine detectors—in front of two tanks near Danang in 1966.

I had a personal bodyguard on my overnight patrol with a platoon of American Marines in what was quaintly called a 'free fire zone'. Sergeant Jim seemed a friendly, affable chap, but was actually spoiling for a fight to avenge the loss of one of his testicles to North Vietnamese shrapnel.

The newly married couple on the lawn at Finella, Cambridge, 20 April, 1968.

Ros in swinging London, 1968.

When I first arrived in New York I had this spectacular view from my studio apartment on Central Park South.

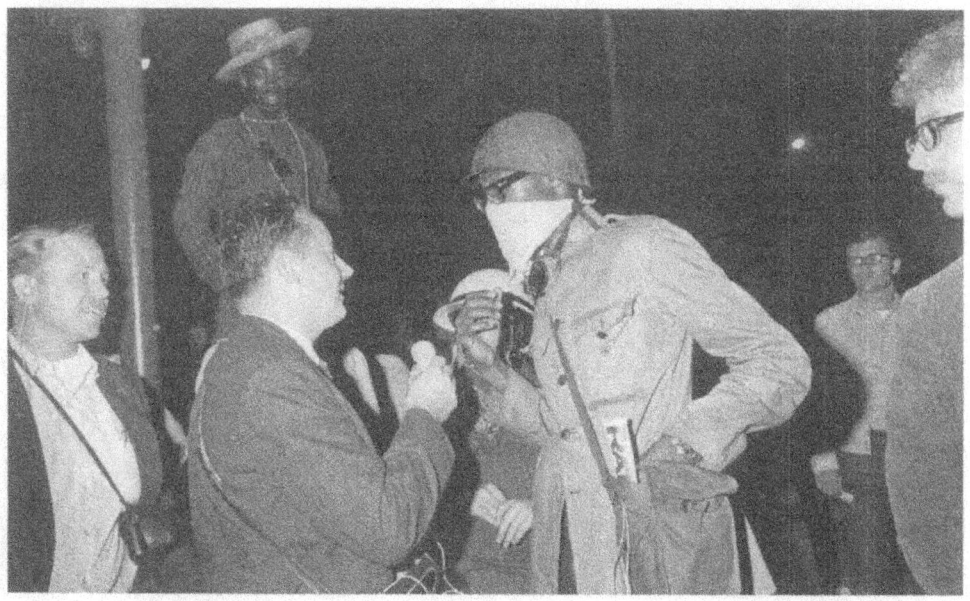

Some demonstrators certainly came prepared. A street interview during the infamous suppression of anti-Vietnam war dissent in the streets of Chicago during the Democratic Convention of 1968.

Talks Department stalwarts celebrate the last News Review *on Friday, 5 July 1969, along with the brash and the new. From left: Paul Raffaele, Linda Conte, John Highfield, Tim Bowden, Frank Bennett, obscured idiot with glass on head, Fred Simpson, Kim Corcoran, Peter MacGregor (partially obscured), BH Molesworth (with bow tie—first Director of Talks), Dennis Harrison, James Pratt (obscured), Murray Gordon, John Hill, Laurie Bryant, Libby Piper, Bill Weir and Russell Warner.*

Some of the inaugural PM team at a morning editorial meeting, Sydney, 1969. From left: Paul Raffaele (reporter), Cathy Munro (researcher), Cliff Neate (reporter), Tim Bowden (executive producer), John Highfield (presenter/reporter) and Anna Wareham (secretary).

TDT *reporters (circa 1974) with flare. From left: Iain Finlay, Mike Carlton, Peter Luck, Vincent Smith and our inimitable compere, Bill Peach.*

Barnaby Bowden (16 months) joyfully perfecting the art of getting up his father's nose.

Navy assault boat driven by a grinning Iban whose brown face and red betel-nut stained teeth were complemented by a sailor's cap marked HMS *Albion*. The navy pilots were all bearded and wore sarongs. Their predecessors (who had lived there for two years) went local so enthusiastically they had themselves tattooed in the Iban style. I think they put on their navy combination overalls to fly their helicopters.

It was nightmare flying country. We couldn't take off next morning until the mists lifted to allow us through a saddle in the mountains at 4500 feet. Our pilot gestured to one of the few emergency landing pads. The top of a mountain had been levelled off into a small cleared area. To achieve this, Ibans had to be lowered down into the jungle that covered even the tops of the mountains, and fell trees and slash the undergrowth with parangs and axes so that a small bulldozer could be winched down to flatten off the top of the hill.

The terrain was so rugged it seemed improbable anyone would want to fight a war anywhere near it, but Long Jawi was fortified with trenches and machine-gun posts. It was agreed we would stay the night to film a supply drop from an Argosy cargo plane the next day. The helicopter landing area was so small that a crewman had to guide the pilot down by saying, 'Six inches to the left Sir', as he watched our wheels put down gingerly on the tiny pad.

There wasn't much room between the mountains for the Argosy pilot to do his stuff, and the efficiency of the operation wasn't helped by the parachute on the first pallet of supplies failing to open. The pallet came down like a bomb, bursting on impact and scattering the Malay soldiers' personally ordered supplies into the jungle. The next box fell into the river, and another was strung up in a tree. I wrote later:

> I know airdrop packers are probably overworked but it does seem to be tempting fate a little to pack bags of cement ON TOP of rice, beer, fruit, brandy, chillies, cigarettes and soap. The resultant mess of those squidged ingredients made a sad sight indeed . . . On one famous day,

the CO at Long Jawi told me, they packed bags of cement on top of a load of eggs!

We were choppered back to the world's most inland naval station at Nanga Gaat in time for a demonstration of fire-power specially turned on for our camera by the Malay regiment garrisoned there, helped by their naval allies. Four 44-gallon drums were moored in the middle of the river to represent Indonesian commando boats. The Malay soldiers had first go, and with admirable soldierly restraint, drilled the drums with automatic rifle fire. Then it was the Royal Navy's turn. With wild yells, saronged and bearded lunatics let fly with their automatic weapons which sounded like the battles of Ypres and the Somme welded into one. One happy warrior blasted off 4000 machine-gun rounds (including tracer) in ten minutes! They kept firing after the drums were well and truly blasted to bits and sunk. Said one beaming bearded pilot, 'I say, that was a bloody good lark wasn't it! I've been saving up my ammo for *months* waiting for a chance like this . . .'

That evening we were invited to the pictures, projected onto sheets strung between some trees. They showed movies every night! 'Stops us boozing, old boy', said one of the pilots—even though they had seen all the films so often they knew much of the dialogue by heart. We finished up at the Anchor Inn, which boasted a rather splendid swinging door—about which there was a story. Apparently every time a local Iban came in, someone would shout at him, 'Shut the fucking door'. When it became necessary for another hut to be built nearby, they asked for a similar door. The Iban carpenter said through an interpreter, 'Yes Sir, but what kind of door? An ordinary door, or a fucking door?'

A British artillery officer I interviewed later in Sabah described the confrontation between Malaysia and Indonesia as 'the last of the fun wars'. It had all the drama of jungle camps, long and difficult supply lines but hardly a shot fired in anger. The Indonesian soldiers didn't really have their hearts in it, knowing that it was just anticolonialist posturing by their charismatic president with absolutely no chance of success.

The artillery officer I spoke to in Sabah described it as 'a jolly good show'. But he wasn't sure what war he would fight next. 'We're not in Vietnam, worse luck. Probably be some shower of a country in Africa. That's why I'm enjoying this while it lasts.' There was a strong air of unreality over the whole affair. The reluctance of the Indonesian Armed Forces, the TNI (*Tentara Nasional Indonesia*), to engage the Malaysian, British and Australian troops stationed in Borneo was confirmed in later years when it was revealed that the TNI literally refused to obey orders from Jakarta during the 1963–65 *Konfrontasi*. Contributing to the *Australia and Security Cooperation in the Asia Pacific* newsletter of November 2001, Group Captain Ian MacFarling wrote:

> ... the operational commander, General Suharto, in an act of high treason sent emissaries to Kuala Lumpur to explain that the TNI was more interested in defeating the Communists at home than fighting the British Commonwealth on the Indonesian/Malaysian border.

I flew on to Jesselton (via the oil rich Sultanate of Brunei which had opted out of joining the Malaysian Federation) and finished up at Tawau, about as far as you could get from anywhere in Malaysia, but close to where there had been some desultory combat on the Kalimantan border. On the morning of 9 August I woke up in my hotel room and tuned in to Radio Australia for the news, only to discover that Singapore was no longer part of the Federation of Malaysia. This was completely unexpected, and a big story. But I was in Tawau, of all places. Fortunately, experienced hands like Tony Ferguson were well able to cope without the likes of me, but I was chagrined to be sidelined and away from Singapore at such a time. I hit the phone to organise my flights back.

At breakfast, rather preoccupied with what I had just heard, I saw a British colonel, attached to a Malay regiment, in the dining room.

Suspecting—rightly—that he may not have heard the news, I thought I should tell him:

TB: Excuse me, we haven't met, but I thought you might be interested to hear the news that Singapore has broken away from the Federation.

COLONEL: Quite impossible!

TB (nettled): Well, I'm only telling you what I heard on Radio Australia a few minutes ago, and I can assure you that is the case.

COLONEL: I can quite definitely tell you, young man, that such a happening would be quite out of the question.

With that he walked out of the room. Despite the colonel's ostrich-like certainty it was true, all right. I made it back to Singapore within 24 hours, which wasn't bad going in the circumstances, but I had missed the main action—the highlight being the 'iron man' of Singapore, Prime Minister Lee, breaking down and crying during his first press conference after the split. My colleague Tony Ferguson had actually asked the question that had caused this extraordinary reaction. I asked Tony what he had asked Lee. He said it wasn't a particularly penetrating question—he had simply asked the Prime Minister to outline the recent events that led to the separation. As he did so, Lee broke down—for reasons one can only guess at, but probably the realisation that his dream of one day becoming Prime Minister of the Federation of Malaysia was over. That dream was one of the main reasons why the Malay administration of Tunku Abdul Rahman in Kuala Lumpur decided to kick Singapore out.

Lee was mortified at his emotional outburst and ordered that the Television Singapura 'pool' film of the press conference be suppressed. But his advisers convinced him that, in Singapore's interest, he should release it. It led news bulletins all over the world.

In Kuala Lumpur there wasn't a peep out of the Malaysian Prime Minister Tunku Abdul Rahman. It was two weeks before his advisers said it was probably time he said something because Lee Kuan Yew was getting all the coverage. This time I was there, and listened in amazement at the press conference while the Tunku described how he had been hospitalised in England with the painful affliction of shingles. Lying in his hospital bed he had mulled over the difficulties in having Singapore, with its 80 per cent Chinese population, inside the Federation, coupled with Lee's political ambitions. (Lee had already enraged Kuala Lumpur by running his People's Action Party candidates in the Malaysian elections in Johore.) The Tunku decided it was all too hard.

Tears seemed far away. The Tunku likened the situation to a couple having problems with their marriage. Giggling happily he explained that when a Malay decided that his wife was incompatible he repeated, 'I divorce you'. And so he simply said the deal was off. He didn't even bother to inform the British Government, which had acted as midwife to the Federation. It was touch and go whether Sabah and Sarawak would stay in—Sarawak, with its close Singapore business connections, would not have joined in the first place without Singapore.

It seemed that the break-up of the Federation of Malaysia saga had barely settled before we were all flat out with another huge and breaking story—the attempted Communist coup in Indonesia of 30 September with its attendant massacres of perhaps half a million Indonesian Chinese, suspected Communists and sympathisers, and political and social chaos in Jakarta.

The first we knew of it in Singapore was a newsflash on the AAP-Reuter news service. I remember crowding around the teleprinter with my colleagues as the first news started to come through on 1 October. The early stories correctly identified the coup plotters as the 30th of September Movement. Who the hell were they? I asked. Then the coup leader was identified as Colonel Qtung. Alan Morris, an expert speaker of Bahasa Indonesia, happened to be in the Singapore office preparing to go to Jakarta for Radio Australia. He rightly said that no Indonesian name could possibly begin with

'Q'. It was a teleprinter typo. Colonel Untung was the man of the moment, but not for long. General Suharto was organising a counter-coup and the position of President Sukarno was ambivalent, to say the least.

My fellow Tasmanian, Philip Koch, was still operating from the ABC office in Jakarta but his problem was to get his material out. The only way was to 'pigeon' his film, audiotape and uncensored copy to Singapore by going to Jakarta Airport and asking a passenger would he or she mind carrying 'a package for the ABC'. People were astonishingly obliging in this regard. The problem in Singapore was we didn't know which flight Philip's material might be on. We had a roster, going to the airport and importuning arriving passengers from Jakarta once they had passed through customs. 'Excuse me, have you got a package for the ABC?' Often the 'pigeon' was looking out for a contact, which made it easier. Others were less obvious. It was time consuming, tedious, but essential. There was no time for tennis.

Living in the Cockpit Hotel had lost its allure and I decided to rent an apartment, sharing costs with a recently arrived Reuters' journalist from London, Robert Hart. We found a fairly basic three-bedroom apartment on the eleventh floor of an apartment block up on the hill behind C K Tang's department store in Orchard Road, and close enough to walk to the ABC. It had a spacious living area and a balcony with a sensational view south over the city to the Straits of Johore. 'Mother Asia', Val Hollinshead, helped us choose furniture, carpets and crockery and we then had to find an amah to cook and clean for us. There was a poky little 'amah's quarters' in 11F Jalan Jintan, but we didn't need anyone living there as we would both be away on assignments for weeks at a time. One of the men carrying our furniture in asked if we wanted an amah. 'Yes', we said, and 'Margaret' (we never knew her Chinese name) came for her interview.

She was young and attractive and we asked her if she could speak English. 'Yes', she said. We quickly discovered that was about it.

We managed to get through to her that we wanted her to come in the daytime and clean, wash and cook for us. She said 'Yes'. I don't think she had ever cooked in her life. Our fantasy of coming home to wonderful Chinese dishes remained unfulfilled. It was not long before she had to go. I had invited a couple of visiting Australians to dinner and arrived home after work to find the flat full of gas. Margaret had put some food in the oven, but neglected to light it, then had gone out. (When she came back I managed, just in time, to stop her lighting a match until the gas had cleared.) The food was impregnated with gas and inedible. In desperation I asked her to heat up some baked beans, so we could have them on toast. She had seen me add some water to a can of soup, so did the same with the baked beans. My guests were presented with bowls of baked beans swimming in water. I cooked something myself, and while doing so, found she had filed some of my papers in the cutlery drawer. Firing someone is never easy, but it had to be done. About five minutes after she had finally left the next day, the phone rang. A Chinese voice said, 'You want amah?' 'NO!'

Bob and I agreed that having travelled the 'young and attractive' route (our strictly adhered to flat motto was DON'T SCREW THE HELP) we would go for age and experience. Enter the unfortunately named Ah Fook Me, a Cantonese woman of indeterminate years, but clearly old enough to be our grandmother. That didn't work out either. The bad jokes visitors perpetrated on her name wore us out in two weeks. Finally Mother Asia came to the rescue and found Ah Wah, a cheerful young married woman with two young children, who bustled in and transformed our lives. She came daily and cooked us fragrant Chinese, Malay and English dishes which we didn't have to think about. When we had to travel we paid her whether she was there or not, and the old hands said we would 'spoil' her by doing this. We were the ones being spoiled, and had no objection to her bringing her kids in to watch television while we were away. 'There'll be six for dinner tonight Ah Wah, a Malay curry would be nice. And please make sure there is plenty of ice in the bucket when we get home.'

Sitting on the balcony, gazing out over the Straits of Johore framed in a magnificent sunset, gin and tonic in hand, the aroma of Ah Wah's latest gastronomic masterpiece wafting past, Beethoven's *Appassionata* sonata playing on my new hi-fi system, I knew that things couldn't get any better. I also knew instinctively that this kind of life was unlikely to last. I was right on both counts, but oh God, it was wonderful while it lasted.

I had taken advice from Anthony A Cane, connoisseur of classical music and fine judge of record-playing equipment, to select my hi-fi. He was about to be posted to New Delhi and was fussing about how his extensive vinyl record collection—including every one of the more than one hundred symphonies that Franz Joseph Haydn ever wrote—would be stored at the ABC. I asked him to visit 11F Jalan Jintan to sample the sound system I'd bought on his advice.

I put on some Vivaldi at a generous volume and he listened carefully till the movement ended. 'Well Bowden', he said—Cane inclined towards pomposity—'I'd say it was a tolerable sound'.

'A *tolerable* sound? What do you fucking mean?' I was beside myself. 'I've bought the amplifier, speakers and record player *you* recommended! So what's wrong with it then?'

Tony Cane was unfazed by this hostile assault. 'I think it's the stylus', he said. 'What is it?' When I told him he replied, 'Ah yes, Bowden, that's it. A compromise head ...'

I could have killed him. Some weeks later, though, I was able to get my own back. We had to move office rather unexpectedly—the previous ABC Representative, Ted Shaw, had neglected to renew the lease, either as a penultimate act of bastardry or through alcoholic amnesia. Tony cabled anxiously from New Delhi to find out what had happened to his hundreds of prized classical records. I replied saying there was nothing to worry about as we had piled them carefully on top of each other and managed to fit them into two vertical stacks so they didn't take up much room. Cane had a fit, because vinyl records should be stacked on edge so they aren't warped by heat or have dust engraved into their grooves. I let him stew for two weeks before telling the truth.

I was relieved to have a new nickname from Hollinshead, not being terribly delighted about Muldoon the Glutton. I was on the phone one day in the office shortly after we moved from Orchard Road to a new location in a back street nearby. I was overheard ordering some grog from a particularly irritating young Chinese girl at Fraser and Neave who kept barking 'ekh' at me over the phone.

'Hello?'

'Ekh?'

I finally got my order through and got around to where it should be sent and to whom it should be billed. 'My name is T G Bowden.'

'Ekh?'

'T for Temperance, G for God, B for Beer...'

Hollinshead happened to overhear me. I became 'God' from that moment. Either God, or Timothy God. Surviving colleagues from that era still call me God. At least I was free of Muldoon—and my nickname was mostly an in-house job.

Not so 'Shoulders' Cook. Arthur Cook was the *Daily Mail* correspondent in Singapore, one of the last of the 'I cover the world' Fleet Street foreign correspondents. During the confrontation between Indonesia and Malaysia, Arthur was particularly irritated that Australian reporters—even though we had troops fighting in Borneo in that bizarre conflict—could travel to Jakarta, while he, a British correspondent, couldn't. It all got too much for the old scoop merchant and he somehow conned himself on a Jakarta-bound flight. The Indonesians wouldn't let him in, of course, and put him on the next available flight back to Singapore. Arthur was able to file a story datelined Jakarta although he hadn't been anywhere other than the airport, but got a bit carried away. 'As I drove past the shoulder-high ruins of the burnt-out British Embassy...', he wrote. Sadly for

Arthur the British Embassy was burnt out all right, but still stood three storeys high. Arthur was known as 'Shoulders' Cook by the other foreign correspondents from that moment.

He used to work for the London *Daily Express* until an assignment in Iran in 1953. The powerful then Prime Minister of Iran, Mohammed Mossadegh, attempted to overthrow the Shah in a dispute on oil policy. But the Shah triumphed. Mossadegh was tried for treason and found guilty. The penalty for treason was death by hanging, and Arthur filed his story reporting the trial and that Mossadegh would hang the following morning. The trouble was Arthur had not fully understood the Iranian system of justice, which was based on the French model. Mossadegh had been found guilty in a committal hearing—the real trial was yet to come. An increasingly distraught Arthur received a cable from his foreign editor Charles Foley asking ominously, WHY YOUR EXCLUSIVE STILL EXCLUSIVE? Followed 24 hours later by another, IT'S MOSSADEGH'S NECK OR YOURS.

Mossadegh died of old age in his bed many years later, and Arthur switched from the *Express* to the *Mail*.

Cook and I first made our acquaintance when the Foreign Correspondents' Association was invited to meet Lee Kuan Yew. After a certain amount of polite chitchat I asked the Prime Minister when he thought there might be a credible opposition allowed in his one-party state. Lee, unfussed by my question, said that if a ship was sinking it was a question of all hands to the pumps and he was busy enough trying to keep Singapore afloat to worry about such niceties. I persisted, perhaps unwisely, saying that once he had the ship dry and sailing nicely—well then what? It was all too much for Arthur Cook who boomed his apologies to Lee for my impertinence and told me I was a wet-behind-the-ears young pup and should shut up. I thought it was a bit much from Cook in front of the Prime Minister who was responding quite affably to my questions, but the moment passed and we didn't meet again.

In late November 1965 I was sent to Vietnam—not specifically to report on the war, although that came later—but to record Christmas messages on tape from Australian Diggers, to be broadcast on the ABC to their families. This quaint tradition dated back to World War II and was already an anachronism as the Diggers could tape their own messages. The first Philips cassette tape recorders had just come onto the market and every duty free store and military PX was full of them. Although Australian warrant officer advisers had been in Vietnam for several years, working with Vietnamese troops in most of the combat areas of South Vietnam, the first detachment of regular troops—1 RAR—had only arrived in May that year. They had not then been assigned to their operational area, Phuoc Tuy Province, but were working with two battalions of the United States 173rd Airborne Battalion, defending the big Bien Hoa air base, about forty-five kilometres north-east of Saigon.

Saigon's Tan Son Nhut airport in late 1965 was one of the busiest in the world, its limited runways coping with jet fighters, lumbering C130 transports, commercial airliners, Cessna artillery spotting planes and the ubiquitous Huey helicopters with their rotors producing that distinctive 'thwok thwok thwok' sound which I will forever associate with the Vietnam War. A familiar, tall, blond-headed, debonair figure, Neil Davis, bless his heart, was at the airport to meet me and spirited me through the narrow Saigon streets crammed with motor cyclos, battered Peugeot taxis, jeeps and heavy military vehicles—to say nothing of the thousands of cyclists making their way through it all somehow. Despite all that, Saigon still had a certain vestige of French charm, with its outdoor cafes and striped umbrellas, although some places featured ugly sandbagged blast walls as well. The Viet Cong's policy of never allowing US soldiers to feel safe wherever they were was in operation well before the Tet uprising of 1968, and the Floating Restaurant on the Saigon River, where westerners tended to congregate, was blown up, crowded with lunchtime diners, shortly before I arrived. (Street urchins used to give GIs heart failure by sneaking up to cafes and bars and rolling Coke cans filled with gravel—then running off giggling as terrified soldiers threw themselves to the floor.)

Neil introduced me to Dema, a nervous Indian money changer who occupied what looked like a large cupboard in the Visnews office in central Saigon. (It was typical of Davis to have his own black market money man living in.) I changed some US dollars for a wadge of Vietnamese piastres (known colloquially as 'disasters') and was then spirited through the accreditation process by Neil (who knew everyone) for both the Army of the Republic of South Vietnam (ARVN) and the United States Military Assistance Command Vietnam (MACV). Journalists covering the war had a lot of clout. I think my press pass gave me the equivalent rank of a lieutenant and I was just a blow-in. My ABC colleague Don Simmons, who was assigned to Vietnam full time, said his MACV pass gave him the honorary rank of captain! With the policy of openness in allowing the press to cover the Indochina war (never to be repeated) in full swing I could even bump serving soldiers off helicopters to get a ride if I was silly enough to do so.

Later that day I made contact with Don Simmons, who had invited me to stay in his flat about ten minutes' drive to the north of central Saigon. He also said I could use the office jeep which was painted white and looked like a United Nations vehicle. Don said it was handy for driving after the 10 pm curfew—the police were likely to stop you and ask questions instead of firing first. We made arrangements to visit the Australians the next day.

Neil Davis hadn't paid a great deal of attention to the arrival of the Australians as he was focusing his camera lenses on a bigger canvas. As early as 1964 he had formed the opinion that the Vietnam War would be won or lost on the ground by Vietnamese troops, despite all the hype of President Johnson sending half a million US soldiers to Indochina. He also knew, as a one-man-band, that he couldn't compete with the resources of the major US television networks, who concentrated on covering what the Americans were doing. So he went out with the South Vietnamese army who did not have the luxury of helicopter evacuations in the event of being wounded in action. This meant going on patrol for up to a week, carrying all his own gear, eating Vietnamese army rations and drinking paddy water. He was the only western cinecameraman to do this and, as a result, had that side of the conflict all on his own. He carried a spring-loaded Bell and Howell camera (which needed no batteries) and one of the new cassette tape recorders strapped to his waist for wild sound. Unbelievably, he continued to cover front line combat in Vietnam and Cambodia for eleven years, despite being wounded several times, once seriously. His unique combat film enabled the British news film agency Visnews not only to compete with the US networks which showed only American-related action, but also to show the world that most of the fighting in Indochina was being done by Asian troops, who sustained horrendous casualties.

(In 1985 Neil Davis was killed by shrapnel in the streets of Bangkok, covering an attempted coup on 9 September. I wrote his biography *One Crowded Hour—Neil Davis, Combat Cameraman, 1934–85* which was first published in 1987.)

The ABC's Saigon-based Don Simmons was a brave and dedicated war correspondent. In his wardrobe I saw at least eight different uniforms. If he went out with the Vietnamese Rangers, he would wear their spotted, camouflaged gear. He had GI clothing with the right sort of hard hat and of course Australian army greens complete with the floppy bush hat preferred by the Diggers. Depending on the circumstances, he would also carry a weapon, and said he was prepared to use it in the event of being overrun. There was a purpose in having the right uniforms. The worst thing a correspondent can do in the field is draw attention to him or herself by wearing different clothes. A sniper's eye can be attracted to a particular individual just because he looks different.

I went to the famous Khu Dan Sinh black market in Saigon where it was said you could buy anything from a helicopter still in its original boxes to cut price Scotch. I had no problem picking up some jungle greens that I hoped would enable me to blend in with the soldierly crowd, plus belts, water bottles and jungle boots—hoping their previous owner hadn't died in them. I also (stupidly as it turned out) bought a tiny hand gun.

The Australians weren't all that pleased to see me. The army has always had an ambivalent attitude towards the press to put it mildly, and were appalled by the American approach. Their instinctive response to visiting news men was to accord them the status of the Viet Cong. When the Australians first arrived at Bien Hoa air base, some American correspondents went down to see what their new allies were doing, and were bewildered by the Australians' attitude to the press. So they went next door to their 173rd Airborne Battalion and simply asked them what the Australians were doing—and were told. The Australians were forced to rethink their approach to public relations, but they still hated the press.

When 1 RAR first arrived in Vietnam, Australian correspondents were agitating to be taken out on a patrol. This was resisted until the Australian command was forced to make some token gestures. Creighton Burns, from *The Age*, Melbourne, was in Saigon at that time and was one of the first correspondents to be taken on a perimeter overnight patrol. Alan Ramsey and photographer Stuart McGladrie (who were living in the 1 RAR camp) were there for AAP, and had to pay a dollar a day for their food, even though they were allotted a tent within the Australian camp. Knowing this, Creighton Burns thought it safer to bring his own tucker. The Battalion CO, Colonel Lou Bromfield, told Creighton that he did not think the patrol would run into anything nasty. When they stopped for dinner, Creighton unwrapped a brown paper parcel he had been carrying and produced his meal—a crusty French loaf, some Camembert cheese, sliced *jambon* and a fresh tomato, all beautifully wrapped in a white, damask napkin. He even had a half bottle of *vin rouge*. He shared some with the Diggers, who admitted it was a lot better than their US C rations.

Some months later Creighton heard that 1 RAR was about to go out with the US Airborne Brigade into an area known as War Zone D, which promised some real action with the Viet Cong. At that time he was sharing an apartment in Saigon with Donald Wise, the correspondent for the London *Daily Mirror*. Donald was tall and moustachioed and bore a remarkable resemblance to David Niven. He was not unused to combat, having been a paratrooper with the British forces in World War II, and had commanded a platoon of Iban trackers during the Malayan Emergency. Burns persuaded him that his readers would relish a story about the Australian Diggers in action.

They were met at the Australian camp by a public relations major who said it was not possible for them to cover the action. Pressed why, he said there were not enough field rations. Creighton responded, saying that if they didn't take them, they would go with the Americans who were in control of the operation anyway, and they would both write stories saying 1 RAR was nervous about being seen in action. The major looked edgy and invited them to have dinner at the officers' mess. Inside a large tent four or five young officers were having dinner. The PR major introduced them, and asked that they be made welcome. As they sat down, all the officers moved further away from them down the table. Creighton Burns was deeply embarrassed. Wise smiled, and said in a voice loud enough to be heard, 'What did you say the motto of this battalion was, dear boy—"Feel free to fuck off"?' Creighton made sure the story got about to other correspondents and Donald's description became the catchcry of journalists trying to do business with the Australians.

There had been official acceptance of my Christmas messages assignment, so I was given a stretcher in a tent and grudging cooperation. I wandered about with my tape recorder asking Diggers if they wanted to send messages home to their folks. Most said no, because they'd sent off their own cassettes. I had prepared a sample form. 'My name is John Smith, and I'm speaking from Bien Hoa air base in South Vietnam. Hello Mum and Dad, I'd just like to say how much I'll be missing you all this Christmas, and wish you all the best. It's pretty hot here at the moment . . . I went on leave in Saigon last week and had a massage and a fuck . . . (That was probably true, but not actually in my sample message.) Well that's about all I can think of to say at this moment, so once again, a merry Christmas to all the family.'

A couple of my subjects actually read out the sample message I'd written. I got myself back to Saigon as soon as I had recorded enough messages to fulfil my ludicrous assignment. I never did it again after writing a fairly savage report to the ABC on the futility of this World War II historical anomaly.

It is difficult now for me to recall how up-beat and optimistic the feeling was in late 1965 and 1966, when I first went to Saigon, given the failure of the Allied assisted efforts to stop a Communist takeover of South Vietnam by 1975. With so many American troops, military and other supplies flooding in to the country it seemed that 'a handful of peasants in black pyjamas' could not possibly withstand the sheer logistic assault of all this good old American know-how. We know now that there was a flood of sophisticated weaponry and supplies coming in from both Russia and China into North and South Vietnam, but this was before the disaster of Tet in 1968. I wrote in a letter home—not in any of my broadcasts as luck would have it—that I didn't see how the Viet Cong and North Vietnamese could win in the present circumstances. I was not alone in thinking this.

The biggest story running in Saigon when I first went there was not the war, but the conflict between the Catholics and the Buddhists, exacerbated by a government crackdown on the Buddhists. One of the manifestations of this situation was the horrendous self-immolation of individual bonzes in the streets of Saigon. A young priest would sit down cross-legged on the pavement, but not to meditate. He would upend the contents of a 2-gallon tin of petrol over his head and robes and set alight to himself—often sitting upright, seemingly impassive through his agony, until only his death caused him to topple over.

In a town made cynical by war, sheer repetition of this ghastly, final method of protest began to dull its impact. I was told of one young monk who poured the petrol over himself and fumbled in his sodden robes for matches. A crowd quickly gathered around him, but because the matches were soaked in petrol, they would not light. Every time he tried to strike a match, the crowd would move back in anticipation, but the match heads disintegrated. There is often a Good Samaritan around. Someone threw him a dry box from the crowd.

Another story Neil Davis relayed to me was of a couple of oil executives in the top bar of the Hotel Caravelle arguing drunkenly over whether the bonzes were preferring Shell or Esso.

The focus of Buddhist resistance was the grounds of the *Vien Hao Dao* pagoda and the Institute for the Propagation of the Buddhist Faith. There were barricades outside the pagoda and daily demonstrations were sometimes broken up by security forces. I had become friends with some of the people at the Australian Embassy in Saigon, and was struck by the insulated lives some of them lived. Looking back now, I think I was wrong to be critical of them. I was just a blow-in, and they had to live there all the time during their assigned term.

One Sunday afternoon, on a whim, I called in to a house occupied by a young Australian I'll call Bill. He was sitting in his living room, nattily turned out in shorts and long white socks, listening to music on his stereo. I insisted that he find out what the real world was like and come with me in the ABC white jeep to take in the scene at the *Vien Hao Dao* pagoda. I said he would find it interesting. Bill wasn't keen, but I made him come and suggested he change out of his white socks into long trousers. I parked the jeep in a side street and we set out to walk the last couple of hundred metres. Something was wrong. There was no one about, and I started to smell the astringent odour of tear gas and the even more foul CS gas. There were missile-sized rocks in the middle of the road where they had been thrown, or placed there ready to be used. When I saw the pagoda, I realised I was on the wrong side. Across a barbed wire barricade I saw camera crews and many familiar journalist faces including Frank McCulloch, the bureau chief of *Time* magazine.

He had a wet white cloth tied around his nose and mouth because of the tear gas. Obviously something fairly nasty had happened. Only hours earlier a revered Buddhist leader, Tich Tien Minh, had been in a car which had a bomb detonated under it, just outside the pagoda, which blew off his testicles as well as causing other injuries. There had been some nasty rioting.

One of the cardinal rules in these situations is never to try to cross over to the other side. Frank saw me, and said as much. I didn't need to be told. Bill was in a certain amount of blissful ignorance about the seriousness of our situation and I wanted to keep him that way. 'I don't think there is much point in staying here', I said in as calm a voice as I could. We turned around and started to walk slowly back the way we had come. I expected a rock in the back at any moment. But nothing happened. We turned the corner to the road where I had left the jeep, and I saw a ring of bystanders around it.

'Oh Christ', I thought to myself. 'It's been booby trapped. If not, then this lot are probably going to turn it over before I can drive away.' We hopped in, and I knew that if the starter motor turned over without us blowing up, that would be a plus. I also knew the battery was getting flat. The starter motor turned over—and ground to a halt. The crowd moved closer. I am not a prayerful man, but I became one at that second. I turned the key in the ignition again. Just as I thought it would die again, the motor fired. I was off like a shot, and drove Bill back to his Sunday idyll, my heart pounding. 'Thanks mate', he said. 'That was quite interesting.'

Early in February 1966 the Prime Minister of Australia, Harold Holt, left Australia to attend an international conference on Vietnam in the Philippines. On the way he decided to visit the Australian troops in Vietnam at Bien Hoa air base, and also at Vung Tau in Phuoc Tuy province, the headquarters of the operational area to which the Australians had just been assigned. This was a big story, and the ABC Singapore office threw us all into it. Tony Ferguson was travelling with Holt's press party to Saigon and Manila, and Don Simmons and I would share the coverage in Vietnam. This was my big moment because Talks correspondents rarely managed to appear on ABC television news, a preserve closely guarded by the news correspondents. My cameraman was none other than Neil Davis, assigned to cover Holt's visit for both Visnews and the ABC. He worked out how we could beat the competition. Before Holt actually flew in to Tan Son Nhut airport, Neil filmed me doing a stand-up beside the aircraft steps, saying that Holt had just arrived and was beginning his historic visit and so on. I also recorded a closer saying what a momentous occasion it had been and he had just left.

Neil was then free to cover the events of his two-day visit, the film of which would be sandwiched between my opener and closer and air-freighted out even before Holt had actually left. By so doing we planned to beat the competition by 24 hours.

The Prime Minister's engagements were in Saigon, including a meeting with the influential General Nguyen Van Thieu who would become President the following year. Holt had an election coming up and the Vietnam issue was already becoming divisive. While Neil chased Holt around Saigon, I headed down to Bien Hoa to be ready for his arrival. The event, with its attendant military, political and press hangers-on, put tremendous pressure on the small Australian military operation. It was stinking hot, of course, and at lunchtime everyone lined up while sweating Aussie army cooks dished out steaks, spuds and salad onto US-style plastic indented trays. The scene in the open-fronted catering tent looked like Dante's inferno, smoke and flames billowing forth, as steaks for the multitude were being barbecued as quickly as possible over half 44-gallon drums. When it came to my turn I caught the eye of the Digger slapping the steaks onto the waiting trays. 'I think I'll have mine just a trifle under-done . . .' I won't detail his reply.

Holt was in electioneering mode and relating well to the Diggers of 1 RAR. The RAAF had an airstrip already operating at Vung Tau so Holt went there as well. The RAAF aircrew had a small bar in their recreation hut, presided over by a diminutive Vietnamese barman the Australians christened 'Joe'. He had been carefully worded up on how to address the most important visitor ever to visit the base.

The Prime Minister, face flushed with the heat, and wearing an open-necked white shirt, entered the bar. Someone asked him if he'd like a beer, and he said he'd kill for one. An RAAF local said, 'Mr Holt I'd like you to meet our Vietnamese barman. Joe, this is the Prime Minister of Australia.' Joe drew himself up to his full five feet eight and a half inches and said proudly, 'Hello Prime Minister. How are they hanging?'

Holt looked puzzled. 'What did he say?'

An aide said, 'How are they hanging?'

The Prime Minister laughed. 'Christ, I dunno—I've been so busy I haven't had time to look at 'em ever since I got here.'

I caught occasional glimpses of Neil Davis filming away and our grand plan seemed on track. Neil drove the film to the airport, packaged it all up, bribed the Air Vietnam clerks to make sure it got on the first flight out, and returned to Saigon for a well-earned drink. The other Australian TV organisations put their film in some hours later, as they would have in Australia, expecting it to leave promptly. It didn't.

Everything worked out. Our film arrived a day ahead of the competition, but it never went to air. The ABC used to shoot reversal film—that is, a positive rather than a negative image. One of the advantages of this is that it can be edited and got to air quickly after processing, while negative film has to be printed to get a positive image. But most overseas news organisations (and agencies like Visnews) shoot in negative because it is easier to make multiple copies of the original. Neil had followed his usual Visnews procedure and had shot in negative, but unfortunately when the Great Harold Holt Scoop arrived in Sydney, it was routinely processed as reversal by the News Department, destroying the images on the film. No one even bothered to tell me. I found out weeks later. Of course, no one was to blame . . .

Saigon at that stage was a curious mixture of war and gracious living—for those who could afford it. You could actually sit in the top bar of the Caravelle Hotel (where Neil had a room while he was in Saigon), sipping a gin and tonic and watching Vietnamese Air Force Skyraiders dropping obscene orange splashes of napalm on Viet Cong guerrillas across the Saigon River in bright green paddy fields only twenty kilometres away. I have done so.

Don Simmons introduced me to Fred Penn, an American oil company executive, who invited us to go water skiing on the Saigon River one Sunday afternoon and come back to his house for a barbecue. I've never been more than a basic water skier—in fact it is one of my least favourite pastimes—and hung on grimly as Fred gunned the motor of his flash speed boat along the glassy brown surface of the river. I wasn't keen to ingest any water and was unamused when Fred did the funny ha-ha stuff and turned around so fast I was hurled away as though I had been fired from a slingshot. I let go the tow rope and grabbed my nose as I sank into the turgid stream. When I was picked up Fred said cheerily, 'An American army captain was shot by a sniper while water skiing here about two weeks ago'.

Journalists covering a guerrilla war with no established front lines had difficult decisions to make about where to go to observe combat. You could either go to an operational area and take pot luck that something might happen, or wait in Saigon until reports of an action came in and hop on the second wave of US helicopters going in with reinforcements and to evacuate the wounded and dead. The North Vietnamese, or Viet Cong, knew this would happen and were always ready. Casualties on 'the second wave' were inevitable. This is how some of the more gung-ho stills photographers, like Tim Page and Sean Flynn, made their names, by risking these flights and grabbing what they could of the chaos and carnage in the short time they spent on the ground. They were known as 'the adrenalin freaks' in the trade, and paid dearly for their derring-do. Page was wounded many times—paradoxically always by so-called 'friendly' fire—and nearly died of shrapnel wounds to the head. Flynn met a horrible death at the hands of the Khmer Rouge in Cambodia in 1970 when he and another freelance photographer, Dana Stone, rode their motorbike through the last checkpoint into no man's land despite the warnings of the Cambodian government troops on the spot.

There was also the political and overall military situation to be covered. All the major international networks and news organisations had staff permanently based in Saigon to feed the news machine which evolved around the daily news conference from MACV (the Vietnamese had one too) known as 'The Five O'Clock Follies'. A po-faced American colonel would address the assembled press from a stage, backed up with maps and charts which he would refer to with a pointer, like a schoolmaster, when he needed to. The jargon was ferocious, his talk peppered with expressions like DMZ (Demilitarised Zone) and 'kill ratios'. One day I heard a briefing officer solemnly point at a map and tell us that a particular area had been 'sanitised'. It was a chilling concept. The briefing officer would say how many bombing sorties had been flown, where they had gone and what was achieved, what ground actions had been fought and the numbers of enemy and Allied casualties suffered. As UPI correspondent Joe Galloway later wrote, it was almost all lies. The Five O'Clock Follies were 'sort of like a pen of mad dogs chewing on each other'. The spokesman would be keenly interrogated by the regulars of the 'Follies', who kept tabs on whether the information given out clashed with previous assessments.

Some of the regular reporters spent their entire time in Saigon, perhaps wisely opting not to go out in the field. One of the most vocal—and totally Saigon-bound—was Joe Fried who worked for the *New York Daily News*. Don Simmons told me that he and some other correspondents once bullied Joe into going on a helicopter flight to an action. Don said Joe returned looking thoughtful and never went again. Some of the American Midwest newspaper reporters used to behave as though they were in a John Wayne movie, swaggering around with six-guns on each hip. The professionals didn't.

Which brings me to my moment of shame and the small pistol I'd bought from the Saigon black market. It was an imitation Beretta, and had a magazine that slotted into its stock. I'd never owned a hand gun, and couldn't resist it. I thought I would take it with me when I went into the field. What I thought I would do with it, I have no idea. I don't think it was even big enough for me to commit suicide with in the event of a position being overrun.

I took this pop gun back to Don Simmons' flat. He was having a quiet beer with Major Joe Da Costa, a military attaché at the Australian Embassy. I showed them my purchase and they were supremely uninterested. To get their attention I asked if either of them could work out how to strip it. Joe took the magazine out and fiddled about, but couldn't do it. There was a trick. You had to cock the weapon (with the magazine in it) and discharge the action before you could unlock the barrel. I carefully removed all the bullets from the magazine, replaced it, cocked the weapon, pointed it under the table and pulled the trigger. Unfortunately there was a bullet still in the chamber. The sound of a pistol unexpectedly going off inside a house is certainly attention getting. Both Don and Joe instinctively grabbed their family jewels—which were fortunately safe. I sat there open mouthed, a smoking gun in my hand. Joe reached out and took it from me and laid it on the coffee table, around which we were all sitting.

No one spoke.

Don broke the silence. 'Where did the bloody bullet go?' This thing was such a Mickey Mouse weapon that the bullet had hit the carpet, flattened out, and bounced a mere ten centimetres. I asked Don to get rid of it and have never owned or fired a gun since.

Far too dangerous! 9

Singapore's York Hotel in Scotts Road was conveniently near both the ABC and my flat. It was the ABC watering hole, and a wonderful pub straight from the pages of Somerset Maugham, with tiled floors, heavy teak furniture, dark wooden panelling, high ceilings with slowly turning fans and a cheerful Hainanese barman, Charlie, who used to make sudden and amazingly obscene sounds with his mouth that cannot adequately be described. Alas, the gracious York Hotel was torn down in the early 1970s and replaced by one of Singapore's ubiquitous high rise buildings. It was a sad loss.

It was at the York that I first met Denny, a charming old colonial relic. He was always impeccably dressed in a long-sleeved white shirt with silver cufflinks and tie, sharply creased trousers and black shoes so highly polished they shone in the dark. (We found out later that he only owned two shirts, and lived in genteel poverty in a rented room on the second floor of a decaying Chinese shop-house near

Chinatown where he used to lower a small saucepan on a string down to the noodle soup stall holder on the pavement below.) We sensed that Denny was hard up, despite his prosperous front. He would sit with his bottle of Tiger beer and hold court at the York with the Australian jockeys who raced in Singapore and Kuala Lumpur—and of course the ABC crowd.

'Good evening Your Grace' was our ritual greeting to Denny. He would solemnly make the sign of the cross and invite us to partake of cold, sparkling, amber fluid. Sometimes, if he was by himself, he would join us and we would buy him a couple of drinks which he accepted with dignity. We weren't sure what Denny did for a living. He told us once that he was the Singapore representative for Patek Phillipe, which made watches that only the very rich could afford. Not much of the profits seemed to be rubbing off on Denny. He and Ron McInnes, The Colonel, were birds of a feather, really. Mac eked out a precarious existence too. He had a room in a Johore Baru hotel which he shared with his delightful Malay girlfriend Fatimah who worked in a Singapore travel agency. Mac drank too much and had the shakes which showed up on his film footage if he didn't use a tripod. Willie Phua, another freelance, was a much better cameraman but Tony Ferguson and Peter Hollinshead tended to give Mac most of the work in those early days because they knew he needed the money and was an amusing drinking companion. Mac used to drive around in one of those big 1950s Yank tanks, a black Chevrolet with tail fins.

It was perhaps inevitable that he and Denny would get together and hatch improbable money-making schemes. They made so much theoretical money in the course of these sessions at the York Hotel they could barely climb over it to get out of the bar. One scheme was to make corporate videos and they did actually make a film. Mac shot some black and white footage of a big construction company operating in Singapore and conned someone he knew into editing it for him. Denny had the directors eating out of his hand and did a deal where, if they liked the pilot, they would pay US$5000 (a fabulous amount in the 1960s) for a 15-minute colour version. Every time Mac blinked, dollar signs appeared in his eyes. The problem was where to show the pilot film. The entire assets of Denny and The Colonel's film business were tied up in Mac's battered Bolex camera. Mac suggested they stretch a sheet across the wall of one of the bedrooms in the York. Denny looked pained. He didn't think The Colonel had the directors' psychology in perspective and he was dead right. Denny managed to con the use of a film projector in sufficiently prestigious surroundings and invited the directors to a screening. 'Everything will be all right', he confided to us, 'if Mac sticks to his bloody camera and leaves the selling to me.' Alas, he didn't.

The Colonel blew it spectacularly. The directors liked the pilot but Mac, full of booze and bonhomie, couldn't stay out of it. He was still earbashing the directors, his hand on their car door, as they drove off. But it was the final touch that nearly killed Denny. 'Here,' said Mac, tossing the pilot film through the car window on to their knees. 'You can have this one buckshee.'

Denny was in shock. 'Buckshee', he said shuddering as we bought him a badly needed cold Tiger beer later. 'I was talking to them in terms of ten thousand dollar deals and he throws in a lousy $20 print—BUCKSHEE!' The Great Film Making Venture died then and there and Mac and Denny didn't drink together any more at the York.

(I was saddened to hear that Denny was killed in a freak accident in the bar of the York, not long after I left Singapore. Two tough Eurasian pimps came into the sacred bar of the York, barged up to Denny's table, interrupting a story he was telling his companion, and offered them women. Denny was outraged and told them to bugger off. Punches were thrown and the old man fell back and hit his head on the side of a marble table. He never recovered consciousness. That is when Tony Ferguson and others discovered where and how he was living in the rented shop-house room, his sole assets the second long-sleeved shirt and a few personal items. Denny deserved a better exit.)

We really shouldn't have preferred The Colonel over Willie Phua, but wily Willie bided his time with Oriental patience knowing that Mac wasn't a long-term threat. The Colonel certainly lived dangerously. Despite his relationship with 'Timah (as everyone called her) Mac was a dreadful racist. He hated Chinese—not a good attitude in a place like Singapore. Once, with 'Timah in the car, he was driving through an area of Singapore where there had been race riots between the Chinese and the Malay minority. Mac hit the brakes a bit late (his eyesight wasn't the best) when the traffic stopped, and the driver behind banged into the bumper bar of his prized Chev. There was only minor damage. Both drivers got out, and Mac raced up to the Chinese driver of the other car and grabbed him by the shirt. 'It must have been a bloody cheap shirt', he told us later, 'because I ripped the front right out of it'. Mac was about to follow up with a left hook, when a Chinese policeman fortuitously arrived. A hostile crowd was gathering, not amused by Mac's aggressive behaviour to one of their own. The policemen looked into the Chev to see 'Timah sitting there. He made an instant decision and told Mac to get into his car and leave quickly. It was just as well he did, or neither of them might have survived.

Eventually Mac ran out of time—and credit. He left owing thousands of Straits dollars to trusting Chinese shopkeepers who, because Mac was a European, did not question his bona fides. It was touch and go whether he would get on the plane to Australia before the authorities caught up with him. His final departure was vintage Mac. As he walked up the stairs to the Qantas 707 for the flight to Sydney, he yelled back to a friend who was to sell his car for him, 'Don't try and flog it on a rainy day—the roof leaks'. And he was gone.

It was dear old Denny who introduced me to the Satay Club. I fell for it completely, and then delighted in dropping my flatmate Bob Hart right in it as well as any other newcomer to Singapore

I could lay my hands on. One night in the York Denny said he would like to invite me to his club. 'I notice you aren't wearing a tie,' he said. 'They may have one they can lend you, but I know the doorman well and can probably talk you in.' We took a taxi (which I paid for) down to the waterfront, near Raffles Hotel. I was a bit nervous about getting in, wearing a short-sleeved open-necked shirt. We walked down towards the bus depot where, among the diesel fumes and roaring engines, Malay stall holders were expertly fanning charcoal in small burners while they marinaded the prawn, chicken and beef satay sticks. There was no doorman. This was the Satay Club. We sat, shouting above the roar of bus engines as the buses came and went, eating delicious satay served on banana leaves with small segments of sticky rice. We even managed to order in some Tiger beer. That was the Singapore I loved, the Singapore which has now been tidied up. There are no more *makan* carts on the streets, no more Satay Club. The eating areas have been corralled into controlled spaces like Newton Circus. They are pleasant enough, but I preferred the old unstructured style. I never got ill eating from any Singapore old-style street stall.

Early in 1966 I had an unexpected and extremely pleasant surprise when Rosalind Geddes arrived in Singapore. By now a fully-fledged nursing sister, she had resigned from her job at the Prince Alfred Hospital in Sydney and decided to head to Singapore where she hoped to get a job. I met her ship and arranged accommodation at the York. Ros was a tropical girl, having been born in Ceylon (Sri Lanka) in 1940. Her father, Eric, was a tea planter and fifth-generation member of the Geddes family to be born there. The Geddes boys were sent off to England for their education, before returning to Ceylon. How to run a tea plantation was all Eric ever knew. Ros and her Australian mother Margaret had to get out during World War II. Ros's grandfather, a Sydney KC, Reginald Bonney, had been to university law school with Bert Evatt—then Attorney General and the Minister for External Affairs—and prevailed on him to get Ros and Margaret out of Ceylon. They were evacuated on an

Australian troopship in 1942 when Japan entered the war—and they got away 24 hours before Colombo harbour was bombed. The Geddes family were united again in Ceylon in the post war, but moved to a tea plantation in South India in 1948 when Ceylon became independent. Ros went to school at Ooty in the Nilgiri Hills. There were stirrings of feminism in her even then. She was furious that the girls had to field for the boys practising the cricket they would play when they went to England for their secondary school education. Unless the girls could bat and bowl too, said ten-year-old Ros, they wouldn't play. Or perhaps the boys would like to play netball? She won the day. At the statutory age of twelve Ros was sent to boarding school in Sydney. The days of the white planters were numbered and two years later Eric bowed to the inevitable and the Geddes family (with Ros's two younger sisters) was reunited in Tasmania where I first met red-headed Ros.

There was no guarantee of work in Singapore, but Ros was hopeful of getting a job in the privately-run Gleneagles Hospital which would also ensure her a work permit. She lived in the York Hotel for a month hoping a job would turn up and loved living in Singapore. We saw a lot of each other. One scented evening, under the slowly turning ceiling fan of her spacious York Hotel room, we put our relationship on a less platonic basis. It was high time for both of us. More than a decade had passed since we first met. Our long-term friendship had blossomed into love.

When Don Simmons came to Singapore on leave from Saigon he was courting petite, blonde Kim Dwyer, who was working as a nanny for the Australian Ambassador's children in Saigon. Kim's parents were also in the Department of External Affairs, which is, I suppose, how she came to be there. One sunny Singapore morning I picked up Don in my newly acquired car—a rather sporty Brabham Viva, the first new car I had ever owned, or to be more accurate, begun to buy on hire purchase—and called by the York to pick up Ros. She saw us, waved and began to walk towards the car. Simmo is a perceptive feller, and there was something about her body language that attracted his attention. He turned to me, 'You're taking advantage of that woman!!' (He used a more colloquial expression.) I blustered and said it was none of his business. 'You *are*, you bastard. I know you are.'

Ros scored a vacancy at Gleneagles Hospital which gave a salary and the essential work permit. She moved into nurses' quarters at the back of the hospital which made intimacy more difficult, but not impossible. There was always 11F Jalan Jintan. We formed the habit of driving down into the city on a Sunday to have a curry lunch at a Muslim restaurant called the Majeed, which not only served brilliant curries, but wonderful *roti*—a delicious offering which began as a small ball of dough and then was rolled and skilfully flung out like a shawl until it was either wrapped around a raw egg or savoury mince, and cooked on a hot plate, sprinkled with oil. Singapore's Indian Muslims were relaxed about Australian unbelievers drinking alcohol on their premises and cheerfully sent out small boys to bring back large cold bottles of Tiger beer. After our exotic lunch we would return to Jalan Jintan to make love under the lazily turning ceiling fan. They were wonderful days.

Regretfully the ABC kept sending me away from Singapore on assignment. It was something to do with my being a foreign correspondent. Ros got more use out of my new sporty Brabham Viva than I did.

Vietnam was becoming a bigger world story as President Johnson's massive military build-up neared its target of half a million US troops on the ground. I flew back to Saigon not only to help out Don Simmons in any way I could, but with a Talks Department brief to produce a radio documentary on the war for a weekly 45-minute program called *Fact and Opinion*. The ABC News Department in those days was suspicious of the tape recorder. Staffed and managed almost exclusively by former newspaper men (there were few women), they ran ABC news rather like a newspaper. Reporters (and foreign correspondents) wrote stories which were read on air by an announcer. Occasionally there were contributions directly from reporters called 'voice pieces'. This was not 'actuality', in the ABC Talks sense, nor as we know it now where news-making people are interviewed, or you have the sound of a street riot and associated commentary recorded by a reporter on the spot, but a reporter lugubriously reading a segment of his own report. Few news journalists were trained how to read a script or use their voices, so these segments were often far from riveting. I recall an edict from on high that no more than two 'voice pieces' were to be included in any one news bulletin. This was a good decision at the time, as the announcer did a far better job of reading than did a reporter. But it wasn't radio in my terms, or as we have come to take for granted these days. Journalists didn't go out with tape recorders.

When I got to Saigon I suggested to Don that he take out a tape recorder with him the next time he went on patrol with the Australians. He snorted his contempt for this stupid suggestion. 'Listen mate, I'm far too worried about keeping my weapon dry swimming across a river than frigging around with tape recorders.' I wondered if Don was tilting the balance too much towards being a fighting soldier rather than a reporter, but was in no real position to judge. That was his way of doing things, and he did have to keep a close eye on what the Australians were doing. If he had taken a recorder he could have captured some amazing stuff. Don had established his own links and credibility with 1 RAR, but there was no way they would let the likes of me loose with a tape recorder so I decided the only way to get close to combat was to go out with the Americans. The American Marines were operating in the north of South Vietnam from Danang, where they maintained a large press centre. I decided to go there, initially at least, in the company of one of Australia's most experienced war correspondents, Denis Warner. (Denis was born in Tasmania, and had also worked on *The Mercury*. Many years before I had written to him asking his advice about whether to leave the paper or not, to seek wider experience. He very kindly wrote back and said, yes, I should.)

Denis had flown into Saigon in the company of His Eminence Cardinal Richard Hughes, as the doyen of the Hong Kong Foreign Correspondents' Association and London *Daily Telegraph* correspondent was inevitably known. Hughes was a monumental figure in every way—all twenty stone (128 kg) and six feet plus (210 cm) of him. Simmo was down at Bien Hoa with the Australians, so I had the office jeep and drove in to the Hotel Caravelle to meet up with Dick and Denis. Shock, horror—there was no room at the Caravelle! This had never happened in the quarter of a century that both men had been covering the Indochina situation. The desk clerk was almost in tears, but nothing could be done. They would have to find somewhere else to stay.

As I had the ABC jeep I offered to help. Denis, no lightweight himself, squeezed into the back seat while Hughes was only just able to manoeuvre his vast bulk into the front. I drove them to the hotel suggested by the desk clerk at the Caravelle. Dick got out to release Denis from the back seat. Denis then stepped awkwardly into the gutter and collapsed in agony with a badly twisted ankle. I stayed with him while the Cardinal headed into the hotel. The rooms they had been offered were on the sixth floor and there was no lift. A purple-faced, furiously sweating Hughes arrived back at the jeep clearly on the verge of a coronary. There was no way Denis could climb up six flights of stairs. I somehow got them back in the jeep and returned to the Caravelle. So piteous was the sight of them that they got in on compassionate grounds alone. Denis thanked me for my help. If he had cursed me I would not have taken it amiss.

I flew to Danang in a C130 transport on the daily 'milk run' that went from Saigon to Danang and back through Pleiku in the highlands, or via the big new coastal air base at Cam Ranh Bay. (I had arranged to meet Denis Warner in Danang later when he could walk well enough to travel.) Sitting opposite me was a huge Marine sergeant, about fifteen stone (96 kg), six feet two inches (215 cm) in height, a granite jaw that would have delighted a cartoonist, dripping with weapons and rugged imperturbability. Sitting beside him

Artist becomes goal

A well-known Saigon artist has been hospitalized with a broken back after being struck with a soccer ball.

Hospitalized was Nguyen Son, 56.

Sources say Son was walking down Ly Thai To Street earlier this week, past a group of Popular Self Defense Force militia playing soccer.

One of the players kicked the ball unusually hard and it struck Son, breaking his backbone.

The incident was termed an accident.

Snuffs out wedding

A 17-year-old bride-to-be has committed suicide because another woman claimed to be the wife of her future husband.

Sources said Lam Ngoc An committed suicide by taking prison.

According to the sources, An was to be married next week.

But another woman came to her house two days ago and created a scence by raving at An, saying she herself was already the wife of the intended.

Her fiance later denied the allegation, but An told her friends and relatives that her sheart has been mortally offended, and subsequently committed suicide.

Telltale sign

Following is a partial translation of item from Thanh Dien News service:

«In yesterday's news release we related the story of the incredibly horrifying suicide by hanging of 20 year old Miss Nguyen Thi Ngoc Lan of Nguyen Thien Thuat street. She hanged herself from the ceiling of the third floor of the family home when none was looking.

Other members of the family found her urine dripped down through ceilings to the floors below...»

The daily column 'Looking Around' in the *Saigon Post* invariably made diverting reading.

was a tiny Vietnamese soldier no more than five feet tall looking like a boy scout pretending to be a soldier. The Vietnamese are small-boned people—I was told the average weight of their babies at birth is about three pounds (1½ kg)—and this soldier looked up at the big sergeant as if in wonder, and then settled his head below his shoulder and fell asleep. He looked like a child on an outing with his father.

In a sense it was an allegory of the current state of the war. The ARVN (South Vietnamese Armed Forces) were understandably weary of the casualties they had been suffering during a long and protracted conflict, and the Americans were anxious to get in there and take over the serious fighting. Mind you, those delicate rather flower-like hands of the Vietnamese soldier were capable of squeezing the trigger of an automatic rifle with just as much efficiency as the sergeant's sausage-sized digits.

The US Marines' Press Centre was attractively positioned on the Danang River among palms and flame trees, with comfortable accommodation, a good dining room, bar and recreation area with pool tables. I didn't really want to leave it but if I was to be reporting a war—or rather, in my case, trying to record it—it was necessary to go near the cutting edge from time to time. A sadistic Marine, one Sgt Babyack (who, I found out after it was too late, hated the press and had a reputation for sending them out on assignments he hoped might kill them) thought it would be just fine for my purposes to go out on a 24-hour patrol with the Marines into what was called a 'free fire zone' near Danang. A free fire zone, I discovered, was marginally government controlled by day and Communist controlled by night. In any case the Marines shot at anything that moved, which was tough on the local farming population, many of whom had chosen to stay on their ancestral land rather than be evacuated to a grotty refugee camp in Danang.

I was to go on the patrol with Serge Brouchard, a Paris-based journalist who had been an officer with the French army before the fall of Dien Bien Phu and who was looking forward to experiencing some combat and seeing if the Americans had any more chance of doing what the French had failed to do. We had our own bodyguard from the Press Centre, a Marine sergeant called Jim, armed with a pump action shotgun. Jim was the recipient of five Purple Hearts, awarded for being wounded in action. The most unusual was being bitten on the field of battle. Jim was trying to pull a Viet Cong soldier out of a foxhole when the VC sank his teeth into his hand.

He locked on and would not disengage. Another Marine smashed the VC in the head with a rifle butt and Jim was left with seven Communist teeth embedded in his palm. (He said he still had six of them.) 'The bite didn't hurt as much as the anti-tetanus shots afterwards.' Another Purple Heart followed a blast by a mortar grenade that blew off one of his testicles and made him sterile. Jim seemed admirably philosophical about this—but even more keen to engage the enemy who had so maimed him.

To record 'actuality' on the patrol I had a cigar-box-sized Swiss reel-to-reel tape recorder called a Stellavox. It was compact, but its three-inch spools could only record about seven minutes of tape at a time, at 7½ inches per second. I had plenty of tapes but changing them under combat conditions would be awkward. The patrol of twenty men was led by a young Marine lieutenant, Sam, who looked about sixteen but was probably in his early twenties. We walked between two huge tanks, which belched smoke, rumbled and clanked as we forged across the countryside, so there was no doubt the North Vietnamese or VC would know where we were. Serge and I were advised by Jim to walk in the tracks of the leading tank, to minimise the risk of stepping on a mine. 'We lose most of our men that way.' It seemed a good idea.

The weather was dry, but dusty and windy—conditions, our bodyguard Jim said, that favoured the VC and their snipers. A village loomed up through the murk and Sam asked the Vietnamese interpreter to round up all the villagers—mostly women and old men. He then instructed them—through the interpreter—to link hands and walk ahead of the tanks to a distant tree line. I thought this was a bit rough and said so to Platoon Commander Sam. 'You reckon?' he said, and gestured to a crater in the paddy field nearby. 'I lost my best corporal there four days ago. He trod on a 105 mm shell, placed point uppermost. It blew the lower half of his body clean away. He lived for about two minutes.' Sam told me the villagers knew where the booby traps were because the VC did not want to waste them by having their own people step on them by accident. If they neared a booby trap they would stop and refuse to go on, and the tank could then roll over and detonate it safely. 'It looks cruel but it isn't really. They know and we don't.'

The Marines certainly weren't winning any friends. One of the tanks crushed and broke through a bamboo hedge behind a farm house, scoring a vegetable garden with its tracks. An old woman scowled at us as we passed through. Sam said we were in Viet Cong territory but behind the river we could see ahead to the east, where army intelligence had told him there was a whole battalion of North Vietnamese regular troops dug in. They were the hard men. I was relieved to hear they weren't on our agenda on this patrol. On the other hand Serge, the ex-French officer, was disappointed.

Search and destroy missions like ours sat uneasily with the 'pacification' program where the US gave food handouts, water pumps, farm machinery and restored or built irrigation systems for rural people to try to counter the fear and terror allegedly inflicted on them by the Viet Cong. The pacification program went by the unfortunate acronym of WHAMMO. I once saw a Zippo cigarette lighter (famously employed in news film footage where US soldiers used them to set alight the thatched roofs of suspected Viet Cong houses) with the inscription: *Let me win your heart and mind or I'll burn your fucking house down.*

At 5 pm we stopped for something to eat and broke out our combat rations. I had pork and lima beans—it was likely to be a windy night—biscuits and a drink of iodine-and-chlorine-impregnated water. One of the tank commanders, who was probably bored and wanted an excuse to shoot something, shouted that he 'thought' he saw the helmet of a 'hard core' North Vietnamese soldier in a village we could see on our left. Sam gave the thumbs up, and the tanks began blasting away. The tanks' big cannons created such a loud explosion that my tape recorder couldn't cope. You could hear the beginning of the shot on tape, a split second's silence, and then the end. It was an unusual effect that, if anything, added to the drama of the moment. There was cheering and shouts of 'Good shot' as the gunners demolished the arch of a Buddhist pagoda and then brought the walls down for good measure. One of the Marines said, 'If there's a hard core there he's now a dead core.' I doubted this, as no fire had come from the village. To make a thorough job of it, our platoon commander called in an artillery strike on the village and gave the co-ordinates. Five minutes later the whole hamlet disappeared in a cloud of smoke and high explosives. I was sure I saw a small boy trying to lead a water buffalo to safety shortly before the unfortunate animal disappeared in thousands of pieces. The Marines thought it was a huge joke. 'Say, did you see that goddamn buffalo go up, man...'

I was crass enough to ask (on tape) about the child I'd seen, and the civilian population of the village in general under those circumstances. Sam said that all the houses had bomb shelters, 'same as every American home has a TV set', and it was their fault if they didn't use them. 'Haven't the VC got bomb shelters too?' I asked but didn't get an answer. It seemed extraordinary that our young commander had the authority to turn on such destructive power at will.

Our plan was to wait till dusk, then move into a previously selected position for the night. There the platoon would put out ambush parties into the surrounding tree lines, scan the area with an infra-red searchlight, and prepare for what might happen. While we were waiting, a huge rifleman came over to speak with me. Speaking softly in a Texan drawl, he said, 'Excuse me sir, I understand you are an Australian'. I wasn't sure where this was going, and said I was. 'I'm very interested in working with handicapped children. Are there many opportunities for that kind of work in Australia?' I told him there were, and he seemed pleased. He also seemed oblivious to the fairly obvious fact that the village he had just helped to demolish would be a good place to start.

It was a telling example to me of what Neil Davis had told me when I first arrived in Saigon—that the cultural differences between the incoming American soldiers and the Vietnamese were so vast that it was easy for the US soldiers to dehumanise the people they had come to save. That was one of the reasons Neil decided to cover the war from the Vietnamese perspective, with the ARVN soldiers. 'I wanted to show the world that they weren't just funny little animals running around as the Americans seemed to depict them—but nice, simple people with ordinary human thoughts and desires.' Neil said later he wasn't surprised when the My Lai massacre was exposed. It was an inevitable consequence of racial contempt. Few Americans tried to learn even the basics of the Vietnamese language with its sung vowels and glottal stops.

Darkness came quickly as it does in the tropics and with it a palpable air of menace. It was a full moon and Sam was unhappy with the position he had chosen for the night, as both tanks and men were silhouetted against the flat, open rice fields around us. The tanks' big engines burst into life again and we moved into a grove of trees where there was a small empty farmhouse, but open ground all around. I heard two disquieting conversations. Sam and his deputy were arguing about where we actually were on the map. This was important, because 'free fire zones' were subjected to random US mortar fire at night to keep the enemy on the move. If Sam wasn't able to pinpoint our position we could be killed by a ball of our own manure, so to speak. Sam's deputy then said, 'I don't like this at all. We can defend this position against any attempt to overrun us, but we are sitting pretty for a mortar attack and there's nothing we can do about it'.

It was reassuring to see the bulk of our two big tanks, one on either side of us. Quietly the platoon went about the business of securing itself for the night. Electrically operated Claymore mines were put out all round us. These were dreadful weapons which spewed out shrapnel in a designated arc, at waist height. One of the tank sergeants explained to me that they had learned through experience to put a bit of white tape on the side facing them. 'The bastards sometimes crawl out and turn them around so that when we let them off we get the lot! Or they try and steal them. This way we know something's up if we can't see the tape any more.' Listening posts and ambushes were set up in the surrounding tree lines and in the grove of trees beside the farmhouse. The rest of the Marines started to dig themselves a hole to lie in with their entrenching tools—the best defence against a mortar attack. I had no entrenching tool and felt naked.

The sound of a rifle fired at you, rather than away from you, has a distinctive sound—a sharp 'crack' that is immediately recognisable once you have heard it. At about 8 pm a crackle of small arms fire rang out, and I didn't need to be told to hit the deck. 'That's just Victor Charlie telling us he knows we're here and wishing us a restful night', said Jim with a happy smile. 'I hope the bastards try something tonight, I'm spoiling for a fight.' So was my companion Serge. I thought they were both mad and wished I had a nice deep hole to crawl into. Jim, who after all was there to look after us, scouted around and found one. It was the bomb shelter in the floor of the abandoned farmhouse, and after checking it for booby traps he asked me to familiarise myself with it, as there would be at least six people anxious to use it too if we were mortared. It was built for Vietnamese, not hulking westerners, but I lowered myself feet first into a claustrophobic tunnel that curved down and to the right, and was about five metres in length.

I went outside again and joined the tank crews. 'This is the time I hate', Jim said quietly. 'The boot's on the other foot now. We can only wait for them to attack us. The day belongs to us, the night is the VC's time.'

As we waited we could hear the random mortar fire from the Marine headquarters start to rain down on the free fire zone and I hoped Sam and his sidekick had got their sums right. There was a distant 'pop', and about twenty seconds later a dull 'kerboom' as the mortar bomb exploded in the distance. John, one of the tank commanders, was telling a jolly story about booby traps when he suddenly stiffened. 'That didn't sound like one of ours. Oh well, we'll know in twenty seconds.' CRACK KERBOOM! An enemy mortar shell exploded about fifty metres from us. I hit the bottom of the bomb shelter in a nanosecond, followed by an avalanche of bodies. There was a moment's silence. An American voice said, 'Say, where's the Aussie?' I replied from the bowels of the earth to much laughter. 'Christ man, you went down there like a gopher.'

A bigger action was going on towards the west, with flares and artillery fire. Sergeant John thought the main action was more likely to be there, rather than us. 'Or they'll wait until 3 am when everyone's at their lowest ebb and then attack.' It was a long night. I dozed fitfully underneath one of the tanks and was pleased that the VC were doing other things that night than giving us a reminder that they were there and knew we were too.

At first light I found Serge had slept through the mortar attack. He was disappointed about that and even more disappointed that we hadn't been attacked more energetically. I thought it was just fine as it was. I'd been able to record some action without losing my testicles. The strong coffee back at Marine HQ was the best I ever tasted, but at the Danang Press Centre Sgt Babyack seemed quite disappointed to see me. When I next saw Neil Davis I told him I'd been out with the Marines at Danang. The man who put his life on the line with South Vietnamese troops almost every day of the week looked shocked. 'Jesus Bowden, you're mad—that's far too dangerous. I'd never do that. Those bastards don't know what they're doing.'

Several days later a still limping Denis Warner arrived and suggested we fly to Hue, the old imperial capital, to check out the political situation there. We took an Air America flight (accurately dubbed CIA Airlines by those in the know) on a twin-engined Beechcraft which was small enough to land on an airstrip inside the old walled city. Ever the frustrated aviator, I sat in the co-pilot's seat and chatted away to the pilot. I asked him if he minded if I flew the aircraft for a while. 'Be my guest', he said, happy to break the boring routine of his milk run. We were on descent to Hue, and there were little, fleecy clouds all around us. Student pilots are forbidden to fly into cloud and I asked the pilot if I could do so. He said it was fine, so I banked and weaved through the little cloudlets. Denis, in the back, was probably wondering what the hell was going on. The pilot said, 'It's a good idea to move her around a bit at this stage anyway. We sometimes get a bit of sniper fire around here'. I redoubled my efforts.

As we lined up on the tiny runway (which ended abruptly against the old city wall, so going around again wasn't an option) I was happy to hand the controls back to the expert. But I made the fatal (well, not quite) mistake of telling him a joke just as we were landing. We had been talking about living in Vietnam and the tummy troubles that seemed endemic to westerners. 'Do you remember', I said on our final approach, 'those wonderful days when a man could fart without fear?' The pilot hadn't heard that fairly well used line and began to laugh uproariously. He was still gasping with uncontrollable mirth as we rocketed down the runway, stopping only metres from disaster. I made a mental note never to tell jokes to pilots during a landing.

Hue was a beautiful place in 1966, with its moats and water-lily-fringed waters ringing the old imperial palace. Sadly the palace and its surrounds were ravaged by bombing and artillery during the Tet uprising in 1968 when the North Vietnamese raised the Communist flag over the old fort as a symbolic, nationalistic gesture, and the American Marines re-occupied it at great cost to life and history. Hue was a university town, the intellectual centre of the country, and Denis wanted to sniff the breeze for an article for *The Reporter* magazine on what the Vietnamese were thinking about the conduct of the war. Accommodation was hard to come by in Hue. Denis, however, had lots of contacts and an obliging US Information Services Officer let us stay in his small house. In the second volume of his autobiography, *Not Always on Horseback—An Australian Correspondent At War and Peace in Asia 1961–1993*, Denis described what happened next:

He had a single-storeyed house with a flooring of white tiles. He left for work early, entreating us to lock the door when he left. I made last use of the bathroom facilities, and failed to notice that the water was still gushing in the toilet. When we opened the front door in the evening we were greeted with a rush of water. Every room in the house had been flooded. Books, papers, shoes, clothing on or close to the floor were saturated. We did our best to explain to our host...

My flying adventures were not over. I decided to spend some time with one of the forward artillery spotters. My pilot and many of his ilk were trained on jet fighters and found Cessnas a bit of an anti-climax. They flew them like an inner-city motorcycle courier rides his motorbike. Their main job was to fly at about 1000 feet during an artillery or air strike and report back to the gunners where their shells were landing, or how effective bombing and strafing from fighter aircraft had been on a target. On this occasion some Vietnamese Air Force propeller-driven Skyraiders were dropping napalm on suspected Viet Cong positions. This frightful weapon is dropped in torpedo-like canisters, which spew petroleum jelly out in a spectacular explosion of red fire and black smoke. It causes the most frightful burns, and can even kill soldiers in trenches nearby through asphyxiation as it consumes all the oxygen from the surrounding air.

'Feel like some lunch?' yelled the pilot over the noise of his engine. I nodded, just as the aircraft bucked and lurched. My pilot started to curse and swear and got on his radio very smartly. 'Those stupid assholes shouldn't be using mortars in this air space without letting me know.' We had nearly been hit by a 'friendly' mortar round. I looked around for an airstrip, but couldn't see one. The pilot simply put down on a dirt road near his Officers' Mess, and we had lunch.

Back in Saigon I wanted to do a story on the RAAF role in Vietnam. An Australian Caribou was heading down to Vung Tau, in the delta region of South Vietnam, and said I could go along for the ride and do some interviews. The two Australian pilots were fairly relaxed about having me moving about the aircraft and I asked if I could stand behind their seats while they were landing. I wished I hadn't. As we turned on final approach, a tropical cloudburst was closing on the airport. The pilot said to his co-pilot, 'I hope that bloody thing holds off for another thirty seconds'. It didn't—and just before we touched down the whole world was blotted out by driving rain. Unfortunately for me I was seeing what the pilots were seeing through the cockpit front windows—which was bugger all. The Caribou swerved from side to side as we skied blindly along the saturated runway. I caught glimpses of buildings and other aircraft on either side as we speared crazily into the murk. The co-pilot said to his skipper, 'Have you got her?' 'I think so', was his not very reassuring reply. It would have been better had I stayed down the back and been in blissful ignorance.

Even commercial flying in Southeast Asia in those days was 'interesting'. On one of my visits to Vietnam I flew through Vientiane, the capital of Laos. I was booked on an Air Vietnam flight to Saigon—booked in a fashion. When the flight was announced a great crowd of passengers, most of them carrying bundles of their possessions (including live chickens), ran towards the aircraft. I thought I'd better do the same, which was just as well. All seats in the DC6B were soon occupied, and bodies and bundles of luggage completely filled the central aisle. I was witnessing strap-hanging on an international flight, that is if there had been any straps to hang on to. Somehow the crew got the door shut and the grossly overloaded piston-engined airliner struggled to get airborne. With all four engines roaring and shuddering we took an agonisingly long time to unstick from the runway and barely cleared the jungle at the end of it. The hostesses couldn't move down the aisle because of the extra passengers, chickens and other cargo. We handed the box lunches over our heads to the passengers behind. So much for First Class service. Four decades on, nothing much has changed. Christopher Kremmer, the distinguished Asia correspondent, told me of a flight he took from Vientiane recently. He found he couldn't do up his safety belt because it had a frayed end and no buckle. He wasn't able to attract the attention of any of the hostesses so finally stuck out his arm across the aisle to stop one and explained his problem. The hostess shrugged and summed up the situation accurately, 'If we crash, we burn, you die!'

In 1966 Neil Davis wearied of life in hotel rooms and set himself up in a flat in Singapore with an amah he swore was twice as good as mine. That was typical of Davis, intensely competitive in his job, sport, love and everything else. If our Ah Wah had a good job with Bob and me, Neil's amah was on clover. (In June Bob Hart got transferred to Saigon, and his successor in Singapore, Alan Thomas, moved in to 11F Jalan Jintan to maintain the Reuters' tradition.) Neil was only in Singapore a few weeks in each year, but at least he had a place to hang his paintings and call home. Through his doors, while he was in residence, went a parade of women—Davis was incorrigible and insatiable. In this department even Section 45D of the Old Mates Act was violated. I was outraged years later when Ros told me he had propositioned her—and in my car, too! I was out of Singapore in Indonesia at the time. The first anniversary of the failed Communist coup was coming up and I went to Jakarta to help cover it and then mind the ABC office while Phil Koch had a much needed break.

At that time Indonesia was in chaos, with galloping inflation and an unresolved political situation. What became known as the 30th September Movement acted when it did because of rumours of President Sukarno's failing health. The wily old man was deeply compromised by his support of the Indonesian Communist Party (PKI) (now defunct) but Indonesia's first president, the man who had welded together the Indonesian nation after Dutch colonial rule—even to the extent of creating a unifying common language, Bahasa Indonesia—was still widely loved and respected by most Indonesians, his portrait having pride of place on the wall of the humblest *atap* cottage. Although the President's powers and influence had been much curtailed by the triumvirate of General Suharto, Foreign Minister Adam Malik, and Finance Minister Sultan Hamengkubowono, they weren't quite confident enough to remove him from the presidency at that stage. Student demonstrations supporting 'The New Order' were growing in strength and militancy, maintaining a rowdy presence at the gates of the *Merdeka* Presidential Palace and President Sukarno was stirring the pot whenever he could, making inflammatory speeches and refusing to go quietly.

The currency had become almost worthless—it was such splendid looking money I papered part of a wall at 11F Jalan Jintan with it—and it was revalued 1000 to 1. There were then Old Rupiahs and New Rupiahs in circulation at the same time with about 115 New Rupiahs to the US dollar, or 115 000 in the old currency. People had to carry around suitcases full of the stuff. Alan Morris, Radio Australia's man in Jakarta, stopped to buy some cigarettes from a hawker on his way to work one morning. Alan bargained the price back down to ten new roops (as they were known), but he only had old roops. Laboriously he began counting out the 10 000 in tattered notes, which took about five minutes, and at the end of this performance the hawker said he owed another 500. How come? asked Alan in his fluent Bahasa. The seller explained that he had taken so long to count the money that inflation had sent the price up in the interim! Alan was very tickled by his cheek and paid over the extra.

Western visitors to Jakarta all stayed at the Hotel Indonesia, one of the few multi-storey buildings in the Indonesian capital which was airconditioned and fully functioning. The hotel management didn't muck about with roops; all transactions were in US dollars. The correspondents used to drink in the Ramayana Bar, looking down on the traffic that crawled around the circular pond and fountain in front of the building. One evening Jack Gillon, a Reuters correspondent, noticed a Pertamina oil tanker grinding its way past the hotel. Oil was one commodity that Indonesia had plenty of, and Sukarno had kept the price of petrol and fuel artificially low. At fifteen old roops a gallon (4.5 litres) most petrol outlets wouldn't even bother to collect the insignificant amounts owing. Jack calculated that the two US dollars he'd just paid for his martini in the Ramayana Bar would buy the whole tanker load. Things were in such a state and the black market was such a fact of life that the Australian Embassy had its own 'official' money changer, and obligingly allowed the ABC to avail itself of this service.

As tensions built towards the failed coup anniversary, Sukarno continued to call press conferences and give speeches at the presidential palace. I went to one of these and was able to see the President, who had a deserved reputation as a great orator, in full flight. Impeccably dressed in military uniform, and wearing his trademark black *pitji* cap, he spoke from a free-standing microphone. To one side was a small table on which were a glass of fruit juice and a plate of biscuits. Neil Davis told me they were always there. Sukarno took off his white gloves, laid them and his swagger stick on the table and moved to the microphone, holding his audience in the palm of his hand even before he started to speak. He began in a low whisper and then, theatrically, built his performance, sometimes quoting in English, Dutch, French or German. I found it somewhat unnerving that when he broke into English to deliver an epigram from Thomas Carlyle he turned and stared straight at me. His oration was a masterly performance. Standing nearby were the three men, Suharto, Malik and Sultan Hamengkubowono, who were currently destabilising him. I don't know what he said in Bahasa, but he pointed to them and said something that made all three smile with some irony. Sukarno was always interested in the foreign press and had noticed my new face among the gaggle of regulars. He asked to meet me and I was introduced to him by Hidayat, the ABC interpreter. He wanted to know the obvious things, who I represented and what I was doing in Indonesia. We made some small talk, and he moved on.

As the 30 September anniversary drew closer, the student protests outside the *Merdeka* Palace intensified. The crack Siliwangi Division from outside Jakarta had been brought in for the occasion, and they were itching to get their batons onto the shoulders and heads of the students who had been massing outside the Palace for several weeks. I happened to be standing with a group of foreign correspondents, including Phil Koch, in open parkland between the troops and the students. Suddenly the Palace Guard charged and I turned sideways to switch on my heavy Nagra tape recorder, thinking that they would let us stay where we were. I was wrong. A rifle butt crashed into the small of my back and I looked up to see a very angry soldier, with his bayonet fixed, who seemed to be suggesting I move on—fast. These soldiers were prepared to use their weapons and there was no safety in being foreign. I shot a sideways glance at Phil Koch being chased by another guardsman with a bayonet inches from his bum. I presumed I had one as close to mine. It was stinking hot and the tape recorder seemed to weigh a tonne as we dashed for the edge of the park fighting for breath, our chests bursting. I hadn't run so fast since school athletics. This incident signalled a change of tactic by Suharto's army against the demonstrators. Several students were killed in the charge, including two girls. (No guardsmen were reprimanded, nor was there any subsequent apology to parents for the murder of their children.) We were lucky to get out of it unharmed. I hitched a ride on the back of a student's Vespa to get away from the area and back to the office. The troops' action was a message to the students from Suharto that they had better find some other way of protesting.

The process of isolating the President went on for another six months. In March 1967 there was a meeting of the People's Consultative Congress, which only took place every five years. Debate about Sukarno—whether he was a traitor and should be put on trial, or whether he should remain as Indonesia's honoured President and father of the revolution—went on for five days. At the end the conference chairman, General Nasution, announced that Sukarno would no longer be known as 'President' but would be called Dr 'Engineer' Sukarno. There was still a nervousness about sacking the old man and General Suharto had to clarify the findings of the congress, telling the press that Sukarno would be treated 'as a president who is no longer in power'. Dr Engineer Sukarno, by then in very poor health, retired to his favourite palace at Bogor in the hills outside Jakarta. He remained under virtual house arrest as Suharto's 'New Order' regime consolidated its power. He died in Jakarta on 21 June 1970.

After the brouhaha of the first anniversary of the attempted coup died down, I was keen to venture into the interior of Java to find out what I could about the post-coup killings, the extent of which will never be accurately known, but which varies from 200 000 to almost a million. How much of this slaughter was anti-Communist, attempted genocide against Indonesia's ethnic Chinese, or simply the settling of old scores, is impossible to know. That there was a frenzy of killing there is no doubt. Rivers were clogged and choked with bodies.

Taking Alan Morris to translate, and a driver, we drove in a venerable, big black Buick from Jakarta through central Java to Bali. (Our fuel costs were modest—a total of five US dollars, due to the ludicrous, controlled fuel prices.) The people in the villages and towns we drove through seemed subdued. I found out later that we had been lucky not to encounter militant black-shirted youth groups still loyal to President Sukarno. They would have seen us as imperialist lackeys. There was not a tourist to be seen so the hotels en route were very pleased to see us.

I was particularly keen to get to Bali, not only for its legendary charms, but because Neil Davis had told me that the killings there had been particularly bad. The Communists had been found guilty of disturbing the carefully balanced Hindu–Buddhist rhythm of village life and communal harmony. This was regarded as a great crime. Councils of village elders tried the Communists and ordered that they be executed—usually by decapitation. There had been group slaughter as well. It seemed difficult to believe that this had happened in serene Bali, of all places.

I found an American missionary who was prepared to talk to me on tape about what had happened. He estimated that on the small island of Bali alone, 70 000 people had been executed or murdered. We looked around for a quiet place to record and sat down on a mound of earth, under the shade of a tree. As we talked, a group of locals gathered around to watch what was going on. After we finished and I was packing up my recorder, one of the group came over and said something in Balinese to the missionary. He looked startled.

'That man told me that the mound of earth we were sitting on is the mass grave of seventeen murdered Communists.'

Alan Morris and our driver took the Buick back to Jakarta while I flew further east along the Indonesian archipelago. The Australian Ambassador in Jakarta, Max Loveday, had arranged to fly to the remote island of Flores—about as far east again from Bali as Bali was from Jakarta. Geoff Miller, the First Secretary at the embassy, was an ex-Tasmanian and in fact we had been to university together. He and his wife Rachel were accompanying the ambassador and his wife to Flores to inspect work being done by two Australian engineers under the Colombo Plan. Geoff said I could come along for the ride and do a story. They were flying in an Indonesian Airlines DC3 which would eventually fly on to West Timor and then return to pick us up from Flores. The ambassador seemed a bit distant when we met and I learned later that he wasn't too thrilled about Geoff having invited me on the Flores expedition.

We landed at the dirt airstrip at Maumere, on the southern side of the island, with the remains of a couple of crashed DC3 aircraft to one side to remind us that we were a long way from anywhere. The port, Ende, was on the northern side of the island, and the road connecting the two places was impassable because the approaches to the bridges had been washed away in recent wet seasons. The two Australian Colombo Plan engineers Max Loveday had come to meet were helping to build and repair both the bridges and the approaches to them in order to restore this vital link. Our DC3 flew on to West Timor but was scheduled to return the next day. We were met by the local *Bupati* (local government chief) and spent the day looking at some of the bridge projects with the amiable Aussie engineers. One of them told me that there was only one fridge at Maumere, in the Chinese store, and he and the owner had come to a very satisfactory arrangement about keeping their beer cold. Flores is mostly Christian and various parts of the island were colonised by both the Portuguese and the Dutch before independence. That night we were entertained at the *Bupati*'s house with a banquet and local dancers before retiring to our beds which unfortunately we shared with some bed bugs.

By 10 am next day we felt we'd exhausted Maumere's charms and were taken to the airstrip where a three-piece brass band banged and blew in our honour. After about twenty minutes, with still no sign of the aircraft, they fell silent, and we sat under the corrugated iron roof of an open-fronted shed, sweltering and waiting. The ambassador was getting more and more grumpy and kept asking Geoff Miller—who spoke fluent Bahasa—to find out what was going on. The airport manager, a small man in a crumpled white uniform and peaked cap, couldn't tell us anything. By midday it seemed the DC3 would not be coming that day and we went back to the *Bupati*'s house for lunch, surreptitiously scratching our bed bug bites from the night before.

Max suggested to the *Bupati* that they radio West Timor to find out what had happened to the aircraft. That would not be possible, said the *Bupati*, via Geoff's translation, because the Colombo Plan project to build a radio network along the archipelago hadn't yet reached Flores. And if something drastic had happened to the aircraft, what then? There was a boat in about a fortnight, said the *Bupati*. The ambassador looked stricken. There he was on a quick junket to Flores in the middle of a critical political and social situation in Jakarta, and he was marooned on Flores perhaps for as long as a month. The day dragged on and we had another dinner and more local dancing. The bed bugs seemed rejuvenated by their feast of the night before and no one slept well.

We were back at the airport again by 10 am with Max positively sulphurous. I stayed well away from him. Fortunately the brass band hadn't bothered to turn up this time. The airport manager was there, trembling with embarrassment and anguish. By 11 am there was still no sign of the plane. Max said to Geoff, 'Ask him if he thinks the aircraft will come today'. Geoff walked over and translated the question. The poor man looked anxiously at the horizon hoping he would see it coming. He thought for a moment and then said something to Geoff, who cracked up. 'How can I pass this on to Max?' Geoff explained. 'He said to me, "It is more than possible—and less than certain".' Mercifully the DC3 did turn up shortly afterwards. It had developed an electrical fault which the crew managed to fix overnight. We flew back along the line of islands and smoking volcanos to Bali, where we changed to a bigger aircraft for the flight to Jakarta.

During the end of my temporary stewardship of the ABC's Jakarta office Geoff and Rachel Miller were invited by their neighbour—an Indonesian judge—to his weekend retreat in the high country near Bogor. I was included in the party and we were entertained in what was obviously a mansion built in the Dutch colonial period. We sat out on wicker chairs, on beautifully manicured lawns, looking out over the plains towards Jakarta, enjoying both morning tea and the cool mountain air. The judge's wife said she would like to introduce her sister to us—a very odd looking woman. She had badly dyed red hair, unusual for an Indonesian, her face was heavily freckled, plastered with makeup and she wore dark glasses. The poor woman was obviously an albino. Our hostess made the introduction, saying that her sister was 'a prostitute from Macassar'. I caught Geoff's eye and looked away quickly. Our tea cups trembled on their fine bone china saucers.

I wondered what to say. 'Do you enjoy your work?' Or, 'How many tricks can you turn in a normal working day?' Something seemed not quite right, so Geoff, Rachel and I played things carefully. This was prudent, because as the conversation went on, it transpired that our hostess's sister was a lawyer, and indeed a prosecutor in Macassar.

Australia's foreign policy at that time was presided over by Paul Hasluck, the Minister for External Affairs. Back in Singapore I joined the jackals of the press at an airport press conference which consisted of Hasluck walking past a line of journalists, ignoring their questions. Paul Hasluck had once been a journalist himself; this experience had not tempered his later loathing and detestation of the profession. I managed to get in front of him with my tape recorder, and he paused briefly:

> TB: Mr Hasluck, does the Australian Government have any plans to assist Indonesia with the current state of its economy?
>
> HASLUCK: (Irritated) Look, I'm not going to respond to leading questions like that. There is an assumption in your statement that there *is* something wrong with the state of the Indonesian economy.
>
> (It wasn't often that Hasluck invited such a free kick, but we both knew that Indonesia was a financial basket case.)
>
> TB: (disingenuously) Well how would you describe the current state of the Indonesian economy, Mr Hasluck?

Got him! He glared at me and walked on without saying a word. No story, but I didn't care.

Wedding bells were ringing in Singapore. Don Simmons and Kim Dwyer had decided to tie the knot with a wedding in Singapore's historic St Andrew's Cathedral and, after a short honeymoon, return to Saigon. In the absence of close family, Peter Hollinshead was to give Kim away, I was to be Don's best man and Ros Kim's bridesmaid. The honeymoon suite at the Cockpit Hotel was booked and arrangements made for Don's bucks' night and Kim's last-night-out with the girls. Don's bucks' night promised to be a rip-roaring affair. Peter Hollinshead thought he had a great scheme to contain the drunks by hiring a barge, suitably stocked with booze and food, to cruise Singapore harbour.

Before we left, Kim took me to one side. 'Tim, you are Don's best man. I know that people get up to all kinds of mad tricks on bucks' nights, but I want you to promise me that you will be responsible for bringing him back to me—in one piece.' It seemed reasonable to say yes to that. Little did I know...

A barge full of cheerful correspondents and various local friends chugged away from the Singapore waterfront while we began to demolish the well-stocked eskies of cold ones. Hollinshead kept the skipper well supplied with beer as well, which was unfortunate as he got pissed and ran us onto a mud bank. He reversed the engines, but we were stuck. We were on a falling tide too, and faced the prospect of twelve hours there unless something was done quickly. There was no alternative to jumping over the side and trying to push the barge off. I was one of about half the barge's complement of drunks that did so. Our feet sank into glutinous black mud as we struggled to get a purchase on the barge to shift it. Those who had gone overboard started to resent the dry-shod bludgers who hadn't. I picked up a handful of mud and heaved it at my boss, hitting him in the face with a splodge of harbour sludge. Others in the water began pelting the other stay-on-boards as well. The bridegroom, who had joined those of us trying to save the ship, climbed back on board. We decided it was time for Hollinshead and Ferguson, who had stayed on board, to get muddy. The unmuddied ones retreated to the stern and prepared to fend us off. Simmo, mud streaked and wearing only his jocks, attempted to rugby tackle Hollinshead. Peter was a big man, who half turned and gave Don a forearm jolt. He hit the bridegroom in the head and shoulders, and Don was bounced overboard. In the melee, nobody noticed. But the skipper had reversed off the mud bank by then and we took off. After a while someone said, 'Where's Simmo?' To our collective horror, we realised he wasn't on board. I could hear the bride's words ringing in my ears. We searched in vain, returned to shore in a subdued frame of mind and went to the Hollinshead house to clean up.

Don, who was fortunately a strong swimmer, was surprised to see the barge heading off without him, and struck out for the lights of Singapore. He swam for about two kilometres, passed on occasions by Chinese pleasure boats who were surprised to see him and told him he shouldn't be swimming there at night because there were sharks. 'None of them offered to pick me up though.'

Unfortunately Don chose a wharf in a security area controlled by the Singapore Navy to try to get ashore. He saw an armed guard and called out to him. The sailor pointed his rifle at Don and said if he tried to come ashore he'd shoot him. Don said, 'How about a cigarette then?' The guard gave him one and Don smoked it treading water. 'Can I come ashore now?' he asked his new friend. 'No' came the reply. 'Well where can I get ashore?' The guard pointed to the lights of Collier Quay further along the harbour front. Don swam off, landed and hired a taxi. It says something for the enduring but fading prestige of the European in the East that a taxi would even stop for him. He didn't have any money either, but directed the driver to the Cockpit Hotel, which was managed by a rather precious gay we nicknamed 'Cufflinks' because he was always jangling and fiddling with them. Cufflinks happened to be in the foyer when a mud-stained Simmo walked in clad only in his underpants, asked the desk clerk to pay his taxi and requested the key of the honeymoon suite. With as much dignity as he could muster in the circumstances he walked up the stairs and disappeared leaving a distraught Cufflinks wondering if his mind had given way.

One of my assignments was to cover the 1966 Philippines elections, when Ferdinand Marcos defeated President Macapagal. It was not immediately apparent that he proposed to assault the country's hard-won democracy so assiduously. I always enjoyed going to the Philippines. English was widely spoken everywhere, the amazingly free and candid press was also in English and the people were delightful with a great sense of humour.

Foreign correspondents then were not slaves to channels of communication as they are today. Most of my copy was still sent to Sydney and Radio Australia by cable—a practice dating back to the days of Morse. You were billed by the word, and there was a cable-jargon where words were run together whenever possible, and the definite article dispensed with. Words like UNPROCEED instead of 'do not go' were more economical. Sentences were separated by the word STOP. I went down to the General Post Office in Manila to file my cable on the latest election news headed MANILA EXBOWDEN UPDATE ELECTION. I handed over my cable and the telegraphist said, 'Why don't you send it by Telex?' I remember asking, 'What's that?' I don't recall exactly what he said but he did say it was quicker. It certainly was. I hung about for a few minutes to buy some stamps and was just walking out when the telegraphist came running out calling my name, 'Oh just a minute Mr Bowden, Sydney has a query on your story...'

'Sydney has *what*?' The awful realisation dawned that this was instant communication. 'Tell them I've left!' It was clear that the era of a correspondent's relative independence was ending.

Cables had been a great journalistic tradition. There are many stories told of the legendary *Daily Express* foreign editor Charles Foley as he attempted to get value for money out of his far-flung correspondents. Most of them were not unfond of a drink, and one had been sent to Cairo on an unusually vague assignment. The correspondent propped up the bar at Shepherd's Hotel and didn't file for a week. Foley cabled him, WHY UNNEWS QUERY FOLEY?

The Cairo correspondent ordered another drink and reached for a message pad, which the well-trained waiters immediately filed for him. UNNEWS IS GOOD NEWS.

Within an hour, an 'urgent' boomeranged from London. UNNEWS UNJOB STOP FOLEY.

Cairo seems to have been a hazardous assignment on the job front. Another correspondent on assignment there for some months for the *Express* had a girlfriend in Beirut—then famous as the Paris of the Middle East. He used to slip off to see her every weekend, but unfortunately for him the Egyptian army chose a Sunday to overthrow King Farouk, on 23 July 1952. Foley knew where he was though, and an ominous rocket arrived from London. FAROUK ABDICATED STOP WHAT YOUR PLANS?

My favourite cable story concerns the wayward foreign correspondent who decided to jump the gun by resigning. His economically worded resignation saved him five words—UPSTICK JOB ARSEWARDS.

Resignation was a concept far from my own thoughts, however. I just loved being a correspondent in Southeast Asia and hoped I could stay in my present job for a long time. I had no way of knowing, as I left Singapore for some home leave in Tasmania just before Christmas 1966, that my days in the region were numbered.

10 How are your teeth?

The terms and conditions of my arduous tropical service (the ABC overseas staff worked under Department of External Affairs guidelines) gave me home leave once a year as well as two weeks in the Cameron Highlands of Malaya. This was a quaint colonial hangover from the days before airconditioning when toiling public servants were permitted a break in the 'high country' to play golf and recharge their heat-exhausted personal batteries. (It was not, however, compulsory. You could take the equivalent of the return train fare and go somewhere else.) I did not regard Singapore as a hardship post, which was how it was officially categorised. Frankly, to quote Harold Macmillan, I'd 'never had it so good'.

I flew home to Tasmania on leave (first class, of course) and enjoyed a Christmas with the Bowden clan at the family weekender Askelon. With consummate journalistic timing I flew out of Hobart the day before the 7 February bushfires-among the most disastrous ever to strike our bushfire-prone continent. A lethal combination of high temperatures and tempestuous winds as high as 80 km/h swept the fires down from the forests on the flanks of Mount Wellington to within two kilometres of the centre of Hobart. At the peak of the disaster the hot winds blew many of the fires together so that they destroyed everything they touched. In some places the temperatures were so high the bitumen on the roads melted and burst into flame. Rogue wind gusts carried the fire from exploding gum trees—and houses—five and ten kilometres in a few seconds. One survivor said, 'It was as though the wind was on fire'.

Fire-fighters could do little because of the scale and unpredictability of the wind-driven fires. Some brick and glass houses simply exploded (or imploded) before the actual flames reached them, while timber houses nearby were untouched. At Middleton, a coastal hamlet to the south-east of Hobart, forty people survived by walking into the sea and standing around a small boat in which pregnant women and small children sat. The fires even burnt the seaweed on the beach and at the water's edge. Thousands of sheep, cattle and other livestock were burnt alive on farms in southern Tasmania. At least 1400 buildings were incinerated, 1500 cars destroyed and 62 Tasmanians lost their lives. One of them was Geoff Davis, father of Neil, who had been fighting fires near Sorell. His life was snuffed out in one of the unpredictable wind and flame shifts.

Communications went down and I sat impotently in Melbourne trying to find out if my parents' and aunts' houses had survived—they were in bush surroundings in the foothills of Mount Nelson. My brothers, Nicholas and Philip, managed to help save several houses in our neighbourhood, in company with their friends. The Bowdens were lucky, but many of their friends lost everything.

(The ABC failed to rise to the occasion during this catastrophe. In the days before I left I had enjoyed several celebratory lunches in the cellar of a photographic studio next to the General Post Office, and just across the road from the ABC. A former photographer from *The Mercury*, Brian Curtis, had gone out into business on his own, and had sponsored what we called 'The Lunchtime O'Booze Club', named after the famed columnist in the British satirical magazine *Private Eye*. The day of the fires Curtis hosted one of his legendary long lunches, attended among others by John Lonergan, the Program Director of the ABC. Down in the cool, protected cellar, shickered and happy, the lunch guests were unaware that Hobart was burning around their ears. Lonergan and the other guests staggered out at 6 pm to find a copper coloured sky and ash raining down. In Lonergan's absence (no one knew where he was) normal programming had continued on the ABC all the afternoon—in contrast to the commercial stations, 7HO and 7HT, who had done a wonderful job co-ordinating rescue efforts and broadcasting warnings from the police and fire-fighting units of when people should abandon their houses and get out of certain areas.)

Having established at last that all my family was safe, I continued on my way back to Singapore to reclaim my car (which Ros had been using happily) and getting back to work. A month later, Peter Hollinshead called me into his office and said that it had been decided to send me to the ABC's North American office, in New York. I said that I didn't want to go, thank you very much.

Peter said that it wasn't for me to say. My former colleague in Tasmania, David Wilson (who had been acting in my old job of Supervisor of Talks), was one of the unfortunate victims of the fire. He and his wife and young children were homeless, having lost absolutely all they possessed. The ABC's new General Manager, Talbot Duckmanton, decided that he would help them with their immediate accommodation problem by giving them an overseas posting. New York had been suggested, but the ABC Representative there, Charles Buttrose, was horrified when he heard that David Wilson was not a trained journalist. He argued that the office was too small to support a Talks man who was not able to file news stories. So it was decided David would go to Singapore—a bigger office—and I would go to New York.

I was a reluctant starter. Ros and I were very happy together and moving on would be sweet goodbye to her and also to flat, servant, new car and a region I found endlessly fascinating. Somehow, I wasn't ready to propose to Ros and in those days the ABC didn't allow non-married partners to accompany their correspondents. Even if Ros had said yes to the then unasked question we would have had to get married in a scrambling rush. So I just gallantly said, 'Cheerio, it's been great', and shot through. Ros told me later that she was surprised by this but got on with her life by signing up with Gleneagles Hospital for a two-year contract

David Wilson and his wife Annette arrived in Singapore in time for a week's handover. I arrived at their hotel with my car and said, 'Well here we are in one of the world's great shopping bazaars. I am at your disposal, where would you like to go?' Annette said, 'Could you take me somewhere where we can buy some plastic coat hangers?'

Peter Hollinshead was putting a brave face on things. He was a quick and shrewd judge of people and he could see David was going to be a challenge. Hollings didn't like mollycoddling people. He liked self-starters who just got on with things. There wasn't much I could show or tell David. He knew about tape recorders and editing. The rest was up to him.

Like poor old Mac I had to unload my car at the last minute. I sold my beloved Brabham Viva to a beaming Chinese who knew (a) that it was practically a new car and (b) that I had to sell it. I wasn't in a good bargaining position and lost heaps. Events moved so quickly there was hardly time for even an office farewell, although a brief drinks and nibbles was arranged. I was quite glum about leaving although I suppose I should have been relishing new challenges. New York seemed a poor swap for my beloved Singapore.

I flew to London on my way to New York and stopped off there briefly. (I was delighted to find that Geoff and Rachel Miller from Jakarta were on the same aircraft. They had been posted to New York with their two small boys, Stephen and Jonathan.) At Bush House things seemed strangely the same with familiar faces along the bar at the BBC Club. One producer said, 'Hello old boy. I haven't seen you around for a while.' It had been four years.

Charles Buttrose, the ABC's North American Representative, was kind enough to meet me at John F Kennedy airport with Peter Barnett who was in town from the Washington office. Peter told me later that as they saw me walking towards them, Charles thought I was wearing suede shoes. (I wasn't.) He said, 'Christ, I hope they haven't sent me one of those Talks poofters'. We drove together into the concrete canyons of New York where the ABC had a suite of offices in the Rockefeller Centre on Sixth Avenue (Avenue of the Americas), while the other ABC—the American Broadcasting Company—had a skyscraper just up the road. The confusion between the two was to cause me considerable anguish later in my New York term.

Buttrose had been a Charles Moses man, with the internal title of D Pub and Con—Director of Publicity and Concerts. He was an ex-newspaper executive, having worked for two notoriously cantankerous press barons—Ezra Norton on the *Daily Mirror* and Frank Packer on the *Daily Telegraph*. As D Pub and Con he had not only been in charge of all ABC publicity and promotions in radio and television, but was also the supremo of the ABC's huge concerts empire, which had symphony orchestras in each state and co-ordinated and looked after a stellar cast of eminent conductors and soloists who toured Australia for the ABC. It was an area close to the heart of the former General Manager Sir Charles Moses, who loved entertaining the visiting conductors, violinists and pianists— many of whom only toured Australia because they liked his style. Buttrose, who had also been a singer in his varied career, knew a lot about the music business and welcomed a good party or two along the way.

Parties and bonhomie were not the forte, however, of the incoming General Manager, Talbot Duckmanton, an austere bureaucrat, who not only distanced himself from this kind of personal relationship with overseas artists, but was quick to move on Moses's inner circle and put in his own team. Buttrose was exiled to New York, but once the initial disappointment of his loss of power and influence had subsided, he recovered his customary ebullience and began to build up the North American office. He and his wife Margot loved New York, and he quickly established a rapport with legendary musical entrepreneurs like Sol Hurok as well as with soloists and conductors. Being an old journo he found it difficult to stop acting like a news editor to the correspondents in North America who certainly weren't responsible to him editorially—but to their Sydney masters. I must say I always found Charlie's suggestions worthwhile and often took them up. If I didn't, he wasn't fussed.

The ABC offices had no studio or broadcasting facilities on site. My Talks predecessors, Keith Mackriell and my Hobart mentor Anthony Rendell, had to take their scripts and tapes to a hired studio to feed their material through a precarious linkage of booked lines to Sydney. Neither of them filed for News. Since Anthony had moved on to London, the gap had been filled by Terry Brown, my old flatmate from Launceston days, and Bob Connolly—a young journalist on a world tour who had lobbed in to New York and was helping out until I arrived. The morning current affairs radio program *AM* began in Australia in September 1967 and was particularly dependent on foreign news. Terry and Bob were feeding the News and Talks machine on a daily basis, using the telephone rather than booking a land-line. With the COMPAC cable by then linking the United States, the United Kingdom and Australia, the sound quality of broadcasts fed down the telephone line was good enough to pass muster. In fact, it was often better than a booked, painfully strung together land-line. All you had to do was bypass the telephone microphone by unscrewing the handset and putting crocodile clips on the wires, then playing your taped items straight down the line to be recorded in Sydney. Both Bob and Terry were trying to justify their existence in New York and had therefore built up a daily service to both News and Talks that I was expected to maintain.

There was certainly plenty of news about. New York, and indeed the whole of America, was beginning a long and dramatic hot summer. There had been race riots in Newark and Detroit just before I arrived in New York—following bad rioting in Watts. The black civil rights movement had become impatient for change and the ghettos had erupted with a powerful combination of frustration, rage and stifling summer heat. New York was edgy. The commuter trains of Wall Street businessmen, who lived in all-white suburbs on Long Island, came into Manhattan on elevated railways over Harlem. I saw a story in the *New York Times* describing the terrified 'suits' lying on the floor of their carriages because snipers were firing at the trains on their way to work.

On my first night in Manhattan Terry Brown suggested we take a taxi and drive around mid-town to show me a bit of New York and also check out the security situation. As we turned into Seventh Avenue I heard a shot and saw a black man crumple to the sidewalk. Terry and I both crouched down in the back seat of the taxi while the driver swerved violently and hurtled into a side street. We had fluked seeing a drive-by shooting by a bunch of red-neck whites, right in the heart of New York. Because it was my first night there and we had actually seen this poor bloke shot, I followed up the next day and found which hospital he had been taken to. I went to see him. He was a bit mystified about who I was and why I was there, and why a foreign news man would be interested in him, but told me he was an encyclopaedia salesman from the South and had just come to New York to work. He liked walking and was on his way home when he was shot in his side, at waist level, just missing his kidneys. His prognosis was good. I asked him how he felt about what had happened and he just shrugged and said that shit happened. He didn't appear to be bitter or angry. I guess if you were black in the US in those days you didn't have high expectations.

Peter Barnett had just left New York to open the ABC's Washington bureau, and Terry Brown had replaced him. Peter had suggested I take over the lease of his studio apartment in New York, which happened to be on Central Park South, near Columbus Circle, with a fabulous view right up the full length of Central Park. I was within walking distance of Carnegie Hall and the Lincoln Centre. It was also close enough to the Rockefeller Centre for me to be able to walk to work. (There was a lot of development going on at the time and I remember seeing fine flakes of asbestos floating down into Sixth Avenue like snow from the new skyscrapers under construction.) The apartment only had one room and a small kitchen and bathroom, but that was fine by me. The sofa pulled out into a king-sized bed that was extremely comfortable. I also inherited 'dear old Miss Etta', Peter's black cleaning lady who was to rob me before I left New York.

Peter had a lot of black friends, some of them dating back to the time he lived in the US while with the Moral Re-Armament Movement a decade earlier. Apart from Miss Etta, I also had an introduction to his dentist. Being a Tasmanian and growing up in the days before fluoride was introduced to the drinking water, I seemed to have more amalgam in my mouth than teeth. After some small talk, the dentist asked me to open wide and shoved in his mirror and probes. He gave a long low whistle. This didn't sound like good news. I managed to mutter, 'What's the matter—decay?'

'Buddy', he said, 'you've got so much metal back there it's not decay that's the problem—it's rust!' We got on just fine, and he was the best dentist I had experienced until then.

Much of the work of the News and Talks staff in New York was to act as a conduit for the 'actuality' broadcast by the major networks. In Southeast Asia you could not rely on the local press for information. The situation was reversed in North America. There was no way we could match the reportorial resources of the *New York Times*, *Washington Post*, CBS, NBC and the American Broadcasting Company. A lot of our work was to put breaking news in context, and incorporate, say, the voice of President Johnson making

How are your teeth?

a statement on the Vietnam War—actuality recorded directly from network television or news radio. Charles Buttrose didn't need much convincing that we had to have an editing space and sound-proofed 'studio' on the premises for our radio reports. We had a desk built with three reel-to-reel Ampex tape recorders incorporated, and a system to patch the output directly down the phone line. There was a Tandberg tape recorder for cut-editing, and dub-editing could also be done on the Ampex machines.

Because *AM* was an early morning program, I was able to pick the eyes out of breaking stories in the US and feed them to Sydney in the mid to late afternoon. Stories with a particular Australian interest had to be obtained in the conventional way. For instance, there was the United Nations Committee of 24 which met every year to review countries still under colonial control. Australia's stewardship of Papua New Guinea was a perennial target, particularly for African and Asian delegates who generally gave us a hard time over Australia's tardiness in preparing Papua New Guinea for independence. That was of little interest to the US news machine and was reported directly by us.

The UN had its own press corps who guarded its territory jealously and was not forthcoming to newcomers like me. I found the UN grindingly boring, and I was not alone in that. If you wanted you could attend some country's reception every day. The UN catering provided uniform canapés whether it was Mozambique or Finland as the host nation. It was always the same: meat balls with a savoury sauce or totally predictable white-bread sandwiches with standard fillings. There also seemed to be a particular breed of large, loud, well-heeled New York matrons, members of the UN Hospitality Committee, who helped host these cocktail parties, invariably drinking lethal martinis.

Accreditation at the UN gave me access to the plush Members Bar, Lounge and Dining Room. Behind the bar was a map of the world with all the countries cleverly shaped from pieces of wood and attached to the wall by wooden ferrules. Under Australia,

Tasmania was upside down. For nearly two years I eyed it off mournfully, planning to absorb enough Dutch courage to vault over the bar and twist it around the right way. But I never did. It is probably still reversed to this day.

The UN beat did produce its lighter moments. My friend Geoff Miller's new post was First Secretary to the Australian Mission to the UN. He told me that a senior New Zealand diplomat told him he was becoming increasingly irritated by the propensity of the Russian delegates to weave banal Russian proverbs into their debates at the UN. Stuff like: 'When the ears of corn are ripe—the farmer sharpens his scythe.' Even the Soviet Premier, Nikita Khrushchev, had been doing it. Geoff's friend told him the next time it happened he was going to respond with an ancient Maori proverb he had just made up. 'The crayfish thinks he is a very splendid fellow, because his coat is red—but his head is full of shit.' He was not able to deliver this inspired fabrication formally, but he made sure it circulated around every UN committee so the Russians would get the message.

In 1967 the biggest international story was the Six Day War launched by Israel against Egypt, Syria and Jordan after the United Nations Emergency Forces (UNEF) were forced to withdraw from the Egyptian–Israeli border, following a request by Egypt's President Nasser. Thus the United Nations was powerless to intervene after Nasser announced a blockade of the Straits of Tiran for all goods bound to and from Israel. In the short and potent action that followed Israel captured the Sinai Peninsula and the Gaza Strip—as well as gaining control over part of Jerusalem and the Golan Heights.

In the United States the nation was rocked by the deaths, on 27 January, of three NASA astronauts—Gus Grissom, Ed White and Roger Chaffee—in a fire during a 'full dress rehearsal' for the Apollo space program. Fires also blazed in the black ghettos of Watts, Newark and Detroit as American blacks rioted and rebelled against the institutionalised discrimination against them.

On a lighter note, the hippie movement spread from California to the East Coast of the United States, the Beatles' album *Sergeant*

How are your teeth?

Pepper's Lonely Hearts Club Band took over the jukeboxes of the nation, the venerable British yachtsman Francis Chichester sailed solo around the world and in South Africa a surgeon, Christiaan Barnard, performed the world's first heart transplant.

One Australian story that strained our slender resources was the coverage of the Americas Cup challenge at Newport Rhode Island in September 1967, when the Australian challenger *Dame Pattie* was pitted against the New York Yacht Club's *Intrepid*. The Americans won, but at one stage it looked as though *Dame Pattie*, skippered by Jock Sturrock, might even win a race.

Iain Finlay was living and working in New York at the time as a freelance reporter and offered his services to the ABC. The Sporting Department was as paranoid about News or Talks people covering for them as the News Department was about non-journalists reporting for the sacred news bulletins. Iain, who had some yachting experience, was hired to report for ABC Sport, and I was to cover for News and Talks. I hadn't met Iain Finlay and his partner Trish Sheppard before, and it was the beginning of a long friendship. Their daughter Zara was a toddler at the time, and Iain rented a flat at Newport and said I was welcome to stay with them. We were allocated office space in a historic building called The Armoury. A local technician organised ship to shore communications to carry commentary from a retired US Navy captain and Iain, who were on the press boat following the races. I would either relay that commentary directly to Sydney, or record it on my trusty Tandberg for later cut-editing and replay down the phone line using the primitive but effective crocodile clips on the phone terminals. It was all rather Mickey Mouse, but it worked perfectly.

The Australians were very popular in Newport where there was a terrific atmosphere. Iain, Trish and I used to frequent the Black Pearl restaurant and bar on the waterfront where the yachties of both teams used to hang out and pick up the latest gossip and news on the competition. I remember the hit tune 'A Whiter Shade of Pale' by a group called Procol Harum that was blaring from every waterfront jukebox. I can never hear that song without thinking of the Americas Cup, 1967.

Iain had an added burden—television. How he did it, I will never know. International satellite feeds for television were in their infancy, very expensive and had to emanate from New York. Each of the Australian networks had its own on-air presenters in Newport to cover the cup. Channel Nine had Mike Ramsden and Channel Seven their quiz king Bob Dyer—of all people. Neither channel, nor the ABC, could afford separate satellite feeds, so there had to be a pool. Nine wouldn't accept Dyer, nor would Seven countenance Ramsden. Charles Buttrose in New York tried to broker a deal where the ABC would provide a presenter. But who? Peter Barnett had his Washington responsibilities and knew as much about yachting as he did nuclear physics. Buttrose then offered Iain Finlay who was not only a personable presenter but did know something about yachting. The fact that he had very little television experience was not emphasised. Nine and Seven reluctantly agreed to the deal, which was for a pooled coverage shot specially by the CBS network. Film would be flown to New York during each race day and edited into a half-hour coverage.

So after working all day doing radio interviews and race commentaries for ABC Sport—as well as two or three television pieces to camera plus interviews—Iain Finlay would collect the last film package of the day from the Press Centre, which included the end-of-the-day press conference, and race to the airport for a flight to New York. There he would work at the CBS Studios until about one the following morning and write a script that would hopefully fit the film footage he had yet to see. He would then see the half-hour package for the first time, and would have an hour, sometimes less, to re-jig his script to actually relate to the edited film which could still change before 2.30 am—the deadline for the satellite feed to Australia. Iain would do his commentary live, keeping one eye on the monitor to adjust for any last minute alterations. At 3 am there would be a post-mortem and planning meeting with the producers for the day that had already begun. Iain—or what was left of him—would then take a taxi to La Guardia Airport to meet a 5 am charter flight that would get him back to Newport in time for the day's racing. He managed a cat-nap in the taxi, on the seats of the airport, and doesn't remember much about the flight back.

He did this for three successive days and nights, until, fortunately for him, the Australians called for a 'lay day', which allowed him to fill up his sleep bucket a bit. Day five—the day of the fourth race—was the end for the Australians. The US, with *Intrepid* skippered by 'Bus' Mosbacher, triumphed over *Dame Pattie* four–nil.

At the end of it all there was a big race dinner in one of the historic Newport waterfront mansions called The Breakers. It was a big deal. Sir Robert Menzies was to be the keynote speaker at the dinner, and Dame Pattie would accompany him. The technician who steered us through the race without incident said he usually did the public address for the dinner, but had lost out to a rival. 'He won't be able to do it', said our man. 'He hasn't got the equipment.'

Charlie Buttrose and Margot flew in from New York for the occasion. As we waited for the dinner to begin, a striking trio walked in the main door. Sir Frank Packer—his face reminiscent of a gargoyle—was supported on each side by his large sons, Kerry and Clyde. Charles was beside himself at the sight. 'Hasn't Frank got a lovely face', he said unkindly. (Ever the consummate professional, Charles had written editorials for Packer in the *Daily Telegraph*, often having to swing their thrust 180° at the last minute after the old man changed his mind.)

The time came for Sir Robert Menzies to speak. As he began, the microphone started to whistle and feedback echoed throughout the elegant surrounds of The Breakers. Always contemptuous of newfangled technology, the PM pushed the offensive apparatus away and continued his speech—now only heard by the few tables immediately around him. To fit everyone in, tables had been set in adjoining rooms. The PA was vital to the diners (who had paid huge sums for the privilege) being able to hear what Menzies had to say. They heard nothing. Our technician had been spot-on.

Among the mix of think pieces, commentaries, current affairs segments and documentaries I produced from New York was the odd light-hearted quickie for the national breakfast show, then compered from Melbourne by the much-loved Peter Evans. I liked his droll style and sense of humour, and used to send him snippets I thought would amuse.

It's when you first move into a new culture you notice things that after a while become part of the furniture. So one day in a hamburger joint I was amused to hear the shorthand jargon of the short-order cooks. The word 'scratch' was the shortening of 'A plain hamburger from scratch'. While I was waiting, a customer ordered a plain 'burger, and the counter jockey yelled 'scratch!' 'Oh, I don't want any butter on the bun', added the customer. 'Hold the bee on that scratch', was the instant cry. I did little items like that for Peter. In one piece—and now I can't remember why—I played a short tune on my teeth, a party trick I'd developed.

As long as I can remember I have played tunes on my teeth. It is done by flicking my thumb nail against my front lower choppers, and using my mouth as an echo chamber. My brother Nicholas does it too, usually in reflective moments. It isn't all that difficult but I haven't found many other people who do it. It is a great way to entertain small children, and even bigger people. Its effect is greatly enhanced by using a microphone and amplification. Over the years I have developed variations, such as smacking my cheek with an open hand, although this is not recommended for long pieces. Great virtuosity can be achieved by using a wooden pencil and strumming between the upper and lower front teeth for fast moving numbers like 'Holiday for Strings'.

Another piece I did for Evans had to do with the telephone. Although every telephone today has buttons and beeps instead of a round cylinder with holes for each number, I found them a new experience in New York. Experimenting in an idle moment, I discovered I could play 'Show Me the Way to Go Home' on the touch tone telephone. To embellish this achievement I managed to record a version complete with ukulele obbligato for Peter's breakfast show.

In October Charlie Buttrose announced that our new General Manager, Talbot Duckmanton, was coming to New York to inspect our operation and go on to Washington—where Peter Barnett had been able to get him a long meeting with President Johnson, a tremendous coup which did much to enhance Peter's prestige in the eyes of the GM. (Peter tells the full story of this quite bizarre meeting in his autobiography *Foreign Correspondence*.)

In New York we didn't have exaggerated expectations of being taken out to a lavish lunch or dinner. Charles told us of a very quaint experience the previous Christmas when Duckers (as the GM was known) had come to town. He announced he would take the office staff out to dinner on Christmas Eve. Everyone had a light lunch and prepared to knock the GM's expense account to leg. Duckmanton led them up Sixth Avenue to the corner of 57th Street, where he ushered them into a Horn & Hardart Automat café. This was a cheap food chain which had sandwiches, snacks and slices of pecan pie in small pigeon holes behind glass panels. Customers helped themselves from this display and took their trays to the cash register to pay. The ABC crew sat down, a bit bewildered. 'Order what you like', said the GM, puffing away at his perennial pipe, which he tamped and prodded with a collection of instruments on a small key ring. As they picked away at their cold sangers Duckmanton finished his coffee and said, 'Well I suppose you are all wondering why I brought you here?' There was a polite but subdued response to this rhetorical sally.

'This is a very sentimental moment for me. The first time I ever came to New York, as a young man, I was alone, it was Christmas Eve, and I ate here at Horn & Hardart.'

Now that's style.

My moment of truth with Duckmanton came as I walked with him back to his hotel from the ABC office. While fuelling and tamping his pipe he told me that he was quite pleased with the work I was doing in New York. But there was one thing that troubled him. He didn't like the jokey spots I was doing for Peter Evans's breakfast show. 'The trouble is, Tim (puff puff), that it is difficult for people to listen to you reporting from the United Nations on *AM*, and then (puff) take you seriously after you have played tunes on your teeth on the breakfast session.'

I thought to myself that he and I had very different views about broadcasting. How many listeners, I wondered, would remember a sententious report of mine from the United Nations on the Committee of 24 ten years on? The situation was even more delicate because it was painfully obvious Duckmanton hadn't heard my latest effort for Evans with the touch tone telephone and ukulele obbligato.

(Ten years later almost to the day I was at a party in Sydney. My host introduced me to another guest. 'Tim Bowden', he said. 'I know that name. You used to broadcast for the ABC from New York.' He turned to his partner, 'Hey Rosemary, this is the bloke who used to play tunes on his teeth!')

Although I pined for Singapore and the Southeast Asian beat, life in New York had its moments. The great pianist Artur Rubinstein—then in his eighties—used to perform every year at Carnegie Hall. Because of the popularity of this concert, he allowed part of the audience to sit up on the stage. I managed to get one of these tickets and sat within a few metres of the old man, watching his huge, gnarled hands stroke the keys of the big Steinway grand, playing Chopin and Schubert. A New York friend also took me to the famous Rainbow Room where I saw Duke Ellington perform in his trademark white suit playing a white grand piano.

On weekends I often teamed up with the Millers and their little boys to visit Bronx zoo or take a ferry to the Statue of Liberty. Long Island beaches were a disappointment to Australians, with grey sand and equally grey water. New York dumped its garbage at sea.

I attempted to throw a tennis ball once and was quickly disciplined by a ranger as that was strictly forbidden. A school friend, Ian Parker, who was a surgeon-commander in the Australian Navy, contacted me from Boston where his ship was in port and I took a train up to see him. Some of my assignments took in the opening of Expo in Montreal and a flying visit to New Orleans where I delighted in the traditional jazz performed by veteran black musicians. My old friend Spike Bryden was doing post-graduate work at the University of Carolina and when I visited him and Elizabeth I discovered that my one-syllable name expanded to two in the deep South—'Tyum'.

One of the unenviable duties of the New York Talks officer was to attend the annual meetings of the Intertel group, composed of the British Broadcasting Corporation, the Canadian Broadcasting Corporation, Westinghouse Broadcasting Company in the US and the Australian Broadcasting Commission. Intertel existed to co-ordinate the production of documentary programs which would be shown in all four countries. My Talks predecessor, Anthony Rendell, had warned me about what happened at these meetings. 'The other members always send top executives, but the ABC sends the likes of us because we never, ever fulfil our obligations and produce the documentaries on time, or even at all. The other members know this, and are always quite nice about it. But it is very embarrassing.'

On this occasion, however, the Intertel meeting coincided with a visit to New York by the ABC's Assistant General Manager (Administration) Wally Hamilton, and I was to attend the meeting under his wing.

Wally's visits to New York were more fruitful than Duckmanton's on the entertainment front. Charles said that Wally always took the staff to a reasonably up-market restaurant and had the endearing habit of ordering wine from the price list rather than by the name. He always chose a high-priced wine near but not at the top of the range. And indeed he did. I hadn't been at the Automat debacle, but had no quarrel with Wally's approach.

Wally Hamilton was a small man with a clipped, severe-looking moustache. He was a devout Catholic and a former Controller of ABC News which he ruled with a rod of iron. He had a reputation of being a hard man, but fair. I hadn't met him before I went to Singapore, and got off to a bad start. Wally was not the kind of man who appreciated practical jokes but on this occasion I couldn't help myself. It was my job to take him to the airport for his flight to London, and a Reuters executive—a pleasant New Zealander, Derek Round—was leaving on the same plane. As we neared the check-in counter, Derek asked me to hold his travel wallet while he adjusted a strap on his suitcase. I noticed his passport, and on a whim, slipped it into my pocket. Derek got to the counter, presented his ticket and looked in his wallet for his passport. It was not there. He quickly searched his pockets and stood there ashen faced. I let him stew for about a minute before handing him his passport. Wally Hamilton had been watching all this and was unimpressed. 'You have no future in our organisation Mr Bowden', he said grimly as he walked through the departure gate without looking back. I hoped he was joking.

We hadn't met since. As we walked together down Sixth Avenue on our way to the Intertel meeting, I was struggling for a safe topic of conversation. Wally wasn't a great man for idle chatter. I found myself burbling about the richness of classical music available on records in New York. I told Wally I'd been able to purchase the entire organ works of J S Bach in a 20-record set for only US$20. There was a pause while Wally considered what I had said. 'Bach was an orderly man', he replied. We walked on in silence. There didn't seem to be anything further to say.

As usual the Intertel players had sent their top guns—and this time so had we. Sir Huw Wheldon was carrying the BBC's baton. I think he was the BBC's head of television. He had made his name on the televised arts magazine program *Monitor*. He was a tall, pompous man and I disliked him instantly. The progress of the various previously agreed documentary projects was discussed. The ABC was in default as usual but Wally got over that by not saying anything. Indeed, he hardly said anything at all during the whole meeting.

Eventually the conversation got around to satellite broadcasting, very much a new toy in world television. Huw Welbred (as *Private Eye* always called him) got terribly excited about the prospect of putting on a debate that could be seen live at the same time by all the participating Intertel countries. He seemed not to care that if British and North American audiences could share a reasonable broadcast time, Australians would have to watch at some graveyard slot in the early hours of the morning.

'What we need is an informed debate on matters of world importance by distinguished world statesmen—not these damned young radicals like Danny Cohn-Bendit—but retired statesmen like Sir Robert Menzies in Australia, Sir Harold Macmillan in Britain, John Diefenbaker in Canada and perhaps Harry Truman in the United States.' (Everyone in the room, except Welbred, knew that Diefenbaker was by then barking mad with dementia.) Wheldon ploughed on. 'We haven't yet finalised a title. We have a working title—look, I know it's not right—*This Shining Hope*.'

This was too much for me. 'Why don't you call it *The Geriatric Hour*?'

I thought Welbred was about to have a seizure. He went brick red with rage and harrumphed that my attitude was just the reason why he didn't want any young contributors to the debate. I could see the WBC representative killing himself with laughter and the CBS Head of English Programs, Gene Hallman, hiding a smile. Wally was stony faced and looking straight ahead. I was never sent to another Intertel meeting.

Life at the ABC office in the Rockefeller Centre was hectic. Bob Connolly had continued his world tour but the programs he had been servicing were howling for more material. I needed a freelance to take up some of the slack, and fast. In the door one day came an Australian, Terry Hughes, who had been working as a television director with the BBC's *Late Night Line-Up* in London. He asked if there was any work. I said there was, if he could do it. Terry had been a behind-the-scenes director, encouraging good performances from others, but had never broadcast himself. He was particularly interested in show business and the arts, so I got him to write a piece on the latest Off Broadway shows. The script was good, but Terry was a softly spoken, shy person and read it without conviction. I was fairly brutal. He had to change his persona for 'on air' work or there was no future for him as a freelance. I read a part of his script to show him what I meant, and pushed him into our new studio to invent the new, forceful, authoritative Terry. He was in there for about half an hour. Every now and then I could hear thumps and bangs as he pounded the desk either in frustration or rage. Eventually he burst out, wild-eyed, with a tape in his hand. I played it. He had made the breakthrough!

Terry Hughes quickly became an indispensable member of the New York ABC team and worked there as a freelance, or on contract, for the next twenty-five years. He developed a faithful following of listeners who shared his enthusiasm for entertainers and artists.

By November I had adjusted to New York on a practical and professional level but emotionally I was a bit of a basket case. I was lonely and I missed Ros, but I wasn't admitting that to myself. There had been no contact between us for seven months. A weekend away changed all that. My fellow cadet reporter on *The Mercury* in Hobart, Michael Philp, had stopped adventuring on yachts in Central America, had married an American girl and become a university lecturer in English at the University of Maryland in Annapolis. He and Susie invited me down to spend a few days with them. I left New York with one of the worst hangovers I have ever had, and resorted to my emergency green pills. These had been given to me by an obliging chemist friend in Launceston for unspeakable hangovers. They were prescription drugs—I think they were probably amphetamines. I only had a few left but I took two of them as I boarded the train to Annapolis. They were magic. Cool streams of water flowed through my numbed brain. I sat in the carriage looking out the window at the bleak winter landscape and admitted to myself that I missed Ros like hell and I had been a bloody fool to leave her in Singapore. At the end of the journey I was still thinking about her and resolved to do something about the absurd situation I had got myself into when I got back to New York.

Mike and Susie had just produced their first son, Tas. Always a boating enthusiast, Mike had built a traditional cat boat and we sailed it to sheltered coves on Chesapeake Bay and picnicked, while Suzie breast-fed Tas. Their obvious commitment and happiness fuelled my determination to try to re-unite with Ros. I had turned thirty in August and wandered miserably around Times Square on my birthday wondering what I was doing with my life. I think many young people get a strong nesting urge at that time in their lives, but before I took the green pills, I had thought marriage was not for me.

When I got back to New York I still felt strongly that I should contact Ros. It was highly likely she would tell me to get stuffed. She might even have another feller. I knew my international times, and put my phone call through to the nursing quarters at Gleneagles Hospital early in the morning to catch Ros before she went to work. What I couldn't know was that she had just got to sleep after finishing a week's night shift. The Chinese hospital switchboard operator misheard 'America'. She told a groggy Ros that a Tim Bowden was calling from Malacca.

I had my spiel all worked out, but it was a difficult and fraught call for both of us. Ros asked me first what I was doing in Malacca. We sorted that out and I blurted out that I had been missing her like hell and I was a bloody fool to leave her in Singapore and how about we got married. There was a long silence. Then she said, 'Tim, that's not fair'.

It was not the answer I expected, but it wasn't a dead-set no. We agreed that Ros could not really respond properly to one telephone call out of the blue after seven months' silence, and that we would write to each other and keep talking on the phone. (I still have

Ros's letters.) She had been deeply hurt at my sudden and cavalier departure, but had, she thought, got over me. We did agree that it would have been difficult to get spliced under duress when I was posted to New York, and perhaps it was better to explore possibilities this way. We kept talking and writing for two weeks, but Ros still hadn't said 'yes'. Then there was utter silence for ten days.

I moped around the office and was grumpy. In Singapore Ros—who had sent a telegram giving the green light to our future together—wondered why I had not responded. Perhaps I had changed my mind. She had sent the telegram to me, care of the ABC, Avenue of the Americas, New York. It arrived at the skyscraper inhabited by the American Broadcasting Company just up the street, and was eventually returned to sender. I got back from lunch one day to find a phonogram in my typewriter. It was in a kind of code. The Malaysians use the expression 'lah' as an emphasis word. Ros's phonogram had been typed out by our office manager, Lydia Hatcher. It said simply, CAN LAH.

I couldn't contain my joy, and confessed to Lydia (who had guessed the truth anyway despite the Malay code) and the rest of the ABC crew who had been finding me difficult to live with. New York suddenly seemed a sunnier and brighter place.

Our long-distance negotiations continued, but in a more buoyant mood. The complications of getting together again were awesome. We agreed that it would be best to get married in England. Ros had cousins in Devon and I had the Bowdens at Cambridge. Margot and Philip Bowden were kind enough to offer us Finella for a wedding reception. Ros's cousin Dick Spurway would give her away. My first Singapore flatmate Bob Hart would be my best man. (As coincidence had it I was able to provide the same service for him a couple of weeks earlier.) The bad news was that Ros could not be released from her two-year hospital contract for three months. We set the date for 20 April 1968. In order to conform with British laws (and to have the banns read in church for three consecutive weeks) I had to be resident in Britain for a month. I had some holidays owing, and the ABC obligingly arranged for me to be transferred to the London office for two weeks, although I had to pay my own air fares to England. It was not possible to get married under a tree in those days—always a risky prospect in England—and since neither of us was keen on a Registry Office job a church wedding it had to be.

In London I had some time to while away before Ros arrived. I met up again with Bruce Allen (the original producer of *Week*) who had cracked a job with the BBC's *Late Night Line-Up* and was doing all kinds of experimental things, including satire, with the program's open-ended format. He had a couple of weeks' holiday due, and we decided to go to either Ireland or Scotland. We tossed a coin and settled for Scotland, unwisely taking with us the Australian novelist Hal Porter (who, even on the strength of only supervising my class for a few hours at Hutchins School, christened me one of his 'Wilkinsons'—Hal-speak for those privileged enough to have been taught by him). Hal, who stayed off the slops when he was writing, was a dreadful piss-pot when he wasn't. Bruce and I decided to take a train to Edinburgh and then hire a car to travel to the Isle of Skye. By the time we were an hour out of London, Hal was blotto and behaving outrageously to those unlucky enough to be sitting next to him. We pretended we didn't know him.

Things only got worse. Hal bought himself a giant-sized bottle of Scotch, the size you usually see in a wooden cradle behind a bar. He settled in the back seat of our hired Mini and started to drink his way through it. It rained constantly. I suppose it did stop every now and then, but mostly it didn't. As we drove over a mountain pass, Hal looked blearily out the window and said, 'If I see another fucking mist-shrouded Scottish loch I'm going to throw up'. Carting around a drunk—even a moderately famous one—was terribly boring. What was worse, we found it hard to get accommodation. Hal would stagger out of the back of the Mini advancing on prim Scottish landladies, stinking of whisky and intoning, 'Greetings dear lady, we have come to honour your humble establishment with our presence'. We got sick of being turned away and made Hal stay in the car until we had done a deal, and then smuggled him in.

The only time we got a break from his nonsense was when he found a pub. Getting him out of a hostelry and back into the car was always a challenge. I remember trying to extricate him from one pub where he was locked in earnest converse with a fairly rough looking bloke in his late twenties with tattoos all over his arms. We finally got him into the car and Hal said that this young man had been confiding in him that he was having all kind of troubles with 'the laddies'. Hal was as camp as the proverbial row of tents and got terribly excited about this. However, after a few more nibbles at his Scotch (he drank straight from the giant bottle) he decided that it might have been his accent and that the young man probably meant 'the ladies'. Bruce and I left him in a pub one night on the Isle of Skye and went to a dance. The local girls were intrigued to find a couple of Australians in their midst and were quite attentive, but we were lucky to get out with our lives. Bruce whispered to me that we'd better leave—fast. One of the girls told him that the kilted lads of the village were not amused at the attention we were getting from their women and were planning to beat us up.

Frankly, it was a bloody awful trip. We'd have been better off in Ireland where Hal would have found no shortage of drinking partners and we would have found pubs where people talked to you. I recall stopping at one isolated Highland hotel thinking that we would sample the local beer and meet some of the locals. It was raining of course. Outside we could hear a convivial murmur of conversation and clinking of glasses. Bruce and I opened the door and walked in. There was absolutely dead silence. We went to the bar and ordered a beer. No one looked at us, or spoke to us. We drank our half pints as quickly as we could and escaped. As we walked out the door, everyone started talking again. I am sure if we had persevered we would have found some traditional Scottish hospitality somewhere. As it was we couldn't wait to get back and unload Hal, although somehow we all remained friends. He was a beguiling old bugger.

Ros arrived in London a week before the wedding. Our meeting was curiously formal. In a way it represented the awkwardness of our strange intra-country courtship. Both of us (we admitted to each other much later) were wondering if we had done the right thing after all. I remember taking Ros to a pub for a drink. We sat at a table talking about the arrangements for the wedding. There were occasional silences. After one of these, I suddenly said to her, 'How are your teeth?'

Ros cracked up. 'What on earth do you mean?' I explained that we were in the land of a beneficial National Health Scheme that encompassed free dentistry. She said her teeth were just fine thanks, and giggled again.

We were married on 20 April 1968 in a little High Anglican church, St Peters On The Hill, near the Backs at Cambridge. My cousin Piers arranged for a friend to take in and play a tiny harpsichord. The rather austere clergyman was surprised to smell brandy on the bride's breath. It was 11 am, and her cousin Dick Spurway said they needed some fortification on their way to church. Ros was in full white bridal splendour and Bob and I were dressed in morning suits, with cutaway coats and top hats. Our wedding photographs cause most Australians to burst out laughing.

Sadly, my uncle Philip Bowden could not attend the reception. He had just been operated on for the lung cancer that was to kill him five months later. Thinking back, we shouldn't really have gone ahead with the reception at Finella under the circumstances, but Margot would not hear of us cancelling.

I mucked up the train bookings and Ros and I had to leave a bloody good party for a slow train to London in time for us to catch a plane to Spain the following morning. We decided to honeymoon in Ibiza, in the Balearic islands where the Polish count and I had so triumphantly sailed *Moonglow* into the superb harbour of Port Mahon six years earlier

I wanted Ros to see a bullfight—I was thinking of the ambience of Hemingway's *Death in the Afternoon*. Ibiza did not have a full-scale bull ring, but some of the local lads turned on a demonstration for the tourists with some young bulls, twirling their capes and stepping nimbly away from the bulls, which did have well developed horns. It was all rather second-rate and some of the audience jeered. The Spanish boys then invited anyone from the audience to come and do better. I remarked to my wife of two days that I wouldn't be so silly. Ros said, 'But they are only very little bulls'. (She now denies ever having said that.) 'Ho', I said, vaulted into the ring and grabbed a cape from one of the Spanish lads. A bull charged towards me and I waved the cape at it. It took no notice and butted me straight in the chest, fortunately with its head and not its horns. I hit the ground, winded, but managed to scramble out of the ring before I was further trampled, to the laughter of both the tourists and the Spanish would-be toreadors.

We took a ferry to Barcelona, hired a car and drove to Toledo. We wanted to see the townscape made famous by El Greco. Ros became obsessed with medieval churches. I don't mind one or two, but she was indefatigable. 'What's that?' she asked, pointing to some carved panels. Sometimes if you say something quickly and authoritatively enough, you get away with it. 'Seven stations of the cross', I said a little too glibly. Apparently there are more. Ros was on to me, and 'Seven stations of the cross' became a metaphor for spouse-engendered bullshit in the years ahead.

Once we'd returned to New York, we found Peter Barnett's studio with the panoramic view of Central Park cramped for two people, and we began to negotiate for a bigger apartment at the back of the building. After the air fares, the expense of the wedding and our honeymoon we were flat broke and I suggested that Ros get a job while I went happily back to my routine of being a foreign correspondent. It was a fairly rugged introduction to New York for her. She found a job as a nurse with an elderly New York plastic surgeon, Dr Aufrich. His speciality was doing nose jobs for young Jewish girls. Although he was in his late seventies, Aufrich could plough through four or five operations in a morning. It was a fairly brutal business, leaving patients looking as though they had done a round or two with Muhammad Ali (or Cassius Clay as he then was). Aufrich had set a style, and there was reference to the 'Aufrich nose'. Ros's nose was much admired by the mothers of incoming patients who wanted to know if it had been 'done' by her boss.

Because of the time difference with Australia, I did not start at the office until 10 am, and the pace did not pick up until the early afternoon. I would be asleep and snoring when Ros took herself off at 6 am to Aufrich's nose factory. Sometimes I would have a game of squash with Charlie Buttrose (who was a fit man in his late fifties) and Terry Brown before a leisurely lunch. Ros would stagger in to the apartment in the late afternoon and try to think about what she might cook for dinner. (She found Peggy Bracken's *I Hate to Cook* an inspiration for quick culinary fixes.) But sometimes I would ring and say I was going to have a few drinks at the United Nations and I'd be late. It is a wonder she stayed with me. Ros didn't like New York much. She found the legendary New York rudeness to be without charm and simply unpleasant after the warm friendliness of Chinese Singapore. She said later that a year in New York with me turned her into a feminist and—later—having teenage sons forced her to be a fascist.

We were both grateful for the Millers. They had an apartment on the east side and we used to go there often for dinner and weekend excursions. Family life in a New York apartment was a challenge. They had to rig up swings in the apartment doorways for their lively boys because it was not safe for them to play unsupervised in the local park.

Geoff was First Secretary at the Australian Mission to the UN, and I used to have long conversations with him about Australian foreign policy. I recall he once mused that if we accepted that Australia was profoundly threatened by Communist nations to our north, and that if the teetering domino 'democracies' like South Vietnam fell and the Communists poured south to invade our big empty country—well then, our foreign policy with its support for the Vietnam War made good sense. But on the other hand, if . . . His voice trailed off and we both stared at our drinks without speaking.

It was Geoff who came up with the Gravity Theory of Communism that was linked to Mercator's Projection—adding to the paranoia of Australia's fiercely anti-Communist foreign policy. 'Consider', he said during one of our discussions, 'if the view of the world most often featured on maps didn't have China and the densely populated countries of Southeast Asia poised over big empty Australia'. We decided (over a few excellent Australian white wines) that it was our position at the bottom of the map that gave the impression that the Asian hordes would seep down—like sand into an empty hourglass—and fill us up.

During one leisurely Sunday when we needed some beer, I said to Geoff that I'd go and get some. He said to use his car, a battered Chev Corvair. It was, of course, graced with diplomatic number plates. On my way downtown to the corner store another driver cut in on my lane and I had to brake suddenly. Without thinking I gave him the finger. To my chagrin and some anxiety, he drew up alongside me at the next lights. People can get shot by road rage maddened lunatics for doing things like that in New York. The driver motioned me to wind down my window. He leaned across and said, 'That wasn't very diplomatic!'

We were fortunate to be living very close to the Lincoln Centre so when we heard Joan Sutherland was to appear in *La Sonnambula* we managed to get tickets. It was an electrifying performance, particularly when a sleep-walking Joan walked across a narrow suspended plank which bent alarmingly under her weight. We were sitting behind a middle-aged gay couple—opera buffs—who had front row balcony seats. At the first intermission they recognised our Australian accents and thanked us effusively for Joan! We said we were pretty pleased about her too. They both stood up and insisted we take their front row seats for the rest of the performance. New York could be like that.

Early in the morning of 5 June 1968 Ros and I were sound asleep (after coming in late from a dinner party) when the phone rang. It was Terry Hughes. 'Bobby Kennedy's been assassinated', he said.

'You're joking!'

'Switch on your television then.' I did, in time to see the chaos in the kitchen of the Ambassador Hotel in Los Angeles shortly after Sirhan Sirhan had shot the Democratic presidential candidate as he was leaving a dinner.

I rang Terry Brown, dragged on some clothes and ran through dark and deserted New York streets to the office. Both of us were battling to get our minds into gear in our early morning stupor. It was coming up to evening news time in Australia. We had only minutes to put something together. Using our brand new studio, we grabbed some sound actuality from CBS and tried to summarise what we had been able to glean from television and radio sources in the time available to us. We rang Sydney and got ready to deliver our package. In the stress of the moment we were unable to work out how to patch in directly to the telephone line. (The 'studio' had only been finished a few days before.)

Terry and I began our Mutt and Jeff routine, but fluffed badly. I shouted down the phone to Sydney, 'Bugger it. Stop the bloody tape and we'll do it again.' I thought we were talking to technicians in the Sydney news room, recording our efforts for rebroadcast later. The thought of television didn't occur to me for a moment, nor did it cross the minds of anyone in Sydney to tell me. Unbeknown to us we had been fed live to ABC TV for the 7 pm national news. I'm told James Dibble smiled genially and remarked that the boys in New York seemed to be under some pressure! Fortunately our second effort went off without more profanity. I didn't hear about my coast-to-coast gaffe until days later. I could well have used stronger language. It was entirely unprofessional not to tell us we were patched in to a live television news bulletin.

Bobby Kennedy's assassination was devastating to a nation still finding it hard to come to grips with his brother Jack's killing. Black Americans knew it was bad news for them. Martin Luther King had been assassinated in April and there was widespread rioting in the ghettos. Opposition to the Vietnam War was also ripping the nation apart and had destroyed Lyndon Baines Johnson who had announced on 31 March that he would not stand again for the presidency. I had missed both these big stories because I was absent on leave getting married. But I was on hand to help report the anointing of Richard Nixon as the Republican candidate for the presidency in Miami in August and his vice-presidential running mate Spiro Agnew. Spiro who? everyone asked at the time.

Ros and I moved into the two-bedroom apartment we'd negotiated at the rear of the same apartment block on Central Park South, losing our spectacular view but able to entertain visiting friends. Robyn Nevin and Barry Crook came to New York, with their daughter Emily, then only six weeks old. The travel had upset the very young baby and no one got much sleep. Evil Nurse Ros Geddes came to the rescue and convinced a doubtful Robyn that Emily had to have a dummy—and not only that, with honey on it! We all slept blissfully.

How are your teeth?

Gay pride was blossoming in New York and Terry Hughes took us to a gay nightclub. I found it an extraordinary experience. They didn't seem to mind straight couples being there, and there was a degree of eroticism on the dance floor that both Ros and I found exhilarating. Robyn stayed at home, as she was looking after Emily. Big Barry did demur when I asked him for a dance, but relented. The only difficulty we had was working out who would lead.

On Thanksgiving Eve we got together with some Australian friends and drank a lethal champagne punch with strawberries floating in it. We woke up the next day with atrocious hangovers, jolted from sleep by the sound of a brass band. Our apartment was on the seventh floor and I looked out into Seventh Avenue to see a giant Snoopy, followed by an even bigger dinosaur, at eye level. I honestly thought I had delirium tremens and called to Ros to make sure she could see them too. They were huge gas-filled, tethered balloons which were part of the annual Macy's Thanksgiving Day parade.

At the Republican Convention in Miami, Peter Barnett, Bob Moore (of *Four Corners* and later *Monday Conference* fame who was in the US on a Harkness Fellowship in journalism at Columbia University) and I endured the hoopla but knew that the Democratic Convention in Chicago in the first week of September would be a tougher call. The brutal put down of Vietnam protesters with tear gas, mace, batons and even tanks by the Chicago police and the National Guard, ordered by Chicago's Mayor Richard Daley, has been well documented—most recently by Peter Barnett in *Foreign Correspondence*. We were all staying in the Conrad Hilton, the Democratic Party headquarters, awaiting the ritual of the quixotic Hubert Humphrey becoming the Democrat's presidential candidate. It was a doubtful privilege. The girlfriend of anti-war activist Tom Hayden managed to impregnate the carpet of the hotel foyer with a frightful chemical that ate into the fibres and produced a smell like human vomit that burnt the nostrils of not only the Democrat heavies, but jackals of the press like us. During the height of the rioting I remember discussing with Peter Barnett whether it was better to move out of the hotel foyer into the street or stay put. We decided, after some discussion, that the acrid and astringent tear gas fumes were a more agreeable alternative to the chunderous stink in the Conrad Hilton lobby.

The infamous clearing of anti-war protesters from Lincoln Park, not far from the Conrad Hilton on 3 September, took place suddenly and with little warning early in the evening. High profile protesters like Yippie leaders Abie Hoffman and Jerry Rubin were there together with notables like William Burroughs, Allen Ginsberg and the French intellectual Jean Genet. So were the press, including foreign correspondents. I saw a line of Chicago's finest start to move in on the crowd. They were so charged up and excited that when I deliberately walked towards their line, sought eye contact and showed my press pass to get through, I was simply shouted at by a glassy-eyed cop and told no one was allowed through their line. Sensing big trouble I moved along to the end of the line and managed to slip around it, just as they charged. Tear gas billowed in acrid clouds as the police went berserk with their batons, hitting out indiscriminately at people who were protesting peacefully. Having got through the line of berserk cops I was able to record and describe this shocking abuse of police power, and edit my report together later that night but still in time for the current affairs program *AM* in the morning, Sydney time. Hooray for crocodile clips! One of the correspondents I interviewed had a distinctive name—Winston Churchill. He was a grandson of the great World War II statesman and said he had never seen a civil protest put down with such savagery outside a third world country. Back in New York Ros arrived home from helping to butcher perfectly healthy noses to see amazing scenes on television. At first when she saw the tanks in the streets she thought she was watching news footage from the Russian re-occupation of Prague, but realised with mounting horror that the soldiers thrusting guns through the windows of cars were in Chicago. She was reassured to talk to me later on the phone and know that the ABC team was safe.

Poor Hubert Humphrey never had a chance, and the man who once told the press they 'wouldn't have Nixon to kick around any more' became President. There was a sense of national relief that the long hot summer—and the election—was over, although what to do about the Vietnam War remained a festering sore.

By 1969 Talbot Duckmanton had been General Manager of the ABC for four years—with another thirteen to go. His taste for overseas travel was already well developed. I think he thought of himself as a kind of foreign minister, with ABC offices abroad as his embassies. He was not the kind of general manager who had much to do with his troops—that is, in Australia. But on overseas trips he had a personality change and became outgoing and, remarkably, even gregarious up to a point. In the comforting ambience of the overseas posts he had time to get to know his ambassadors. Although Charles Buttrose, the dyed-in-the-wool Moses man, had been exiled to New York, constant visits there convinced Duckmanton that he should be brought back to a senior job at HQ. But that was not until 1970. Peter Hollinshead got the nod first, and rang me in March 1969 to say that Duckmanton had appointed him head of all current affairs in both radio and television. Peter said that he wanted me to return to Sydney to be responsible for starting up the evening radio current affairs program *PM*, to complement the morning's *AM*.

Ros was delighted, as her ambivalence about New York had never really diminished. She knew Sydney well, although I had never lived there. We started making plans for our return. The Millers had made us clucky and we started to talk of children. When it was announced that we were leaving, our cleaner Miss Etta used her last visit to relieve us of a portable radio, Ros's prized antique sapphire brooch and fur stole. (We were stupid enough not to pack small items ourselves and the New York movers added to the tally by helping themselves to a rose jade Buddha that Ros had given to me as a wedding present, silver nick-nacks, and various other little treasures we didn't miss till months later.)

I took myself around New York's radio news operations, including the Westinghouse Broadcasting Company. In 1965 one of its stations, WINS, had been the first to attempt a 24-hour all-news coverage. It divided the hour up into four 15-minute segments with major news bulletins on the hour and half hour, and news headlines in between. Breaking news was aired and immediately backgrounded by other journalists, researchers, and whatever telephone interviews with participants could be obtained. Big stories took priority, but in the normal course of events national, international and local news were skilfully juggled through the hour—and onward through the day and night. News anchors and presenters in the United States were working journalists. In Australia, ABC radio and television news were presented by announcers, and *AM* was compered by an actor. This made no sense to me, and I determined that *PM* would be fronted by working journalists. It seems quaint these days to think that this was ever regarded as a radical notion.

Walking along 59th Street at the rear of our apartment block—a narrow one-way lane—I saw a motorist about to reverse back into a parking spot he was lucky to spot. A taxi, which could have held back until he got in, ran right up behind him and the driver started blaring his horn. The man who was trying to park had no choice but to abandon his precious parking space and drive off around the block again. I raced up to the taxi driver's open window and shouted at him that he was an inconsiderate mother-fucker and why did he have to bully some poor bastard who was only trying to park. 'Bloody typical of you New York taxi drivers', I heard myself shouting. 'Why don't you wake up to yourself you miserable prick!' He put his head out the window and replied in kind. I think we both felt better.

I took the elevator up to our apartment and told Ros I thought I'd been in New York too long.

11 Aussie is the place for me

In the 1960s the ABC produced an LP record called *Australian Birthday*. One of its more bizarre tracks was *Australiana*. For some strange reason it was set to a Latin American beat and sung in a phoney foreign accent which made the lyrics seem even more banal. From memory, the song began:

> Australiana, Australiana
> The kookaburra and the kangaroo.
> Australiana, Australiana
> Where everything is bright and blue ...

Each verse ended with the refrain:

> Aussie is the place,
> Aussie is the place,
> Aussie is the place for me.

Ros and I used to sing it at parties, and it became a bit of a catchcry in the ABC's New York office. The LP was produced by

Darrell Miley who once headed the ABC's Federal Entertainment Department but was later Controller of Radio Programs. In this latter role, everything was not always bright and blue—as I would discover when I returned to the harsh realities of Head Office.

One of the continuing dilemmas of a highly sought after ABC overseas posting is what to do with a returning foreign correspondent. Mercifully well away from domestic political wrangling, the overseas-based reporter can report fearlessly on corrupt foreign governments or the peccadillos of overseas prime ministers, presidents and heads of state. The correspondent becomes well known to ABC listeners and is often the subject of envy by colleagues who imagine —often accurately—the overseas reporter leading a glamorous life, hopping on and off international flights and meeting the great and influential. The long hours, lack of weekends and the sometimes dangerous assignments to trouble spots are conveniently overlooked. There was a certain punitive joy in putting the perceived high flyer back on the subs desk for a year or two on his return, 'That'll cut him down to size'. That was why Ray Martin, who followed me to New York, eventually went to Channel Nine after failing to get assurances from Duckmanton that he would get a position of any consequence back at Head Office.

At least I was going back to an exciting job—starting a daily current affairs radio program from scratch—and, exciting as the Big Apple had been despite its rough, raw side, both Ros and I were looking forward to living in Australia again. The chorus of *Australiana* took on a new significance. We couldn't wait to experience the simple pleasures of boiling a billy under a gum tree and enjoying that sense of space and light that Australians take for granted.

On our way back through London I asked to see the BBC's radio current affairs operation. They had a 15-minute current affairs program on Radio 4 at 6 pm, later dropped for a program called *PM* at 5 pm which ran for nearly an hour. (They may have 'borrowed' our name, as the BBC *PM* started after ours in Sydney—although it is a fairly obvious title.) I also wanted to see the prestigious evening radio current affairs program *Ten O'Clock* go to air. In these days of satellite communication it is easy to whistle up commentators or experts wherever they may be in the world. But in the 1960s arranging debates between experts in different countries and time zones involved complicated booking of land-lines and radio circuits arrangements which did not always succeed. This was the stock-in-trade of *Ten O'Clock* and they were very good at it. I wanted to see first hand how they did it. It went on late so that they could be long-running and serious—and also react to the last vote in the House of Commons so that MPs would have time to get to the BBC to continue a particular debate on *Ten O'Clock*.

After the program went to air, the compere, producers, technicians and other guests crowded into the adjacent hospitality room as the traditional BBC trolley was wheeled in, groaning with delicious cheeses, dips, salami, ham, olives, fruit and of course bottles of wine. Attractive studio managers and secretaries flitted about filling glasses and making sure we were all well fed. I thought this was absolutely wonderful. At the ABC you would be lucky to get a cup of tea. The executive producer came over to apologise to me for the standard of the hospitality. 'Damn BBC bean counters, old boy. Didn't you notice? No more French wine. We have to put up with Algerian...'

Sydney Harbour looked fantastic as we flew in to Mascot in May 1969. After a brief stint at the Gazebo Hotel in Kings Cross we found a flat in Kirribilli, almost in the shadow of the bridge, with a view of the incomplete Opera House filling our front window. The post-Utzon architects and builders were struggling with how to hang the glass fronts onto the open maws of both the big concrete shells. I could take a small ferry just in front of our flat to Circular Quay in the city and walk up Macquarie Street across Hyde Park and down to the ABC offices at 171 William Street—which I often did.

Returning foreign correspondents could claim rent assistance for a year before real estate reality set in.

The Talks Department was on the third floor of the Bryson Building, an old brick pile near Forbes Street. From the ground floor, a car showroom, a temperamental lift with one of those concertina metal inner doors creaked its way up to a collection of shabby offices floored with brown linoleum. The corner office of the Federal Supervisor of Current Affairs (Radio), Selwyn 'Dan' Speight, had a square of carpet, but it was not wall-to-wall. Under the strict public service rules of the time that was the prerogative of more senior executives. The *AM* team, under its Executive Producer Russell Warner, were first in best dressed and naturally had snaffled the offices along the William Street frontage of the building. *AM* had started in September 1967 and was considered the jewel in the Talks crown, although it was only broadcast in the major capital cities on the Second Network (now Radio National) and its ratings were a disappointment—7 per cent in its first year, and that figure was only achieved in one capital city, Melbourne. The *PM* team had to make do with some windowless partitioned offices in the back of the building. There was no airconditioning, and we sweltered in the humid Sydney summer.

Our leader, Dan Speight, was a wonderful shambling bear, who gazed at us through thick, horn-rimmed glasses with a mix of pride and bewilderment. Dan was an old newspaper man (he was nearly sixty) who had come to radio late in his career. He had been a war correspondent in China, and had a metal plate in his head as a result of a shrapnel blast—courtesy of a Japanese air raid in Chonkqing while he was covering Chiang Kai-shek's Nationalist forces there in World War II. This may have contributed to Dan's vagueness, but we all loved him dearly. Everyone has a Dan story. His grasp of radio technology was never strong, and one evening he was standing in what we called the 'lines' room, where incoming broadcast circuits from foreign correspondents came in and were recorded on quarter-inch tape. There was no studio in the Talks area, but we did have a small cubicle equipped to gather incoming material. Dan rushed in one day to speak to Malcolm Downing in London, after he had sent through his story. 'Malcolm, are you there?' shouted Dan. There was silence from Malcolm, who had been told Dan wanted to speak to him. 'Hello Malcolm', said Dan again.

'I can't hear you Dan', said Malcolm from London. 'Can you hear me?'

'Yes Malcolm, I can', bellowed Dan. One of the techs spotted the problem and gently took the microphone Dan was holding to his ear, and put it in front of his mouth. Malcolm could hear him quite well after that.

Dan's difficulties with radio technology made him even more dependent on *AM*'s Russell Warner who, unlike Dan, was not loved dearly. I thought his management style was somewhere between Attila the Hun and the Emperor Caligula—and he spoke well of me too. Warner, who relished his reputation as a chauvinist authoritarian, was well on top of radio technology and the cut-editing of quarter-inch tape—which Dan found an enduring mystery. *AM* was a formula program and Warner ran a tight ship. He decreed that no story would run longer than ninety seconds. That was achieved by lopping the top off every piece that ran longer, no matter how good it was, and including the guts of the truncated report in the scripted introduction. He also continued the ABC tradition of having presenters who were not journalists. Robert Peach (Bill Peach's cousin) was an actor who presented *AM* for most of its first year. But as Ken Inglis points out in his excellent history *This is the ABC*, Duckmanton (who was an ex-announcer himself) took an obsessive interest in the program and decreed that it should be shortened to twenty minutes and a new compere found. Announcer Brian Wright presented the program in 1968 and fruity-voiced announcer Tony Lee was in the chair when I arrived at 171 William Street in 1969. (*AM* had clawed back an extra five minutes of air time by then.)

I thought Lee—an amiable fellow personally—represented all that was wrong with the detached 'trained voice' style of presentation of current affairs and grew even more determined to have journalists fronting *PM*.

Many of Australia's best-known radio and television journalists cut their teeth on the early *AM*. Paul Murphy, Richard Carleton and Alan Hogan were trainees under Warner's stern regime. John Highfield was there and, indeed, the future Premier of New South Wales, Bob Carr. Bob was already laying the foundations for a political career and was the State President of Young Labor. This was a great source of concern to Dan Speight, who knew that an active political commitment by a reporter—even by a trainee—was a potential source of embarrassment to the ever impartial ABC.

In 1969 the protest movement against Australia's involvement in the Vietnam War was building, and students used to hold occasional rallies outside the ABC Radio News building, opposite us. They were alleging a pro-government bias in the ABC's reporting of the war—and they had a point! One morning a Foundation Day group of university students was drifting up William Street with no immediate focus. In a moment of inspired madness, Bob Carr provided one. He opened a window overlooking the crowd and began haranguing them from above in a Ruritanian accent accusing them of being 'Butchers of Hungary' and 'Rapists of Poland'. The students loved it, and began cheering, booing and waving their placards. Dan Speight heard the noise and came to see what was going on. Later he took Bob into his office to counsel him. It soon became clear to Bob that Dan thought he had arranged the whole demonstration so he could address them and thus further his political career! He blanched at the prospect of shifting Dan from this view and resignedly gave up any attempt to do so. I think it says a great deal for both men that Bob kept his job—and his Labor affiliations. Bob was also an excellent cartoonist and used to post his daily offerings around the office, lampooning his ABC superiors including his immediate boss Russell Warner.

Peter Hollinshead, now Director of Current Affairs, radio and television, told me to devise, organise and staff *PM*. I jotted down a wish list on the back of an envelope—senior and middle ranking reporters, a studio producer, researcher, secretary and a trainee or two for good measure. Including me, the staff numbered about ten. When I trotted up to Broadcast House at 145 Elizabeth Street, always referred to as 'Bullshit Castle' by the troops as there was not a single broadcaster in it, and gave this to Hollings, he nodded and passed it over to his administrative assistant, Arthur 'Pappy' Papastatis, who had a seizure. 'There's no way we can get away with creating ten new positions', squeaked Arthur. 'You can fix it Art', said Peter genially, 'you always do'. And, by God, he did!

Pappy was an Australian-born Greek who had served in the AIF in New Britain. He was an administrative genius. He came into the ABC from Treasury, in Canberra, and knew the Commonwealth Public Service system (under which the ABC operated) inside out. In his time Arthur had worked for the General Manager, and the Assistant General Manager. But they had a problem with Pappy's cheerfully admitted addiction to the gee-gees, the TAB and a fondness for a drink. So they gave him to Peter Hollinshead. Peter knew nothing about how the ABC bureaucratic system worked and Pappy was a godsend. Hollings wasn't censorious about Arthur's gambling, and he enjoyed a drink himself. In Peter's hands, Pappy was a powerful weapon and he flourished under Peter's friendship and patronage. I can see him now, swarthy, thick-set, with heavy black horn-rimmed glasses which he constantly dropped down his nose and had to push back, cigarette in hand with a phone grafted to his ear. He conducted the public service orchestra like the maestro he was, and *PM* got its staff.

Russell Warner's nose was out of joint. He knew I was a Hollinshead insider, getting resources he would have killed for. Being young—and arrogant—I did not hide my disdain of Warner as a person and as a producer. But as I was to find out later, patronage is seldom permanent and can backfire on the unwary. At that stage in our careers we were equally ranked as Executive Producers, under the amiable Dan, with whom Warner admittedly had the inside running. Meanwhile, I had the joyous challenge of getting a new program on air.

There was no shortage of reporter recruits in Sydney, partly because of the excitement of the new and the relief of not having to work for Warner. I decided—wrongly as it turned out—that the compere's job should be shared between two people, to lessen the strain. John Highfield and a New Zealander Laurie Bryant were to take alternate nights. The following year Huw Evans took on the anchor role and began a tradition that endures to this day, with outstanding broadcasters like Paul Murphy, Iain Finlay, Ellen Fanning, Monica Attard and Mark Colvin—all capable of conducting penetrating live interviews and departing when necessary from a prepared script in the interests of topicality and breaking news. Other reporters in at the start were Paul Raffaele for whom no assignment was too challenging, Cliff Neate, an experienced Talks hand, and Tony Joyce, recently arrived from England and about to make his name as one of the ABC's best current affairs reporters. Cathy Munro got the job as researcher, the extremely efficient—and acerbic—Anna Wareham was unit secretary and radio veteran Bill Weir our studio producer with the job of physically getting us to air.

That was harder than it should have been. The studios were 500 metres away in upper Forbes Street. Most were at basement level and protected like Fort Knox by thick reinforced concrete fortifications that were deemed necessary during World War II. (They were also riddled with asbestos.) It was hard for the *AM* staff too. As many stories as possible were prepared in advance. The edited tapes were put in small labelled aluminium cans, each on top of a script which had a suggested introduction, beginning and ending words, and the timing of the item—say two minutes, forty-five seconds. At five minutes to six (remembering that we were preceded by a 5-minute news bulletin) Bill Weir would scoop up all the tapes and scripts into a leather bag and dash madly up 'Coronary Hill' to the Forbes Street studios, probably shortening poor Bill's life. Reporters who were still working on late-breaking stories would stay at 171 William Street, keeping in contact with me or Bill by phone, giving an estimation of when they could get to us with their story. We would thunder into Studio 707 throwing tapes at the long-suffering ABC techs who would put the *PM* theme on one machine, and the first three or four stories on other replay tape machines while John Highfield or Laurie Bryant tried to get their breathing under control after their run up the hill.

Before *PM* started I had to kill off *News Review,* which then was chugging along from 7.15 to 7.30 pm on the Second Network—still heralded by Jim Pratt's stentorian bellow of 'neeooos revieeew' with the triumphant fanfare that I had first heard in Tasmania when I contributed to the program in 1959. I devoted the last edition to a history of the program, interviewing the legendary Fred Simpson, and old hands like Kim Corcoran and Frank Bennett—by then the most senior reporter on *This Day Tonight.* Tragically, Frank—who was only in his forties—died a few weeks later. The advent of television news at 7 pm had made *News Review* a non-event. We had a party to see off *News Review,* and one of the guests was the much-loved and respected B H Molesworth, who had been the ABC's first Director of Talks from 1938 until 1955.

I put out a press release to spell out the differences between *AM* and *PM* and—partly to get up Warner's nose—emphasised the advent of 'presenter reporters'.

> This does away with the old format of having an announcer or compere reading a script written for him to link the various items ... The presenter can react to late news developments by himself without waiting for someone to tell him what to do.
>
> Perhaps the most important difference is that he speaks with the authority of the man who has been living and breathing current affairs all day—and I think this feeling will reach the listeners.

PM first went to air on 7 July 1979, at 6.05 pm on the ABC's Second Network fronted by John Highfield. (He scored his moment of history by the tossing of a coin; Laurie Bryant lost.)

Sadly there was no audio record kept of that first program in Radio Archives. It began with an overseas story—which was not typical—the assassination of Tom Mboya in Kenya. While *AM*'s strength was overseas news—the world was awake while we were asleep—*PM* had the day's breaking news to react to, and indeed the Southeast Asian region was in our time span. I determined that stories would run as long as necessary, and included what I called 'mini documentaries' for up to four minutes on softer, social topics to emphasise that we were a flexible, unpredictable program. John Gorton was then into the second year of his rocky ride leading the Liberal Party, and the Prime Minister with the battered face had already survived one challenge to his leadership. An election was looming, so the daily doings in federal parliament were grist to our mill.

Reporting parliament on radio and television was difficult because, although the ABC—by law—had to broadcast every word that was uttered in the House of Representatives, not a syllable could be recorded for later replay. Draconian penalties existed for any breach. Nor were any television cameras allowed inside either the lower house or the Senate. So we began broadcasting reports by Paul Murphy, our Canberra correspondent, in which he wove brilliant word pictures of what was happening in the chamber. His candid—some said irreverent—descriptions of antics at Question Time were thought to be sailing close to the awful spectre of breaching parliamentary privilege. Paul has a wonderful way with words and gave vivid, gripping reports. I believe he changed the way politics was reported on radio.

A big plus for *PM* (and I don't remember ever asking for this—it just happened) was that we were broadcast simultaneously on the ABC's Third Network, which went to every transmitter in the land outside the capital cities. This gave us an enormous reach, and letters from grateful country people flooded in thanking us for this new conduit of information. The ABC used to regard its Third Network as catering for farmers, the brain dead, or a combination of both.

Apart from the endless stock reports and weather forecasts (and the long-running rural soapie *Blue Hills*) the Third Network broadcast straight news bulletins, middle-of-the-road music and light entertainment. In Third Network programming policy five minutes of Arthur Fiedler and the Boston Pops Orchestra was the equivalent of a symphony concert on the Second Network, now Radio National. The advent of *PM*, bringing serious current affairs to so many homes, was warmly welcomed. Duckmanton didn't interfere with what we were doing. It was probably a bad time of day for him to listen. He wouldn't have liked the 'untrained' voices that were introducing our items, but we certainly didn't get the kind of unwanted nitpicking on production that the *AM* team had to endure.

In the capital cities *PM* pinched half an hour of dinner music— *Familiar Classics*. The classical music lobby screamed in protest because in those days there was no Classic FM, dedicated to serious music. Duckmanton did interfere in this case, and we were delighted. We were shifted to The First Network, which had a bigger audience. (*AM* was a beneficiary of our move, because the program was also shifted to the First Network in the mornings and inherited a big follow-on audience from the 7.45–8 am news.)

I was well aware that ABC News correspondents in Tokyo, New Delhi, Jakarta, Singapore, Kuala Lumpur and Saigon were all in our 'window' of daily coverage. Because the News Department still regarded tape recorders as instruments of the devil—'proper' news was a story written by the reporter and read by an announcer—most journalists were completely untrained in microphone technique and in writing for something to be 'said' rather than 'read'. To give some semblance of credibility to actually having journalists overseas, occasional 'voice pieces' from our foreign correspondents were included in some bulletins. This was the reporter reading a segment of his written story. These voice pieces were invariably wooden and deadly dull. I began to have the ABC foreign correspondents interviewed and recorded on the phone about a big battle in Vietnam or the latest coup in Thailand. It's done every day now and it worked well because the journalists answered naturally and were able to draw on their specialist background knowledge that did not get a guernsey in their hard news coverage. And as I remembered from my own experiences in Southeast Asia, if you did have a scoop, sometimes your story was not used by News until the news agencies like Reuters or AAP put it out first!

By September I was getting more mileage out of the ABC correspondents in Asia than the News Department was—and they were paying them. When the Controller of News, Keith 'The Turk' Fraser, realised what was going on, he slapped a ban on his men being interviewed by current affairs programs like *PM*. His reason for doing this was, he said, that it was not the job of journalists to express their personal opinions on events or politics in the countries they were covering, and this question and interview technique 'could inadvertently cause journalists to stray too far into the area of personal opinion or subjective comment'. Their job was to report hard news, and that was that.

I wondered why we had foreign correspondents if all they did was parrot the news agencies. Fraser decreed that no ABC News foreign correspondent could be approached by current affairs people directly, but only through the Supervisor of News Gathering, Fred Miles (who affected green suits and was consequently known as 'The Green Stoat'). This effectively meant 'no'. It was a serious blow to *PM* and I asked Dan Speight to take up our cause. He rang 'The Turk' and then put out his own memo clarifying when we might approach News correspondents directly:

> The specified exception is what Mr Fraser calls 'an act of God' story: for example, a disaster of any kind where a report must depend on facts, and opinion has no place. With such a story the interview technique is permissible.

Everyone knew it was a nonsense, even Fraser himself. (His other nickname was 'Boots' because it was said he wore his ex-policeman's boots to work. In later years Fraser claimed to have been offended by this as they were orthopaedic boots!) We didn't push our luck for a while and then snuck in the odd 'illegal' interview until the passing of time and an outbreak of commonsense inevitably overtook Fraser's Gilbertian decree.

Ros and I were extremely happy to be back in Sydney and enjoyed life in the Kirribilli flat. We started to talk about having kids and tore down all the contraceptive barriers—with no immediate results. I might have had the impressive title of Executive Producer, but that carried a salary of only $6000 a year, which wasn't much even in 1969. We agonised how we could afford a house. From New York we had seen in the *Sydney Morning Herald* that Mosman houses were selling for $16 000—how on earth were we going to afford that kind of money? By the time we got home the prices had shot up to the high twenties. We decided to start saving for a deposit, and brought in some economies. Home-brewed beer was one of them. It was before the days of home-brewing shops with sealed fermenters and fancy recipes. It was also illegal to brew beer above 2 per cent alcohol, although I figured if my hand shook a bit as the sugar went in, the home-brewed beer police would perhaps give me the benefit of the doubt. We brewed in an open plastic bucket. The result was barely drinkable but it was cheap. We drank most of it ourselves— our guests politely declining. The open bucket fermentation let in bugs that gave it a slight taste of cider. It was a perfect demonstration of my father's deeply held belief, 'Home-brewed beer is like farting—your own seems all right!'

We shared a half-cabin motor boat on Middle Harbour with fellow expatriate Tasmanian Brian King, who was then a reporter with *Four Corners*, swam on the outer-harbour beaches and had picnics. Ros did not miss New York. She was, however, surprised at how backward attitudes were in Australia towards women. Ros's interest in the growing feminist movement was not only triggered by being in New York married to me, but by very quaint rules and

Spooling Through

regulations still restricting what women could and couldn't do in Australia. Take pubs for instance. Women were not allowed in a public bar—apart from the barmaids who worked there. They could only be served in the Ladies Lounge. We had just spent time in London and New York where such absurd rules and regulations were unknown.

Not long after we arrived in Sydney in 1969, Ros and I decided to see a movie in the city. It was a hot summer's night, we were early and felt like a drink. Knowing Sydney's strange drinking habits I didn't want any trouble. Surely a hotel of international standing would be safe enough? We walked into the Wentworth and headed for the cocktail bar. Unfortunately I could not go in with Ros because I was not wearing a tie. Where could we drink together then? 'Alas, sir, the public bar doesn't serve women and we have no other area where you can both be served.' This got Ros's dander up and she shot the messenger with great vigour. (Sydney was even hosting an International Tourism Convention at the time.)

We walked up the street, still thirsty, I saw a tavern on George Street and headed up the stairs looking for the Ladies Lounge but there wasn't one. The publican trotted down the stairs very agitated and said Ros could not have a drink on the premises. I said, 'Well, I suppose you won't mind if I do', and walked into the public bar, ordered a schooner of VB and went back to where Ros was standing at the bottom of the stairs. I handed it to her so we could share it. The publican was suspicious and had stayed in the background. He came charging down the stairs and tried to grab the glass from Ros's hand. With some skill she directed the entire ice-cold contents of the schooner into his crutch. Had she not been a woman he would have clocked her. I thought it wise that we left fairly quickly before he had a go at me—but we still didn't get a drink before seeing our movie.

Duckmanton had hired Peter Hollinshead to be Head of Current Affairs because he admired the way he ran the Asian operation, and because of the GM's addiction to foreign travel, he had seen quite a lot of him. But Hollings had no idea of the diplomatic minefield he was entering in Bullshit Castle. Always a straight shooter, he scorned the machinations of 'the claret pickled pontiffs of the eleventh floor'—as Bob Ellis memorably dubbed them. Notionally he worked to Ken Watts, the Federal Director of Television Programs (who regarded himself as the father of *This Day Tonight*), who in turn worked to Neil Hutchison, the Controller of Television Programs. (Their close relationship was reflected in their collective nickname of 'Wattchison'.) Peter Hollinshead saw no need to defer to them in his editorial control of *This Day Tonight*. In fact, Watts was known to be a hands-off editorial executive.

Hollings didn't like the content of *This Day Tonight*, nor the way executive producer Bruce Buchanan was running it, and began the time-honoured process of bringing in his own people. Don Simmons was brought in as a producer and Philip Koch retrieved from Asia and sent to Canberra to conduct *This Day Tonight*'s political interviews.

With an election due in October and actually threatening a change of government, senior ABC management became even more paranoid than usual about the irreverence and hard-hitting style of *This Day Tonight*. In August Hollinshead and Bruce Buchanan (a Watts appointment) were called before Wally Hamilton—who was then the most senior executive after Duckmanton—and the Deputy Managing Director, Clement Semmler. As Bill Peach wrote in his book *This Day Tonight—How Australian Current Affairs TV Came of Age*:

> Hamilton tersely informed them that the Commission and management were unhappy about the state of current affairs and that all television and radio current affairs programs were now under management control in the person of himself.

'Wattchison' were bypassed, and sat back to wait their time—which would come again. Dan Speight, Russell Warner and I were also paraded before Hamilton and given the same news. But the real message was directed at *This Day Tonight*. It was not long before the pot boiled over.

Only weeks before the election, Gorton had gone for a much publicised swim on Bondi Beach to show, presumably, that he was a man of the people. David Salter, on *This Day Tonight*, prepared a very funny film story contrasting Prime Minister Gorton's Bondi swim with Chairman Mao's 1966 epic swim down the Yangtze River—employing the same hysterical voice-over that the Chinese used for their propaganda films. But it never made it to air. Peter Hollinshead (and this wasn't his finest hour) noticed it on the daily rundown. Because it was lampooning the Prime Minister, Hollinshead went over to *This Day Tonight* at Gore Hill to view the segment. He didn't think it was funny—particularly just before an election.

Bruce Buchanan and senior producer Gerald Stone disagreed and asked that it be referred to Hamilton. As it happened, that was a bad move. Wally (who had no sense of humour) thought it so appalling that he promptly suspended Buchanan as Executive Producer, pending the arrival of Duckmanton who was in Western Australia. The press took up the matter and Buchanan was reinstated a week later. But he received a formal written rocket from the General Manager which did not bode well for his future.

The election was close. Had it not been for the DLP–Labor split, the Coalition would have lost. Nationally Labor's vote exceeded the Coalition's by 3.6 per cent. Labor gained eighteen seats, mostly from the Liberals. Gorton managed to hang on to the Prime Minister's job, but the vultures were gathering.

Over the Christmas break Buchanan was replaced as Executive Producer of *This Day Tonight*. Hollinshead decided to bring in Tony Ferguson to replace him. Don Simmons and Phil Koch were already on board. Naturally, the existing *This Day Tonight* team did not regard any of this as good news. Hollinshead's men became tagged as SEAP—the Southeast Asian Push. Hollinshead told me to get ready to move over to *This Day Tonight* for reasons which horrified me. He wasn't sure whether Bill Peach, Gerald Stone or Ken Chown would accept the 'New Order' of SEAP, and might walk. If Bill Peach went, I—according to Peter—would take over as compere! I knew bugger all about television at that stage, and I was aware—more than Hollings was—how well Bill did that job, and of his iconic status. He was the public embodiment of *This Day Tonight*. I went clammy in the palms and hoped he wouldn't depart. He didn't, and neither did Gerald Stone or Ken Chown.

Gerry decided he would like to go back to reporting, and Don Simmons moved into one of the producer's jobs. (There were two daily producers, taking alternate days.) Ken Chown stayed in his producer's chair, and things settled down. The *This Day Tonight* team found that Tony Ferguson did not have a forked tail or carry a trident and the program continued its independent and idiosyncratic approach to politics and Australian life. If anything, Ferguson sharpened its edge and because he and Peter Hollinshead trusted each other, there were seldom editorial difficulties. Curiously enough, the advent of Wally Hamilton did not have an adverse effect on the program's freedom or impact. In fact, as President Johnson memorably said when he was asked why he kept J Edgar Hoover on as Director of the FBI, it was better to have him inside the tent pissing out, than outside the tent pissing in.

At least Wally made an effort to quell the paranoia *This Day Tonight* seemed to engender in the higher ranks of ABC management. Ferguson invited Wally to come over and have a cuppa at morning tea time and meet some of the reporters. He was surprised by his response. 'I will', said Wally, 'as long as you guarantee that I won't be personally humiliated in any way'. (I thought that a telling example of the fear and loathing at Bullshit Castle towards a talented group just trying to do its job.) He was as good as his word, and chatted amiably with Stuart Littlemore, Caroline Jones, Peter Luck,

Gerald Stone and Bill Peach, who were delighted to meet him. It wasn't Talbot Duckmanton's style to mix with the troops—unless they were overseas, of course.

Ros and I decided to start looking for a house somewhere on the lower North Shore. We had no money, but building societies were lending generously in those days, and we hoped for the best. John Power had been a producer at *TDT* and had moved on to *Four Corners*. We went to a party that he and his then wife Jan held in the garden of their Lindfield house. Ros and I agreed we were sick of living in units, and told Jan Power we were looking for a house. Jan said, 'Well Gerald Stone is selling his in Northbridge—why don't you buy that?' I hadn't then met Gerry, but when he happened to walk past, Jan said jokingly, 'Meet Tim and Ros Bowden. They want to buy your house'. I shook hands with Gerry and he said, 'OK, consider it's a done deal'.

Jan rang us later to say that it was an unusual house, on a cliff, and that she thought we would like it. When Gerry and Beth asked us over to see it, we were smitten. Ros says quite rightly that I made the decision on looking at the magnificently decorated plaster and timber-beamed ceiling of the dining and living rooms. We certainly didn't consider things like a backyard big enough for children to play in. The agreed price was $27 000. But could we raise the money? We found out that the building society would lend us $23 000. My sainted Uncle Max Lovett said he would lend us the extra $4000 as an interest free loan.

I went in to the building society, filled in the form and it asked about the bridging finance. I put down 'loan from Uncle Max', or words to that effect. The clerk at the counter didn't seem happy. I asked if there was a problem and he said that the building society didn't like me having two loans. I asked what would he prefer to see in the application? He said, our own savings. We looked at each other.

'I don't think I've made a very good job of filling that form in', I said brightly. He said he didn't think so either, tore it up, and gave me a new one. I filled it out detailing 'savings' for the $4000. 'That looks better', said the clerk, smiling at me. We got our loan and the house.

I had barely been with *PM* a year before Hollinshead decided he wanted me to join my SEAP colleagues at *This Day Tonight*. I arranged for Clive Speed to come up from Melbourne and take over as executive producer of *PM*. He did so, and stayed for the next decade, giving the program a harder political edge—which it needed.

My status with *This Day Tonight* was ambiguous, neither reporter (I didn't know enough about television then) or producer. Eventually I was dubbed Assistant Producer. Hollinshead wanted me at *This Day Tonight* because he wasn't sure whether Ken Chown would stay. I got on well enough with Ken—a tall Londoner with a quick wit, a distinctively hoarse voice, and a penchant for suddenly singing hymns like 'O God Our Help In Ages Past' at quiet times of the day. Ken had a wonderfully quirky eye for stories. I was able to assist in the filming of a couple of local items that he seized on with great delight. One was on a small firm in Sydney still manufacturing piano rolls—the star of the segment was an Edna Everage-like pianist who belted out tunes on a special piano which punched holes in the rolls as she played, a cigarette held in the corner of her mouth. Another profiled a little factory still manufacturing wooden mouse traps from timber grown on its own poplar plantation. Ken was not unaware that I was understudying him, and tested me on occasions by suddenly asking me to do videotaped studio interviews—always a strain unless you are doing them regularly—or assigning me to film stories I found hard. One, I remember, was to interview Charlie Fitzgibbon, head of the Maritime Workers Union, about an industrial dispute. I'd never worked in Sydney and knew next to nothing about industrial relations in that town. Like the man at the sewerage farm, I went through the motions, but the item did not make it to air.

The first film story that I did on my own for Ken and that got to air was on the Sydney Opera House. The architects who had taken over the project from Utzon had a large wooden model made to scale of the redesigned interior. It was just big enough for me to crawl inside, giving viewers their first glimpse of what the main Concert Hall would look like. I also managed to get an interview with the controversial Minister for Public Works, Davis Hughes, who had engineered Utzon's departure. We both hailed from Tasmania—indeed he was my second cousin. I didn't tell Ken Chown that. It would only have confirmed his somewhat jaundiced view of Tasmania as a backward, in-bred island which produced people like Hughes and me.

Ros still wasn't pregnant and we got a dog as a child substitute. We got him from the public pound as a puppy, hoping he wouldn't grow too large. We should have looked more carefully at his feet. He was a cross between some sort of hound and—well no one ever really knew. Spike was a singular dog, and soon worked out that when he heard the closing theme of *This Day Tonight*, Ros would let him ride in the car when she came to pick me up. As soon as he heard the music, he would rush to the screen and howl with joy. I think we managed to get his performance filmed and replayed on the program.

We started having tests to see why Ros wasn't conceiving. Mine were straightforward enough, although I remember getting a bit bored with it all. Sperm samples had to be got in for testing within an hour. We got short of containers and my last effort was delivered—with raised eyebrow by the female technician who received it—in a Chinese sweet and sour pickle bottle.

It would have been better if Ros had gone immediately to a fertility specialist. Instead, the gynaecologist she attended had a pet theory that red-heads were uptight. Ros isn't. She is a most relaxed and calm person—well most of the time. So he prescribed a sedative, but as she wasn't uptight anyway, this treatment was ludicrous.

Eventually we got sick of all this and decided to adopt. As a final check we did visit a fertility specialist—expecting him to confirm infertility. He explained there were three basic tests for this, enough wrigglies in my ejaculation, confirmation that Ros was ovulating, and the density of mucus in the tubes leading to the ovaries. The first two were OK, but what about the third? While I was standing by he busied himself with some glass rods, and stepped back from a reclining Ros, stretching a strand of mucus between them. 'Look!' he said triumphantly. 'No self-respecting sperm could swim through that.' The pompous ass who prescribed a sedative for Ros had not even bothered to test her for that essential link in the elementary fertility trilogy. I'd like to name him, but he may not be dead.

I mentioned that we were planning to adopt. 'Why?' asked our genial specialist. 'You don't get rid of your car just because it needs a new carburettor . . .' He was a droll fellow. Prescribing some pills for Ros, he said there were too many in the bottle. 'If you use them to fertilise dahlias, you'll have some prize-winning blooms.'

We were rather attracted to the idea of adoption anyway, and decided to go ahead. Social attitudes to unmarried mothers were about to change and the Whitlam Labor Government would make single-parent benefits more available, but in 1971 it was still possible to adopt babies within Australia with only a relatively short waiting time. We didn't even need to consider the possibility of an inter-country adoption—which we would have, of course, if babies had been unavailable locally. Social workers came to interview us, and we settled down to wait, not knowing how lucky we were.

On 10 March 1971, Billy McMahon challenged Prime Minister John Gorton for the leadership. The vote was tied and Gorton famously fell on his sword using his chairman's casting vote. He then popped up as the deputy leader of the party. It was the end of a brief era during which Gorton had actually behaved like a small 'l' liberal rather than a large one. *This Day Tonight* turned on a cracker program that night with Richard Carleton securing the first television interview with the new Prime Minister. Producer Don Simmons and Stuart Littlemore put together one of the most memorable closing items of current affairs television ever—a film montage of Gorton's political career set to Frank Sinatra's 'I Did It My Way'. The song has been over-used now, but on that night its effect was electrifying. The final shot was Gorton slung in a harness being hauled between two RAN ships, ending in a close-up frozen frame of that cheeky, battered face. Gorton adopted 'I Did It My Way' as his trademark in later years.

Meanwhile, leadership ructions were going on in Broadcast House. Duckbert Talmanton and Hollinshead had fallen out disastrously. Peter was furious when Duckmanton had reinstated Bruce Buchanan as EP of *This Day Tonight*, which he saw as a challenge to his authority. Duckmanton, in the harsh political power-plays of feuding factions of Broadcast House, was a far different animal from the relaxed and friendly Singapore tourist. I don't think there was one decisive incident that destroyed their relationship, but the rot set in after the Buchanan affair. Hollings was utterly unforgiving about what he saw as a betrayal of loyalty. He referred to Duckmanton from then on as 'The Bald Eagle'. One of them had to go, and it wasn't going to be Duckers. The only sweetener for Peter and Val was a return to their beloved Singapore. The downside for Tal was that he could no longer have his suits and shirts tailored in Singapore and had to go overseas via less attractive ports like Jakarta and Manila. He wasn't all that keen on Hong Kong either. But relations were so poisonous with Peter he dared not set foot on Singapore Island. It was very inconvenient for him.

Conservative allegations of bias continued to swirl around *This Day Tonight*'s head (nothing changes!) and with the Liberal Party falling into terminal disarray, right-wing academics published papers attempting to prove left-wing bias. Meanwhile, the new Prime Minister Billy McMahon bumbled about making satire irrelevant.

Lachlan Shaw, a former foreign correspondent and experienced journalist, succeeded Hollinshead as Director of Current Affairs. Lachie had been News Editor of Radio Australia—in which role he had been courageous in resisting improper editorial directives from the Department of External Affairs.

Walter Hamilton, the ABC's Assistant General Manager (General), retired in April 1971. The once feared ex-News czar had proved to be a staunch defender of *This Day Tonight*'s editorial independence. Duckmanton, who had never been a journalist, was uneasy in his role as 'editor in chief' of the ABC and was happy to leave current affairs and news decisions to Wally, who was most happy to handle them. Alas, Wally had gone when one of the most outrageous government assaults ever on the ABC's news and current affairs independence took place a matter of weeks later. On 13 May the Postmaster General Alan Hulme wrote to the ABC Chairman Sir Robert Madgwick saying that the ABC's budget appropriations for 1970–71 would be reduced by $500 000 and directed that $250 000 of that be applied to current affairs television. The letter was leaked, and in the furore that followed Hulme had to pull his head in, and Madgwick was properly principled and tough in his rejection of the government's improper interference in how the ABC spent the money it was allocated.

(An excellent account of this turbulent period of *This Day Tonight*'s history is contained in Bill Peach's book *This Day Tonight—How Television Current Affairs Came Of Age*.)

It was an indication of how seriously the McMahon government regarded the influence of *This Day Tonight* and *Four Corners* on the general public. And an election was not due until the end of the following year. Duckmanton felt that *This Day Tonight* needed to be sorted out. Despite the Hollinshead fiasco, he turned again to a man he had come to know in the warm glow of an ABC overseas office, Charles Buttrose. Neither Charlie nor his wife Margot wanted to leave New York, but their marching orders could not be ignored. Charles was to have a big job—Assistant General Manager (General) with responsibilities for current affairs, concerts, publications, Radio Australia and the chairmanship of the Artists Tours Committee. One of his first priorities was to sort out the *This Day Tonight* and *Four Corners* lot and I know this because of a letter sent to him in Singapore by Neil Hutchison—the Wattchison duo was back in the power game. Curiously enough, Charlie does not mention his stewardship of current affairs in his book on his time with the ABC, *Words And Music—Press Barons And Coping With The ABC,* other than saying that current affairs was 'a hot potato'. It was certainly one that was too hot for him to handle.

The following account of ABC politicking has never been published but since both Hollinshead and Buttrose are now dead, there is no reason not to tell the story. Peter Hollinshead, back in Singapore, was aware that Buttrose was flying to Sydney via Singapore. Some days before he arrived, a letter from Neil Hutchison, marked 'private and confidential', arrived for Charlie. (Hutchison, who had just been appointed to the cushy job of ABC Representative in London, was acting in the position Charlie was about to assume.) Peter felt instinctively that this was an important briefing for Buttrose on the situation awaiting him in Sydney. He looked at it longingly and considered steaming it open, but managed to restrain himself. Eventually Charlie breezed into the Singapore office, ebullient and cheerful as ever. He told Hollinshead that he was 'an old carpenter and will carpent the way they want it' when he got back. Peter said there was a letter for him and handed it over. Charlie opened it, glanced at it briefly, put it back in the envelope and into the breast pocket of his coat.

Would he like a fish head curry for lunch? Charlie said he would, and Peter summoned the faithful Omar (of the amazing dentures) to get the office car. Peter was in shirt-sleeves, as is the Singapore way, and he suggested to Charlie that as they would be eating outside he wouldn't need his coat and tie. Charlie agreed and draped his coat over a chair, and walked down with Peter to the waiting car. There, Peter excused himself saying he had forgotten something, raced back into the office, took the envelope out of Charlie's pocket, and sweating and stuttering with nervousness told the office manager, Eileen, to copy it and put it back in the same pocket. He would take the responsibility. They then went out to lunch.

Peter sent a copy of the letter on to Tony Ferguson at *This Day Tonight*. It was a remarkable document and a breathtakingly cynical outline of a pre-emptive strike to gut ABC current affairs television. This was to be achieved by immediately sacking Tony Ferguson, Bill Peach, Richard Carleton—and, interestingly enough, Allan Martin, the Executive Producer of *Four Corners* who was a Ken Watts man. There would be a public outcry for a few weeks, said Hutchison, but that would die down and a new style of current affairs would be devised that would be objective—a journal of informed opinion like *The Scotsman* newspaper. ('Like what?' yelped Bill Peach when he was told.)

Forewarned and forearmed, Ferguson leaked the letter to the editor of *Nation*, George Munster, and the story and public outrage that followed spiked the plot. Duckmanton himself assured Peach, Ferguson, Carleton and Martin that their jobs were safe. Like a returning foreign correspondent, Buttrose was to find that overseas politics were far more benign than those at home.

Charlie began to call for the daily rundown of *This Day Tonight* stories, keeping a weather eye out for anything that smacked of being anti-government in tone, or satirical. The old newsman was aware that priorities changed during the day, and asked for updates in the rundown as the day went on. Short of demanding that the program be taped and sent to him for vetting—which would ruin *This Day Tonight*'s immediacy and was impractical—he could not totally control the output. We were aware of what he was doing, of course, and a surprising number of our controversial stories did not emerge on the rundown until very late in the day, after Buttrose had gone home.

One of these concerned a live interview with a draft resister, a young teacher, Michael Matteson, who had been technically 'on the run' for three years. As resistance to the Vietnam War grew, a great many young men whose birth dates had been pulled out of the barrel in that obscene lottery that accompanied conscription chose to avoid their call-up. We knew the government was running dead on this, to use an unfortunate analogy. There were 44 000 young men who had not registered for service in Vietnam, and only four in gaol. Clearly, the law was not being enforced and on 16 November 1971 Gerald Stone asked the Commonwealth Attorney-General Senator Ivor Greenwood to debate the matter. Contrary to what was said afterwards, the Attorney-General was also advised early that same afternoon that a draft resister would be in the *This Day Tonight* studio in Sydney. Gerald Stone thought that Matteson only had a 50 per cent chance of getting out of the studio without being arrested.

Reporter Peter Manning had located Matteson at Sydney University and convinced him to risk appearing on *This Day Tonight*. Stone interviewed Matteson—a long-haired, bearded, rather hippie looking teacher—about his reasons for not joining up. (He said he was an anarchist who opposed conscription for any purpose because it was slavery.) Gerry then asked an embarrassed Senator Greenwood how the Commonwealth Police, with all their resources, could not find Matteson when we could find him in a few hours. Greenwood responded by saying that as there was a warrant out for Matteson's arrest, it was Stone's public duty to keep him there until the Commonwealth Police arrived to arrest him. As soon as these words were spoken, Matteson leapt from his chair, and with Peter Manning following, ran up the steep steel-treaded stairs that led to the control room of Studio 21, two floors up. The Commonwealth Police, in the meantime, waited politely outside the studio door at ground level obeying the red 'DO NOT ENTER' sign signifying the program was still on air.

As Assistant Producer I was standing in the rear of the control room and Don Simmons was in the producer's chair. There had been no pre-planning about an escape route, but in the heat of the moment Peter Manning and I agreed that it was not our role to deliver

Matteson into the hands of the law—particularly as he had been courageous enough to come on the program. We all headed out of the control room into the corridor and headed away from the front of the building where the plods were, and down the fire stairs to ground level at the back of the Gore Hill tower block. Peter and I hoped that the gate to the staging and props area would be open, but it wasn't. In some desperation we opened the door of a wooden hut, tacked onto the back of the building, and opened a window. Matteson was out of there like a startled possum. There was no security fence around the television complex then (an omission rectified days later) and he met up with his friends and their car and disappeared into the night.

There was no question Peter and I had broken the law, albeit a bad one. The only person who saw us was a large stage-hand called John. I hoped he was discreet, and he was magnificent. (We never spoke about what had happened. Sometimes I would run into him at the 729 Club at St Leonards, where television people gathered. 'Hi John', I'd say. 'Hi Tim', he would reply with an expressionless face.)

Then the shit hit the fan. Although *This Day Tonight* had not concealed from the Attorney-General that we planned to interview a draft resister and it was a legitimate story by any measure, the government was predictably furious. A Liberal backbencher, Les Irwin, called for Duckmanton's resignation. The General Manager—by then already angling for his longed-for knighthood—called in Buttrose, the new Director of Current Affairs Lachie Shaw, and Tony Ferguson, and berated them for rotten judgement. Buttrose was incandescent because he hadn't even known about it, and Shaw was dressed down for not telling him. With an election year coming up the *This Day Tonight* crew tightened their already taut safety belts.

There was movement at the station in staffing for *This Day Tonight* at the beginning of 1972. Gerald Stone departed temporarily to do some documentaries, Peter Luck, a foundation *This Day Tonight* staffer, went overseas on a Churchill Fellowship, Alan Hogan and Peter Ross were in London, and Peter Couchman went to Singapore. Caroline Jones, Stuart Littlemore, Tony Joyce, Peter Manning and Bob Connolly were joined—in the Sydney/Melbourne axis—by Mike Carlton, Kerry O'Brien, Paul Murphy, Andrew Olle, Colin Chapman, Tom Finlayson, Jim Downs, John McIntosh and Paul Barber. Ken Chown left *This Day Tonight* during the year for a stint at *Four Corners* and at Hobart's *This Day Tonight* after its Executive Producer Harry Holgate stood for the Labor Party in the Tasmanian House of Assembly.

Don Simmons and I were the daily producers for most of that year. Morning conferences with that quick-witted and stroppy bunch could be a challenge. Tony Joyce had a wicked sense of humour and, like Mike Carlton, was a superb mimic. Ken Chown was late coming into one of his morning conferences one day. Tony Joyce, a Londoner himself, had his back to the door and was mimicking Ken Chown's distinct, hoarse voice, conducting the meeting. The room fell silent as Ken appeared, unseen by Tony, still in full cry. He saw where the rest were looking and turned around. 'Having trouble with your vocal chords Tony?' asked Ken genially.

During one of my morning meetings I summed up by saying that the day was shaping well. We might have Caroline Jones's film story ready by the end of the day. Dick Carleton would almost certainly have something live from Canberra. Bob Connolly's story that was held over from the night before could certainly run that night. And the day was yet young. However, what we really needed was a good funny, something to make our audience clasp their sides and roll all over the living room floor. Stuart Littlemore leaned forward over the desk and pointed dramatically at me, 'Well why don't *you* do a studio interview!'

Over time there had developed an expectation that *This Day Tonight* would have a lighter item towards the end of the program—usually a satirical political sketch. Sometimes this resulted in inspired moments, others perhaps not so inspirational. One of the latter was undoubtedly the time Bill Peach, Gerald Stone and I attempted to perform the closing theme for *This Day Tonight* with Bill on ukulele, Gerry on comb and paper and me playing my teeth on camera. Eric Hunter, from *This Day Tonight*'s Melbourne unit, said, among other even less complimentary things, that it was one of the most outrageously indulgent pieces of television ever broadcast on an Australian current affairs program. Bill and I could only agree with him.

This Day Tonight reporters like Tony Joyce knew how important it was for Bill Peach to be the public face of the program, but sometimes they were irritated by public perceptions that he ran the whole show. Tony told me he would be filming in an outback New South Wales country town and would see a local eyeing him off, trying to place him. Tony said the conversation inevitably went like this:

'You're Tony Joyce from *This Day Tonight*.'

Tony would admit that was the case.

'One of Bill Peach's boys.'

'Yes.'

'What's he like to work for?'

'Firm but fair', Tony said he always replied.

A pause.

'Gee, you must meet a lot of interesting people in your line of work.'

According to Tony he would check his exit and say, 'No, strangely enough most of the people we meet are rather dull and ordinary—like yourself!' Perhaps the story was apocryphal—but knowing Tony you couldn't be sure.

Technical hitches on air happened all too often, partly because of the primitive nature of our equipment. These days, captions and interviewees' names and titles can be tapped instantly on screen by computer. We had to have letters attached to a black-velvet-covered board and framed by a studio camera, then superimposed onto the transmission picture from the control room. Unlike my earlier adventures in Tasmania with *Week* we did have videotape. But these machines took ten seconds to come up to speed and stabilise the picture. That meant that Bill Peach, once he had embarked on the last sentence of his link, had to maintain a steady pace and not change a word so that the item he was introducing would come up on cue and not leave him gazing into space with nothing happening. There was no autocue in those days so Bill had to memorise the last vital words and deliver them straight to camera. Often there was not time to rehearse this timing and we had to try to wing it.

One evening my Uncle Max Lovett was visiting Sydney from Melbourne and I brought him in to watch *This Day Tonight* go to air from the control room. The director, David Poynter, called for the film titles to roll and the familiar *This Day Tonight* theme was heard. Up came Bill to introduce the first item, which happened to be a film story. No great drama there because the telecine chain can bring a film up to speed in three seconds. It was not until halfway through the program that we went to the first videotape item. Bill read his link, and then—nothing. No picture. I rang the phone on his desk and suggested he went to the next item. Bill apologised—he was good at that—and ploughed through his next introduction, also videotape. Still nothing. I rang him again and suggested he go to the next story—the last available. It was also videotape, and Bill was left stranded again. By this time we had word from the videotape suite that their 'sync pulse generator' had gone down and we could roll videotapes all night, but the picture wouldn't stabilise. It was time for a standby item. These were timeless film stories that we had ready for an emergency. This certainly seemed to be one. As I rang Bill to tell him to go to the first standby a startled squawk came from telecine to say that as it was so late in the half hour, they had taken it down. I remember that Bill, who was extremely experienced at apologising for technical glitches, had been reduced to asking the viewers a desperate rhetorical question, 'What can I say to you all now?'

This disaster was unfolding in Sydney, Canberra and Melbourne as we were linked live to those three centres. The Melbourne producer came onto the intercom and said they still had their standby up, but there was no introduction for it. It was called 'Horses'. I rang

Bill, still dying slowly in vision, and said, 'There's a standby in Melbourne but no intro. It's about horses'. Bill more or less said that, at last, we had something going to air. He signed off after that, five minutes early. Uncle Max said he found the whole thing very interesting.

As the countdown towards an end-of-year election continued, relations between *This Day Tonight* and Broadcast House deteriorated into trench warfare. Buttrose, frustrated that he could not exercise more control over *This Day Tonight*, even forbade Bill Peach to make any unscripted remarks. Other strictures were imposed by the board of the ABC, concerned about alleged editorialising. It was decreed that if someone had been invited onto the program and declined to appear, this could not be referred to. The corollary of this, of course, was that if an item could not be 'balanced' by such a refusal, the item should not go to air—a death knell for any investigative reporting. The situation was degenerating into high farce, pointed up by the banning of any cartoons by Bruce Petty.

On the personal front, things were much brighter. Early in September the Bowdens had a welcome phone call. After a wait—appropriately enough—of nine months, we were told that a baby boy was awaiting collection at Crown Street Hospital. Barnaby John Bowden was only nine days old, small but perfectly formed at a modest five pounds—and not much longer than a wine bottle against which he was photographed soon after we got him home. Only Spike the dog looked crestfallen. He seemed to know he would no longer be top dog in the family hierarchy and he was right.

Back at Gore Hill there was to be more blood letting. The censorship of *This Day Tonight* by Buttrose was reaching ludicrous proportions. We soon realised that any proposed story with the initials PMG in it would get the chop from Charlie. The PMG was our parent department, presided over by the Postmaster General Alan Hulme, the same man who had tried to cut the current affairs budget directly. After five separate PMG-related items had been banned, we started to get the message. One was an interview Tony Joyce conducted with John Baker, the secretary of the Union of Postal Clerks and Telegraphists, who alleged that the equipment used to monitor STD calls by the PMG was faulty and that some customers were being grossly overcharged. Buttrose killed the item on the usual premise that it had to have balance, and the Director General of Posts and Telegraphs, Mr Ebenezer Lane, had refused to appear. It was patently obvious that Lane would never appear. Indeed, he told *This Day Tonight*'s Jeff Watson at a press conference (having refused a request for an interview) that '*This Day Tonight* cooked up the Post Office stories to get back at Sir Alan Hulme for his remarks about bias in the ABC'.

When news of this extraordinary statement was relayed to Lachie Shaw, he sent a memo to Buttrose reporting the conversation and saying that as it was obvious Lane was not going to come on *This Day Tonight*, we should run the J S Baker interview on STD call overcharging. Buttrose reiterated the ban, and wrote on his copy of the memo, 'This is typical'.

In September the Post Office announced a record profit of $60 million. On the same day, in the Senate, there was an inquiry about a refund of $51 000 to Parliament House from the Post Office. The explanation given was that Parliament had been overcharged for 100 000 phone calls. On that day, Friday 29 September, I was the daily producer. It seemed to me that this gave the J S Baker interview new legs, and I again put it on the daily rundown as 'PMG Post Office Records Record Profit, Sydney film, Tony Joyce'. Buttrose was away from Sydney and Keith 'Boots' Fraser was Acting Assistant General Manager. The magic letters 'PMG' had rung the usual alarm bells and Fraser banned it again. Tony Ferguson was furious, and at 4 pm he said he was going home to consider his future. We were to abide by Fraser's instructions. His actual words were, 'Don't do anything silly'. It was obvious that Tony intended to resign over the matter. I called a meeting of all the *This Day Tonight* staff available, which included my brother producer Don Simmons who happened to be in the unit. I said that I thought the time had come when we had to make a stand, that this was a blatant attack on freedom of speech and information by our pusillanimous management and we should put the item on against Fraser's explicit instruction, to support Tony. The meeting agreed unanimously. We were certainly aware that this was a very serious thing to do and that there would be grave repercussions for those involved.

Having made the decision, I felt curiously at peace. Although drastic, we knew it was the right thing to do. Bill Peach wrote later:

> The management appeared to think that the ABC's responsibility was to the government of the day. We in *This Day Tonight* thought that the ABC's responsibility was to the public. It was the public who paid for the ABC and we thought they had the right to know what was going on.
>
> Ken Inglis quoted me in *This Is The ABC* as saying, 'We thought we were the ABC more than they were'. 'They' were the management, and I was talking about this night when *This Day Tonight* ran the PMG story. As far as I know it was the only time a story was ever run on the ABC against the express edict of the management. It was not done lightly. Everybody knew it was an act of mutiny, and the consequences would be serious for those held responsible.

The next problem was to make sure the story actually got to air. I decided to run it as lead item, but not to inform the Director of Current Affairs, Lachie Shaw (whom I liked and respected), until the last moment so there would be no time to contact the technical people concerned to abort the segment. A minute before the clock ticked over 7.30 pm I rang Lachie at his home. By that stage he could hear the title music in the background. I told him that we could not accept Fraser's directive on the J S Baker interview and we were running it. Lachie took the news calmly and asked if it was possible for him to stop the story at this stage. I said that it wasn't, and terminated the call. He then rang Fraser, but by then Bill had introduced the item and the film was running. They both knew that nothing could be done to stop it then.

The curious thing about this much-banned story was that it was relatively innocuous—just a low key interview by Tony Joyce with the Post and Telegraphs union leader detailing failures in Post Office systems which were denied by management. *The Age* newspaper was the first to cotton on to what had happened and rang Tony Ferguson for a comment. Tony immediately took full responsibility for having put the item to air and, as was his style, did not mince words:

> Mr Ferguson said he knew he could lose his job by speaking out publicly as an employee of the ABC.
>
> 'They might dismiss me—there is probably no alternative. But I either had to stand on this issue or to go along like a tamed cat. I'm not prepared to do that. It was such a brazen thing—protection of the Postmaster-General, our arch-critic. What happened tonight was just too sick for words. Finally you are forced to say something...'

Fraser carpeted Tony the next day, demanded a written report and directed he take forty-nine days' leave.

There was better news on the PMG front. Flushed out at last, the Director General Ebenezer Lane came on the program in Melbourne to be interviewed by Doug Stanley to defend the Post Office's performance. In Sydney John Baker was interviewed by Tony Joyce again, and demanded an inquiry into the administration of the Post Office—not only to scrutinise the STD debacle, but also the alleged practice of the Post Office in awarding expensive contracts to outsiders under questionable circumstances. As Bill Peach said later, 'The story which the management had previously assured us was "old hat" (a term invariably used by ABC executives to undermine ideas, programs and people they personally resented) had now become so important it rated a national *This Day Tonight* telecast on the Monday night'.

The management spokesman, Peter Lucas, said that Tony's absence on leave was not a suspension, but staff thought otherwise. On Tuesday afternoon there was a big protest meeting in the grounds of the ABC's Gore Hill studios. A senior ABC executive, Alan

Ashbolt, Head of Radio Special Projects, spoke courageously at the meeting, making the point that the decision to run the banned PMG item was not made by Tony Ferguson alone, but supported by both Don Simmons and myself. Don and I also addressed the meeting. I said that one of the most important things to come out of the whole affair was the identification of a widening gap between senior ABC management executives and program makers.

> If management thinks it can treat its program makers with such contempt, there is a cause for grave concern for the future of broadcasting in this country. It is simply not good enough to ban programs, not only without viewing them, but also without any rational discussion why they must be banned.

A further mass meeting of ABC staff was held at the Teachers Federation Hall in Sydney the following Monday, passing strong resolutions to reinstate Tony Ferguson, for an end to the intimidation of *This Day Tonight* staff, better consultation between management and staff, and an end to the abuse of management power, with strike action threatened if these demands were not met. The press reaction was generally sympathetic with the *This Day Tonight* position.

The buffoonish performance of Buttrose and Fraser finally flushed the General Manager, Talbot Duckmanton, out to take control of the affair. Sadly, Lachie Shaw resigned from his job, and the ABC. He was an honourable, caring professional and could no longer stomach dealing with the likes of Buttrose and Fraser. I was sad about this, as my actions had contributed to his leaving. With a federal election only weeks away, Duckmanton now had no Director of Public Affairs, no Executive Producer of *This Day Tonight* and a groundswell of industrial anger about what had happened. There was a strong possibility of a general strike. Every executive producer of the state-based *This Day Tonight* programs, reporters and staff, signed letters to Duckmanton which attacked the management in very blunt terms, accusing them of suppressing the truth,

Spooling Through

TV producer ordered to take leave

Speakers at yesterday's ABC Staff Association meeting (from left): Mr Don Simmonds and Mr Tim Bowden, producers of "This Day Tonight" and Mr Alan Ashbolt, head of the special projects of the ABC.

distorting the guidelines and diminishing the credibility of ABC Current Affairs. The President of the ACTU, Bob Hawke, weighed in saying that the ABC's management would be an impediment to a Labor government granting autonomy to the national broadcaster. He said ABC management was, in effect, handing out political protection to the McMahon Government—and the *This Day Tonight* incident was yet another example.

Duckmanton bowed to the inevitable and reinstated Tony Ferguson as executive producer of *This Day Tonight* twenty days after he had been sent on leave. The face-saver was a statement by Tony that he would not make unauthorised statements to the press and would accept future management directives. Duckmanton appointed the ABC's Tasmanian Manager, Arthur Winter, to act as Director of Current Affairs. I knew Arthur well, and welcomed the appointment. He was a fair-minded man, and in fact smoothed the troubled waters with his customary aplomb.

Although Tony Ferguson had shouldered the responsibility for airing the banned PMG item, I knew that senior management were not unaware of the role I had played.

I didn't think I could look forward to a great future in ABC television current affairs—and I was dead right.

12 Naked came the stranger

In January 1969, a raunchy novel, *Naked Came The Stranger,* was published in New York. Its author, Penelope Ashe, did not exist. 'The demure Long Island housewife' was the alter ego of a group of twenty-five hard-bitten journalists on the Long Island weekly *Newsday*. Aimed at out-pulping the wildly successful schlock of Harold Robbins and Jacqueline Susann, they set out to prove that their badly written, sex-filled novel could become a best-seller too. Each journo did a chapter, and passed it onto a colleague who wrote the next, and so on. Each writer ended his chapter with the heroine, talk show hostess Gillian Blake, in a hopelessly compromising position from which the next journo in the chain had to rescue her. Some of the characters bore an uncanny resemblance to *Newsday* executives. I'm told their first effort was a bit too well written so they dumbed down the manuscript a few extra notches. *Naked Came The Stranger* did become a best-selling novel. Later, one of the writers involved, Mike

McGrady, cashed in even more by writing another book, *Stranger Than Naked—Or How To Write A Dirty Book For Fun And Profit*.

The concept of this book struck a chord at *This Day Tonight*, during the dark times of 1971 and 1972. We felt the almost total breakdown between the unit and management had reached the point where black humour seemed the only way through. I can't remember who suggested that we write a novel about the ABC in the same way that the *Newsday* journos had pumped out *Naked Came The Stranger*. The advantage of doing it that way was that it would not take too much time—providing each writer agreed to do their chapter within a week and pass it on.

The working title was *Work Work, Shuffle Shuffle*—taken from a cartoon by Bruce Petty who used the phrase to caricature Billy McMahon scratching away busily and ineffectually at his prime ministerial desk. Our book was to be about a public service bureaucracy called the Australian Organisation. Nowhere in the narrative was the reader to be told what the AO actually existed to do. The book would be about the sterile corridor games, vicious in-fighting and indulgent private extravagances that characterised the lives of the denizens of Broadcast House, at 145 Elizabeth Street—which were more important to our executives than broadcasting. So what the Australian Organisation was created to do was irrelevant.

The most remarkable thing about the whole exercise was that we actually did it. Deadlines were kept, and the manuscript grew week by week. Everyone you can think of at *This Day Tonight* at that time—including the producers—contributed. We had to be responsible for two chapters each. Caroline Jones only completed one, for the quite understandable reason that she followed Mike Carlton's effort and that was so raunchy and sexually explicit that she passed on the grounds there were no greater depths to plumb.

I can't find out what happened to the finished MS. I do have copies of chapters six to twelve in a file and the text is—well—uneven, and somewhat unsubtle. The Chief Executive of the AO was Ruggles Ranton, a pipe-smoking over-promoted clerk who was desperate for a knighthood. One of our writers gave him a rubber underwear fetish. (As far as I know this was a fictional add on.) Ken Watts was the inspiration for a confirmed bachelor, Charles Claw, whose predatory sexual habits were a great worry to a good looking (and straight) young trainee, Alistair Trueblood, who became enmeshed in the personal politics of the AO to an extraordinary degree. Priscilla 'Pussy' Trantilla, Ruggles Ranton's personal assistant, lusted after the young Trueblood. But then again, so did Charles Claw. The bureaucratic nemesis of Claw was Bill Bloat, a robustly heterosexual director of publicity and internal affairs, whose extroverted ways were reminiscent of the ABC's Assistant General Manager (General), Charles Buttrose.

My memories of this improbable tale are fading but I do recall that the real power in the Australian Organisation resided in Priscilla 'Pussy' Trantilla, Ruggles Ranton's PA, and Bert Bugley, the commissionaire, who used to occupy a desk in the foyer of the executive building, Orgas House. Ken Chown drew the short straw of the first chapter. I remember he had Pussy Trantilla riding a crowded morning lift in Orgas House which stopped at each floor. She mused, as she noted the various levels and the departments they housed, that it was a bit like passing the stations of the cross—as she slowly ascended to the heights of CEO Ruggles Ranton's executive suite with its commanding views across the park.

Work Work, Shuffle Shuffle was, if nothing else, therapeutic for *This Day Tonight* staff as the December 1972 election drew closer. It helped get us through those dark times, but unlike our *Newsday* mentors, we never made it through to publication.

There was still time for the important things of life, and our friends (including a substantial *This Day Tonight* contingent) gathered at our Northbridge house for a delightfully pagan Naming Party for our son Barnaby. Gerald Stone anointed the baby's brow with Italian *grappa* and various guardians were appointed in lieu of godparents. (Beth Stone became Barnaby's Jewish mother—because it was felt no boy should be without one—and still performs that role admirably even though Barnaby is now thirty.)

At around that time Ken Chown arranged for a bulk bottling of red wine for those at *This Day Tonight* who wanted to take advantage of it. There was considerable interest and I offered our house for this pleasant exercise. Three huge casks were unloaded in our carport, plastic tubing inserted and umpteen dozen washed bottles were filled and corked. Not all the wine went into the bottles and it was a good day. As not everyone was able to take their bottles with them our dining room had some thirty cartons of freshly decanted red stacked against the walls.

I mention this because Ros and I had been interviewed for a second adoption and were told that a social worker would call one day on a surprise visit to have a look at our house to be sure there was enough room for a family with two children. The day after the great Bacchanalian communal wine bottling, Ros had a group of her women friends to lunch—including her mother Margaret. They were sitting out on our deck drinking champagne and becoming somewhat merry. Behind them the house was literally awash with grog—cartons of wine as far as the eye could see. There was a knock on the door, not heard at first due to the cheerful chatter, and of course it was the adoption house inspection visit. Ros introduced the social worker to her guests and showed her through the house with as much aplomb as she could muster considering that the living and dining room looked like a winery cellar and the whole house reeked of stale plonk. The visitor seemed unfazed by this and departed. Ros and I hoped for the best.

As the election countdown continued, *This Day Tonight* did profiles of marginal electorates. One of them was the Prime Minister's own seat of Lowe in Sydney. It attracted a large field of fringe candidates, one of whom represented CAMPAIGN, the newly-emerging gay rights movement. Tony Joyce interviewed all the various candidates in Lowe, including the CAMPAIGN hopeful. In what must be one of the more bizarre television moments of the election campaign,

Joyce asked the gay candidate whether he had any chance of being elected. He solemnly assured the reporter that he wouldn't be contesting the seat if he didn't think he could win. Pushing him, Tony suggested that his standing in Lowe was a waste of time for him and everyone else. The CAMPAIGN candidate gazed earnestly into the camera lens and said, 'On the contrary, Mr Joyce, I can assure you now that a homosexual *will* win the seat of Lowe!'

We became aware of plans to split up the Sydney–Canberra–Melbourne axis of *This Day Tonight* the following year so that each state would have its own program with a local compere. This would weaken its national impact, which is what Duckmanton wanted. Support for the national program came from Wally Hamilton in retirement. He wrote a letter to *The Australian Financial Review* opposing any move to parochialism and the parish pump. 'On balance, for all its faults, *This Day Tonight* has not just been good TV but has been a fine and important program to the ABC and to Australia. And Australia needs *This Day Tonight*—heaven knows it needs it—even if the ABC thinks it doesn't.' This from the man it was once feared was put in to nobble *This Day Tonight*.

Hamilton also made the point that it had been difficult for the Commission and management to accept 'unflinchingly' that *This Day Tonight* would inevitably go wrong at times. But it should be accepted for what it was, even if it did sometimes tilt at their own hallowed windmills. The Methodist Church also weighed in, supporting a national *This Day Tonight* and expressing concern about political control and censorship. Arthur Winter, acting as the Director of Current Affairs, recommended that the program continue in 1973 as before, but be removed from the News Department and put back under the control of the Program Division. Good news for the program, but not for me. This would mean Ken Watts would be back in control and I would not be part of the family any more.

All the political leaders fronted up for their *This Day Tonight* interviews in the last days of the election campaign—except the Prime Minister. Gough Whitlam's interview was recorded on a Sunday morning when Ros and some of the other partners came in to watch from the control room. David Poynter was directing and as we waited for everything to be put in place he looked critically at the shot of Whitlam sitting in his chair. Speaking to the floor manager, Bill Phillips, through his headphones, he said, 'There's something not quite right with that shot. Ask Mr Whitlam if he'd mind crossing his legs the other way.' Bill did so, and the famous eyebrows shot up. 'But I usually dress to the left.' There was much laughter in the control room, and the interview got under way. Whitlam was already assuming a prime ministerial air, and his minders were confident that federal Labor's period of twenty-three years in the political wilderness was about to end.

After the interview, Ros said to Gough, 'Mr Whitlam, I really liked your remark about dressing to the left'. Gough actually blushed. He seemed uncomfortable that his wisecrack had been heard by women as well as the crew.

At the eleventh hour, Billy McMahon plucked up enough courage to come on *This Day Tonight*—although he insisted that Richard Carleton not interview him alone, and Tony Joyce was included to share the gig. The PM had been experimenting with using an autocue for some of his televised Liberal Party advertisements but was obviously uncomfortable with the technology. Gough, who had called McMahon the 'Tiberius of the telephone', now gleefully dubbed him the 'Augustus of the autocue'.

There was the stench of political death about McMahon's entourage, many of whom were speculating openly about where they might get jobs after Labor won the election. I was given the job of taking the Prime Minister to make-up, and then to Studio 21. The make-up took so long I thought they were attempting a face lift. Even Billy's bodyguard got bored and departed, leaving me to guarantee the safety of the nation's leader. Finally the job was done and I said I would take him to the studio. 'Is there somewhere near here where I could take a leak?' asked the PM.

I led the way to the gents and pondered about protocol. Should I wait outside or go in and have one I didn't want? I decided on the latter. The Prime Minister and I stood together at the urinal concentrating on the job in hand. Shaking the drops off Billy turned to me and said, 'I've just come down from Queensland today where I've been talking with the Women's Electoral Lobby. Do you know much about them? I didn't understand one single word they said to me.'

I got him to the studio where his wife fussed about him, trying to boost his confidence as he sat in his chair looking bewildered and rather pathetic. He did not give a convincing performance and his prime ministership was all over a couple of days later.

So was my tenure with *This Day Tonight*. Unfortunately, unlike Tony Ferguson, I wasn't important enough for the 'New Order' to have to find a job for me. (Tony Ferguson was offered the position of Executive Producer of *Four Corners* for 1973, and accepted it.) Allan Martin, the original Executive Producer of *This Day Tonight* who had moved on to *Four Corners*, called me in to his office to tell me in blunt terms that I was not wanted at *This Day Tonight*, and I'd better find myself another job somewhere else in the ABC. This was Watts's payback for my role in airing the J S Baker interview against management instructions—but I don't think I would have lasted even if that hadn't happened. I was not prepared for Martin's final words: 'Anyway, Tim, you're such a happy, cheerful fellow I'm sure you'll take what I've just told you in good spirits with no trouble at all.'

I glared at him, for once speechless, and left the room chewing over what I should have said to the prick if I hadn't been so taken aback at this bizarre statement.

A phone call from my old friend Anthony Rendell cheered me up a couple of days later. Anthony had been Duckmanton's personal assistant during these troubled times. I hadn't seen much of him. He told me he had applied for, and won, the job of Director of Current Affairs (Radio) that was advertised after Dan Speight retired.

'Why don't you come back to William Street and we'll do some good things with current affairs radio?' he asked. I was delighted and agreed on the spot. My status was that of 'Executive Producer Without Portfolio', but I was sure I'd work something out with Anthony. I had relinquished my *PM* position in favour of Clive Speed, who was now well established as Executive Producer—but I would not have wanted to go down that particular road again.

Anthony arranged that I would oversee the Sunday morning program *Correspondents' Report*—in fact I, would present and produce it, as well as look after the daily *News Commentary* and *Notes On The News* (once introduced by an announcer in an aberrant moment as 'Newts On The Nose'). I went back to 171 William Street in good spirits, set up shop in a spare office and waited for Anthony to walk in the door. He never did. Two weeks later he rang again to say that he'd changed his mind, as he'd won a job with the BBC World Service and that he and Anne Marie were off to London.

My old nemesis Russell Warner was acting as the Director of Current Affairs (Radio), and I had been delivered into his hands. He was not pleased to see me and the feeling was mutual. I attempted to smooth the waters by seeking him out to say that if there had been difficulties in the past I wanted to assure him that was now history and I hoped we could work well together. His only response was to grunt—and add, not encouragingly I thought, 'We'll leave that for the time being'. Warner was boorish, rude and unpleasant when we did have to meet, but I was used to that. I was not invited to staff meetings, nor involved in any current affairs policy matters. But I was happy enough to run *Correspondents Report*, and liaise with colleagues like Ray Martin in New York and Paul Murphy, by now in London. It was a welcome relief from the stresses and strains of producing *This Day Tonight* which was the toughest job I ever had in the ABC. However, Warner's behaviour towards me was becoming increasingly bizarre and unpleasant.

One of the regular contributors to *News Commentary* was a Consolidated Press journalist, Emery Barcs. He wrote mostly on

European politics—and I say wrote, because his scripts were always read by an announcer. One day I asked Emery why this was so. He looked embarrassed and said it was because of his heavy Hungarian accent. Sure he had an accent, but I had no problem understanding him and I didn't think the listeners would have either. Today, of course, his accent would not only be unexceptional but unnoticed in multicultural Australia. I said he ought to record his own script. Emery looked worried and said he thought there might be trouble. He was right. Warner appeared breathing fire and brimstone. Someone had told him I had recorded Emery Barcs. He demanded I do no such thing. I told him to calm down and said that I thought it was time this anachronistic ban was lifted. I thought Warner would have a seizure. Eyes bulging, the veins on his neck standing out and his face flushed an unhealthy red, he hissed at me that it 'was a Commission directive' and I was not to broadcast Barcs. It wasn't worth nailing my colours to the mast on that one, so I shrugged and junked poor Emery's quite acceptable tape.

I would have been content if Warner had just ignored me but he could not resist rubbing my nose in the fact that he was top dog. Most of it was silly stuff. Together with the admirable John Hinde, I produced a weekly 10-minute program, *The World's Press*, reviewing what the major overseas papers were saying in their editorials. John wrote it, and I read it. Hinde told me that Warner had asked him for a report on the program's deficiencies. As Hinde was a freelancer and I was the program's Executive Producer, I thought Warner might well have asked me, and went to his office to have what I hoped would be a civilised chat about it.

His reaction was quite extraordinary. He said I was impertinent and the matter was none of my business. I attempted to say that as I was responsible for the program I thought it was, and he went off his face. He shouted that I was in no position to ask questions about anything, and he would tell me what he thought I ought to know. In any case, I was a 'known troublemaker' and was in his department 'under sufferance'. Further dialogue was impossible because he melodramatically ordered me out of his office.

Only hours later he abused me in front of junior staff. He accused me of misappropriating an ABC radio (it was listed as my official property). I did not respond at the time but went to his office again to protest against this appalling behaviour in front of staff. He flew into a manic rage and said again that I was a troublemaker and had been for the last three years. He threatened to 'parade me' before Ken Watts, and again ordered me out of his office. He was certainly behaving like a sergeant major in a boot camp.

There was no alternative. I had to confront the bully in the playground—particularly if I was to continue working in radio current affairs. In my foreign correspondent days the General Manager had been very friendly even though I never got the nod to call him Tal. (Peter Barnett earned that ultimate accolade only after getting him in to see President Lyndon Johnson—twice!) But he did once say that I could contact him directly if a 'crunch' situation ever developed. Of course, back in Australia I did not see him at all—together with 99 per cent of the staff. There was one fairly terse meeting after the J S Baker/PMG imbroglio when he said he was far from pleased with me. Despite that, I decided to write to Duckmanton directly about Warner's impossible behaviour and concluded:

> My immediate concern is for my own position. I like the work I am doing and I want to continue. But I am being deliberately goaded into a situation which will result in an act of insubordination and a further smear on my ability to perform a useful function within the ABC.

He did reply, saying that he had 'some concern' about the matters I had raised, but that as he was going on leave he felt I should make my complaints about Warner's behaviour to Darrell Miley, as the officer responsible for the work of the Radio Division. 'If you are not satisfied with the outcome of your approach to Mr Miley you may then come to me.'

I thought that was a reasonable line to take, although both Duckers and I knew that Warner was great mates with Miley, and that they saw each other socially. I didn't have any high expectations that much would come of mediation through Miley. At best I thought I might succeed in making Warner back off.

In my submission to Miley I did not mince words. After detailing the harassment by Warner I said:

> Other people in the department may wish to speak out about Warner's contempt for normal courtesies and his arrogant behaviour ... Since my few weeks in the department there have been occasions upon which secretaries have been reduced to tears by outbursts of unnecessary behaviour. However, it is not my wish, nor intention, to appear to be a spokesman for discontented staff.
>
> I am concerned with my own position and professional reputation, which I have reason to believe are being actively undermined by Warner.

The mediation session with Miley was a farce. Warner was there, sulphurously puffing on his pipe. He denied every aspect of my complaints, saying they simply didn't happen. Miley, a nice human being even if he didn't have the fastest mind in Broadcast House, said at the end of it that he hoped everything was now all right. I said that it wasn't, that absolutely nothing had been resolved. Miley threw up his hands in some despair and asked the ceiling what he could possibly do. There was no immediate response from above.

I weighed in again saying that there were clearly irreconcilable differences, but that I could live with those—providing Warner stopped his petty harassment and rudeness to me, particularly in front of staff. If he at least behaved with reasonable civility towards me, I would not press for further action. I thought that was not much to ask—but I would reserve the right to go to the General Manager again if his behaviour degenerated. Warner grunted. I think we actually shook hands, and Darrell Miley seemed relieved.

It worked. Warner didn't speak to me unless he absolutely had to, and that was fine by me. He just left me alone to get on with my job—which is all I'd wanted in the first place. I did not discover until recently how precarious my situation was. Because I had relinquished my executive producer position to Clive Speed at *PM*, I was on what was called 'the unattached list'. This meant I was paid the same money as my previous position. It did not, however, give me the public service job security I thought I enjoyed. I could have been sacked without any appeal process and, had I over-reacted to Warner's treatment of me, this may well have happened. Fortunately, Graham Taylor—with whom I had worked in Singapore—was appointed Duckmanton's personal assistant during this period. While he was acting briefly as Head of Personnel Services & Establishment, he reinstated my permanency—to the rage, he recently told me, of 'the claret pickled pontiffs'. Graham said he didn't enhance his own career by doing this. I had not realised that the Controller of Programs, Ken Watts, the man who had originally chosen me for the Singapore Talks job, had become so vindictive towards me.

The position of Director of Current Affairs (Radio) was advertised a few months later. I applied, but didn't hold my breath. At least I got an interview. With all the surprise of a morning sunrise, Warner was appointed. (An impeccable inside source who had seen his application told me, in some disbelief, that it actually said Warner was about to undergo an operation to have his gallstones removed—which would ameliorate his bad temper, or words to that effect.)

The day I heard the news I was walking down the stairs at 171 William Street and met the Chancellor of Sydney University, Sir Herman Black, coming up to record a *News Commentary*. I said, 'Have you heard the news? Caligula's horse has been made a consul'. He immediately twigged and chuckled.

I have fond memories of the rest of that year. *Correspondents Report* was a delight to produce and the overseas correspondents relished the chance to escape from the shackles of straight reporting and share their personal impressions of living in the countries of their posting. With regular office hours, there was time to enjoy family life. We went boating on Middle Harbour at weekends, continued to brew our own beer and enjoyed Barnaby who was a delightful toddler. I noted with interest that *This Day Tonight* was in the gun again for being anti-government. Even the new emperor, Edward Gough Whitlam, had been satirised by Peter Luck and Mike Carlton for his Messianic tendencies. 'In the Beginning there was Gough...' But conservatives howling about balance have selective amnesia when a Labor government gets a hard time from the ABC and vice versa.

I carved out a barbecue from a solid sandstone ledge near our back door—nearly losing my toes in a sudden rock fall—and life was good. Our application for another adoption could not be satisfied for a statutory two years. In fact, it took nearly three years before we got Guy Philip Bowden because social attitudes to adoption were changing so rapidly. The Whitlam Government introduced a single mother's allowance and the women's movement encouraged the belief that it was better for the mother and the child to stay together.

One day I had a call from Michael Symons, a producer with the ABC's Science Unit, asking if Ros and I, as adoptive parents, would take part in a debate on adoption. The main issue at the time was whether adopted children should be allowed, or indeed encouraged, to locate their birth mothers after they reached the age of eighteen. He asked what my attitude was. I hadn't given this question much thought and replied that I was against it. Michael seemed pleased, and signed us up for the live debate. On the way into the studio Ros asked me what the issues were. I told her what I had said. 'But that's not what I think', she said. 'Adopted children *should* be encouraged to find their birth parents. I think that is terribly important.'

Michael Symons met us at the door. Being a producer myself, I was embarrassed about what I had to say. 'Michael, there is good news and bad news. Ros doesn't agree with me, and thinks adopted children should be able to find their birth mothers.' His face fell. 'But I'm hard line.' He looked relieved.

The fulcrum for the debate was a Scottish woman who had, against the odds, managed to find her birth mother in South Africa through a new organisation called Adoption Triangle which facilitated such meetings. It had been an emotional and cathartic experience which she had ultimately found rewarding and she had gained a large extended family. However, there were stories of attempted reunions which did not have good outcomes. Some birth mothers, in new relationships, who had not told their partners about having had a child, rejected contact completely. Such a rejection could be devastating to the adopted person. My spinal cord reaction as an adoptive parent was to feel threatened by the possibility of a birth mother entering the picture. The Scottish woman eyed me off with some distaste. As the debate proceeded I realised I was talking absolute crap. Because of my promise to Michael I batted on as a critic, but I had really changed my views as the discussion went on and they stayed changed.

The real drama concerned with this particular debate had already happened within the Science Unit. Michael Symons wanted to find a young adopted adult, prepared to talk about the issue from his or her perspective on air. One of the Science Unit's support staff thought she might be able to help: she had a nephew then in his early twenties who had been adopted, and she would sound him out. She telephoned her nephew, explained about the adoption debate and asked him if he would come on the program to talk about his own adoption. There was a rather long pause—and he said that, if she didn't mind, he'd need to think a bit more about it before deciding. 'You see, before your telephone call I didn't know I was adopted...'

While I enjoyed my stewardship of *Correspondents Report* and overseeing the daily commentaries, I had plenty of spare time and cast about for a radio project which would enable me to explore a topic in more depth than a 5-minute segment in a current affairs weekly magazine. During my time with *This Day Tonight* I had met Rupert Lockwood, a former Communist journalist who had featured prominently in the 1954 Royal Commission. This had been set up by Menzies to investigate Soviet espionage in Australia following the defection of Vladimir Petrov, Third Secretary at the Soviet Embassy in Canberra, in April of that year. Rupert was the alleged author of 'Document J', one of the documents handed over by Petrov, which mentioned the names of some people who worked for the Leader of the Opposition, Dr Evatt. By the time I met Lockwood he was no longer a member of the Party, having resigned in disgust—together with many other Australian Communists—when the Soviet Union invaded Czechoslovakia in 1968.

Rupert and his wife Betty had bought a run-down weatherboard cottage at St Albans, in the MacDonald Valley, a short drive from Wisemans Ferry on the Hawkesbury River. Ros and I were invited up there for weekend barbecues and met an interesting collection of people including judges, journalists, priests, lawyers, university lecturers, a professional punter, teachers and indeed some of the locals. On occasions festivities lasted through the weekend with a whole sheep roasted over a spit carefully tended by a small, wiry, grey-bearded man, Arthur Ellis. Rupert called him 'the Passionate Plumber' and he was a long time member of the Communist Party who had also quit in 1968. It was better to be a friend of Arthur's than an enemy. He believed that the justice system did not always deliver appropriately just results. Arthur favoured a more individual approach.

During one of the weekend parties at St Albans, Arthur noticed a Mercedes Benz with a picnicking party pull up in a parking area near the MacDonald River, just across the road from the Lockwood weekender. Before they drove off, the Passionate Plumber noticed that they chucked all their rubbish—food scraps, plastic cups, bottles and paper—out onto the grass of the parking area beside their car. He noted the registration number as they drove off, collected all their rubbish and put it in a green garbage bag. Through connections he found out their name and address through the registration number. He told me that he waited a week until the garbage matured nicely then drove to their address late one evening. It was a big house on the North Shore with a swimming pool. The owners woke the next morning to find their rancid picnic detritus of the week before floating on the pool's formerly pristine surface. I determined, come may what, to stay friends with the Passionate Plumber.

Rupert Lockwood's background made him an unlikely recruit to Communism. He was brought up in the small town of Natimuk in the western Victorian Wimmera region, and his father was the proprietor of a country newspaper. His mother was deeply religious and taught music and art. His brother, Lionel, became Surgeon Rear Admiral Lockwood in the RAN and Rupert was in no doubt which fork and spoon to use or in what order. He attended Wesley College in Melbourne, and one of his contemporaries there was Harold Holt. Sir Robert Menzies had also been a pupil at Wesley College.

Rupert followed his father's example and became a journalist—first working on the Melbourne *Herald* during the depression of the 1930s when he was appalled by the plight of ordinary working people. He left Australia for Europe in 1935, travelling through Asia. He was unimpressed by the brutal and oppressive Japanese government of Manchukuo in China, and the Russian Communist regime seemed benign by comparison. But it was his experience of the Spanish Civil War that radicalised him, and he reported from Republican lines in 1937, as did Ernest Hemingway and Arthur Koestler. In Madrid he broadcast over Republican Radio EAQ warning of the march of fascism, and in Britain contributed anonymously to the Communist *Daily Worker*. The Madrid broadcasts alerted British Intelligence and, Rupert believed, started his security dossier.

He became the Chief Reporter for Sir Keith Murdoch's Melbourne *Herald* in the Canberra press gallery, but did not last long in that job. His downfall followed an invitation to him to propose the health of Robert Gordon Menzies, then Deputy Prime Minister, Attorney-General and Minister for Industry, at the press gallery's Christmas dinner. (Menzies had also been accorded the title of 'Pig Iron Bob' by the Port Kembla watersiders incensed at his role in approving the export of scrap metal to Japan.) Refreshments flowed generously at the dinner. Rupert later described what happened in his book *War On The Waterfront—Menzies, Japan And the Pig-Iron Dispute*:

> I rose to pay tribute to our honoured guest's humanitarian concern for the Chinese People. Mr Menzies had long realised that the Chinese suffered a shortage of iron in their diet. He was seeking to remedy this deficiency by shipping the iron to a clearing house in Japan, from where it would be speedily delivered to the Chinese from bomb-racks. Alan Reid, veteran Canberra journalist then with the Sydney *Sun*, recalled that up to this point everything had been going along merrily—until I, white-faced and intense, proposed the toast in those terms. I have never seen Menzies' face so black with anger. Gone was the ornamental wit and ironic elegance...
>
> Massey Stanley, doyen of Canberra political journalism, then holding the daunting post of publicity officer for the Country Party, went berserk, rushed up and king-hit me on the nose. Blood spurted over my white dinner shirt... Arguments flared and a few more scuffles hastened dispersal. Never would Canberra know such a Christmas press gallery dinner as the one that came under the shadow of the Port Kembla pig-iron ban.
>
> Menzies never forgave insult...

Lockwood was a good hater too. He died in 1997 two days before his eighty-ninth birthday, in a nursing home near Natimuk where he had been brought up. Although in failing health, he managed to write an essay in 1995 tilting at his old enemy Robert Gordon Menzies. He had unearthed a pro-Nazi quote from Menzies from the *Sydney Morning Herald* of 25 October 1938: 'If you and I were Germans sitting beside our fires in Berlin, we would not be critical of a leadership [Hitler's] that has produced such results.' He never forgave Menzies' pre-World War II appeasement of the Japanese and his failure to enlist in the armed services in World War One.

I was still at school when Petrov defected from the Russian Embassy, and knew almost nothing about that era of Australian politics. Debate still goes on over Menzies' sudden calling of the 1954 election after Petrov's defection—a heaven-sent opportunity to kick the Communist can, some cynics say; the entirely proper actions of a principled man, maintain Menzies' supporters.

At St Albans I talked to Betty Lockwood and her daughter Penny about some of the effects on the family of Rupert's 9-day grilling in front of the Royal Commissioners in 1954. The windows of the Lockwoods' Merrylands house were shattered by stones, and both Rupert and Betty were distressed when their six-year-old twin girls arrived home looking crestfallen and saying that some of their friends had been told not to play with them. There were threats against Rupert's life, countered effectively by a formidable bodyguard from the Seamen's Union in Sydney and the notorious Painters and Dockers in Melbourne.

A project took shape in my mind to do an extended documentary on Rupert Lockwood, eventually titled *The Making Of An Australian Communist*, in which Lockwood described the process which impelled him to join the Party—from his upper-middle-class upbringing through journalism, travel in Asia, the Spanish Civil War, the Petrov Royal Commission and his eventual disillusionment with the Russian Communist model after the rape of Czechoslovakia.

There was no outlet for an extended profile like this in Current Affairs, and I discussed the project with Richard Connolly, Director of the Radio Drama & Features Department of ABC Radio. He and his deputy, Julie Anne Ford, liked the concept and said to go ahead. The hour-long program was broadcast on Sunday Night Radio Two, now known as Radio National, on 16 September 1973. It was well received, and there were many requests for transcripts. I really enjoyed the luxury of being able to compile what I hoped was a significant contribution to the history of the Cold War in Australia. In a sense the program was unbalanced because it gave Lockwood a platform to express his point of view. But, on the other hand, this was not like a current political debate: we were dealing with history. In later years I recorded more programs with Rupert which included responses from his conservative critics. Julie Anne Ford and Richard Connolly were pleased with what I had done.

By early 1974 I was becoming increasingly frustrated with Warner's attitude to me—or, rather, complete disregard of me. Although *Correspondents Report* was judged a successful program as far as I could tell, I became increasingly frustrated by my inability to contribute to the philosophy and future of radio current affairs. As long as Warner was there, I was going nowhere. I began to think of changing direction—supported by Ros. There was no dramatic event which triggered this, just the sterile attrition of Warner's contemptuous refusal to acknowledge I existed in the department. It could be said that he won—as far as radio current affairs was concerned, he held all the cards.

I needed a circuit breaker. I didn't know it at the time, but I had chased my last fire engine. News and current affairs had been my whole life since I joined *The Mercury* in Hobart twenty years before.

Fortunately I had been at the ABC long enough to qualify for three months' long service leave on full pay. There was an option of taking six months' leave on half pay. If I added in my holidays for the following year we could make it seven. There are only so many windows in your life when you can take an extended break like that. Most people travel before they marry and settle down then have to wait until after their children have grown up and they retire. Barnaby was only eighteen months old, so schooling didn't have to be considered. Ros had been doing some part-time journalism, writing happy migrant stories for the Department of Immigration—and we had even been able to pay back Uncle Max the $4000 he lent us to help buy our house. Later Ros started doing freelance interviews for the ABC, despite my helpful advice that her voice was too light for radio (which, had I stopped to think, I'd have recalled James Pratt had once said about me!). She soon proved me wrong and in view of what we were about to attempt, that was just as well.

We decided we would buy a second-hand VW Kombi and head north in June up the east coast to Cairns, across to Normanton and Cloncurry, across the Barkly Tablelands to Tennant Creek and up to Darwin. Then we could consider how we would get back. Tasmania seemed a good place to spend Christmas, and after that we would face up to whatever professional future beckoned in the ABC, if there was one.

I broached the possibility of an attachment with Radio Drama & Features with Dick Connolly and Julie Anne Ford. They had no positions vacant, but things might be different in seven months' time. They were keen, however, to have me on board, which was a welcome change.

We followed up an advertisement for a 1967 split-screen Kombi which had been converted, by its owner, into a camper. It had a small gas and electric fridge just inside the van door, and a table and bench seats which converted into a double bed. The rear compartment would be a bed for Barnaby. For reasons I can't remember we called the Kombi Gertrude, shortened to Gertie. The Italian guy who sold it to us nearly cried when we drove off. Kombis do that to people. I never met anyone who drove one who was not a splendid human being.

To carry our gear we found a 6 × 4 trailer, and I installed a full-length rack on Gertie's roof to carry a big marquee tent, and chairs and tables to put up if we camped for a week or so in a nice place. I installed a wooden bench and storage bins across the back of the trailer as a travelling kitchen, and a 60-litre water tank with a pump attached. There was still plenty of room for an axe, spade—essential for bush camping—stocks of tinned food and other gear. I also fitted an awning along the side of Gertie above the door so we could have shade when we stopped. How on earth I expected Gertie's tiny 1600 cc engine to pull all this around Australia was an unanswered rhetorical question. A baby seat for Barnaby fitted in snugly between the two front seats and we decorated his sleeping area with transfers. By the time we equipped ourselves with all this gear, we had less than

$1000 to last us for the next seven months. Even at 1974 values, that wasn't going to be enough. We hoped to support our travel by Ros's freelancing for ABC Radio. I was not able to work as I was staff, and on long service leave. If Ros could not sell her interviews, we would have to come back with our tails between our legs.

A German mechanic in North Sydney, Karl, checked out Gertie's engine. I asked him about having a temperature gauge fitted. 'Vat for', shouted Karl. 'You vant to get ulcers?' He was right. It's a wonder that little air-cooled engine didn't melt, considering the load we were carrying and pulling. But it just kept right on chuntering away with that distinctive Volkswagen sound.

We rented our house to a current affairs colleague, Hilary Roots, and prepared to head off on our odyssey. Ros's parents lived at Mount Colah, on Sydney's northern fringe, and we called in to spend our last night in Sydney with them. Their driveway fronted onto a rather steep hill. The following morning, after our farewells, I revved the motor, and engaged first gear. To my horror, Gertie—with loaded trailer and full roof rack—ground to a halt before we got to the top of the hill. If we couldn't get out of Ros's parents' drive on Day One, how the hell were we to get around Australia? It was tricky backing the trailer back into the drive but I managed it. With even more revs I engaged the clutch and tried again. It happened again. I simply couldn't get a decent run on the hill from the driveway. Sweating and cursing I managed to back the trailer right down to the bottom of the hill—which anyone who has tried to back cranky trailers with a short wheel base will know is no easy task. At least we could get a run on the hill, and to my enormous relief, Gertie just made it over the top on our third go—although I had to slip the clutch a bit at the last moment. 'At least most of outback Australia is flat', I said to Ros.

I can still remember the wonderful surge of exhilaration and excitement of embarking on that adventure. The sun was shining, one of Barnaby's favourite tapes was playing on the cassette player to his great delight, and the whole of Australia was waiting for us.

Postscript

I am surprised, writing about these events nearly thirty years later, how strongly I still resent Warner's brutish behaviour—but I suppose I should be grateful to him. He caused me to embark on a new course in life and in the ABC which took me into immensely rewarding areas of radio and later television. That might never have happened had I stayed with current affairs.

Ahead lay a new career with Radio Drama & Features, during which I developed skills as an oral historian. Under Dick Connolly's benevolent regime I was able to undertake major oral history projects including *Taim Bilong Masta—The Australian Involvement With Papua New Guinea* and *Prisoners of War—Australians Under Nippon*. Each of these documentary series was more than two years in the making. As a result, in 1985 I was able to found the ABC's Social History Unit, which, I am delighted to say, has flourished and is still doing great work in exploring the living and past history of Australia. While recording interviews for the POW series I wrote my first book, *Changi Photographer—George Aspinall's Record Of Captivity*, and began a series of oral history-related books including *The Way My Father Tells It—The Story Of An Australian Life* and a biography of my friend and colleague Neil Davis, *One Crowded Hour—Neil Davis, Combat Cameraman, 1934–85*.

An invitation to write and present ABC-TV's *Backchat* for eight years from 1986 was entirely unexpected. I never considered I had the kind of face that was suitable for a television presenter. Indeed, Jim Oram, the Sydney *Daily Telegraph* television critic at the time, agreed. 'Tim Bowden (who reminds one of a koala and therefore should be protected) sits in front of a camera introducing written comments from the viewers.'

Nor could I have foreseen my first journey to Antarctica in 1989, which resulted in a book, *Antarctica And Back In Sixty Days*. In 1993 I was commissioned by the Australian Antarctic Division to write their Jubilee history, *The Silence Calling—Australians in Antarctica, 1947–97*. I was also able to present an associated six-part travel and adventure series for ABC-TV, *Breaking The Ice*, on Australians living and working in Antarctica. I have now been to Antarctica six times.

Heading off with Ros, Barnaby and Gertie in 1974 was the first of many driving and adventure expeditions in outback Australia, some with children and some without. (In 1975 we celebrated the arrival of our second adopted son Guy.) I did not write a book about our first and second journeys with Gertie, but in more recent times Ros and I have joined the 'grey nomads' with a Toyota diesel Landcruiser we called Penelope and a camper trailer Ros christened The Manor. Penelope has considerably more power than poor old Gertie (who faithfully served us for eleven years) and spawned two travel books, *Penelope Goes West—On The Road from Sydney To Margaret River And Back* and, most recently, *Penelope Bungles to Broome*.

I spent twenty-nine years and eleven months on the staff of the ABC and loved (almost) every moment of it. Now I am deeply concerned about the cumulative budget cuts inflicted on the ABC over the last two decades that have crippled the national broadcaster's ability to experiment and innovate with its radio and television productions. In the early 1980s I was permitted to work on major oral history projects for two years at a time. I can't imagine a radio producer being allowed to work for more than two weeks on a single project these days. Perhaps two days would be more accurate. (Sadly, even the Radio Drama & Features Department, which was itself a great Australian cultural institution, has been dismembered.)

For the moment though, I have passed the *Will You Still Need Me, Will You Still Feed Me* birthday and can feel another travel book coming on. Not only that, but Ros says she will come with me.

Index

30th September Movement, 232–3
3TR Sale, VIC, 15

abalone industry, 162–3
ABC
    budget cuts to, 336–7
    radio networks, 286–7
    TB applies for job at, 77–8
actuality broadcasts, 250–1
Adams, Mary, 132
aeroplanes, *see* flying
Agricultural Department, TAS, 163–4
airdrops in Sarawak, 187–8
Ajaccio, Corsica, 137–8
Allen, Bruce, 165–6, 265–7
AM (radio show), 251, 280
American Army in Vietnam, 217–26
America's Cup, reporting on, 253–6
Amnesty International, 127
Antarctica, travels to, 336
Anthony, Rex, 31–2

Argosy cargo plane, 187–8
army trucks, 71
Arve River, TAS, 59–60, 62
ARVN (South Vietnam Army), 219–24; *see also* Vietnam war
Ashbolt, Alan, 310–11
Ashe, Penelope, 314–15
Askelon (beach house), 10–11, 158, 243
Athenaeum Club, 154–5
Attard, Monica, 284
Aufrich, Dr, 269
Australian Army in Vietnam, 197, 201–2
Australian Birthday, 277–8
Australian Broadcasting Commission, *see* ABC
Austria, holiday in, 111
aviation, *see* flying

Babyack, Sergeant, 220, 226
Backchat, 336
Baker, David, 36
Baker, John, interviews with, 308, 310

Balearic Islands, 133, 149–52, 268
Balfe, Eric, 27
Bali, Communists killed in, 234–5
BAPH states, 84–5, 160–2
Barcs, Emery, 321–2
Barnett, Peter, 249–50, 273–4
BBC, 115–21, 278–9
Bearup, William, 113–14
Beechcraft, flight to Hue, 226–7
bees, report on, 163–4
Bell, Corporal, 69
Benenson, Peter, 128
Bennett, Frank, 285
Bernacchi, Diego, 51
Betjeman, John, 128
Bicheno, TAS, 162–3
Bien Hoa, Vietnam, 205
Bigges, Oscar, 12
Binchy, Maeve, 118
Bishopscourt, 14–15
Black, Sir Herman, 325

Index

Blackwood, Donald (bishop) and Ida, 14–15, 89
Blain, Doug, 44–5, 82–3
blood donation, 75–6
Bloodworth, Dennis, 180–1
boats and ships
  at Maria Island, 51–2
  Canopic, 143
  motor boat on Middle Harbour, 289
  on *Moonglow*, 143–54
  reporting on America's Cup, 253–6
  Sydney to Hobart Yacht Race, 35–6
  TB holds up *Oriana*, 141
  trip to Europe, 93–9, 102–4
Bonney, Reginald, 214–15
Borea D'Olmo, Gian Marco, 146, 151
Borneo, 185–8
Bowden, Barnaby John (son), 307, 315–16
Bowden, Dorothy (aunt), 14–15, 89
Bowden, Eric (uncle), 155
Bowden, Guy Philip (son), 326, 336
Bowden, Humphrey (cousin), 109, 132–4
Bowden, John (father), 3, 5, 10–11
  death at ninety-one, 155
  meets at bush hut, 63
Bowden, Jonathan (cousin), 109, 132–4
Bowden, Lisa (sister), 5
Bowden, Marge (aunt), 13–14
Bowden, Margot (aunt), 109–10
Bowden, Nicholas (brother), 5, 244, 256
Bowden, Nora (aunt), 6, 10, 13–14
Bowden, Peg (mother), 5, 77, 157–8
Bowden, Philip (brother), 5, 244
Bowden, Philip (uncle), 3
  cancer operation, 268
  farewell to, 154–5
  holiday with family, 132–4
  life in England, 89–90, 109–11
Bowden, Piers (cousin), 109
  at wedding, 267
  holiday with, 132–5, 137–8
Bowden, Rosalind
  arrives in Singapore, 214–15
  at farewell party, 175
  early life, 214–15
  family life in Sydney, 288–9
  Kim Dwyer's bridesmaid, 238–9
  life in New York, 269
  marriage to, 267–8
  moves to Sydney, 83
  part-time journalism, 332, 334
  postcard sent to, 134–5
  schooling, 72
  TB leaves in Singapore, 245–6
  TB proposes to, 262–5
  travels with in Australia, 333–4, 337
Bowden, Sophie (cousin), 109
Bowden, Tim
  and firearms, 18, 65–7, 199, 209
  and music, *see* musical interests
  aviation interests, *see* flying
  birth, 1–2
  boating, *see* boats and ships
  childhood, 3–5, 10–11
  education, 4–5, 11–12, 15–16, 42–3, 89
  fights bull in Ibiza, 268
  hearing loss, 18, 65–6
  holidays in Europe, 132–5
  sand bank collapses on, 11
  sport, 17, 19, 34–5
  vehicles used by, *see* vehicles
  wedding to Rosalind Geddes, 265
  writings, 10, 336
Bradley, Athol, 39–40
Bradman, Donald, 17
Brettingham-Moore, Hubert Mansel, 32–3
Brighton Camp, TAS, 1, 18
Brisbane, QLD, 95
British Broadcasting Corporation, *see* BBC
British Colonial Office interview, 111–13
broadcasting, *see* radio shows; technology; *This Day Tonight*
Broadcasting House, *see* BBC
Bromfield, Lou, 200
Brouchard, Serge, 220–2, 225–6
Brown, Terry
  coverage of Bobby Kennedy assassination, 271–2
  reports from New York, 248–9
  shares house in London, 159
  squash games with, 269
Bryant, Laurie, 284–5
Bryden, Bill, 86
Bryden, Mike 'Spike', 64
  at college, 95
  bushwalking with, 58, 61–2
  shares house in Launceston, 159
  TB visits in Carolina, 259
Buchanan, Bruce, 291, 292, 298
Buckey, Harry, 57
Buddhists vs Catholics in Saigon, 202–3
Bugis Street, Singapore, 180–1
bullfight in Ibiza, 268
Burbury, Stanley (Governor of Tasmania), 33–4
Burns, Creighton, 200–1
Burns, Doug, 10
Bush House (BBC), 115–21, 278–9

bushfires in Tasmania, 243–5
bushwalking, 5–8, 57–63
Butler, Chris, 59
Buttrose, Charles
  and political interference in programming, 311
  at America's Cup, 255
  in New York, 245, 247–8
  management of *This Day Tonight*, 299–301, 306–10
  return to Australia, 275
  squash games with, 269
  Talbot Duckmanton stories, 257

cables, terminology in, 241
cadet corps at school, 18
Cairo, Egypt, 104–5, 241–2
Calling Australia, 141
Cambridge, UK, 89–90
  first visit to, 108–9
  wedding in, 267–8
Cane, Tony, 178, 194–5
Canopic, 143, 152, 155–7
Caribou (plane), flying in Vietnam, 228–9
Carleton, Richard, 298, 301, 303–4
Carlton, Mike, 315
Carmichael, Alan, 174
Carr, Bob, 282
Carter, Len, 35–6
Catholics vs Buddhists in Saigon, 202–3
Cavendish Laboratory, Cambridge, 111
CEB (clockwork tape recorder), 78–9
Cessnas, flying in Vietnam, 228
Chicago Democratic Convention, 273–4
childhood, 3–4, 10–11
Chinamans Bay, TAS, 50–1
Chipmunk (plane), flying in, 48–9
Chown, Ken
  leaves *This Day Tonight*, 303
  on *This Day Tonight*, 295
  starts *Work Work Shuffle Shuffle*, 315

wine bottling, 317
Christmas messages from Vietnam, 197, 201–2
Chung, Helene, 4
Citizens' Military Force, 65
Clayton, Clyde, 55–6
clockwork tape recorder, 78–9
Cochin, India, 101
Cockpit Hotel, Singapore, 185
Collegiate school, 16
Colvin, Mark, 284
Communism
  attempted coup in Indonesia, 191–2, 234–5
  gravity theory of, 270
  in Australia, 328
  Menzies exploits fear of, 331
  Sukarno support for, 230
COMPAC cable from New York, 248
Connolly, Bob, 248, 261
Connolly, Richard, 331–3, 335
Conrad, Peter, 2
Cook, Arthur 'Shoulders', 195–6
Cooke, Alistair, 126
Corcoran, Kim, 285
Correspondents' Report, 321, 325–6
Corsica, holiday in, 137–8
Cosgrove, Robert, 9
court reporting, 31–3
Cradle Mountain, TAS, 5–8
Crater City, Aden, 102–4
crime reporting, 31–3
Crook, Barry, 272–3
Cunningham, Don, 163–4
Curtis, Brian, 244–5

Da Costa, Joe, 209
Daily Devotional, 173
Dalton, Patricia, 57
dancing class, 15–16
D'Argaville, Barry, 37–8
Darlington, TAS, 51
Davis, Neil
  father dies in bushfire, 244
  in Saigon, 197–8, 226
  in Singapore, 177–8, 230

killed in action, 199
TB's biography of, 336
travels with Holt in Vietnam, 205–6
De Havilland Comet, 185–6
Democratic Convention, Chicago, 273–4
Denning, Warren, 168–9
Denny (Singapore drifter), 210–14
Dibble, James, 272
Dickinson, Jim, 44
Dingwall, John, 90
documentaries, 86–8, 162–3, 259–61
dogs
  on the *Canopic*, 156
  radio reports on, 123–4
  Spike, 296, 307
Dolan, Bert, 29
draft resister, interview with, 301–3
Drambuie incident, 29–30
Duckmanton, Talbot
  attitude to *This Day Tonight*, 299–300
  cancels piano smashing competition, 171
  deals with Warner affair, 323–4
  enmity with Hollingshead, 298
  interest in *AM*, 280
  moves Charles Buttrose to New York, 247–8
  on Matteson interview, 303
  on overseas trips, 275
  on political interference in programming, 311
  posts David Wilson overseas, 245
  shakes up Singapore office, 178
  shifts *PM* to First Network, 287
  visits New York, 257–8
Dwyer, Kim, 215, 238–9
Dyer, Bob, 254

Eastley, 'Bud', 44
Edison, Alistair, 44–5
  in Paris, 132–3

Index

shares house in London, 90, 139
takes berth on *Moonglow*, 152–4
election campaign, coverage of, 317–19
Ellis, Arthur, 328–9
employers
  ABC Hobart, 77–93
  ABC Launceston, 158–75
  ABC New York, 246–76
  ABC Singapore, 174–246
  ABC Sydney, 276–333
  BBC, 115–21, 140–2
  Cavendish Laboratory, 111
  Examiner (Launceston), 90–1
  Mercury (Hobart), 21–46
England, 89–90, 108–15, 246–7
  beer in, 130–1
  wedding in, 265
Europe, 93–9, 102–4, 132–9
Evans, Huw, 284
Evans, Peter, 256–8
Evers, Nick, 66, 68
Examiner, 34–5, 90–1

Fact and Opinion, 216–17
Fahan school, 4, 16
family life in Sydney, 326
Fanning, Ellen, 284
Farquhar, Hedley, 167–9
feminism, 289–90
Ferguson, Tony
  and Matteson interview, 303
  brought into *This Day Tonight*, 292
  in Singapore, 182, 190, 211
  moves to *Four Corners*, 320
  plans to sack, 301
  runs PMG story, 308–12
  travels with Holt, 204
Ferrographs, 116–17
Fiat 500, 73
financial news, TB reports on, 23–4
Finella (house), 89–90, 109–10
Finlay, Iain, 253–5, 284

firearms
  cadet corps, 18
  demonstration in Sarawak, 188
  on National Service, 65–7
  purchased in Saigon, 199, 209
First Network, 287
Fitzgibbon, Charlie, 295
Fleming, Doug, 88–9
floods, radio coverage, 91–3
Flores, Indonesia, 235–7
flying
  Beechcraft to Hue, 226–7
  Caribou in Vietnam, 228–9
  Cessnas in Vietnam, 228
  commercial flights in Vietnam, 228–9
  in De Havilland Comet, 185–6
  in Lancaster bomber, 183–4
  in navy helicopters, 187–8
  in Tiger Moth, 47–8
  out of Flores, 236–7, 236–7
Flynn, Sean, 207–8
Foley, Charles, 241–2
Ford, Julie Anne, 331–3
Ford, Penny, 71–2, 82–3
foreign correspondents, 287–8
fouled propellor, 152–3
France, holiday in, 132–3, 135
Franklin Hotel, TAS, 29
Fraser, Keith, 288–9, 308–9, 311
free fire zones, Vietnam, 220
Fried, Joe, 208–9
Fry, Fred, 160
Fulton, Dick, 23, 30, 43, 83–4

Galard, Lahra de, 146–7
Galloway, Joe, 208
Garland, Nicholas, 114–15
gay pride in New York, 273

gay rights, campaign for, 317–18
Geddes, Eric and Margaret, 214–15
Geddes, Rosalind *see* Bowden, Rosalind
General Overseas Service (BBC), 115–21
Genoa, first visit to, 106–7
Giblin family, 10
Gillon, Jack, 231–2
Gladwyn School, 4–5
Good, Bad and Indifferent, 160, 172–3
Goodfellow, Alan, 16
Goodwood Park Hotel, Singapore, 181, 185
Gorton, John, 286, 292, 297–8
Gourlay, Fred, 51
Grabowski, Christopher de, 144–52, 154
Green, Kenneth, 39
Greenwood, Ivor, 302
Gregory, Graham, 159
Grubb, Marietta, 2
Guiler, Eric, 165–6
Gulf of Lions, sailing across, 147–8
guns, *see* firearms

Hallman, Gene, 261
Hamengkubowono, Sultan, 231–2
Hamilton, Wally
  at Intertel meeting, 259–61
  management of *This Day Tonight*, 291, 293–4
  retirement, 299
  support for *This Day Tonight*, 318
Hart, Robert, 213
  shares house in Singapore, 192
  TB's best man, 265
  transfer to Saigon, 230
Hasluck, Paul, 238
Hatcher, Lydia, 264–5
Hawke, Bob, 312
hearing loss, 18, 65–6
Henry, Neville, 73
Highfield, John, 284–5
Hinde, John, 322

hippie movement in US, 252–3
Hobart, 2
  attitudes to police, 32–3
  bushfire devastation, 243–5
  flooding, 91–3
  piano smashing competition cancelled, 170–1
  shipping news, 23
  see also Tasmania
Hobart Temperance Alliance, 31
Hobart Town Hall, wool auctions, 78–80
Hodgman, Michael, 4–5, 17
Holgate, Harry, 303
Holland, Barry, 90–1, 139
Hollinshead, Peter
  assigns TB to New York, 245–6
  cuts Gorton segment, 292
  enmity with Duckmanton, 298
  gives Kim Dwyer away, 238
  letter from Neil Hutchison, 300–1
  management of *This Day Tonight*, 291, 293
  nicknames given by, 185–6, 195
  plans for *PM*, 282–3
  return to Australia, 275
  work assignments from, 185
  work in Singapore, 178–9, 181–2
Hollinshead, Val, 192
Holt, Harold, 204–6
Home Service (BBC), 117
Hotel Indonesia, Jakarta, 231–2
Hue, Vietnam, 226–8
Hughes, Davis, 296
Hughes, Richard, 218
Hughes, Terry, 261–2, 271, 273
Hulme, Alan, 299, 307–10
Hume, Alan, 56
Humphries, Barry, 114–15, 128

Hutchins School, 11–12, 15–20
Hutchison, Neil, 291, 300–1
Hydro-Electric Commission, TAS, 168

Indonesia
  Communist coup attempt, 191–2
  Communists killed in, 234–5
  deposition of Sukarno, 230–8
  first visit to, 99–101
  see also Konfrontasi
Intertel group, 259–61
Iran, attempted coup, 196
Italy, first visit to, 106

Jack, Grahame, 58
Jakarta, 99–101, 230–8; see also Indonesia
Jantzen, 'Scotty', 159
Johnson, Lyndon Baines, 257, 272
Jones, Caroline, 315
Jones, Lloyd, 48, 56
journalism, training in, 26–7; see also newspaper industry
Jowett, Wilf (uncle), 47–8
Joyce, Tony
  interview banned, 307–8, 310
  interviews election candidates, 317–18
  on *PM*, 284
  on *This Day Tonight*, 305

Kemp family, 19, 38–9, 41
Kennedy, Robert, assassination of, 271–2
Keon-Cohen, Russell 'Blurt', 17, 19
Kerr, John (teacher), 19
Khu Dan Sinh black market, 199–200
Kimber, Christopher, 10
King, Brian, 289
King, Deny, 55
Koch, Christopher, 2
Koch, Philip
  brought into *This Day Tonight*, 291, 292

chased by guardsman, 233
  interview advice, 111
  moves to London, 89
  reports from Jakarta, 192, 230
  TB inherits flat, 113
  work in Singapore, 178
Konfrontasi, 176, 188–9
Kremmer, Christopher, 228–9
Kuching, Sarawak, 185–8

Laird, John, 126–7
Lake Pedder, TAS, 56–8
Lake St Clair, TAS, 5–8
Lancaster bomber, 183–4
Lane, Ebenezer, 308, 310
Launceston, 158–60
Lee Kim Chwee, 179
Lee Kuan Yew
  address by, 182–3
  interview with, 196
  reaction to exclusion from Malaysia, 190–1
Lee On Wing, 186
Lee, Tony, 280–1
Lenah Valley Progress Association, 28–9
Lilley, Ted, 95
Limb, Arthur, 172–3
Lincoln Park, Chicago, 274
Lineup, 172
Littlemore, Stuart, 298
loan, application for, 293–4
Lockwood, Rupert and Betty, 327–32
London
  accommodation in, 139–40
  temporary transfer to for marriage, 265
  Underground railway, 141–2
  visit en route to New York, 246–7
Lonergan, John, 244–5
Long Jawi, Sarawak, 186–7
Lord Montague of Beaulieu, 129
Louthan, David, 144, 151–3
Loveday, Max, 235–7
Lovett, Don (uncle), 19
Lovett, Dot (aunt), 48
Lovett, Max (uncle), 306–7

Index

Luck, Peter, 303
Lunchtime O'Booze Club, 244–5

Macbeath, Alexander, 43
MacFarling, Ian, 189
Mackenzie, Compton, 127
Mackriell, Keith, 248
Madgwick, Robert, 299
Majorca, 133, 151–2
Malaysia, 176, 188–90
Malik, Adam, 231–2
Manning, Barbara, 173
Manning, Peter, 302
Maria Island, TAS, 10, 50–5, 158
marriage, 267–8; *see also* Bowden, Rosalind
Marshall, Graham, snakebite incident, 7–8
Martin, Alan, 301, 320
Martin Baker Aircraft Company, 141–2
Martin, Ray, 278, 321
Maslin family, 11
Mason-Cox, Bill, 18–19
Mathew, Lisl, 18
Matteson, Michael, 301–3
Maumere, Flores, 235–7
May, Lucien, 83–8, 90, 158
McCulloch, Frank, 203–4
McGarry, Annie, 9
McGladrie, Stuart, 200
McGrady, Mike, 315
McInnes, Ron, 182, 211–13
McMahon, Billy, 297–8, 319–20
McWatters, Aubrey, 24, 26
Mercury, 21–46, 82–4
Mediterranean, sailing on, 147–8
Menzies, Robert
  life under, 8–9
  signed letter from, 106–7
  speech at America's Cup, 255–6
  tribute from Rupert Lockwood, 330–1
Middleton, TAS, 244
Milanov, Kajica, 39, 43
Miles, Fred, 288
Miley, Darrell, 278, 323–4
Miller, Geoff
  in New York, 246–7, 258, 270
  trip to Flores, 235–8
Miller, Lionel, 24–6
minefields in Vietnam, 221–2, 224
Minorca, 149–50, 268
Mitchell, David, 26, 90, 139–40
Mitchell, Vic, 45–6
Molesworth, BH, 285
Montgomery, Bob, 162–3, 168–9
Moonglow (yacht), 143–54
Morris, Alan, 191, 231, 234–5
Moses, Charles, 113–14
  appoints Ted Shaw, 178
  support for Charles Buttrose, 247
Mossadegh, Mohammed, 196
motoring reports, 45
Mount Wellington, TAS, 2
mountain climbing, 134–5, 138
Muir, Frank, 83, 124–6
Munro, Cathy, 284
Murphy, Paul, 284, 286, 321
musical interests
  at school, 19
  classical concerts, 131–2, 134, 258, 271
  hi-fi system, 194
  on the *Canopic*, 156
  piano lessons, 9
  rock 'n' roll, 64–5
  tunes on teeth, 256, 304–5
  tunes on telephone, 256–7
mutton bird harvest, report on, 164–6
My Word, 83, 124–6

Naked Came the Stranger, 312–13
Nanga Gaat, Sarawak, 186–7
napalm drops, 228
National Service training, 64–71
Neate, Cliff, 284
'negative projection', 129
Nelson, Hank, 81–2

Neptunia (ship), 93–9, 102–4
Nettlefold, Len, 143
Nevin, Robyn, 272–3
New Norfolk, TAS, 91–3
New York, 247–64, 269–76
Newell, John, 118, 123
Newport, Rhode Island, 253–6
News Commentary, 321–2
news conferences in Vietnam, 208
News Review, 80, 84, 285
newspaper industry, 21–3, 26–7; *see also* journalism
Nguyen van Thieu, 205
Nixon, Richard, 272
Norden, Denis, 83, 124–6
Northbridge, NSW, house in, 293–4
Northern Tasmanian Magazine, 160
Notes on the News, 321

Oram, Jim, 336
Orchard Road, Singapore, 179–80
Oriana, 141
Orr, Sydney Sparkes, 38–43
Outside Broadcast van, 173–4

Pacific Service (BBC), 115–21
Packer, Frank, 255
Page, Tim, 207–8
Palma, *see* Majorca
Papastatis, Arthur, 283
Paris, holiday in, 132–3
Parker, Ian, 259
passport stolen in Genoa, 106
Peach, Bill
  forbidden unscripted remarks, 307
  in London, 129
  on management of *This Day Tonight*, 291
  plans to sack, 301
  public face of *This Day Tonight*, 305
  runs out of material, 306–7
  supports PMG stories, 309–10

343

throws farewell party, 175
Peach, Robert, 280
Penn, Fred, 207
People's Consultative Congress, Indonesia, 233–4
Petty, Bruce, 307, 315
Philippines, reporting from, 240–2
philosophy, 42–3, 93
Philp, Michael
  breaks wrist twice, 74–6
  holiday with, 50–5
  marries and settles in Maryland, 262–3
  reports on yachting, 35–6
  sails in *Moonglow*, 143
  shares house in London, 90, 139
  starts on *Mercury*, 26
  tribute to Chris de Grabowski, 145–6
phone interviews, 287–8
piano smashing competition, 169–71
Pirates of Penzance, 19
Pitt, Edie and May, 15
Playford, Malcolm (relative), 132
PM, 275, 280, 282–9
police, attitudes to in Hobart, 32–3
political coverage
  Australian Parliament, 286
  in Tasmania, 27
  marginal electorates, 317–18
political interference in programming, 171, 299, 307–10
Port Mahon, Minorca, 149–50
Port Sorell, TAS, 11
Porter, Hal, 265–7
Postmaster General's Department, 299, 307–10
Pratt, James, 77–8, 285
press, 21–3, 26–7; *see also* journalism
Pritchett, Bill, 182–3
program transmission, *see* technology

propellor, fouled, 152–3
protests
  against Vietnam War, 282
  by ABC staff, 310–11
  in Indonesia, 232–3
  in Lincoln Park, 274
Pybus, Cassandra, 39
Pyramids, 105–6

Queensborough Cemetery, TAS, 73–4

RAAF, role in Vietnam, 228–9
race meetings, 34–7, 44
race relations, 3–4, 249, 252
Radford, Paul, 12, 18
radio shows, 78–80, 123–5, 140–2
  3TR Sale, 15
  AM, 251, 280
  Calling Australia, 141
  Correspondents' Report, 321, 325–6
  Daily Devotional, 173
  Fact and Opinion, 216–17
  Good, Bad and Indifferent, 160, 172–3
  Lineup, 172
  My Word, 83
  News Commentary, 321–2
  News Review, 80, 84, 285
  Northern Tasmanian Magazine, 160
  Notes on the News, 321
  PM, 275, 280, 282–9
  Report from London, 131
  Tasmania Today, 78–80, 80
  Ten O'Clock, 279
  The World's Press, 322–3
  Week, 160, 166, 169–70, 173
Raffaele, Paul, 284
Ramsden, Mike, 254
Ramsey, Alan, 200
Randell, Ken, 26
rear gunners, fate of, 183–4
recording technology, *see* technology
Reed, Wilbur, 85

religious broadcasting, 173
Rendell, Anthony
  arrives in Hobart, 78
  invites TB to work on radio, 321
  links tape recorders, 80
  on Hobart radio, 84–6, 158
  on Intertel, 259–60
  precedes TB in New York, 248
  television productions, 160–2
Report from London, 131
Riedle Bay, TAS, 52
Roberts, John, 172
Robertson, E Arnot, 83, 125–6, 132
Rodwell, Emerson, 17
Rome, first visit to, 106–7
Round, Derek, 260
rowing team, 17
Royal Australian Air Force, role in Vietnam, 228–9
Royal Australian Army Service Corps, 71
Royal Commission into Soviet espionage, 327–8
running prowess at school, 19
Rural Department, ABC TAS, 167
Russell, Bertrand, 126–7
Ryan, Leo, 10

Saigon, reporting from, 197–209, 216–30
sailing, *see* boats and ships
Salisbury, Wyn, 90–1
Sambell, Craig, 167
sand bank collapses on TB, 11
Sands, Basil, 116
Sandy Bay, TAS, 73–4
Sarawak, reporting from, 185–8
Saturday Evening Mercury, 45
scallops, documentary on, 86–8
schooling
  Fahan school, 4
  Gladwyn School, 4–5

Index

Hutchins School, 11–13, 15–16
University of Tasmania, 42–3, 89
Science and Industry, 123–5, 140–2
Scotland, holiday in, 265–7
Screaming Lord Sutch, 169–72
Searle, Leon, 30–1
  walk from Lake Pedder, 58, 61, 64
seasickness, 148
Second Network, 287
self-immolation of Buddhists, 202–3
Semmler, Clement, 291
Shannon Rise, TAS, 168–9
Shaw, Lachlan, 299
  and Matteson interview, 303
  on political interference in programming, 308–9, 311
Shaw, Ted, 178, 194
Sheppard, Trish, 253–5
Shone, Roy, 30, 37–8
shorthand, 27, 39–40
Simmons, Don
  brought into *This Day Tonight*, 291, 292–3
  gun goes off in flat, 209
  on Matteson interview, 302–3
  on Ros Geddes, 215–16
  political coverage, 298
  reporting from Vietnam, 198–9, 208–9, 217–18
  supports PMG stories, 308–9, 311
  swim on bucks' night, 238–40
  travels with Holt in Vietnam, 204
Simpson, Fred, 84, 285
Singapore, 101, 174–246
Singapore–Australian Alumni Association, 182–3
Six Day War, 252
Small, Angus, 24
Smith, Les, 88
Smith, Major, 65, 69–70
Snaithe, Cecil (radio character), 123, 140

snakes, 7–8, 54
Snell, Gordon, 118
Snow, CP, 109
soccer, reporting on, 34
Social History Unit, 335
Sorell, John, 26, 31, 89
sound recording, *see* technology
sound tests, 79
South Vietnamese in wartime, 219–24; *see also* Vietnam war
Southeast Asia
  Malaysia, 176, 185–90
  Singapore, 101, 174–246
  Vietnam, 197–209, 216–30
Spain, honeymoon in, 268–9
Spain, Nancy, 83, 125
Speed, Clive, 295, 321
Speight, Selwyn 'Dan', 280–3, 288, 291
Spring Beach, TAS, 10
Spurway, Dick (Ros's cousin), 265, 267
St Tropez, France, 147
Stanwix, John, 57
Steedman, George, 118–19
Stein, Andrew, 16
Stellavox recorder, 221
Stilwell, Nic, 94, 98, 103, 105–8
Stone, Beth, 294, 316–17
Stone, Dana, 208
Stone, Gerald
  at naming party, 316
  management of *This Day Tonight*, 292
  Matteson interview, 302
  on *This Day Tonight*, 304–5
  TB buys house from, 293–4
student protests, *see* protests
Suez Canal, 104–5
Suharto, General, 189, 192, 230–8
Sukarno, President, 176, 230–8
Surrey pub, 119–20
Svensen, Peter, 55
Swedish cyclist story, 28
Switzerland, 132–4

Sydney, NSW, 95–6, 279–80, 289–90
Sydney Opera House, story on, 295–6
Sydney to Hobart Yacht Race, 35–6
Symons, Chris, 161
Symons, Michael, 326–7

Take It From Here, 124
Talks Department, ABC Sydney, 279–80
Tanner, Bill, 160, 167
Tanner, Nick, 49–50
Tanner, Peter, 57–8
tape recording, *see* technology
Tasmania
  bushfire devastation, 243–5
  bushwalking, 5–8, 57–63
  Labor government, 9
  radio broadcasting from, 84–5
  return to from England, 157–8
  upside down at UN bar, 251–2
  wilderness regions, 55–6
  see also Hobart
Tasmania Today, 78–80, 84
Taylor, Graham, 185, 325
TDT, *see This Day Tonight*
technology
  actuality broadcasts, 250–1
  broadcasting *PM*, 284–5
  cable and Telex, 241
  clockwork tape recorder, 78–9
  COMPAC cable, 248
  early television, 160
  Ferrographs, 116–17
  film negative processing, 206–7
  for Menzies speech, 255–6
  hitches in *This Day Tonight*, 305–7
  newspaper industry, 21–3
  Outside Broadcast van, 173–4
  phone interviews, 287–8
  sound recording, 78–82

345

Stellavox recorder, 221
teeth, TB's, 250, 256, 304–5
television, reporting for, 160–2
Temple, John, 26
Ten O'Clock, 279
Terraine, John, 114–16, 119–20, 130
The Labyrinth, TAS, 6
Third Network, 286–7
This Day Tonight
   inspiration for, 172
   management by Peter Hollinshead, 291–3
   plans to split up, 318
   political coverage, 297–300
   TB joins, 295–6
   TB's departure from, 320
Thomas, Alan, 230
Tich Tien Mink, 203–4
Tiger Moth, 47–8, 56
tiger snake, 7–8
Togatus (student newspaper), 47
training films, National Service, 68–9
Trefoil Island, TAS, 164–6
Truchanas, Olegas and Melva, 53–5
Tunku Abdul Rahman, 190–1

Underground railway, 142–3
United Nations, reporting on, 251–2
United States, reporting from, 247–64
University of Tasmania, 42–3
   graduation from, 89, 93–5
   military platoons, 65
   Royal Commission into, 38
Urquhart, Mac, 63

US Marines, reporting with, 217–26

Van Hee, Tony, 152
vehicles
   army trucks, 71
   Fiat 500, 73
   Kombi van, 333–4
   Landcruiser, 336
   road testing of, 45
   Underground railway, 141–2
   Vespa motor scooters, 106–7
   Willys car, 72
   see also boats and ships; flying
Vespa motor scooters, 106–7
vets, sharing house with, 159
videotape, hitches with, 305–7
Vien Hao Dao pagoda, Saigon, 203–4
Vietnam war
   draft resisters, 301–3
   protests against, 282
   reporting on, 196–209, 216–30
Villiers, Alan, 84
voice pieces, 217
Vung Tau, Vietnam, 205–6

Wareham, Anna, 284
Warner, Denis, 84, 217–18, 226–8
Warner, Russell, 291
   in Current Affairs (Radio), 321–5
   jealous of resources, 283–4
   management style, 280
   relations with TB, 332
Warren, John, 114
water-skiing in Singapore, 207

Watson, Jeff, 308
Watts, Ken
   inspires fictional character, 315
   interviews TB, 174
   management of *This Day Tonight*, 291
   revenge on TB, 320, 325
   wedding in Cambridge, 267–8
Week (radio show), 160, 166, 169–70, 173
Weir, Bill, 284–5
Welsh, Keith, 27
Westinghouse Broadcasting Company, 276
Whalers Cove, TAS, 53–4
Wheat, 'Hooks', 44
Wheldon, Huw, 260–1
Whitlam, Gough, 318–19
Williams, Jack, 166
Williams, Mal, 34–5
Williams, Michael, 128–9
Williams, Robyn, 81
Wilson, David, 165–7, 171–2, 245–6
Wilson, George, 41
Winter, Arthur, 170–1, 312, 318
Wise, Donald, 201
women barred from hotels in Sydney, 289–90
wool auction, reporting on, 78–80
Work Work, Shuffle Shuffle, 315
World's Press, The, 322–3
Wright, Brian, 280
writing by TB, 10, 336
Wyndham, Arthur, 91–3

yachting, *see* boats and ships
Youd, Doug, 173–4
Young, Archbishop Guildford, 37
Young, Gavin, 180–1

www.ingramcontent.com/pod-product-compliance
Lightning Source LLC
Chambersburg PA
CBHW031307150426
43191CB00005B/116